Asian Defence Review 2022

# DIPLOMACY IN TURMOIL

## A Year of Turbulence

## Asian Defence Review 2022

# DIPLOMACY IN TURMOIL

## A Year of Turbulence

Edited by
Air Marshal Anil Chopra PVSM AVSM VM VSM (Retd)

Centre for Air Power Studies
New Delhi

*in association with*

KNOWLEDGE WORLD
KW Publishers Pvt Ltd
New Delhi

The Centre for Air Power Studies is an independent, non-profit, academic research institution established in 2002 under a registered Trust to undertake and promote policy-related research, study and discussion on the trends and developments in defence and military issues, especially air power and the aerospace arena, for civil and military purposes. Its publications seek to expand and deepen the understanding of defence, military power, air power and aerospace issues without necessarily reflecting the views of any institution or individuals except those of the authors.

Centre for Air Power Studies
P-284, Arjan Path
Subroto Park
New Delhi 110010

Tele: (91-11) 25699131

E-mail: capsnetdroff@gmail.com
website: www.capsindia.org

**Editor:** Air Marshal Anil Chopra PVSM AVSM VM VSM (Retd)
**Associate Editors:** Air Commodore Savinder Pal Singh, VSM (Retd) and
Ms. Neha Mishra



ISBN 978-93-94915-06-0 Hardback
ISBN 978-93-94915-07-7 ebook

Published in India by Kalpana Shukla

KW Publishers Pvt Ltd
4676/21, First Floor, Ansari Road
Daryaganj, New Delhi 110002
Phone: +91 11 43528107
Marketing: kw@kwpub.in
Editorial: production@kwpub.in
Website: www.kwpub.in

Printed and bound in India

## CENTRE FOR AIR POWER STUDIES

### VISION

To be an independent centre of excellence on national security contributing informed and considered research and analyses on relevant issues.

### MISSION

To encourage independent and informed research and analyses on issues of relevance to national security and to create a pool of domain experts to provide considered inputs to decision-makers. Also, to foster informed public debate and opinion on relevant issues and to engage with other think-tanks and stakeholders within India and abroad to provide an Indian perspective.

# Contents

# Editor's Note

Russia launched a full-scale military invasion of Ukraine on February 24, 2022. As the fighting continues, there has been a significant loss of Ukrainian lives, and has pushed millions of Ukrainians to flee to neighbouring countries. With clear military asymmetry in their favour, Russia was expecting quick gains and achieving its military and political objectives of a favourable regime in Kiev. The same did not happen. Russians had perhaps underestimated the Ukrainian resolve to fight. Russians had also not brought all its major military assets into conflict to keep as reserves for a possible escalation by NATO. They also made some tactical operational mistakes. NATO's tacit support of Ukraine through supplies of defensive military equipment, intelligence information, and financial support also made things tough for Moscow. Russia has more or less taken control of the pro-Russian Eastern regions of Ukraine and have made significant gains in the south to be able to control the Black Sea.

NATO was formed in 1949 to defend from a possible attack from the Soviet Union. Warsaw Pact alliance pact was created in reaction to the integration of West Germany into NATO in 1955. After the USSR dissolved in December 1991, the Warsaw Pact came to an end. In the next 20 years, all the Warsaw Pact countries outside the USSR, each joined NATO (East Germany through its reunification with West Germany; and the Czech Republic and Slovakia as separate countries), as did the Baltic states which had been part of the Soviet Union. The Russian annexation of Crimea led to strong condemnation by NATO nations. Ukraine was considered an important buffer between NATO and Russia. Russia had repeatedly insisted that Ukraine's joining NATO was unacceptable to them. Discussions for Ukraine's entry into NATO had begun in 2008. On June 12, 2020, Ukraine joined NATO's enhanced opportunity partner interoperability program. On September 14, 2020, Zelenskyy approved Ukraine's new National Security Strategy, "which provides for the development of the distinctive partnership with NATO with the aim of membership in NATO." On June 28, 2021, Ukraine and NATO forces launched joint naval drills in the Black Sea codenamed Sea Breeze 2021. On November 30, Putin stated that an expansion of NATO's presence in Ukraine, especially the deployment of any long-range missiles capable of striking Moscow or missile defence systems similar to those in Romania and Poland, would be a "red line" issue for the Kremlin. On December 17, Russia put forward proposals to limit US and NATO influence on former Soviet states. On January 28, Putin said the West has ignored "Russia's fundamental concerns" on NATO's expansion and said that NATO had "strike weapons systems near Russia's borders". On February 24, 2022, Russia invaded Ukraine. The end state of the war maybe that Russia will retain control over Donetsk and Luhansk regions of eastern Ukraine, and the southern regions connecting Crimea.

The second area of global action continues to be the Indo-Pacific. It is all about preventing aggressive Chinese expansion and hegemony without getting into a catastrophic conflict. The Quadrilateral Security Dialogue (Quad) members have been meeting more regularly at the apex and ministerial levels. In a joint statement in March 2021, "The Spirit of the Quad," was described as "a shared vision for a Free and Open Indo-Pacific," and a "rules-based maritime order in the East and South China seas" through which the Quad members state need to counter Chinese maritime claims. The first Quad Plus meeting, under the pretext of Covid's response, included representatives from South Korea, New Zealand and Vietnam. In May 2021, Brazil and Israel, two countries with no border to the Pacific Ocean, were also invited into the Plus format. Following the 2020 Malabar naval exercises, the American secretary of state and former CIA director Mike Pompeo met with members of the Quad to discuss about converting the security arrangement into an "Asian NATO" with "shared security and geopolitical goals." There has been a flurry of ministerial-level meetings in the last one year. US President Joe Biden hosted the first Quad Leaders' Summit on September 24, 2021, at the White House. The leaders pledged to work towards peace and prosperity in the Indo-Pacific region. Quad is not a military alliance, but the militaries of the partner countries are regularly exercising to improve interoperability.

On September 15, 2021, a trilateral security pact between Australia, the United Kingdom, and the United States, termed AUKUS was announced for the Indo-Pacific region. Under this pact, the US and the UK will help Australia to acquire nuclear-powered submarines. The pact will also support cooperation on advanced cyber, artificial intelligence and autonomy, quantum technologies, undersea capabilities, hypersonic and counter-hypersonic, electronic warfare, innovation and information sharing. With NATO active attempts against Russia in Europe, Quad and AUKUS would sandwich the Eurasian region and effectively attempt to contain both China and Russia, and any collaboration between them. The real first test in Indo-Pacific would be, if and when China choses to invade Taiwan.

This issue of the Asian Defence Review (ADR) covers the theme "Diplomacy in Turmoil: A Year of Turbulence". ADR is further divided into three sections. Effectively we cover the entire regional arc from West Asia to Indo-Pacific. Xi-Jinping remains a tall powerful leader and is hoping to get an unprecedented third term in power. In many ways, he shapes the global reactions in the Indo-Pacific. We track the current trends of Chinese modern weapons. We also study China's nuclear missile modernization and its implications for India. We also look at China's artificial islands in South China Sea having geo-economic implications in addition to geo-strategic. They give them an additional three million sq km of the exclusive economic zone (EEZ) making it a great case for India-South East Asia security cooperation. The world continues to be concerned about geopolitical aspects of the Belt and Road Initiative and yet many of its projects seem to be faltering. We look at India's status as 'Net security provider' in the Indian Ocean region (IOR), and what more needs to be done.

The resurgence of the Taliban post-9/11 has many lessons. US exit from Afghanistan has left a vacuum that has still to be filled. The region has got relegated in importance because of the power-play in Ukraine and South China Sea. Meanwhile, the Taliban takeover in Afghanistan has regional dynamics in Central Asia. Israel has one of the most significant air power in West Asia. The same is backed by the high technology defence industry. India Air Force has been increasingly engaging in multilateral exercises with countries across the globe. India got global recognition for its Covid vaccine medical support during the pandemic. All this and much more has been covered in this issue.

Knowledge is power, and an asset for individuals and organisations. Knowledge must reach the right person at the right time, so that they can imbibe the same. Knowledge management has thus become important. The Indian air force is encouraging strategic thinking and reading. We in the Centre for Air Power Studies are trying to cultivate an intellectual bias through our publications. We also continue to invite scholars and veterans to write for us.

Happy Reading

Air Marshal **Anil Chopra** PVSM AVSM VM VSM (Retd)
Director General
Centre for Air Power Studies

# Editors and Contributors

---

## Editor

Air Marshal **Anil Chopra** PVSM, AVSM, VM, VSM (Retd), is a fighter pilot, test pilot, and a pioneer of the Mirage-2000 fleet, who has commanded a Mirage 2000 Squadron and the Flight Test Centre, Aircraft and Systems Testing Establishment (ASTE) of the Indian Air Force (IAF). He was the Team Leader of the MiG 21 Bison Upgrade project in Russia. He has commanded operational air bases in both the Western and Eastern Sectors. He was head of the IAF in Jammu and Kashmir (J&K), and head of Operational Inspections of the IAF. He retired as the Air Officer Personnel. He has been a member of the Armed Forces Tribunal, Lucknow Bench, and member of the Executive Council of Jawaharlal Nehru University (JNU). He has also been an advisor on a committee of the National Green Tribunal. In addition to the four Presidential awards, he is recipient of the Gandhi Family Peace Medal for his work in J&K. An avid writer, Air Marshal Chopra has more than 600 articles published in various magazines, newspapers and books. He has recently written a book titled *China, The Rising Aerospace Power: Implications for India*, and was also the co-editor of a book titled *The 1971 Indo-Pak Air War: Reflections and Projections.* Air Marshal Chopra is presently the Director General of the Centre for Air Power Studies (CAPS) and runs "Air Power Asia" (airpowerasia.com), a website that puts Asia's aviation and military power into the correct perspective.

## Associate Editors

Air Commodore **Savinder Pal Singh** VSM (Retd), was commissioned in the fighter stream of the Indian Air Force (IAF) in December 1985. He has flown more than 3,000 hours on various fighter aircraft including the MiG-

21 Bison and Su-30. He is a Qualified Flying Instructor, Fighter Combat Leader and Instrument Rating Examiner. He commanded a Fighter Squadron and later a Su-30 Fighter Flying Operational Base. He has held several prestigious appointments, including Air1, Western Air Command, principle Director (Air Defence and Weapon System) Air Headquarters (HQ), with two tenures at the Strategic Force Command. He is an alumni of the prestigious National Defence College (NDC), Army War College (AWC) in Mhow, and Defence Services Staff College (DSSC) in Ooty. He is also a recipient of the Presidential award and commendation by the Chief of the Air Staff (CAS). Post retirement, he has worked as a strategic analyst and advisor and has written many articles on various issues covering air power, theatre command, China and Pakistan. He has covered a series of podcasts on various combat assets of the IAF, which were recorded by BharatShakti.com. Presently, Air Commodore SP Singh is working at the Centre for Air Power Studies (CAPS) as a Senior Research Fellow and is heading the team for research and analysis on Indo-Pacific issues.

Ms. **Neha Mishra** is a Research Associate (Indo-Pacific Group) at the Centre for Air Power Studies (CAPS). Her research interest focuses on India-China Geo-economic Engagement or Competition, Role of Energy or Resource Strategy in International Politics, and China's Resource Diplomacy. Before joining CAPS, she worked as research intern at the Institute of Chinese Studies (ICS) and then in the Indian Council of World Affairs (ICWA). Ms. Mishra has a M.Phil and Master's degree in Political Science from the Department of Political Science, University of Delhi. She is pursuing her Ph.D from the University of Delhi on 'India—China Geo-economic Engagement'.

## Contributors

Air Vice Marshal **Anil Golani** (Retd) was commissioned in the Flying Branch of the IAF in December 1982 and superannuated in November 2019, with varied experience having served across the country and abroad. Presently working as Additional Director General CAPS since May 21. He likes to play golf, read and write on issues concerning air power, security and strategy and national interest.

Group Captain **Amitabh Mathur** (Retd) was commissioned in the Aeronautical Engineering (Electronics) Branch in 1987. He has a wide experience in the field of Guided weapons, Electronic Warfare, Specialist Air-to-Air and Air-to-Ground weapons, and Chemical, Biological and Nuclear Weapons.

Ms. **Mahima Duggal** is a Research Associate with the Centre for Air Power Studies (CAPS) in New Delhi. Her research is focused on the changing balance of power and security issues in the Indo-Pacific region. Ms. Duggal has written extensively on subjects like Indian foreign policy, India-China ties, East Asian security dynamics, US alliances and partnerships in the Indo-Pacific, and Europe's interest in the Indo-Pacific for both national and international platforms, including The Diplomat, Asia Times, South Asian Voices, 9DashLine, Council on Geostrategy (UK), and the Canon Institute for Global Studies (Japan). She has authored several journal articles (including for the *Journal of Indo-Pacific Affairs*, *Journal of Indian Ocean Studies* and *Air Power Journal*) and numerous individual and co-authored chapters in edited volumes published internationally. Ms. Duggal is also an Associate Research Fellow at the Stockholm Centre for South Asian and Indo-Pacific Affairs (SCSA-IPA) of the Institute for Security and Development Policy (ISDP) in Sweden, and the Editorial Assistant to Series Editor for Routledge Studies on Think Asia.

Dr. **Anu Sharma** has been associated with the Centre for Air Power Studies (CAPS), as an Research Fellow with research interests in the West Asian region. She has recently published a book titled *Through the Looking Glass: Iran and Its Foreign Relations* in 2020. She has also published and presented various papers on foreign and domestic politics of Iran and the broader West Asian region both nationally and internationally. Her core interest area includes area studies, foreign policy and defence politics. She has graduated from Delhi University's Kalindi College in Journalism and Mass Communications. She has credible experience as a freelancing journalist with *The Statesman*, New Delhi as part of her Graduation programme. She holds Masters in International Relations from School of International Studies (SIS), JNU and M.Phil from the American Studies division of Centre for

Canadian, US and Latin American Studies (CCUS & LAS), SIS, JNU. She has done her Ph.D from Centre for International Politics (CIP), School of International Studies (SIS), Central University of Gujarat, Gandhinagar.

Ms. **Nasima Khatoon** is a Research Associate at the Rashtriya Raksha University (RRU), Gandhinagar. Previously, she has worked as a Research Associate at the Centre for Air Power Studies (CAPS), New Delhi and the National Institute of Advanced Studies (NIAS), Bengaluru. Her areas of research interest are India's foreign policy, nuclear strategy and security and borderland studies of northeast India. She holds a Master's degree in Defence and Strategic Studies from the Savitribai Phule Pune University, India. She has written book chapters, journal articles and short analytical articles for the Springer, Routledge, *Air Power Journal*, *The Hindu* and *The Diplomat* among others.

Wing Commander **Swaim Prakash Singh** was commissioned into the Indian Air Force in June 1997 in the Administration branch. He is a cat AYE, Master Fighter Controller, qualified Assistant Provost Marshal, and AWACS Mission Commander with over 1000 hours of flying and Directing Staff at the prestigious Defence Services Staff College, Wellington. He is an alumnus of DSSC Wellington and served as Directing Staff (psc+) for two years. The officer was part of the Tri-Services Indian Expert team to review the course curriculum of the Command and Staff College of Tanzania in 2016. He was instrumental in achieving a significant diplomatic feat in opening the Indian Armed Forces Training Team (IAFTT) at C&SC Tanzania, which commenced functioning in 2017. He has also been to Israel, Russia, and China. The officer has been commended by the Air Officer Commanding-in-Chief of HQ Western Air Command in 2006 and by the Chief of Integrated Defence Staff in 2016. The officer holds an MSc, M.Phil, and psc+ in Defence and Strategic Studies and is currently working on a Ph.D in the same field. The officer is also a keen orator, critical analyst, and learner. The scholar warrior officer is currently employed as a Senior Fellow at the New Delhi-based think tank, the Centre for Air Power Studies.

Professor **Sanu Kanikara** is a Distinguished Veteran IAF, fighter pilot, who is a Qualified Flying Instructor as well as a Fighter Combat Leader, with vast experience in flying various fighter aircraft of IAF. He took VRS as Wing Commander and soon earned his reputation as a Political and Defence Analyst specialising in military strategy, national security, and international politics. He did his Ph.D in International Politics from University of Adelaide, Australia and Executive Masters in Public Administration, ANZSOG. He is an Adjunct Professor, University of New South Wales, Distinguished Fellow Institute for Regional Security (IFRS) and Distinguished Fellow Centre for Air Power Studies (CAPS).

Dr. **Temjenmeren Ao** is a Research Fellow on Southeast Asia at the Indian Council of World Affairs (ICWA), New Delhi. Prior to which he worked as an Associate Fellow at the Centre for Air Power Studies, where he completed a project titled, "China's Aerospace Sector: A Study on its Rise through Transfers of Technology". His area of interests includes the study on international economics, India's foreign relations in the contemporary political, economic and security environment and issues of dual-use technology transfers. He completed his Masters of Arts in Economics from the Centre for Economics Studies and Planning, School of Social Sciences, Jawaharlal Nehru University (JNU), New Delhi, and holds a Ph.D in International Relations from School of International Studies, JNU.

Mr. **Mohit Sharma** is a Research Associate at the Centre for Air Power Studies, New Delhi. He is working on a book project which explores Taliban's administrative structure, Leadership, various factions within the Taliban, and their relationship with neighbouring countries. He has been tracking developments in South Asia with focus on extremist groups operating in the Af-Pak region, alongside Counter-Terrorism and Counter-Insurgency strategies. He has delivered lecture on Taliban resurgence in Squadron Officer's Capsule Course for the Indian Air Force. His research interests also include study of radical ideologues, and understanding Jihadi literature in theological framework. His works have been published in *Defence and Diplomacy Journal*, *Financial Express*, and *South Asian Journal*. He has a post-graduate degree in International Relations and Area Studies from School of International Studies, Jawaharlal Nehru University, New Delhi.

Dr. **Poonam Mann** is an Associate Fellow at the Centre for Air Power Studies, New Delhi. She is engaged in academic research on Central Asian region, Caucasus and Eurasia. She has published various research papers on a wide range of security and strategic issues and contributed chapters in edited volumes. She has presented papers in various national and international seminars and participated in Track-II dialogues with multilateral institutions like Shanghai Cooperation Organisation (SCO). She has authored a book titled, *India's Foreign Policy in the Post-Cold War Era*. She holds a Ph.D from the Department of Political Science, Kurukshetra University, Kurukshetra. From 2000-2005, she has worked as a Researcher with the Institute for Defence Studies and Analyses, New Delhi. Besides research, she has also worked as a lecturer of Political Science in various colleges in India.

Dr. **Joshy M Paul** is a Research Fellow at the Centre for Air Power Studies (CAPS), New Delhi, focusing on the Chinese Navy and the Indian Ocean. He has seventeen years of research and academic experience in Asian Security, East Asian Affairs and Maritime Security of the Indo-Pacific. Before joining CAPS, he worked as an Assistant Professor at the Department of International Studies, School of Law, Christ University (Bangalore) and also with a premier naval think tank, National Maritime Foundation, New Delhi. He has published a number of articles in reputed journals, including *India Review*, *South Asian Survey*, *International Studies*, *Air Power Journal*, and *Maritime Affairs*. He was the RSIS MacArthur Associate Visiting Fellow (Singapore) in 2010, NIDS Visiting Research Fellow (Japan) in 2011, and Salzburg Global Seminar Fellow in 2009, 2015 & 2021. He earned an M.Phil and Ph.D in International Politics from CIPOD, School of International Studies, Jawaharlal Nehru University, New Delhi.

# List of Tables, Maps and Figures

## Tables



## Maps



## Figures

# Abbreviations

| | |
|---|---|
| AAI | Airports Authority of India |
| ADGES | Air Defence Ground Environmental System |
| ADMM | ASEAN Defence Ministers' Meeting |
| ADSS | Automatic Dependence Surveillance System |
| AEP | Act East Policy |
| AI | Artificial Intelligence |
| ALBM | Air Launched Ballistic Missile |
| ALCM | Air Launched Cruise Missile |
| ANDSF | Afghanistan National Defense and Security Forces |
| ANSP | Air Navigation Service Provider |
| AOIP | ASEAN Outlook on the Indo-Pacific |
| ARF | ASEAN Regional Forum |
| ASCM | Anti-Ship Missile |
| ASEAN | Association of South East Asian Nations |
| ASPC | Air and Space Power Centre |
| ATMS | Air Traffic Management Services |
| AUKUS | Australia, the United Kingdom, and the United States |
| BMD | Ballistic Missile Defence |
| BRI | Belt and Road Initiative |
| CAA | Citizenship Amendment Act |
| CAPS | Centre for Air Power Studies |
| CARs | Central Asian Republics |
| CASA | Central Asian-South Asian Electricity Transmission Project |
| CMC | Central Military Commission |
| COC | Code of Conduct |

| | |
|---|---|
| CORPAT | Indo-Thailand Coordinated Patrolling |
| CPEC | China Pakistan Economic Corridor |
| CSP | Comprehensive Strategic Partnership |
| CSTO | Collective Security Treaty Organisation |
| DF-5, DF-41, DF-4, DF-21, DF-26, DF-31, DF-15 | Dong Feng-5, Dong Feng-41, Dong Feng-4, Dong Feng 21, Dong Feng-26, Dong Feng-31, Dong Feng -15 |
| DOC | Declaration on the Conduct of Parties in the South China Sea |
| DRDO | Defence Research and Development Organisation |
| EAEU | Eurasian Economic Union |
| EAM | External Affairs Minister |
| EAS | East Asia Summit |
| EEZ | Exclusive Economic Zone |
| EEZ | Exclusive Economic Zone |
| EWGs | Experts Working Groups |
| FATA | Federally Administered Tribal Areas |
| FOC | Final operational configuration |
| HF | High Frequency |
| HGV | Hypersonic Glide Vehicles |
| HIDE | Handheld Interagency Identity Detection Equipment |
| HPR | High Powered Radars |
| HSR | Health Silk Road |
| IACCS | Integrated Air Command and Control Centre |
| IAF | Indian Air Force |
| IAI | Israel Aerospace Industry |
| ICBM | Intercontinental Ballistic Missile |
| IDF | Israeli Defence Force |
| IED | Improvised Explosive Device |
| IMU | Islamic Movement of Uzbekistan |
| IOC | Initial operational configuration |
| IONS | Indian Ocean Naval Symposium |
| IONS | Indian Ocean Naval Symposium |

| | |
|---|---|
| IPOI | Indo-Pacific Oceans Initiative |
| IRBM | Intermediate Range Ballistic Missile |
| IS | Islamic State |
| ISAF | International Security Assistance Force |
| ISI | Inter-Services Intelligence |
| ISIS | Islamic State of Iraq and Syria |
| ISKP | Islamic State-Khorasan Province |
| ISRO | Indian Space and Research Organisation |
| JAD | Jamaah Ansharut Daulah |
| JCM | Indonesia-India Joint Commission Meeting |
| JDCC | Joint Defence Cooperation Committee |
| JI | Jemaach Islamiah |
| JL-2 | Julang-2 |
| JORN | Jindalee Operational Radar Network |
| LEP | Look East Policy |
| LLLWR | Low-Level Light Weight Radars |
| LLTR | Low-Level Transportable Radars |
| LOS | Line of Sight |
| LTTE | Liberation Tigers of Tamil Eelam |
| MALE | Medium Altitude Long Range |
| MaRVs | Manoeuvrable Re-entry Vehicles |
| MDA | Maritime Domain Awareness |
| MIRVs | Multiple Independently-Targetable Re-entry Vehicles |
| MPR | Medium Powered Radars |
| MRAP | Mine-Resistant Ambush Protected vehicles |
| MRBM | Medium Range Ballistic Missiles |
| MRSAM | Medium Range, Land Based Missile Systems |
| MTCR | Missile Technology Control Regime |
| NATO | North Atlantic Treaty Organisation |
| NDN | Northern Distribution Network |
| NGO | Non Governmental Organisation |
| NLOS | Non-Line of Sight |
| NOSTRADAMUS | New Trans horizon Decametric System Applying Studio Methods |

| | |
|---|---|
| NPT | Non-Proliferation Treaty |
| NSCN | National Socialist Council of Nagaland |
| NVD | Night Vison Devices |
| OEM | Original Equipment Manufacturers |
| OTH | Over the Horizon Radars |
| OTH-B | Over the Horizon Backscatter |
| OTH-SW | Over the Horizon Surface Wave |
| PLA | People Liberation Army |
| PLAAF | People Liberation Army Air Force |
| PLARF | People's Liberation Army Rocket Force |
| PLASAF | People's Liberation Army Second Artillery Force |
| PRT | Provincial Reconstruction Team |
| QUAD | Quadrilateral Security Dialogue |
| RASP | Recognised Air Situation Picture |
| RATS | Regional Anti-Terrorist Structure |
| RPA | Remotely Piloted Aircraft |
| RPG | Rocket-Propelled Grenade |
| SAARC | South Asian Association for Regional Cooperation |
| SAGAR | Security and Growth for All in the Region |
| SALW | Small Arms and Light Weapons |
| SCO | Shanghai Cooperation Organisation |
| SCS | South China Sea |
| SII | Serum Institute of India |
| SIMBEX | India-Singapore naval exercise |
| SITMEX | Trilateral Maritime Exercise between India, Singapore and Thailand |
| SLBM | Submarine Launched Ballistic Missile |
| SLOCs | Sea Lanes of Communications |
| SOP | Standard Operating Procedures |
| SRBM | Short Range Ballistic Missile |
| SSBN | Ship Submersible Ballistic Nuclear |
| SSM | Surface to Surface Missile |
| TAC | Treaty of Amity and Cooperation |

| | |
|---|---|
| TAP | Turkmenistan-Afghanistan-Pakistan Power Interconnection |
| TAPI | Turkmenistan-Afghanistan-Pakistan-India |
| TAR | Tibet Autonomous Region |
| TNT | Trinitrotoluene |
| TRU | Transportable Radar Units |
| TTP | Tehrik-e-Taliban Pakistan |
| UAV | Unmanned Aerial Vehicles |
| UN | United Nations |
| UNAMA | United Nations Assistance Mission in Afghanistan |
| UNCLOS | UN Convention on the Law of the Sea |
| US | United States |
| US DoD report | US Department of Defense report |
| USINDOPACOM | US-Indo-Pacific Command |
| USP | Unique Selling Point |
| USSR | Union of Socialist Soviet Republics |
| UUV | Unmanned Underwater Vessels |
| VA/VPs | Vital Area/Vital Point |
| VAP | Vientiane Action Programme |
| VR | Virtual Reality |
| WANA | West Asia North Africa |
| WHO | World Health Organization |
| WPNS | Western Pacific Naval Symposium |
| WTO | World Trade Organisation |
| XUAR | Xinjiang Uyghur Autonomous Region |
| ZOPFAN | Zone of Peace, Freedom, and Neutrality |

# 1

# Ambitious Xi Jinping: Curbing Dissent and Antagonising the World

ANIL CHOPRA

---

Xi Jinping is currently the paramount leader of China, holding all the three most powerful posts, General Secretary of the Chinese Communist Party (CCP), President of the People's Republic of China (PRC), and Chairman of the Central Military Commission (CMC). The very authoritarian Xi's hold over his country is more like that of a dictator. He has built a cult-like personality. To exercise a greater hold over the party, he has tried to quell and finish dissent or even mild opposition. He has also tried to reign in possible power blocks. Xi has used the entire state machinery for censorship and mass surveillance. To stay in power for indefinite periods, he had the existing term-limit removed. Like the all-powerful Chairman Mao, he has had his political thoughts and approaches embedded in the party thinking. He directly controls all instruments of power including national security, military, economy, and social reforms. He is thus de facto "Chairman of all things".

Xi has followed a very assertive foreign policy. Some of his signature campaigns have been the claiming of most of the South China Sea (SCS), and the Belt and Road Initiative (BRI) which is meant to extend China's influence to Eurasia and Africa. Internally, he used every means to consolidate his position, more prominent being the anti-corruption campaign to reign in the corrupt and the opponents. He is clearly a man in a hurry to make China a superpower. On June 30, 2020, Xi implemented the National Security Law (NSL) in Hong Kong to ostensibly curb the democratic movement and protests, and to integrate it fully with communist China. His most important unfinished agenda is the annexation or unification of Taiwan with mainland China.

## Youth Full of Turmoil

Born in Beijing on June 15, 1953, Xi was the second son in the family. He had a communist lineage, and tried joining the CCP when very young. When he was just 10, his father was purged from the Party. Xi's secondary education was cut short by Cultural Revolution. Xi's sister committed suicide, and his mother publicly denounce his father, when he was labelled as an enemy of the revolution and sent to prison in 1968. Young Xi was forced to work in the villages, but was unable to withstand the hard rural life, and escaped to Beijing. He was arrested, and sent to a work camp to dig ditches, and later worked in a village for seven years. Clearly, he had a tough, and at times humiliating childhood.

After being repeatedly rejected, Xi managed to join the Communist Youth League of China in 1971 by enticing a local official. Similarly, after being rejected many times, he managed to finally join the CCP in 1974. He enrolled on a chemical engineering course in Beijing under the "worker-peasant-soldier" student quota. A significant time of the course under such quota was spent reading about Marx-Lenin-Mao Zedong's thoughts and doing fieldwork with the People's Liberation Army (PLA).

## Political Rise

Xi's first exposure to political work was as secretary to the Vice Premier Geng Biao, who was also the secretary-general of CMC. In 1985, he went to the USA in a Chinese delegation to study US agriculture. During this two-week visit, he stayed with an American family, and that left a lasting impression on him. He served in various political posts in the coming years. In between, Xi enrolled at Tsinghua University and studied Marxist theory. He finally graduated with a doctorate in law and ideology. Xi was Governor of Fujian, not far from the coast facing Taiwan. He came to the national stage in 2002, when he was elected as a full member of the 16th Central Committee. His political career was marked by a tough stance against corrupt officials. This was watched closely both by the public and the party leadership. Later he was the Governor and Party Secretary in Zhejiang, a province in eastern China, along the East China Sea. In 2007, he was elevated to be the Party Secretary of Shanghai, and became a member of the CCP Politburo Standing Committee. In March 2008 Xi was elected as the Vice President of PRC and Vice Chairman of CMC. He was ranked above Li Keqiang, and it was generally presumed that he would succeed Hu Jintao as China's next leader.

He was also appointed the president of the Central Party School of the CCP. After the global financial crisis of 2008, Xi visited many Latin American countries to promote Chinese trade ties. He also visited most European countries, Japan, South Korea, Cambodia and Myanmar. He visited the United States, Ireland and Turkey in February 2012. In the US he was invited for a meeting with then US President Barack Obama at the White House and he also met the then Vice President Joe Biden.[1]

Xi was elected[2] to the posts of general secretary of the Communist Party on November 15, 2012, and also made chairman of the CMC by the 18th Central Committee of the CCP. He is the first General Secretary born after the formation of PRC in October 1949. Clearly, Xi had gone through many trials and tribulations. Singapore's Lee Kuan Yew had said,[3] "I would put him (Xi) in the Nelson Mandela class of persons. A person with enormous emotional stability who does not allow his personal misfortunes or sufferings affect his judgment".

## Initial Years as the Supreme Leader

During his first speech as general secretary, he did not resort to any political sloganeering, and spoke primarily about the aspirations of the ordinary people, better education, jobs, income, social security, health care, and better living conditions. Xi also spelt out the need to take-on corruption at the highest levels. Further economic reform and a strengthening military were his most important agendas. He also sent other signals by choosing to eat at a regular hotel buffet, and by travelling in a bus with his colleagues rather than a convoy of large cars. He was elected as the president, on March 16, 2013.[4]

## Xi's Anti-Corruption Drive

From day one Xi had decided to crack down on corruption, and he mentioned the same in his inaugural speech. He then issued an "eight-point guide" to arrest corruption and discipline the party officials. He emphasized the need to crack down on both "tigers"and "flies", implying the powerful leaders and lowly bureaucrats.[5] That was his way of enforcing discipline. Early in his tenure, he created central investigation teams, and an anti-corruption agency,and began legal proceedings and criminal cases against many senior corrupt functionaries. Many high-ranking officials and military officers were implicated.[6] A few hundred thousand lower functionaries were given written warnings or fines/demotions imposed.[7] Many Xi critics labelled this drive as an equivalent of a political purge. The National Supervision Commission[8] set up by Xi had higher status than the Chinese Supreme Court. Amnesty International also questioned having a government commission with higher legal status, and that it was a threat to human rights.

## Censorship and Document Nine

Within a year after coming to power, in 2013, Xi circulated "Party Document No. 9", which forbade intellectuals, particularly college instructors, from talking about universal values, media freedom, civil rights, and any digressions in CCP's history, the "crony capitalist class," and any references to a desire for judiciary's independence.[9] The document cautioned against seven "Western values". Clearly, what was bothering the staunchly communist and autocratic Xi Jinping, the Chinese talking about constitutional democracy and judicial independence; universal values encompassing morality, human traits, human endeavour, and social order; individual rights; pro-market globalization; media independence; and questioning Chinese style socialism. These subjects were forbidden to be covered in any educational materials. Internet censorship saw a sudden rise.[10] Xi took a very strong stand to control internet usage inside China. Google, Facebook and Twitter are still all blocked[11] in China due to the country's "Great Firewall" to safeguard internet sovereignty. Even Wikipedia stands blocked. Weibo is a Chinese microblogging website and one of the biggest social media platforms in China since 2009. The interactions on the website are closely monitored by the CCP and any defamatory[12] comments could invite prison. Most

Chinese avoid controversial or critical comments. The government also asked the telecommunications operators to block individuals' use of Virtual Private Networks (VPNs). Comparisons between Xi and the Disney character Winnie the Pooh[13] had the government enraged, and all such references were banned on Internet.

## Centralising Power

Xi has clearly consolidated his power and become the most powerful leader since Chairman Mao Zedong. Practically he has done away with the collective leadership that was being practised for long. The maximum two-term restriction for Presidency has been done away with[14] since March 2018. The logic used was that the General Secretary of the CCP, and Chairman of the CMC have no term limits, and so why does the President. He, de-facto exercises direct institutional control over the CCP, the military, internal security, the economic structures, and many cases, bypasses existing institutions. He has literally got all his blue-eyed boys from his earlier tenures in the districts and provinces. He has also tried to build a cult personality for himself. He is often referred to as "Xi Dada" (Big Daddy),[15] though one is not sure whether it is in awe or fear. The levels of sycophancy are when people in the streets singing in his praise "Xi Dada! Xi Dada! Every one of us loves him!" Some call him the "Great Helmsman".[16]

## Greater State Control over Economy

While his predecessors opened up control over the economy and that resulted in over 10 per cent annual growth, Xi actually increased state control over China's economy. While allowing the private sector to continue, albeit within party dictated norms, he ensured greater support for state-owned enterprises (SOE).[17] Rather than allowing the private sector more space, Xi wants a tool for the implementation of government policy.[18] He has also been working closely to increase the global role of the Chinese currency Renminbi (RMB),[19] and of creating a stable international monetary environment for its own economic development. He wants the RMB for trade, lending, borrowing, and investing internationally. The International Monetary Fund (IMF) announced on December 1, 2015, that the Chinese Yuan too would be treated as a reserve currency.[20] The basket already included the US dollar the Euro, the Japanese yen, and the British pound. The Yuan currently accounts for about 2 per cent of global foreign exchange reserve assets, and Morgan Stanley analysts[21] predict that it will account for 5 to 10 per cent of global foreign exchange reserve assets by 2030. His motto, continue to reform but don't take China or its government for granted. Since Trump administration imposed economic sanctions, Xi tried to push self-reliance, especially on high technology. China unveiled plans to boost spending and research on cutting-edge chips and artificial intelligence in a bid to achieve "major breakthroughs in core technologies."[22] Yet he chose to convey his strength to the private business community in 2020 when Jack Ma made an adverse comment on the Chinese banking regulatory system. Angry Xi stopped Ant Group's IPO and cracked a whip on Chinese high-tech business to curtail their monopoly. In late 2021, Beijing issued many new industrial regulations covering from"Big Tech"to private education.[23]As a reaction, many analysts felt that such centralised control over a technology-driven economy is bound to have adverse consequences in the long-term. Clearly,China's economy is at an 'inflexion point'.

Many have wondered about the timing of Xi's crackdown on big businesses.[24] By the time Xi began his second term in 2017, he now assessed that China's development was "unbalanced and inadequate", and required greater direct involvement to fix it. The party "wants to first halt the source that is creating inequality,"said Feng Chucheng, a partner at research firm Plenum in Beijing.[25]

## One Child Policy Review

China's one-child policy began in 1979 to control rapidly growing population. In the mid-1980s, it was modified to allow rural parents a second child if the first was a daughter. The policy was enforced through a financial penalty in the form of the "social child-raising fee." There was a very significant demographic impact of the policy over nearly half-century. It also began impacting economy through older population profile. China finally shifted to a two-child policy from January 1, 2016. But even this failed to bring an upsurge in births, as the cost of raising children in cities was a deterrent.[26] After the latest Census showed a continued decline,

China announced that it will allow couples to have up to three children. Experts felt that there was no need to tread too cautiously and it would have been best to remove all birth-related restrictions.

## Xi's Legal Reforms Push

Since 2014, Xi began legal reforms, essentially to reinforce Chinese socialistic rule of law. Effectively it is an instrumental use of laws by rulers to facilitate social control and to impose punishment. Reforms were meant to deliver justice that had been ridden by local government interference,corruption, and lack of constitutional oversight. Effectively it meant centralising the system under the garb of transparency and professionalisation of the legal workforce. Cross-jurisdictional circuit legal tribunals were introduced as check and balance. Xi personally oversaw these reforms, which were aimed at more power for the Party, and less everyday arbitrariness. Building a "socialist rule of law with Chinese characteristics" and "law-based governance".[27] Xi's plan closely looks at the outside world, and how interventions by "foreign forces" should be opposed and prevented. The law is meant to support peaceful reunification and against aspirations of independence. This is fuelling speculation about a Taiwan-specific "anti-secession law".[28]

## Xi's Military Reforms

From the day he came to power, military reforms and a complete overhaul of the People's Liberation Army (PLA) was on Xi's agenda. The reforms were directly overseen by himself as the CMC Chairman and as head of the military reforms committee. He made it clear to the top military officers that the party has absolute control over the army. Reducing party hold over the military would result in the organisational collapse like the Soviet Union, he felt. To reduce costs and modernise the military, PLA strength was cut by 300,000 troops to two million. This was not the first time troop strength was being cut. The PLA's size had been cut four times, by one million in 1985, by 500,000 in 1997, by 200,000 in 2003, and now by 300,000.[29] The country was divided into five theatre commands. Four autonomous general departments were expanded to 15 entities that reported directly to him through CMC. A Strategic Support and a Joint Logistics Support Force were also created. In April 2016, Xi declared himself as the Commander-in-Chief, a clear politico-military statement of power. A commander in War or Peace. The military reforms were unprecedented in scale, scope and ambition.[30] The key reform drivers were, a major overhaul for efficiency, building a joint force, modernisation, integrating with society, and most importantly centralising authority under Xi. The key takeaways of the Military reforms are in Figure 1.1 below.[31] The CMC structure is in Figure 1.2.[32]

**Figure 1.1: Key Chinese Military Reform Takeaways in Recent Years**

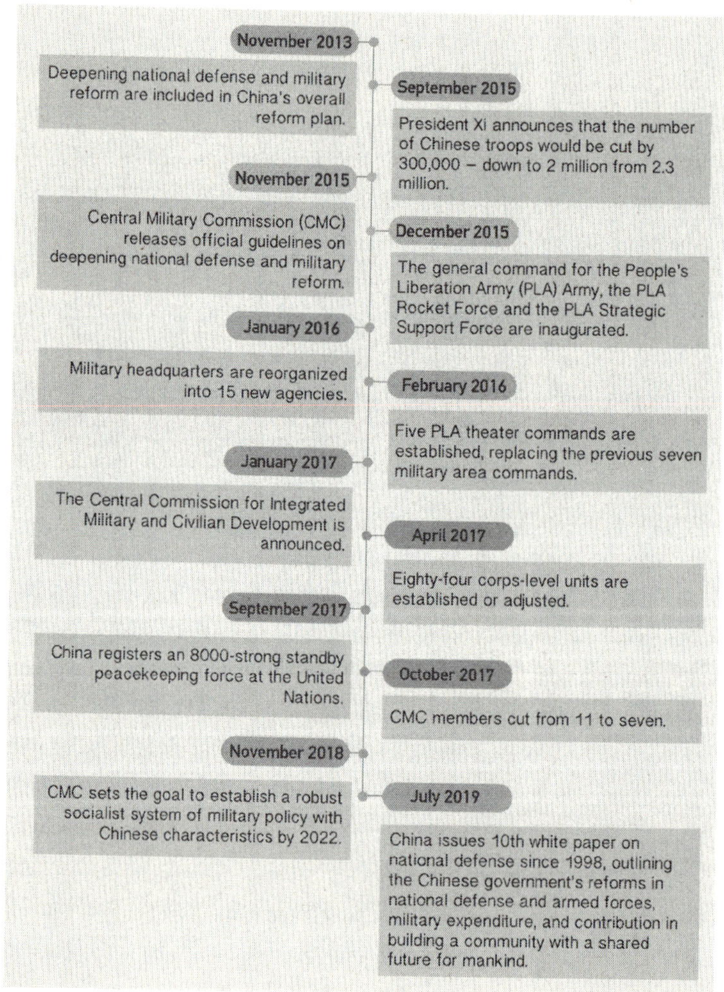


Source: CGTN. Credit: Ministry of National Defense of the People's Republic of China

**Figure 1.2: Reform in China's National Defense and Armed Forces**

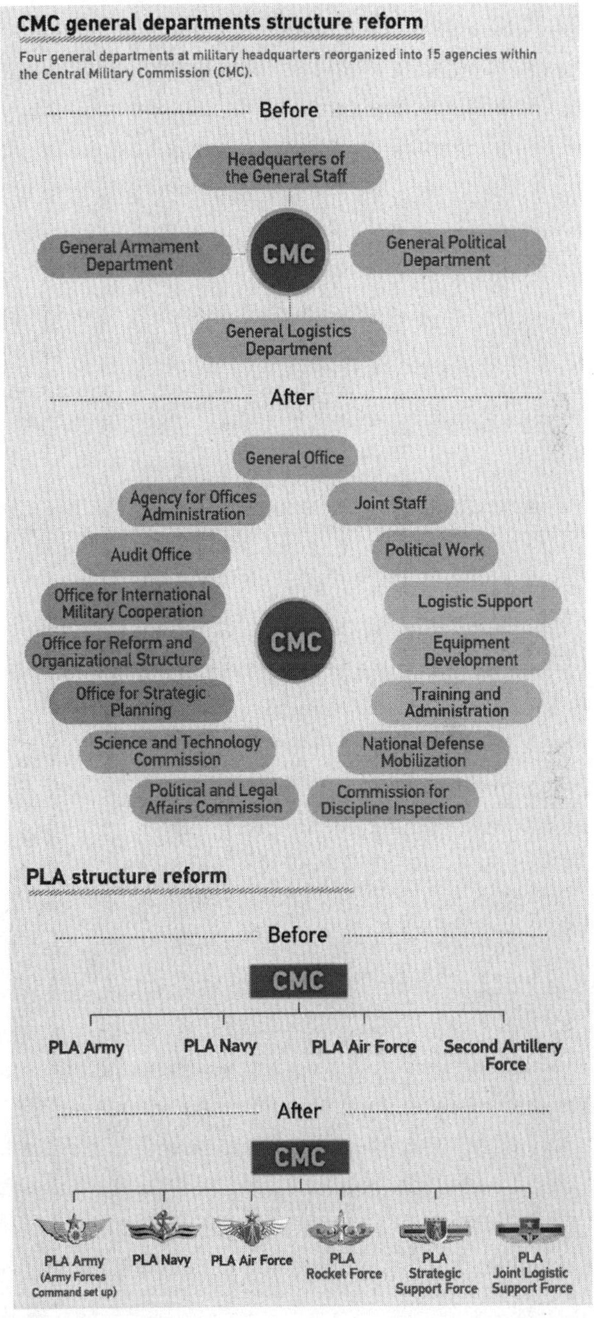


Source: CGTN

## Xi's Signature Belt and Road Initiative

Xi unveiled his BRI project in September 2013. Xi made the announcement in Kazakhstan, and called it a "golden opportunity".[33] BRI which is touted as the ancient Silk Road, is meant to build massive infrastructure projects taking roads, rail lines and sea routes connecting East Asia to Europe. The economic model is through relatively cheaper yet significant interest loans. The USA or any other country does not have any competing projects or visions. The projects have found resistance in many countries due to the mounting debt and the ensuing arm-twisting by the Chinese.[34] Also all these projects ultimately benefit the Chinese contractors who by design are the only ones who can execute them. Chinese paramilitary provides security to these projects resulting in further Chinese footfalls. Many projects have been cancelled or put on hold by recipient countries later. Further, BRI has been added to the CCP constitution in 2017, thus making it more permanent.

## Xi Pushes Territorial disputes in the South China Sea

The South China Sea (SCS) is a vast area measuring 3.6 million sq km (Figure 1.3). Several countries have made competing territorial claims over the SCS.[35] These disputes are potential flash points. China claims the entire SCS as their own by drawing and demarcating the "nine-dash line". China's claim overlaps literally with every other country in the region. Some of the more prominent disputes are over Natuna Islands with Indonesia and Taiwan; The Scarborough Shoal with the Philippines and Taiwan; the Spratly Islands with Vietnam and Taiwan; Paracel Islands with Taiwan and Vietnam; areas in the Gulf of Thailand with Malaysia, Cambodia, Thailand and Vietnam. The entire ASEAN is concerned that the disputes may accelerate into armed conflict. Xi has accelerated building military assets on even the smaller Islands by reclaiming part of the sea. China prefers bilateral discussions but the ASEAN countries find that a disadvantage to deal with more powerful China, and prefer multilateral talks. By making such territorial claims, China has also claimed a large Exclusive Economic Zone (EEZ). China has also claimed a large Air Defence Identification Zone (ADIZ). The USA has accused China of arm-twisting the smaller

**Figure 1.3: Dispute in the South China Sea**

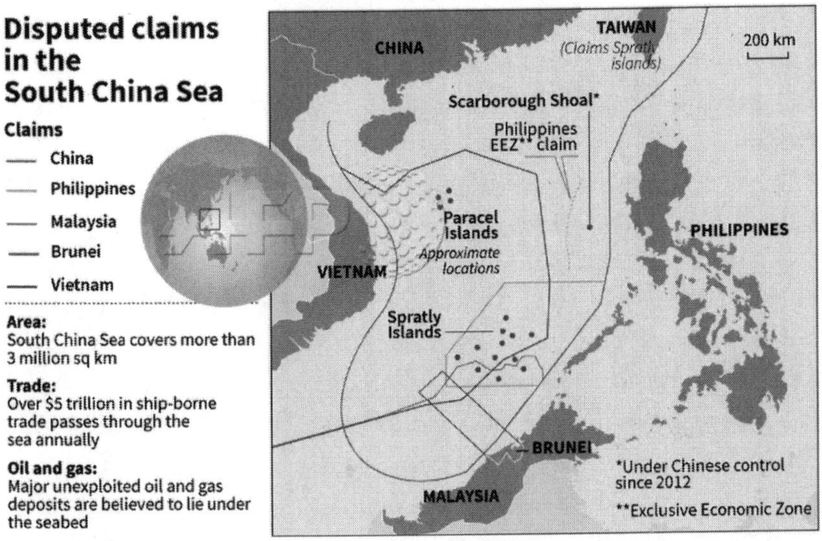


Source: CSIS/AMTI

countries in the neighbourhood and that the Chinese claims have no basis.[36] There has been some show of force incidents between the neighbouring navies. Most countries, including many from Asia and Europe, have been insisting on freedom of navigation operations (FONOPS), and the right of passage in accordance with accepted principles of international law, including the United Nations Convention on the Law of the Sea (UNCLOS). The statement issued after the virtual ASEAN summit on June 26, 2020, said the UNCLOS is "the basis for determining maritime entitlements, sovereign rights, jurisdiction and legitimate interests over maritime zones." China has been often seen to be flexing its military muscle in the region. In January 2013, the Philippines had formally initiated arbitration proceedings against China's claims. On July 12, 2016, the Permanent Court of Arbitration backed the Philippines,[37] saying that there was no evidence that China had historically exercised exclusive control over the waters or resources. Xi's China rejected the ruling, calling it "ill-founded". The US has been working with regional allies and acting as a "stabilising force" in Southeast Asia. This has heightened tensions with China which till now was getting away without check.

## Human Rights Offensive

Early enough, Xi decided to rule with an iron hand. Some of his actions have overshadowed even the Tiananmen Square massacre. He launched an aggressive campaign against activists. The "709 Crackdown" began in July 2015, and is still going on.[38] Many lawyers, and human rights activists were detained. So have been Chinese women's rights and labour rights activists. Being a closed society, the outside world hardly comes to know about the atrocities. In 2017, many Chinese provinces asked Christians to replace pictures of Jesus Christ with Xi Jinping.[39] Believe party instead of religion was the theme that was set. Some pastors have alleged that it involved "destroying crosses, burning bibles, shutting churches and ordering followers to sign papers renouncing their faith".[40] Xi also launched a "Strike hard campaign against violent terrorism" in Xinjiang in 2014.[41] It involved mass detention, and surveillance of ethnic Uyghurs. Xi personally visited Xinjiang in early 2014. Over a million Uyghurs are held in the so-called re-education camps, which have living conditions worse than concentration camps to forcibly convert the local Muslims to Han way of thinking. The famous Maoist term 'People's Democratic Dictatorship', the dualistic policy that means a short painful, intervention treatment[42] has been in action. Despite UN Human Rights Commission's intervention, nothing seems to have changed, and forced labour camps continue. Xi Jinping's calls for the sinicisation of Tibet[43] has been another human rights issue. This involves Buddhism with Chinese characteristics, political and ideological education in Tibetan schools, and building an impregnable fortress around Tibet to dissuade against separatist ideas.

## Integration of Hong Kong and Macau

Xi pushed for total integration of Hong Kong and Macau with the mainland China. It all began with road and rail connectivity. The Hong Kong security law was passed on June 30, 2020.[44] This law criminalises all acts that were perceived by the state as secession, subversion, terrorism, or collusion with external forces. Xi supported stern action by the Hong Kong police to enforce the law. Xi also warned of "foreign forces" interfering in Hong Kong and Macau. The law effectively put an end to the "One country, two systems" that China had promised to maintain in Hong Kong.

## Xi's Thought and Chinese Dream

Xi and the Communist Party ideologues coined the phrase "Chinese Dream",[45] a term he first used on 29 November 2012. It was meant to achieve "great rejuvenation of the Chinese nation". Since then, it has become the political slogan of the Xi era. In October 2017, Xi made a speech at the party congress outlining his political plan for the next 30 years. It is officially called "Xi Jinping Thought on Socialism with Chinese Characteristics for a New Era". Its core goal is to restore the country to its past glory, through economic prosperity and make China a respected world power. It emphasises Xi's leadership of the party and the importance of strengthening its rule over all aspects of Chinese society. Reliance on traditional Chinese political thoughts, culture and practices was important. Xi Jinping's 'Thought' was incorporated into the constitution of the CCP by the 19th Party Congress.[46] "Xi Jinping Thought" has become the most popular smartphone app in China, meant to regularly remind and educate the cadres of the political doctrine.

## Xi and the Communist Party

During July 2021, celebrations marking the 100th anniversary of the founding of the Chinese Communist Party (CCP), Xi further endorsed his views on strengthening the communist party. Highlighting the achievements of the countrymen, he praised the 95 million-member CCP, and said, never had the party been able to unify the people as they were now.[47] Xi proclaimed that CCP had never represented individual interest groups, and that the party was the guardian of China, and that all must uphold the leadership of the Party for China's success. Xi vowed to advance China's influence globally by building a "community of common destiny for all mankind". His agenda clearly is to push the party's preferences and urged the Chinese diaspora to serve the goals of the CCP. For Xi nationalism means supporting the CCP. He is conscious that the party derives legitimacy through mass mobilisation. The strong authoritarian government is an integral part of the "China model".With the sudden collapse of the government in Afghanistan in August 2021, China openly spoke about the failure of "neo-imperialism" and the failure of the Western approach of imposing "alien models on countries which have a distinctively different history, culture and national conditions.

## Xi's Common Prosperity Campaign

One of the drives being run by Xi is the "Common Prosperity" campaign. It is a fundamental requirement of socialism and is necessary to balance growth and financial stability. Xi felt that there was a need to balance income distribution across different groups of population and regions, and was "an essential requirement of socialism and a key feature of Chinese-style modernisation".[48] Ostensibly it is meant to reduce the rich-poor divide. Xi made significant changes to reformist Deng Xiaoping's philosophy that "to get rich is glorious.[49]" There have been crackdowns on businesses and individuals. The term being used is "reasonably adjusting excess incomes" and encouraging high-income individuals and businesses to "give back more to society.[50]" "We can allow some people to get rich first and then guide and help others to get rich together"[51] is the theme. Many policymakers, investors, and journalists have been targeted. Mostly they were the ones who made suggestions that were seen by Team Xi as questioning the party line of thinking. Xi clearly seems to be using the so-called "common prosperity" to impose greater control over, the fast-becoming independent, very rich private enterprises.[52] Over $1 trillion market value of China-listed firms was wiped out by Xi's drive. Domestically, Xi realises that China's miracle is ending. China's growth has slowed in recent years.[53] The urban unemployment rate at nearly 15 percent could cause stability. As per the World Bank report of 2020,[54] China's absolute per capita income was US$ 10,500.4 (US$ 17,312 PPP) compared to USA's US$ 63,543.6. Common prosperity may be retrogression of the Mao era. The common prosperity pilot program demonstrates the party-state's inability to realise successful socio-economic models for common prosperity. Xi has simultaneously cracked down on the nation's charity-related civil society units.

## COVID-19 Pandemic Cover-up

The German news outlet, Der Spiegel, reported that in January 2020 Xi Jinping telephonically pressured WHO Director-General Tedros Adhanom to 'delay a global warning' of the coronavirus outbreak, and especially not mention about the virus's human-to-human transmission risk. The newspaper cited intelligence from the country's Federal Intelligence Service.[55] The WHO denied the allegations. The US accused the WHO of endorsing 'Chinese propaganda', and stopped aid to the organisation.[56] On 22 September 2020, the Chinese billionaire Ren Zhiqiang was jailed for 18 years for questioning Xi's COVID-19 handling, albeit, the charge was of corruption.[57]

## Xi Projects Himself as Climate Change Statesman

At 28 per cent of global emissions,China is one of the biggest sources of carbon dioxide. But President Xi announced that China will aim to hit peak emissions before 2030 and for carbon neutrality by 2060.[58] He outlined the steps during a video talk to the UN General Assembly in New York. This announcement was seen as a significant step in the fight against climate change. Climate Action Tracker, the research group monitoring action to reduce greenhouse gas emissions, says it would make a significant contribution to reducing the expected rise of global temperature. Li Shuo, an expert on Chinese climate policy from Greenpeace Asia said, "It demonstrates Xi's consistent interest in leveraging the climate agenda for geopolitical purposes."

## Xi's Foreign Policy Approach

Like the military, Xi also has a hard-line approach to foreign affairs, with clearly a nationalistic agenda, and forcefully asserting China's influence on the international stage. Xi has picked fights with many of his neighbours and antagonised others.[59] Xi is impatient with the status quo, and displays a high tolerance for risk. He wants to make China united and confident when asserting externally. But often Xi's foreign policy signals are difficult to read. Beijing has an interest, in denuclearisation of North Korea as it perceives it could cause instability in its backyard.[60] Xi was very concerned about South Korea positioning THAAD air defence system on its soil. Yet, it pursues a double game to keep USA hanging on a hook, by offering South Korea to improve relations. Meanwhile, Japan finds Xi's aggression in SCS and ECS a thing of worry. Japan is concerned about possible forced takeover of Senkaku Islands which China calls their own Diaoyu Islands.

Also,China's promulgation of the ADIZ in November 2013, covers these islands. Xi and the Japanese Prime Ministers have met repeatedly. While there has been increasing dislike and hatred among the people on two side, the very high volume of trade between them, especially after the China—US trade war remains the main positive. Once the US and its European allies imposed sanctions against Russia after the Ukraine crisis, Xi found a good opportunity to woo Russia. Xi built a strong personal relationship with Russian strongman Putin. Xi signed the $400 billion gas deal with Russia, and soon became Russia's largest trading partner. They also meet regularly in regional groupings like SCO, RIC and BRICS. China has also closed to Iran after the US imposed sanctions. More recently China has been openly offering support to the Taliban regime in Afghanistan, ostensibly to fill the vacuum left by US withdrawal.

## US-China Relations

The very rapid rise of China and its expansionist designs and desire to be the second global power is seen by the US as a direct threat to its sole superpower status. On China-US relations, Xi said at the beginning of his tenure in 2014, "If China and the United States are in confrontation, it would surely spell disaster for both countries".[61] Xi has been very critical of US's "Strategic Pivot[62]" to Asia. US finds Chinese expansionist actions in SCS; its tacit threats for forced unification of Taiwan; and China's Belt and Road Initiative (BRI) to increase global influence as a threat to its global position. Both sides are also strengthening military forces in the Western Pacific region. The US has also been critical of Chinese cyber-attacks and intellectual property theft. In response, the US has been trying to rally the West in what he calls a battle between "autocracies versus democracies."[63] Beijing is now preparing for a period of increasing global uncertainty and geopolitical hostility. The trade war between US and China is likely to intensify further.

## International Image Building

Xi has also been conscious of building his image as a global leader. Xi has made state visits to most major countries of the world. Xi's state visit to the US in 2015, became very memorable as he met the chief executives of

America's top 10 technology companies,with a market value about $2.5 trillion.[64] He uses the state-controlled media to build a larger than-life image at home and to project himself as a responsible global statesman abroad. This has been accompanied by a resurgence in patriotic nationalism whipped up by state media, with a particular focus on Mr Xi as China's strongman, leading some to accuse him of developing a personality cult.[65] Xi has made visits to Africa to get greater acceptance and bring the countries into Chinese fold. Xi made an early state visit to India in September 2014, and had one on one with PM Modi again in Wuhan later. Xi's visit to Pakistan in April 2015, cleared the way for the China-Pakistan Economic Corridor (CPEC), the flagship of BRI project. Pakistan confirmed on him their highest civilian award, the Nishan-e-Pakistan. Xi was the guest of honour at the 70th Anniversary of the World War II Victory Day parade in Moscow in 2015. During his visit to the UK in 2015, Xi also visited Manchester City's football academy as a part of his image-building exercise. In the 2017 World Economic Forum event at Davos, Xi became the first paramount Chinese leader to attend, and was a keynote speaker, and promised on "economic globalisation" and climate change. Later, Xi also visited the United Nations, World Health Organisation and International Olympics Committee, to showcase his global image and responsibilities. Xi also became the first Chinese leader to visit Japan since 2010 when he attended G 20 summit in Osaka in June 2019.[66]

## Unification of Taiwan

Xi met the then Taiwanese President Ma Ying-jeou in 2015, the first-ever meeting since 2015. Xi said that China and Taiwan are "one family" that can't be pulled apart. "No force can pull us apart because we are brothers who are still connected by our flesh even if our bones are broken, we are a family in which blood is thicker than water," Xi said.[67] But in 2016, President Tsai Ing-wen's pro-independence Democratic Progressive Party won a sweeping victory in Taiwan. Therefore, during the 19th Party Congress in 2017, Xi mentioned Taiwan and unification, using a little stronger language. In March 2018, Xi warned Taiwan will face "punishment of history" for separatism.[68]

In January 2019, Xi said "Taiwan's unification with China is inevitable," and threatened to use military force, if required.[69] Xi also said that they "are willing to create broad space for peaceful reunification, but will leave no room for any form of separatist activities."[70] The Taiwanese President Tsai retorted, that Taiwan would not accept one country two systems scheme. China has been making aggressive aircraft and maritime forays to threaten Taiwan since then. The number of incidents is increasing. Some say it is a dress rehearsal for actual assault.

## China and Afghanistan

China has offered $31 million in emergency aid to Afghanistan, which would essentially include food supplies and coronavirus vaccines.[71] This is also a Chinese way of engaging the Taliban. The formation of the new interim government was a "necessary step to restore order" in Afghanistan, feels China. China is also trying to closely coordinate with other neighbours Pakistan, Iran, Tajikistan, Uzbekistan and Turkmenistan. Meanwhile, China has been critical of the US's handling of Afghanistan and creating a mess. "What the US did in Afghanistan over the past two decades is a textbook example which shows us the consequences of wanton military intervention and attempts to impose one's own ideology and values on others," said Foreign Ministry Spokesperson Wang Wenbin.[72] Afghanistan could become a key player in expanding Xi's flagship BRI. Also keeping control over Afghanistan would help China secure its Xinjiang region from possible external intervention and export of revolution. China is also looking at unexplored wealth of minerals residing in Afghanistan. China's success in Afghanistan would not only embarrass the US but also increase China's global standing and reach.

## Personal life and Public Image

Xi married Ke Lingling, the daughter of Chinese Ambassador to the UK, in 1979. The two were said to fight "almost every day". After the divorce in 1982, she immigrated to the UK. Jinping's second wife, Peng Liyuan is a charming celebrity singer. Team Xi Jinping tries to showcase them as an ideal couple through songs such as "Papa Xi loves Mama Peng". Ironically this is for the Chinese masses to whom the government has always dictated on the number of children they can have.[73] Unlike many of her predecessor "first ladies", Peng has maintained high visibility. Xi Mingze, their daughter is a graduate of Harvard University. Members of Xi's extended family have substantial business interests, but all became low profile when Xi started the anti-corruption campaign when he took over thereins.

Xi was considered supremely pragmatic, a realist, with his "eyes on the prize" from early adulthood.[74] A down-to-earth, cautious, and hard-working person. There aren't many 21st Century leaders who lived in a cave and laboured as a farmer before clawing their way to power.[75] He is known to enjoy American films like the God Father, and likes playing football and climbing mountains. Xi has a very high public rating in China. In 2018, Forbes ranked him as the most powerful and influential leader in the world. Xi was the fourth Chinese to be honoured with Pakistan's highest civilian award Nisha-e-Pakistan in April 2015.

## Antagonising the World

Other than Pakistan, China hardly has any real friends. Many countries are dependent on China mainly for cheap goods coming out of China's mass-producing factories. An unfavourable balance of trade is of concern to all. The BRI debt-trap is forcing all countries to review projects. Russia-China's current friendship is of convenience. In the long term, Russia cannot have a belligerent superpower on its border. Communism is failed ideology. Are the Chinese masses happy under an undemocratic autocratic leadership, unlikely? Most ASEAN countries have lost their EEZs in SCS, and are angry. Xi is trying to show its anger to India and after Galwan has lost major goodwill with over a billion people. Major world powers are rallying around the US. The QUAD and other tri-laterals are all aimed to contain China. No one can make friends through arm-twisting. Can China become a global leader without genuine friends? I don't think so.

## Xi-Modi Personal Equation

PM Modi made a great start in 2014, with the neighbourhood-first policy. Modi developed a personal rapport with Xi. In 2014, Xi arrived for a three-day visit and red carpet was rolled out in Modi's home state Gujarat, in Ahmedabad. Modi's first visit to China was in May 2015. Xi too received Modi in his home town of Xi'an. The next one-on-one was at Wuhan, China in April 2018. There were many optics of the Modi-Xi summit meeting in

Mamallapuram in 2019. Unprecedented camaraderie was visible between leaders of the world's most populous two nations. Modi visited Hangzhou in September 2016 for the G20 Summit, Xiamen in 2017 for BRICS Summit, and Quindao in 2018 for SCO summit. Effectively Modi met Xi around 18 times after becoming PM in 2014. Modi is the only Indian PM who made nine official visits to China, five times as PM and four times as Chief Minister,the most by any Indian PM. He did invest significant personal capital with Xi. Modi and Xi had agreed to maintain peace and tranquillity between the two countries.

China has been concerned about India's participation in the so-called anti-China QUAD grouping. Xi perhaps wanted to give a signal to India, and to put it in place. Then Galwan happened. China's intrusions and actions in eastern Ladakh in 2020 put Modi-Xi one-to-one equation into cold storage.

## Powerful Xi Push—Implications India

Xi has continued to push the Chinese initiatives to strengthen their position in the Indian Ocean region. They have invested large sums in most South Asian countries surrounding India. China is currently the largest overseas investor in Myanmar, Pakistan, Sri Lanka and the Maldives.[76] Chinese investment is mostly in hard infrastructure—power, roads, railways, bridges, ports and airports. While Pakistan remains China's major arms importer, India's other neighbour Bangladesh is the second biggest. China has been supporting the governments of Pakistan and Myanmar who are otherwise under international pressure on terrorism and human rights. China's approach to gaining access to new countries has been through arms sales and loan-based infra projects. The contracts clearly specify that arbitration for disputes in projects would be by China-based courts. Loans are conditional, and the contracts are given to Chinese companies. China taking a stake in the Karachi and Dhaka stock exchanges makes get deeper into the country's economy. China has pumped investments in land-locked Nepal and has also got involved into the local politics to increase influence and have them tilt away from India. China has also been using its strength in telecom technology and large-scale production to enter global markets, especially in Asia and Africa. Their network and systems hardware is suspected to be embedded with cyber devices that can have security implications for the recipient country. "China is behaving how emerging superpowers generally tend to behave, they try to flex muscles and project power, all of which China is trying to do at the moment," says Happymon Jacob, associate professor of disarmament studies at Jawaharlal Nehru University (JNU).[77]

It's continued strengthening engagement with Pakistan, and deeper forays into Bangladesh, Myanmar and Sri Lanka have implications for India. While the BRI projects are meant to be economic in nature, but these projects are making the recipients indebted to a more powerful China, who then makes inroads into the masses and institutions, and may actually impact sovereignty. Ports have great military potential.

The Pakistan-China nexus has much greater implications. They both are occupying the Indian Territory. Both have serious boundary issues with India. The commonality in military hardware, and regular joint military exercises between them, increase the threat of a two-nation war for India. The number of exercises has increased exponentially and high-level military to military visits are on the increase. China learns Western combat tactics and philosophy from Pakistan who has been part of the Western military system for many decades. Pakistan gets to know about some of the Russian platforms of Su-30 class that are also operated by India.

The Regional Comprehensive Economic Partnership (RCEP) will give Xi greater political and economic control over Asia. India has chosen not to be a part of the arrangement. This puts pressure on India to have stronger bilateral trade arrangements and also on the US to increase its presence in Asia. Xi's military modernisation pitch has also cemented its leadership claim in the region. The world is reacting. The Quad is being strengthened. More trilateral security arrangements are evolving like the AUKUS between Australia, the United Kingdom, and the United States. China is pushing multi-polarity and ideological plurality. CCP represents China's authoritarian state-capitalism, a model that it wants to push as a successful alternative to the liberal world order. India believes in democratic, rule-based order.

Xi is a man in a hurry. He has thrown to the winds Deng Xiaoping's approach of "hide your strength, bide your time". Xi will continue to rule as an absolute leader for some time to come. India has to contend with rising China and an aggressive Xi. India has to become economically and militarily stronger. India cannot expect outsiders to fight our battles. India has to build a strong deterrent so as to prevent Chinese aggressive designs. India has to prepare for hybrid war. India has to sit out if required. India and a united polity can face the Chinese challenge. It has to use diplomacy, and to find more free-thinking friends and build alliances.

## Notes

1. Priyanka Boghani, Xi Jinping, Obama meet at White House, The World, February 14, 2012, at https://www.pri.org/stories/2012-02-14/xi-jinping-obama-meet-white-house. Accessed on September 5, 2021.
2. Melissa Albert, "Biography of Xi Jinping", Britannica, Updated August 13, 2021, at https://www.britannica.com/biography/Xi-Jinping. Accessed on September 5, 2021.
3. Simon Elegant, "China's Nelson Mandela", *Time*, November 19, 2007, at https://world.time.com/2007/11/19/chinas_nelson_mandela/. Accessed on August 30, 2021.
4. Melissa Albert, n. 2.
5. Zhao Chenggen, "President Xi Jinping's Anti-Corruption Storm Is Here to Stay", *Global Asia*, September 2014, at https://www.globalasia.org/v9no3/debate/president-xi-jinpings-anti-corruption-storm-is-here-to-stay_zhao-chenggen. Accessed on September 5, 2021.
6. "Agence France-Presse in Beijing, China's former military chief of staff jailed for life for corruption", *The Guardian*, February 20, 2019, at https://www.theguardian.com/world/2019/feb/20/chinas-former-military-chief-of-staff-jailed-for-life-for-corruption. Accessed on August 31, 2021.
7. Heilmann, Sebastian, *China's Political System*. Rowman & Littlefield, 2017, pp. 62–75.
8. Pratik Jakhar, "China's anti-corruption campaign expands with new agency", BBC, March 20, 2018, at https://www.bbc.com/news/world-asia-china-43453769. Accessed on August 31, 2021.
9. Willy Wo-Lap Lam, "The June 4th Massacre and the Militarization of Chinese Politics", The Jamestown Foundation, June 4, 2019, at https://jamestown.org/program/the-june-4th-massacre-and-the-militarization-of-chinese-politics/. Accessed on September 5, 2021.
10. Elizabeth C Economy, "The great firewall of China: Xi Jinping's internet shutdown", *The Guardian*, June 29, 2018, at https://www.theguardian.com/news/2018/jun/29/

the-great-firewall-of-china-xi-jinpings-internet-shutdown. Accessed on August 31, 2021.

11. Arjun Kharpal, "An app that let Chinese users bypass the Great Firewall and access Google, Facebook has disappeared", CNBC, October 11, 2020, at https://www.cnbc.com/2020/10/12/chinese-app-that-let-users-access-google-facebook-has-disappeared.html. Accessed on August 31, 2021.
12. Angus Grigg, "How China stopped its bloggers", *Financial Review*, July 4, 2015, at https://www.afr.com/technology/how-china-stopped-its-bloggers-20150702-gi34za. Accessed on August 31, 2021.
13. "Why Xi Jinping is called Winnie the Pooh on Twitter? It's a long story",*Business Today*, June 18, 2020, at https://www.businesstoday.in/latest/trends/story/india-china-border-dispute-twitterati-twitter-xi-jinping-winnie-the-pooh-ladakh-galwan-valley-261566-2020-06-18. Accessed on August 31, 2021.
14. Shi Jiangtao and Kristin Huang, "End to term limits at the top may be start of global backlash for China, analysts say", *South China Morning Post*, February 26, 2018
15. Tom Phillips, "Xi Jinping: Does China truly love 'Big Daddy Xi'—or fear him?", *The Guardian*, September 19, 2015, at https://www.theguardian.com/world/2015/sep/19/xi-jinping-does-china-truly-love-big-daddy-xi-or-fear-him. Accessed on August 31, 2021.
16. Jeremy Goldkorn, "An oath, and tears of joy in the Great Hall of the People", SupChina, March 19, 2018, at https://supchina.com/2018/03/19/oath-tears-joy-great-hall-people/. Accessed on August 31, 2021.
17. Orange Wang and Sidney Leng, "Chinese President Xi Jinping's show of support for state-owned firms 'no surprise', analysts say", *South China Morning Post*, September 28, 2018, at https://www.scmp.com/economy/china-economy/article/2166261/chinese-president-xi-jinpings-show-support-state-owned-firms. Accessed on September 5, 2021. https://www.lowyinstitute.org/the-interpreter/has-china-given-state-owned-enterprise-reform. Accessed on September 5, 2021.
18. Nicholas Borst, "Has China given up on state-owned enterprise reform?", *The Interpreter*, April 15, 2021, at https://www.lowyinstitute.org/the-interpreter/has-china-given-state-owned-enterprise-reform. Accessed on September 5, 2021.
19. Edwin L.-C. Lai, "Renminbi Internationalization: The Prospects of China's Yuan as the Next Global Currency", The Hong Kong University of Science and Technology, June 2015, at https://iems.ust.hk/publications/thought-leadership-briefs/renminbi-internationalization-the-prospects-of-chinas-yuan-as-the-next-global-currency. Accessed on September 5, 2021.
20. Kimberly Amadeo, "How the Yuan Could Become a Global Currency", *The Balance*, November 30, 2020, at https://www.thebalance.com/yuan-reserve-currency-to-global-currency-3970465. Accessed on September 25, 2021.

21. Evelyn Cheng, "China's yuan could become the world's third largest reserve currency in 10 years", Morgan Stanley predicts, CNBC, September 4, 2020, at https://www.cnbc.com/2020/09/04/chinas-yuan-rmb-to-become-third-largest-reserve-currency-by-2030-morgan-stanley.html. Accessed on September 25, 2021.
22. Bloomberg, "Why Xi Jinping waited years to launch his crackdown on tycoons", *Business Standard,* August 11, 2021, at https://www.business-standard.com/article/international/why-xi-jinping-waited-years-to-launch-his-crackdown-on-tycoons-121081100067_1.html. Accessed on September 5, 2021.
23. Amanda Lee, "China's economy at an 'inflection point' as Xi Jinping embarks on sweeping regulatory crack down", *South China Morning Post,* August 22, 2021, at https://www.scmp.com/economy/china-economy/article/3145764/chinas-economy-inflection-point-xi-jinping-embarks-sweeping. Accessed on August 31, 2021.
24. Business Editor, "Why Xi Jinping waited years to launch his crackdown on tycoons", *Business Standard,* August 11, 2021, at https://www.business-standard.com/article/international/why-xi-jinping-waited-years-to-launch-his-crackdown-on-tycoons-121081100067_1.html. Accessed on August 31, 2021.
25. Ibid.
26. Stephen McDonell, "China allows three children in major policy shift", BBC News, May 31, 2021, at https://www.bbc.com/news/world-asia-china-57303592. Accessed on August 31, 2021.
27. Moritz Rudolf, "Xi Jinping Thought on the Rule of Law", SWP Berlin, April 22, 2021, at https://www.swp-berlin.org/10.18449/2021C28/. Accessed on August 31, 2021.
28. Ibid.
29. Shannon Tiezzi, "The Real Reason China Is Cutting 300,000 Troops", *The Diplomat,* September 8, 2015, at https://thediplomat.com/2015/09/the-real-reason-china-is-cutting-300000-troops/. Accessed on September 5, 2021.
30. Edited by Phillip C. Saunders, Arthur S. Ding, Andrew Scobell, Andrew N.D. Yang, and Joel Wuthnow, Chairman Xi Remakes the PLA, National Defense University Press, Washington, D.C. 2019, at https://ndupress.ndu.edu/Portals/68/Documents/Books/Chairman-Xi/Chairman-Xi.pdf. Accessed on August 31, 2021.
31. Wang Xinjuan, "Graphics: China's military reform in past 5 years", CGTN.com, September 1, 2020, at http://eng.mod.gov.cn/news/2020-08/01/content_4869047.htm. Accessed on September 5, 2021.
32. Liu Hui, "Graphics: Reform in China's national defense and armed forces". CGTN.com, December 26, 2019, at http://eng.chinamil.com.cn/view/2019-12/26/content_9704070.htm. Accessed on September 5, 2021.

33. Wu Jiao and Zhang Yunbi, "Xi proposes a 'new Silk Road' with Central Asia", *China Daily*, September 8, 2013, at http://usa.chinadaily.com.cn/china/2013-09/08/content_16952304.htm. Accessed on September 11, 2021.
34. Andrew Chatzky and James McBride, "China's Massive Belt and Road Initiative", Council on Foreign Relations, January 28, 2020, at https://www.cfr.org/backgrounder/chinas-massive-belt-and-road-initiative. Accessed on September 11, 2021.
35. Greg Austin, "The Conversation, How did the South China Sea dispute begin and where is it headed?", Scroll.in, July 29, 2020, at https://scroll.in/article/968918/how-did-the-south-china-sea-dispute-begin-and-where-is-it-headed. Accessed on October 2, 2021.
36. AFP, "China's sea claims have no basis", says US, *The Hindu*, July 27, 2021, at https://www.thehindu.com/news/international/chinas-sea-claims-have-no-basis-says-us/article35570625.ece. Accessed on October 2, 2021.
37. Robert D. Williams, "Tribunal Issues Landmark Ruling in South China Sea Arbitration", Lawfare, July 12, 2016, at https://www.lawfareblog.com/tribunal-issues-landmark-ruling-south-china-sea-arbitration. Accessed on October 2, 2021.
38. William Nee, "China's 709 Crackdown Is Still Going On", *The Diplomat*, July 9, 2021, at https://thediplomat.com/2021/07/chinas-709-crackdown-is-still-going-on/. Accessed on September 11, 2021.
39. News Desk, "China Asks Christians to Replace Pictures of Jesus Christ With Xi Jinping", India.com, November 15, 2017, at https://www.india.com/news/world/china-asks-christians-to-replace-pictures-of-jesus-christ-with-xi-jinping-2636115/. Accessed on September 11, 2021.
40. Christopher Bodeen, "Group: Officials destroying crosses, burning bibles in China", Associate Press, September 10, 2018, at https://web.archive.org/web/20191008144601/; https://www.apnews.com/c09b2ee4b71540c8a7fd6178820c5970. Accessed on September 11, 2021.
41. "Eradicating Ideological Viruses", Human Rights Watch, September 9, 2018, at https://www.hrw.org/report/2018/09/09/eradicating-ideological-viruses/chinas-campaign-repression-against-xinjiangs. Accessed on September 11, 2021.
42. Richard Baum, "Mao Zedong and 'People's Democratic Dictatorship'", *The Great Courses Daily*. June 19, 2021, at https://www.thegreatcoursesdaily.com/mao-zedong-and-peoples-democratic-dictatorship/. Accessed on September 11, 2021.
43. Edited by Palki Sharma, "Xi Jinping's three-step plan to sinicize Tibet", WION, August 31, 2020, at https://www.wionews.com/world/xi-jinpings-three-step-plan-to-sinicize-tibet-324367. Accessed on September 11, 2021.
44. Grace Tsoi and Lam Cho Wai, "Hong Kong security law: What is it and is it worrying?", BBC News, June 30, 2020, at https://www.bbc.com/news/world-asia-china-52765838. Accessed on September 14, 2021.

45. William Zheng, "Communist Party jargon: from tigers and flies to the Chinese dream", 10 slogans used in the Xi Jinping era, *South China Morning Post*, June 16, 2021, at https://www.scmp.com/news/china/politics/article/3137393/communist-party-jargon-tigers-and-flies-chinese-dream-10. Accessed on September 14, 2021.
46. Yamei. "Full text of resolution on amendment to CPC Constitution", Xinhua, October 24, 2017, at http://www.xinhuanet.com/english/2017-10/24/c_136702726.htm. Accessed on September 14, 2021.
47. Scott W. Harold, "What Xi Jinping's Communist Party Valedictory Speech Can Tell Us About His Conception of China and Its Role in the World", The Rand Blog, July 7, 2021, at https://www.rand.org/blog/2021/07/what-xi-jinpings-communist-party-valedictory-speech.html. Accessed on September 14, 2021.
48. Willy Wo-Lap Lam, "Early Warning Brief: Implications of Xi's Revival of the Maoist Slogan 'Common Prosperity", The Jamestown Foundation, August 26, 2021, at https://jamestown.org/program/implications-of-xis-revival-of-the-maoist-slogan-common-prosperity/. Accessed on September 15, 2021.
49. Ibid.
50. Ryan Hass, "Assessing China's 'common prosperity'" campaign, Brookings, September 9, 2021, at https://www.brookings.edu/blog/order-from-chaos/2021/09/09/assessing-chinas-common-prosperity-campaign/. Accessed on September 14, 2021.
51. Willy Wo-Lap Lam, "Implications Of Xi's Revival Of Maoist Slogan 'Common Prosperity'—Analysis", The Jamestown Foundation, August 29, 2021, at https://www.eurasiareview.com/29082021-implications-of-xis-revival-of-maoist-slogan-common-prosperity-analysis/. Accessed on September 15, 2021.
52. Ibid.
53. Bill Conerly, "China's Economic Miracle Is Ending", *Forbes*, May 4, 2021, at https://www.forbes.com/sites/billconerly/2021/05/04/chinas-economic-miracle-is-ending/?sh=507b0aeeaa9d. Accessed on September 15, 2021.
54. World Bank national accounts data, and OECD National Accounts data files., World Bank, 2020, at https://data.worldbank.org/indicator/NY.GDP.PCAP.CD?locations=CN. Accessed on September 15, 2021.
55. Express Web Desk, "Xi Jinping dialed Tedros to 'delay global warning' on Covid-19 outbreak; WHO denies", *The Indian Express*, May 10, 2020, at https://indianexpress.com/article/world/coronavirus-who-china-xi-jinping-tedros-adhanom-phone-call-6402951/. Accessed on September 14, 2021.
56. Ibid.
57. Associated Press, "Chinese tycoon Ren Zhiqiang jailed for 18 years for criticising Xi Jinping's COVID-19 response", *Business Today*, September 22, 2020, at https://www.businesstoday.in/latest/world/story/chinese-tycoon-ren-zhiqiang-jailed-for-18-years-for-criticising-xi-jinping-covid-19-response-273670-2020-09-22. Accessed on September 14, 2021.

58. Matt McGrath, "Climate change: China aims for 'carbon neutrality by 2060'", BBC News, September 22, 2020, at https://www.bbc.com/news/science-environment-54256826. Accessed on September 14, 2021.
59. Jude Blanchette, "Xi's Gamble", *Foreign Affairs*, July/August 2021, at https://www.foreignaffairs.com/articles/china/2021-06-22/xis-gamble. Accessed on September 5, 2021.
60. Oriana Skylar Mastro, "China's Dangerous Double Game in North Korea", *Foreign Affairs*, April 2, 2021, at https://www.foreignaffairs.com/articles/china/2021-04-02/chinas-dangerous-double-game-north-korea. Accessed on September 5, 2021.
61. Teddy Ng and Kwong Man-k, "President Xi Jinping warns of disaster if Sino-US relations sour", *South China Morning Post*, July 9, 2014, at https://www.scmp.com/news/china/article/1550184/confrontation-us-would-be-disaster-says-president-xi-jinping. Accessed on September 11, 2021.
62. Kenneth G. Lieberthal, "The American Pivot to Asia", Brookings, December 21, 2011, at https://www.brookings.edu/articles/the-american-pivot-to-asia/. Accessed on September 11, 2021.
63. Zolan Kanno-Youngs and David E. Sanger, "Biden Speaks With Xi Amid Low Point in U.S.-China Relations", *New York Times*, September 10, 2021, at https://www.nytimes.com/2021/09/10/us/politics/biden-xi-china.html. Accessed on September 11, 2021.
64. Jane Perlez, "Xi Jinping's U.S. Visit", *New York Times*, September 29, 2015, at https://www.nytimes.com/interactive/projects/cp/reporters-notebook/xi-jinping-visit/china-tech-market. Accessed on September 11, 2021.
65. "Xi Jinping: From princeling to president", BBC, May 12, 2021, at https://www.bbc.com/news/world-asia-pacific-11551399. Accessed on September 11, 2021.
66. Official Statement, Xi Jinping Arrives in Osaka, Japan for the 14th G20 Summit, Ministry of Foreign Affairs, PRC, June 17, 2019, at https://www.fmprc.gov.cn/mfa_eng/topics_665678/xjpcxesgjtfh/t1676587.shtml. Accessed on September 11, 2021.
67. Reuters, "China and Taiwan presidents meet for first time", AlJazeera, November 7, 2015, at http://america.aljazeera.com/articles/2015/11/7/taiwan-china-leaders-make-history-at-Singapore-talks.html. Accessed on September 14, 2021.
68. Reuters, "Xi Jinping warns Taiwan will face 'punishment of history' for separatism", *The Hindu*, March 20, 2018, at https://www.thehindu.com/news/international/xi-warns-taiwan-will-face-punishment-of-history-for-separatism/article23299005.ece. Accessed on September 14, 2021.
69. Lily Kuo, "'All necessary means': Xi Jinping reserves right to use force against Taiwan", *The Guardian*, January 2, 2019, at https://www.theguardian.com/world/2019/jan/02/all-necessary-means-xi-jinping-reserves-right-to-use-force-against-taiwan. Accessed on September 14, 2021.

70. Ibid.
71. BBC News, "China offers $31m in emergency aid to Afghanistan", September 9, 2021, at https://www.bbc.com/news/world-asia-china-58496867. Accessed on September 22, 2021.
72. Ibid.
73. Olav Albuquerque, "Power and divorce are wed to each other?", *The Bridge Chronicle*, July 4, 2020, at https://www.thebridgechronicle.com/opinion/power-and-divorce-are-wed-each-other-52750. Accessed on September 15, 2021.
74. Carrie Gracie, "The thoughts of Chairman Xi", BBC, October 13, 2017, at https://www.bbc.co.uk/news/resources/idt-sh/Thoughts_Chairman_Xi. Accessed on September 15, 2021.
75. Ibid.
76. Amit Bhandari and Chandni Jindal, "Chinese Investments in India's Neighbourhood", Gateway House, March 12, 2018, at https://www.gatewayhouse.in/chinese-investments-in-indias-neighbourhood/. Accessed on September 23, 2021.
77. Nikita Kwatra and Sriharsha Devulapalli, "Mapped: How China has raised its clout in India's neighbourhood", *The Mint*, June 30, 2020, at https://www.livemint.com/news/india/mapped-how-china-has-raised-its-clout-in-india-s-neighbourhood-11593498026189.html. Accessed on September 23, 2021.

# 2

# Military Power Play Amidst the Changing Regional Dynamics

SP SINGH

President J Biden, on August 31, 2021, nearly two decades after the US began military operations against the Taliban in Afghanistan, declared that the last US combat troops had vacated the soil of Afghanistan. President Biden, earlier on April 14, 2021, had declared the withdrawal of US combat troops from Afghanistan before the twenty-year anniversary on September 11, 2001. In mid-August, the Taliban, in less than two weeks' time were able to capture most of Afghanistan's provincial capitals and finally entered Kabul on August 15, 2021. President Ashraf Ghani fled the country as the Afghan government collapsed. The US and other countries conducted a major airlift operation throughout the month of August, to evacuate their nationals and Afghans who were considered at risk of Taliban reprisals.[1] Despite such efforts, many were left behind amid risks of renewed civil war and humanitarian crisis along with a large arsenal of arms and state of art military equipment at the hands of the Taliban.

For the world, it was not only the concern for the future of democratic values, human lives, peaceful existence of society, resources, and fate of long-term development projects and investments, but also the danger of politico-military power play and the turmoil that would engulf the region after the withdrawal of US forces from Afghanistan. With the Taliban in control, Pakistan rejoicing on their take over and China moving in stealthily to seize the opportunity for politico-military and economic gains, the region was staring at another long period of instability and power struggle. India of course was affected the most by this development in the neighbourhood.

## Background

On October 15, 1999, the UN Security Council created the Al-Qaeda and Taliban Sanctions Committee through a resolution, that linked both these groups as terror outfits and accordingly imposed major sanctions on their funding, arms shipments, and travel. The UN move came in almost after two decades of ascendency of Al-Qaeda and its leader, Osama bin Laden, who controlled the terrorist groups across the region. The Taliban, which rose from the ashes of Afghanistan's post-Soviet civil war, became the central point of all terror activities as it provided Al-Qaeda with a safe sanctuary for terror operations.

On the infamous day of 9/11 (September 11, 2001), four commercial airliners were hijacked by Al-Qaeda operatives and crashed into the World Trade Centre in New York and the Pentagon in Washington, DC. President Bush, on September 18, 2001, authorized the use of force against the perpetrators of these attacks by signing a joint resolution. Immediately after this, the US military supported by the British, commenced a bombing campaign against Taliban forces, by launching "Operation Enduring Freedom". Al-Qaeda and Taliban forces were obviously the main targets of this operation and in the early phase of this campaign, the US forces made their intent amply clear.[2]

On November 14, after the retreat of the Taliban, the UN Security Council passed a Resolution, calling for a "central role" for the United Nations in establishing an interim administrative controlling authority in Afghanistan. UN further requested its member nations to dispatch peacekeeping forces to ensure stability in the region as well as provide requisite humanitarian aid. After the fall of Kabul in November 2001 with the escape of Osama Bin Laden from Tora Bora cave complex, Hamid Karzai was installed as the interim administration head through the signing of the Bonn Agreement, endorsed by the UN Security Council Resolution. However, despite the official fall of the Taliban on December 9, 2001, Al-Qaeda leaders continued to retain certain hide out in the mountains. In March 2002, "Operation Anaconda", the first major ground offensive operation, was launched against an estimated less than a thousand Al-Qaeda and Taliban rebels in the valley of Paktia Province.[3] On August 8, 2003, North Atlantic Treaty Organisation (NATO) took control of International Security Forces (ISAF) in Afghanistan, expanding NATO/ISAF's role across the country. President Karzai becomes the first democratically elected head of Afghanistan under the safety umbrella of NATO/ISAF. However, the perceived peace was short-lived and barely three weeks later on October 29, Bin Laden released a videotaped message, just days before the US election, challenging the US-led coalition in Afghanistan.

Despite these threats, in a unique democratic election ever in Afghanistan, more than six million voter turnout was observed in September 2005. Surprisingly, more than half of those casting ballot were women. It was seen as a sign of political progress in a powerful patriarchal and conservative society reeling under the threat of terrorist attacks by Al-Qaeda and the Taliban. Once again, this progress towards peace did not last long and July 2006 saw a bloody resurgence of violence across the country with a manifold increase in suicide bomber attacks as well as increase in remotely detonated bombing. On May 2, 2011, nearly after five years of the resurgence of Al-Qaeda terror activities in Afghanistan, their leader Bin Laden, perpetrator of the 9/11 attacks, was eliminated by US forces in Pakistan.[4] Immediately after this, President Obama set upon to announce the troop withdrawal from Afghanistan and accordingly declared the withdrawal of troops by the summer of 2012. However, the Afghan government's capability to ensure security of the country, seemed to remain under serious doubts. US efforts in eliminating terrorism continued to be undermined by Pakistan becoming a haven for terrorists. In just 10 years of war against terrorism, the US suffered about 1,700 troop casualties and a financial loss amounting to about $500 billion.

In June 2013, Afghan forces took over the security responsibility nationwide as NATO handed over control of the remaining 95 districts. After almost a year of observation of capability of Afghan forces, President Obama, on May 27, 2014, announced a phase-wise withdrawal of US troops. Overturning this commitment, Trump administration in 2017, announced the troop withdrawal to be conditional, based on actual security situation on the ground. Taliban, miffed with this change of decision, in a series of audacious terror attacks in Kabul killed more than hundred people giving a stern message of escalating the violence. In February 2019, Negotiations between the United States and the Taliban in Doha picked up pace again and on February 29, 2020, an agreement was signed between the US envoy Khalilzad and Mulla Baradar. While on one end the agreement Taliban guaranteed to scale down terrorist activities, on the other it paved the way for a significant reduction of US troops in Afghanistan. However, the peace once again eluded the Afghan and amidst the change of guard in the US, Joe Biden flip-flopped on withdrawal, Taliban fighters in a surprise move rapidly advanced towards Kabul to take over control. During this move, Taliban fighters took control of most of Afghanistan's provincial capitals except two and also took full control of border crossings. Taliban fighters, in the face of very little resistance, quickly overran the capital Kabul, and took over the presidential palace. The last US troops left Afghanistan by the end of August with the Taliban taking over full control. A chaotic two weeks evacuation period followed this final troop withdrawal, in which more than a hundred thousand people were evacuated.[5]

## Aftermath of US Withdrawal

The Taliban launched a sweeping offensive in early May 2021, capturing large swaths of the country's rural provinces and solidifying the group's authority in locations where it already had a major presence. Other districts were taken over by the Taliban with greater surprise, with almost negligible military opposition. In May and June 2021, the Taliban grabbed control of almost 100 of Afghanistan's 400 districts. The Taliban took control of Zaranj, the provincial capital, on August 6, 2021. The Taliban's subsequent conquest of half of Afghanistan's provincial capitals stunned many onlookers, including, of course, US authorities. According to reports, US officials were anxious on August 13, that the Taliban could attack Kabul within days. The Taliban took the last major cities and destroyed the last strongholds of organised Afghan government resistance with the fall of Jalalabad in the East and Mazar-e-Sharif in the North. The Taliban entered Kabul on August 15, 2021, effectively completing their control of the country. The rapidity of events threw the entire US withdrawal plan into disarray. The civilian populace was terrified, and chaos reigned across the country. The US forces were compelled to make an impromptu pull-out, leaving behind not only military equipment, but also millions of their Afghan supporters.

The country has descended into turmoil as ISI-backed Taliban have taken control of most districts, including the capital Kabul, following a rushed and poorly managed withdrawal of US forces from Afghanistan. As NATO forces left the war-torn country and US Marines flew out, they left behind a considerable amount of weaponry, ammunition, and military equipment that the Taliban now control. When the Taliban overran Afghan forces who failed to protect district centres, they took a large amount of modern military equipment with them. When the Taliban rolled into provincial capitals and run over military outposts with stunning speed, they made even bigger gains, including combat aircraft. They took not only political control, but also US-supplied armament, such as rifles, ammunition, and helicopters. The Taliban now have aeroplanes, 11 military bases, and an army of well-trained warriors with the latest weapons and gadgets, as well as well-planned military bases with cutting-edge aviation and ground warfare equipment.[6]

US forces had built a huge arsenal of high-tech state-of-the-art weapons, aircraft, multipurpose wheeled armoured vehicles, ammunition, Night Vision Devices (NVD), special clothing and electronic equipment in Afghanistan. The US forces, between April and July 2021, barely a few months before their withdrawal, had handed over a huge arsenal of weaponry to the Afghan National Defense and Security forces (ANDSF). This included six A-29 light attack aircraft, more than a hundred High Mobility Multipurpose Wheeled Vehicles (Humvees), about 10K high-explosive rockets, 60K high explosive rounds, 9000K rounds of .50 calibre ammo, and 20000K rounds of 7.62 mm bullets. Taliban immediately on assuming control of Kabul, and took control of these weapons and equipment also.[7] Afghanistan's neighbours are in awe and shock at the rapidity of turn of events. They are still trying to adjust to a changing geopolitical landscape following the Taliban's quick return to power after two decades.

## Diplomacy being held hostage in the Region

The Taliban's takeover represents a shock to regional diplomatic and security dynamics as well as emerges as a threat to the democracy in the Asian region. With neighbouring and other countries responding in a variety of ways to the Taliban's new position, threat looms large on the stability of the region in protecting democracy, human rights and the peaceful co-existence through strong diplomatic relations. Afghanistan, post-US withdrawal, under the Taliban is fast emerging as not only the epicentre of terrorism but also a region for contest of power and control amongst the regional powers. Such a scenario is detrimental to the safety, security and peace in the region. The power play within the Islamic group is also weaponised and has the potential to destabilise the entire region.

## Al-Qaeda

Various Islamist extremist terrorist groups have operated in Afghanistan for decades, and the Taliban have had different relationships with them. Al-Qaeda and the regional Islamic State-Khorasan Province (ISKP) are two of the most powerful terrorist organisations in the region, and the Taliban's control is likely to have varying effects on both. Al-Qaeda has very strong ties with the Afghan Taliban and sees it as a vital partner in its pursuit of global jihad. The loyalty that Al-Qaeda leaders have shown to successive Taliban leaders stands testimony to this relation.[8] Al-Qaeda-Taliban relations have been strengthened by the groups' joint battle in Afghanistan and personal bonds, according to the UN sanctions monitors' assessment. The ISKP, also known as ISIS-K, has been fighting the Taliban since its inception in 2015, and the two groups have frequently clashed. ISKP perceives the Taliban's nationalist political ambition in Afghanistan as incompatible with its own concept of a global caliphate. ISKP may suffer a setback because of the Taliban's takeover. Such hardliner groupings are a potential for continuing internal faction war for supremacy, leading to highly volatile and destabilising period ahead. With the huge arsenal of US weapons left behind, the power struggle could see fierce fighting in the years ahead.

## Pakistan and China

Pakistan has historically had a disruptive and destabilising role in Afghan affairs, according to numerous assessments, notably through providing active and passive assistance to the Taliban. A large number of weapons and military equipment abandoned by US forces during their withdrawal have, apparently, found their way into Pakistan and this not only adds to military power of Pakistan, but also may fall into the hands of jihadi groups working against peace and stability in India. China and Afghanistan share a small, thinly populated border, and China has had a limited role in Afghan affairs in recent years, primarily due to China's perception of a threat from Islamist terrorists in Afghanistan. Nonetheless, Afghanistan's potential mineral wealth, along with the Taliban's takeover, may lead to further Chinese economic and military involvement in Afghanistan.[9] Since the Taliban's seizure of Afghanistan's government, the Chinese government has expressed its support for the group, meeting with them both before and after the takeover. Despite its prior requests for the Taliban to develop an "inclusive political structure," China appears to be supporting the Taliban's government. The Taliban, on their part, have stated that they wish to work closely with China, with a Taliban spokesperson apparently indicating in a foreign media interview that China would be the Afghan government's most important partner moving ahead, especially in terms of security cooperation.

## Iran, Central Asian Region (CAR) and Russia

Iran's objectives in Afghanistan include retaining its traditional influence in western Afghanistan, defending Afghanistan's Shia minority (the Hazaras), and decreasing refugee flow into Iran. For obvious reasons, the Iranian regime supported the withdrawal of US forces from Afghanistan. Iran may back Afghans in northern, western, and central Afghanistan against the Taliban, as it did in the 1990s, especially if Hazaras reject and strive to fight a Taliban-led administration. While on one hand, Iran rejoices in the shameful exit of US forces from Afghanistan after being defeated by the Taliban, it is also taking very measured steps to work towards safety and security of Hazara community. In such a scenario the instability in the region is bound to increase.

Tajikistan, Turkmenistan and Uzbekistan, as Afghanistan's Central Asian neighbours, have reacted to the Taliban's takeover in a variety of ways, including the sole regional rejection of the group's government. Turkmenistan and Uzbekistan appear to be putting economic connections first, especially the projected Turkmenistan-Afghanistan-Pakistan-India (TAPI) natural gas pipeline, and have held official talks with the Taliban on the subject.[10] However, Tajikistan has not only rejected the Taliban's government, but also has emerged as the group's most powerful regional foe, owing to both the country's history of Islamist militancy and ethnolinguistic ties with Afghan Tajiks (the country's second-largest ethnic group) who oppose the Taliban's rule. Despite concerns about the Taliban's takeover affecting traditional Russian issues, the initial Russian statements indicate that the Russian government wants to strengthen its ties with the Taliban. They are even considering of inviting the group to participate in multilateral negotiations in Moscow in October 2021. Russia has also expressed support for Tajikistan, which hosts Russia's largest external military base.

### *India*

India, with the ouster of the Taliban regime in 2001 and Northern Alliance leaders holding key positions, had found a congenial environment for progressing its diplomatic ties with Afghanistan. A major focus of India's diplomatic effort was on humanitarian aid along with focus on education and infrastructure development in Afghanistan. It is not surprising that very soon India in 2011, became the first country to sign a strategic partnership agreement with Afghanistan. India, after being a strategic partner, was not only involved in training of but also provided limited support in terms of certain specialist equipment including helicopters. However, with the return of Taliban rule in Afghanistan and with Pakistan and China pushing to take advantage of situation, the road ahead for India is going to be filled with one of the most difficult diplomatic and military challenges. Though during the Doha agreement peace deal, the Taliban had successfully created an impression of having been changed to a moderate political entity, there has been little or no evidence to prove it. The challenge for India becomes even more complex with Haqqanis getting the all-powerful interior ministry and intelligence along with control of Afghanistan's eastern region. The list of ministers includes some of the old hard-line clerics as well.

## Military Power Play in the Region

The conflict in Afghanistan has featured elements of proxy warfare since it began in 1979, primarily between the Soviet Union and the United States. Despite having a centralised government as required in the constitution, no central administration has exerted control over the entire country, and power struggles have remained an inherent aspect of governance in Afghanistan. Several entities, including neighbouring states and others, have political and economic stakes in Afghanistan's protracted conflict. Iran, China and Pakistan are concerned about spillover effects from the country's instability, such as the rise of radical Islamism, terrorism, and illicit drug and refugee flow. Anger toward the US and the perceived threat of its presence in the region also impact their objectives. All of these factors, particularly the fear of radical Islamism spreading throughout Central Asia, have caused Russia to adopt a pragmatic strategy of backing the Afghan government, political opposition, and Taliban. Pakistan and India are competing in Afghanistan to limit each other's influence. Pakistan is attempting to preserve strategic depth, while India is one of Afghanistan's primary international aid providers. Since Pakistan has mostly been a suspect of harbouring terrorism, many experts have recently questioned Pakistan's involvement with the Afghan Taliban. As a result, the competition for military space in Afghanistan continues to be primarily between the Taliban, Pakistan, and China for various reasons, and India, which is threatened by all three, has no choice but to pay much more attention to its security as a result of this new turn of events in Afghanistan. Therefore in subsequent paragraphs, we would analyse the power balance or imbalance around only Taliban, Pakistan China and India

## Taliban Forces

The Taliban surged through Afghanistan when US President Biden declared the exit date of April 2021, while many Afghan forces surrendered and gave in their guns. The Taliban were also able to grab substantial stockpiles of small arms and light weapons (SALW) left behind due to the hasty and chaotic nature of the US withdrawal. SALW such as assault rifles, handguns, and machine guns, as well as Handheld Interagency Identity Detection Equipment (HIDE), are among the weapons left behind, while major weaponry and military equipment include missiles, aircraft, helicopters and armoured vehicles. These weapons now being used as tools of coercion and not merely a trade commodity. Taliban was already controlling a considerable amount of arms, most of which were Kalashnikov-pattern automatic assault rifles, light and heavy machine guns, rocket-propelled grenade (RPG) launchers, as well as mortars, shotguns and handguns.[11] As a result of the

Soviet-Afghan war in the 1980s, a major number of these weapons were said to be Cold War-era types. In recent years, terrorist groups' arsenals have grown as a result of purposeful and incidental diversion of military material from state forces. Furthermore, cross-border arms trafficking is a significant concern in South Asia, and another source of weaponry for terrorists operating in Afghanistan. The Taliban's acquisition of more advanced technologies, like night vision devices or infrared lasers for weapons, has prompted worries because of the tactical advantage it gives them.

The US claims to be having difficulty in coming out with exact number of all of the equipment that its troops surrendered, and it's also unclear as to how much of it was in working order when insurgent Taliban forces seized it. However, records of what was supplied to the Afghan army over the past two decades provide an indication of the problem's scope. Almost over a third of nearly a hundred billion spent on the ANDSF, was spent on material, which included nearly six hundred thousand small guns and ammunition. In the last two years before pulling out, the US supplied the Afghan military with about seven thousand machine guns, around twenty thousand grenades along with more than 18 million rounds of ammunition. Taliban is believed to have taken over 73 aircraft including twelve A-29, nine Black Hawk attack helicopters, and fourteen MI-17 helicopters, 20 ScanEagle drones, 70 Mine-Resistant Ambush Protected vehicles (MRAPs), and 27 Humvees as in fully functional condition left behind by US forces.[12] The Taliban now have access to all the military weapons depots existing throughout Afghanistan. The ScanEagle is likely to be used as a 'suicide' drone as it does not carry any weapon as a combat drone.

The unknown quantity of this huge arsenal, as well as how much of it has been taken by the Taliban and how much remains unattended on bases and tiny combat outposts across the country, is causing substantial regional security worries. The Taliban's projected combat capabilities could push Central Asian countries like Uzbekistan and Tajikistan to reinforce bilateral security ties with both Russia and China, or to be more open to dealing diplomatically with the Taliban de facto government, which they might not have considered before. Another question is whether al-Qaeda and ISK-P, two competing worldwide jihadi groups that oppose and fight against Western countries, would obtain access to the Taliban's weapons.

So far, the Taliban has maintained tight relations with al-Qaeda, with no indication that these ties will be severed, raising concerns about whether the Taliban will continue to offer al-Qaeda officials with safe haven just or weapons as well. In addition, the Taliban will have to protect their stockpiles against growing attacks by ISK-P, who may try to expand their own arsenal through similar insurgency action. The Taliban's ability to manage this is important for the West because the greatest security concern is that these weapons could fall into the hands of a terrorist group with a global agenda, such as IS/ISK-P or al-Qaeda, both of which have increased their attack frequency in Afghanistan since the Taliban took control.

The military might be obtained from recent war spoils extends beyond the direct impact they may have on the Taliban's current and future firepower; it also includes its instrumental use as coercion, fundraising, and propaganda tactics. While the Taliban's capacity to utilise and maintain newly obtained weapons to execute assaults will be primarily dependent on their ability to use and maintain this equipment over time, these weapons are not required to control territory, finance, or spread propaganda. To utilise and maintain the various types of guns and munitions now in the Taliban's possession, different levels of expertise are required. For many years, mostly Russian-made guns circulated throughout Afghanistan, and they are likely to remain the Taliban's favourite armament, particularly among lower-ranking members. Having access to a larger stockpile of US-made weaponry may help the Taliban control the land and combat ISK-P and other terrorist groups in the short term, but it may not be the best option in the long run. As a matter of fact, since the Taliban does not possess any expertise to maintain weapons and produce enough ammunition, it appears that US weapons will be only contributing to regional arms proliferation through illegal sales. A more plausible scenario is that the Taliban will continue to expand their grip over the country with the new vehicles, aircraft, and weaponry with the help of supporters of the Northern Alliance, such as Russia and Iran.

### *Pakistan*

Afghanistan grew more fragmented and split domestically in 1996, a few years after the Soviet invasion ended, and the Taliban emerged as a major political and military power. They received political and material backing from Pakistan, as well as hosting Osama bin Laden, who was engaged in the 9/11 attacks. Pakistan opted to support the United States' anti-terrorism stance, which effectively declared war on the Taliban. Pakistan and the Taliban in Afghanistan are on the verge of a huge conflict. The Taliban have rejected Pakistan, its principal state backer during the fight against the US forces and the overthrown Afghan government, since taking control. It has done so by challenging the Afghan-Pakistan border's status and providing a safe haven for the anti-Pakistan insurgent group Tehrik-e-Taliban Pakistan (TTP). Pakistani Taliban or TTP, which has killed thousands of Pakistanis and pursues to establish a Taliban-style, Shariah-compliant state in Pakistan is the bone of contention with the Taliban.[13]

For decades, Pakistan and the Afghan Taliban have been partners, with Islamabad providing safe havens for Islamist terrorists in Kabul in order to construct a sympathetic administration. Border confrontations and unprecedented Pakistani air attacks inside Afghanistan have heightened already simmering tensions since the Taliban reclaimed power in August. According to residents, Pakistan began air raids over eastern Afghanistan in April, killing a large number of civilians. Pakistan was quick to cover it up by claiming said it was targeting TTP militants. There was an unusual reaction by the Taliban, against the air strikes, issuing threats against its long-time ally Pakistan. It seems that the relations are strained over the Taliban's reluctance to take any action against TTP, an ideological ally. The extremist group TTP under shelter of the Taliban has intensified its terror activities against Pakistan and that has irked Islamabad.

After almost twenty years of narrative-based policy of a "good Taliban-bad Taliban", Pakistan is now faced with the backfiring of this policy by Taliban pushing for a "good Pakistan-bad Pakistan" strategy. Ill designs of Pakistan of using Taliban against India were shattered when the Taliban released thousands of TTP prisoners, immediately after taking control of Kabul. TTP on their part swiftly reciprocated by welcoming the Afghan Taliban for their "friendly" gesture. Meanwhile, west of the TTP's tribal heartland, in Pakistan's dry, mineral-rich Balochistan province, which borders Afghanistan and Iran, an ominous new front is forming. Separatists have maintained a low-level insurgency in the southwestern province for years, motivated by resentment over Balochistan's political and economic marginalisation, despite the area's enormous natural resources.

### *China*

Following the withdrawal of US troops from Afghanistan in 2021 and the subsequent Taliban attack, China signalled its willingness to collaborate with a new Taliban-led administration. The Chinese administration was concerned about possible Taliban assistance for Xinjiang insurgents. There have been concerns that the Taliban may transfer some US military hardware to China. However, the majority of the US weaponry left in Afghanistan are designated as "low-tech" systems, for which China has built equivalents. Furthermore, with the United States out of Afghanistan, China is largely expected to become a Taliban backer. This leaves the door open for Beijing to sell weapons to Afghanistan in the future. This includes support and servicing for equipment such as the Mi-17, which is also used by the Chinese military.[14]

In the current environment, China is confronted with both chances and challenges in Afghanistan. On the one hand, China stands to receive significant economic benefits if it can keep the Taliban together; on the other hand, if the Taliban disintegrates and begins fighting, China may face a spillover effect in Xinjiang. The Taliban intend to rebuild Afghanistan and have openly requested China's assistance in economic development, as China is the only country in Afghanistan's immediate vicinity that is capable of doing so and has accepted the Taliban's legitimacy to some extent. China may utilise its clout with the Taliban to secure concessions in mining and exploration, as well as persuade and coerce the Taliban to break relations with terrorist groups like al-Qaeda. Beijing is attempting to align with a Taliban-led administration that appears to be doing and saying the right things, after which it will almost definitely be willing to provide quick economic assistance. This will be nothing compared to the level of aid the former government received from the West, but China may be able to provide some direct money and small economic projects.

China has a number of immediate objectives. It wants to see a Taliban government develop in Afghanistan that can strengthen its influence both at home and abroad. This entails the Taliban emulating a politically inclusive administration and smoothing off some of its rougher edges, especially when the world's attention is focused on them. Beijing does not want a sanctioned, pariah state in its neighbourhood, nor does it want a government that would provide the appearance of total control only to see things unravel into a new round of violence later. China will play a larger role in Afghanistan than it has in recent decades, while it is leery of becoming engulfed in the same way that the USSR and the US were. It sees a too prominent role as risky, which led to the withdrawal of the USSR and the US from Afghanistan after a long campaign. China isn't naive enough to believe that putting the Taliban in charge of Afghanistan will miraculously turn a country that has been at war for decades into a location where they can do business. Even when the Taliban is mostly able to maintain order, local grievances, Islamist groups, foreign intelligence, guns for hire, factional rivalries, and a variety of other variables can endanger their investments. China's motivation for extending support to the Taliban is to use the US's hasty withdrawal from Afghanistan as proof that the US is an untrustworthy friend and a failing power. Following the global financial crisis and the COVID-19 outbreak, China sees the quick withdrawal of US troops from Afghanistan as the third indicator of US hegemony eroding. Beijing has also taken advantage of the chance to mock US military adventures throughout the world. Beijing couldn't resist the urge to take advantage of the upheaval in Afghanistan to undermine public trust in Taiwan's institutions.

In a situation where the Taliban knows they won't get substantial financial support from the West—at least not without terms, they won't accept—China is one of the few options available to them. There is a residual goodwill because Beijing provided the Taliban with money and guns when they were in exile and made investments during their last era of authority. The Taliban merely need to consider China's diplomatic protection and economic obligations to Pakistan. Since their existing international standing is anathema to them, the Afghan Taliban need international legitimacy in order to construct a functional state, a coherent political society, and a functioning economy. As a result, the Taliban want China to bolster their international legitimacy and aid with Afghanistan's national rehabilitation.

Once the two countries reach a mutual understanding, China is likely to gradually expand its military influence in the region, with the dual goal of ensuring the security of its own projects in Afghanistan while also posing a major military challenge to the US and NATO for any future direct or indirect intervention in the Asian region, thereby projecting itself as a regional superpower.

### *India*

The US withdrawal from Afghanistan has increased the challenges manifold, for the Indian subcontinent. In the previous two decades, the US military presence had put a lid on extremist forces and produced a favourable atmosphere for India to collaborate with Afghanistan. The withdrawal will very certainly result in an increase in worldwide and regional terrorism, a resurgence of Taliban power in Pakistan, and political instability in the region. A military engagement by China with the Taliban will be another security dilemma for India in the neighbourhood that is already facing terrorism in J&K, border conflicts both with Pakistan and China, emerging geopolitical power contest in the Indo-Pacific and economic instability and internal disturbance in the immediate neighbourhood Sri Lanka.

The Taliban's violent overthrow of India's democratically elected government was a serious setback for the country's security. India's security fears were largely alleviated in 2001, when the Taliban was deposed following the US-led invasion of Afghanistan. India has invested over $3 billion in Afghanistan over the last 20 years, demonstrating its strong engagement with the new regime in Kabul. The Afghan parliament, education and health infrastructure, a significant hydropower dam, and the 218-kilometre Zaranj-Delaram motorway are among the projects. With the Taliban regaining power in Kabul, India fears that these development efforts will be in vain, exacerbating its security concerns. The Indian security establishment worries that a hardline Islamic Sharia-based administration might spread its radical ideological influence across the subcontinent, bolstering the morale of India's Islamist terror groups and resulting in increased recruitment and violence. The Taliban's insistence on establishing an "Islamic Emirate" rather than a "Republic," which could have indicated an attempt to create a more inclusive polity, adds to this belief. New Delhi is concerned that Pakistan may use Afghan soil more freely to train, equip, and encourage anti-India terror groups such as the Lashkar-e-Tayyaba and JeM, and then use them to sow instability in Jammu and Kashmir under the Taliban's supervision (J&K). The lack of a democratically elected government, as well as the law and order situation in Afghanistan under Taliban rule, has further added to those concerns. As in the past, New Delhi's immediate priority is to guarantee that Pakistan does not take advantage of Afghanistan's instability and use its soil for anti-India terrorist activities, particularly in J&K.

In the goal of gaining diplomatic recognition, the Taliban leadership is working with the international community and warring ethnic Afghan tribes to create greater stability. Pakistan is assisting the interim Taliban government in this process by organising international negotiations to press for recognition. As a result, the Taliban is growing more reliant on Pakistan, strengthening Islamabad's grip on Kabul. A "Pakistan-dependent" administration in Afghanistan is not desirable for India because it will certainly cause security concerns in J&K and other parts of the nation.[15] India is concerned that the Taliban's over-dependence on Islamabad may lead to increasing anti-India terrorist actions on Afghan soil, threats to Indian-funded projects in Afghanistan, and disruption of India's land connectivity to Afghanistan and Central Asia.

India, being the only stable democracy remaining in this turn of events in the region, while watching the developments post US exit, will have four key areas to concentrate on while dealing with the Taliban, namely:

(a) To protect its billions of rupees investments in Afghanistan.
(b) Taking diplomatic measures to prevent the Taliban from becoming a pawn of Pakistan.
(c) Ensuring that anti-India terrorist groups that are backed by Pakistan, do not get support from the Taliban.
(d) Preserving the democracy in the region "under fire", with the Taliban having destroyed one in Afghanistan, Pakistan being the historical perpetrator of military take-over and China being with non-democratic governance ever and the US having failed to preserve the democracy even after two decades of presence.

## Conclusion

The emergence of the Taliban with the US's exit from Afghanistan has triggered geopolitical flux and thus, instability in the region. The road to prolonged peace and establishment of democratic governance in Afghanistan, secured by the US military presence, has come to its end with the hasty exit of US forces and the Taliban re-establishing its fundamentalist grip once again after two decades of exile. These developments have placed Afghanistan into the court of regional powers that now have the burden of managing the military vacuum created by the US retreat, leaving behind the bruised diplomacy and democracy in turmoil.

The idea of a regional solution to Afghanistan has always piqued political interest, but differing regional geopolitical viewpoints restrict the chances of a long-term agreement under Taliban leadership. Though Russia, the Central African Republic, and Iran as regional players have their own non-military interests in the region, the real threat to the subcontinent is the military nexus between China, Pakistan, and the Taliban, which aims to crush freedom and a peaceful democratic way of life in the region. Pakistan is keen on establishing strong ties with the Taliban to further its agenda of terrorism against India, while China on the other hand wants a stable government, irrespective of whether it is a democratic or non-democratic, primarily to secure the security of its own strategic projects and establish itself as a regional superpower.

In Afghanistan and elsewhere, this scenario directly challenges India's political, security, and economic interests. If India wishes to protect its interests, it needs to realign its policy in Afghanistan, notably its relationship with the Taliban, following the exit of US forces. India has always backed the Afghan government while remaining neutral toward the Taliban. India, since 2001 Bonn conference, which prepared the ground for the formation of an interim administration in Afghanistan, has maintained a consistent strategy of engaging with successive Afghan governments toward regional peace and development. These multiple factors will increasingly push India into a geopolitical tough spot in the region, smart statecraft, therefore, is required to deal with changing dynamics in Afghanistan to preserve not only the democratic values of India but also to work towards re-establishing democracy in this fast-emerging collusive danger of Taliban, China and Pakistan that is holding democracy and diplomacy a hostage to rule of gun.

## Notes

1. "U.S. Military Withdrawal and Taliban Takeover in Afghanistan: Frequently Asked Questions", CRS report US, September 17, 2021, at https://crsreports.congress.gov/product/pdf/R/R46879. Accessed on February 4, 2022.
2. Ibid.
3. Adam Geibel, *Military Review* May-June 2002, at https://www.govinfo.gov/content/pkg/GOVPUB-D110-c8aaef82e26966248e7c3ab0267dc0a9/pdf/GOVPUB-D110-c8aaef82e26966248e7c3ab0267dc0a9.pdf. Accessed on February 6, 2022.
4. Akshobh Giridharadas, "The Rashomon Effect: Retelling the Killing of Osama Bin Laden, 10 Years Since", ORF papers, May 20, 2021. Accessed on February 9, 2022.
5. Adam Geibel, n. 3.
6. Jack Detsch, "The U.S. Left Billions Worth of Weapons in Afghanistan", FP April 28, 2022, at https://foreignpolicy.com/2022/04/28/the-u-s-left-billions-worth-of-weapons-in-afghanistan/. Accessed on March 14, 2022.
7. Ibid.
8. "Terrorist Groups in Afghanistan", CRS report US, April 19, 2022, at https://sgp.fas.org/crs/row/IF10604.pdf. Accessed on April 24, 2022.
9. Elizabeth Threlkeld and Grace Easterly, "Afghanistan-Pakistan Ties and Future Stability in Afghanistan", USIP, August 2021, at https://www.usip.org/sites/default/files/2021-08/pw_175-afghanistan_pakistan_ties_and_future_stability_in_afghanistan.pdf. Accessed on April 24, 2022.
10. Soraya Parwani, "The TAPI Pipeline in Post-U.S. Withdrawal Afghanistan ", South Asian Voices, July 12, 2021, at https://southasianvoices.org/the-tapi-pipeline-in-post-u-s-withdrawal-afghanistan/. Accessed on April 26, 2022.
11. Jack Detsch, n. 6.
12. Ibid.
13. Asfandyar Mir, "Pakistan's Twin Taliban Problem", USIP, May 4, 2022, athttps://www.usip.org/publications/2022/05/pakistans-twin-taliban-problem, Accessed on May 6, 2022.
14. Justin Paul George, "Real threat or hype: Should US weapons in Taliban hands worry us?", August 31, 2021, at https://www.theweek.in/news/world/2021/08/31/real-threat-or-hype-should-us-weapons-in-taliban-hands-worry-us.html. Accessed on May 7, 2022.
15. Sarral Sharma and Sameer Patil, "India's Strategy towards Post-August 2021 Afghanistan", ORF papers, February 28, 2022, at https://www.orfonline.org/research/indias-strategy-towards-post-august-2021-afghanistan/. Accessed on May 10, 2022.

# 3

# Tracking the Current Trends of Modern Chinese Weapons

AMITABH MATHUR

While addressing the Chinese National People's Congress in March 2021, the Chinese President proclaimed that his country had been the first to tame COVID-19,[1] thereby exhorting his countrymen to resume work and regain positive economic growth. As a result, China is on the cusp of occupying a position of centrality in the international system, and most analysts predict that China's real GDP will surpass that of the United States by 2030.[2] Moreover, it is the world's most significant trading power and most prominent source of global lending; it boasts of the largest population, most significant military, and innovation centre.

Alvin and Heidi Toffler, in their book "War and Anti-War", have surmised that the *war follows the wealth*.[3] No surprise that China has been extensively modernising its military for two decades. President Xi Jinping dreams of making the PLA mechanised by 2020,[4] informative by 2035, and a world-class army[5] by 2050. The growth in its defence spending has almost always outpaced even the spectacular growth of its economy. There is no doubt that the task of complete reunification of the motherland, as asserted during the October 2021 speech in terms of its core interests: Hong Kong, the South China Sea, and Taiwan, has already begun. The imposition of the national security law on Hong Kong in 2020[6] has effectively ended its autonomy and has improved China's air and missile capabilities. China has thus modernised and expanded its navy and adopted more aggressive postures, particularly in the South China Sea, because it perceives a more significant threat from the sea in the East than from the West. China is also improving its anti-access/area-denial capabilities to counter the US's ability to project military power throughout East Asia. Over the next decade, China will likely impose an air defence identification zone on parts of the South China Sea.

The US-China strategic and military sparring continued in the South China Sea (SCS) in the recent past. The US and Japan held anti-submarine drills in the SCS reportedly to practise "targeting PLA Navy's conventional submarines" for the first time. Continuing the trend of deepening Sino-Russian defence partnership, bombers from the two countries (Chinese H-6K and Russian TU-95MC aircraft) concluded a joint strategic patrol over the Sea of Japan and the East China Sea.[7]

China's powerful navy, newly armed coast guard, and vast fishing fleet intimidate the five neighbouring nations with overlapping claims—Brunei, Malaysia, the Philippines, Taiwan, and Vietnam—and assert control in disputed waters.[8] Several recent activities endorse this understanding—Chinese vessels sailed into waters off Japan and around several contested islands, which are called Diaoyu Islands by China and Senkaku Islands by Japan; a Chinese coast guard vessel rammed and sank a Vietnamese fishing boat; Chinese military aircraft flew over disputed waters claimed by both China and Malaysia; and China and India engaged in their first deadly border conflict in four decades.[9]

So far, President Xi's efforts to intimidate Taiwan have failed to convince the island nation to embrace unification. The US lawmakers visited Taiwan in October '21 to discuss a military deal, a move that China strongly condemned. President Xi has conceived BRI, the Confucius Institutes, and global governance leadership as a conduit to project its political and cultural values as soft power.

## Military Expenditure

The People's Republic of China has steadily reached its standing as the second most powerful and financially stable country. It now threatens to overthrow the US and take its place as the world's fastest and strongest GDP in the world, with two-thirds of global net worth accumulated in China. China's military expenditure was $252 billion in 2020. China's share of global military spending in 2020 rosc by 76 per cent compared to its spending in 2011.[10] China's military spending has now increased for 26 consecutive years. However, in 2019, China's latest defence white paper—*China's National Defense in the New Era*—said the PLA was yet to complete this task and was also 'in urgent need of improving its informatisation'. The communiqué issued at the Fifth Plenum of the Chinese Communist Party's 19th Central Committee in October 2020 continued the call to 'accelerate mechanisation, informatisation and intelligent integration'. Mechanisation refers to the replacement of legacy equipment; informatisation refers to improving technical sophistication ('net-centric capability); while intelligent integration refers to the improvement of automation, big data and artificial intelligence by integration. In addition, the white paper also outlines a 'demand-oriented' approach to planning and funding. Thus, unless there is a severe political or economic change, Chinese military spending can continue to increase in the coming years.

## Role as an Arms Supplier

China was the world's fifth-largest arms exporter in 2016-20, with 5.2 per cent of the total volume of arms exports. After an increase of 77 per cent between 2006-2010 and 2011-15, Chinese arms exports decreased by only 7.8 per cent between 2011-15 and 2016-20.[11] The number of countries to which China delivers arms has grown significantly from 40 in 2010 to 51 in 2016-20. Nearly all of China's arms exports in 2005-19 were to developing states, and it has now clearly emerged as a competitor to Russia and Western arms exporters in selling arms to such states. Pakistan was the primary recipient of Chinese arms exports in 2016-20, receiving 38 per cent of the total exported.

## Non-Contact Warfare

A close look at the theoretical construct and security dynamics worldwide points to a volatile, uncertain and complex international order where the major powers like the US, China and Russia are constantly engaged in a competitive slugfest.[12] Shifting the security landscape from traditional to non-traditional arena and new forms of warfare propagated by security planners have changed the character of warfare. Show of restraint has led the security experts to look for the non-military measure to non-contact military measures to influence the politico-military decision outcomes.[13] It may be kinetic or non-kinetic and lethal or non-lethal with low-cost options on the use of an intelligent power—a combination of soft and hard power. The balance of power game is still on display with dominance and counter-dominance strategy in play. The world has been devising a strategy of winning without fighting. Hence, using terms like hybrid warfare, unrestricted warfare, asymmetric warfare, information warfare, and political warfare has gained popularity.

Information is so central to modern-day warfare that, unlike traditional warfare, even a little piece of information can have enormous and far-reaching consequences. Consequently, it is important to address every technological or tactical issue that affects speedy gathering, sharing, and exploitation. This places an enormous burden on the modern military today, where strategy, training, organisation and courage are required to effectively carry out their duties in the chaos, confusion, fear and violence, characterising modern warfare. The most critical military skill is understanding how best to wage this struggle for information, as the technology systems have inherent weaknesses. As a result, strategists will almost certainly find themselves struggling to keep up with (let alone regulate) new technologies, which could reshape the international economy, politics, and the military balance of power.

Growth in Information and Communication Technologies has connected people, the economy and governments as never before, impacting people, governments and the military. With its penetration into all aspects of governance, economy and society, the digital world has exposed people, political leadership, governance structures and the economy as never before. Technology is not only fuelling growth but competition. Hence, remote and invisible means and methods can perpetuate the crisis. That is how Non-contact warfare in this digital world can be fought where unlike conventional warfare, where the focus was to defeat the military or the leader. Non-contact warfare aims to weaken the opposing military before the onset of conflict or make the conflict irrelevant without fighting. Non-contact warfare is done by employing all elements of national power and non-state groups to influence across multiple domains to target adversary's population, sovereignty, governance structures and economy through non-military or military, both kinetic and non-kinetic means to intimidate or paralyse its politico-military response capabilities.

Technological change is also transforming how we think about and prepare for warfare. As Carl Philipp Gottfried von Clausewitz observed, "war's nature doesn't change, only its character." The nature of war has always been and remains violent and political.[14] But the character of war—its conduct—is profoundly and visibly influenced by technology attacks, surprises, or calamities that we cannot anticipate or deter.

Contrary to popular belief and the needs of policymakers, intelligence is not about predicting the future. Since no nation showcases its capabilities, it is all about collecting and analysing information that helps explain the physical and political world. By doing so, intelligence helps leaders make better decisions. The renowned physicist *Neils Bohr*, who developed a model to predict the seemingly random movement of electrons, liked to observe, "Prediction is tough, especially if it's about the future". The inadequacy of prediction is like a law of physics, a constant in human affairs.

This chapter attempts to carry out an environment scan of Chinese technological growth.

## China's Military Modernisation

### *The PLA's New Joint Doctrine*

On November 13, 2020, the Xinhua News Agency announced that the Chinese Communist Party's (CCP's) Central Military Commission (CMC) had issued the **Guidelines on Joint Operations of the Chinese People's Liberation Army**. The promulgation of this document speaks to the core of what the PLA aspires to achieve. Specifically, the PLA seeks to become a force capable of prosecuting "integrated joint operations" in multiple battlespace domains in an era of information-centric warfare and future intelligent warfare.[15] With this, the PLA now has a warfighting doctrine to be employed by the joint warfighting organisation.

*Modernisation*

The modernisation is to be done by creating combined arms group armies capable of combined arms and all domains operations with coherent integration of air, land, sea, and information towards operational/strategic goals. China's 2019 white paper states that the goal is to: "generally achieve mechanisation by 2020 with significantly enhanced informationitisation and greatly improved strategic capabilities."The modernisation of the PLA is to be completed by 2035, turning the force into a world-class military. Chinese are developing a multi-domain wall to prevent any kind of intrusion. Therefore, it needs an advanced ISR capability in all domains, secure communications, and domain-specific walls in air, space, surface, and subsurface. In addition, it needs systems of systems to complete the kill chain by modernisation on the following three main processes:[16]

- **Informatisation:** This is essentially digitisation. It relates to the sharing of information between PLA units.
- **Intelligentisation:** builds upon informatisation and is a leading element of future force development. It states that artificial intelligence and machine learning should improve informatisation.
- **Military-Civil Fusion (MCF):** China elevated its Military-Civil Fusion objective to a national development strategy in 2015. Although its roots date back to the 1990s, this transformation is designed to leverage technological developments in the civil sphere to help the military. It is assessed that at present, it is in its early stages.

## Informatisation

In conjunction with precision-guided munitions, information technology is now crucial to success in war. The objective is to achieve information dominance. The information must be processed so that the entire military situation, including terrain and climate, can be described almost immediately to the relevant commanders. This description will identify the enemy's most critical vulnerabilities and enable the commanders to employ their information systems to ensure that the most appropriate assets are used to target these vulnerabilities. These forces will react with greater accuracy, carrying their destructive power over extended ranges. A significant advantage of such a system is that high-quality information on the battlespace should make it easier for critical forces to remain a safe distance away from the battlefield and strike with precision over great distances.

The domination of information is viewed as an essential criterion for modern warfare. The PLA believes that by controlling the flow of information and disrupting the enemy's access to information, it can change the course of the conflict. PLA has an operational system consisting of five component systems: the command system, firepower strike system, information confrontation system, reconnaissance-intelligence system, and support system. In addition, it also envisages a "systems confrontation" approach, in which PLA presumes that by targeting key elements of an enemy's system such as C2 nodes, etc., it can defeat each element of an enemy's interconnected system.

The roll-out of 5G, 6G and beyond, along with "Standards 2035" for such networks being implemented, will revolutionise communications speed as enumerated below.

### *5G roll-out*

With increases of up to 100-fold in speed, 50-fold in reliability, and 10-fold in device connections, 5G would usher new applications, which may be beyond imagination today. President Xi Jinping stated in 2020 that the 5G infrastructure is a top priority in the $1.4 trillion New Infrastructure Plan for its post-COVID economy. China is all set to incorporate nationwide 5G networks that will enable AI applications and the Internet of Things to reach further deep into everyday life. The roll-out spans the defence domain from military telemedicine to UAV swarm communications, border security and integration with Beidou. In telecommunications infrastructure, China is all set to repeat in 5G technology what the United States did in the case of 4G. If successful, China will have a first-mover advantage in technology with significant commercial, intelligence, and military applications.

Qualcomm's Economic Strategy Team estimates that over the next 15 years, China shall have a lion's share of the world's 5G market. Global System for Mobile Communications Industry Association (GSMA) candidly states that "China now represents the world's largest 5G market, with 5G connections in China itself accounting for 87 per cent of global

5G connections." Similarly, Huawei's telecommunications infrastructure increase from 0 per cent to 28 per cent has made it the world's leading supplier of 5G equipment.

### *6G & Beyond*

China has concentrated on R&D for shifting the band to THz spectrum for applications such as communications, ISR, targeting, countermeasures, precision guidance.

## Intelligentisation

The Next Generation Artificial Intelligence Development Plan—2017 of the Chinese Communist Party (CCP) called for China to become the world leader in artificial intelligence (AI) by 2030.[17] For China, AI plays a supporting role in diplomacy, information, military, and economic strength at national power levels. China's AI strategy appears to be sharply focused on AI's economic potential and applications in other domains, especially the military.

Wargaming is a method for studying military operations and has developed indigenous wargaming capabilities to impart realistic training for preparing for future operations. The widespread adoption of 'Artificial Intelligence (AI)' and 'Autonomous Weapon Systems' portends a new revolution in Chinese military affairs.[18] The People's Liberation Army (PLA) is now conceptualising a future battlefield environment dominated by AI and autonomy, which it calls 'intelligent warfare'. It combines human and machine intelligence with extensive AI in all military applications.

Intelligent warfare will comprise of three main features, the use of "big data", the "algorithms", and the "computing power". PLA's experimentation with AI in wargaming predates but was also inspired by the success of Google's AI, AlphaGo. PLA researchers envisioned using AI for simulations and operational planning and analysis to model complex dynamics and interactions. The application of AI in wargaming has become the centrepiece of some national wargaming competitions in China.

Most PRC writers envision that humans will remain in command of autonomous systems, especially at the strategic level, and have only limited control of machines at the tactical level. The writers argue that no matter how advanced intelligent weapons and equipment become, they will still require human innovation, design, production and management. Wars are a conflict between people and primarily is the ability to defeat a human enemy. Hence, machines at no stage can replace human ingenuity, creativity, and flexibility of humans. Therefore, intelligent warfare will accelerate the observation, orientation, decide, act (OODA) loop from intelligence collection to transmission, processing and decision-making.

AI and autonomy are set to take conventional warfare into outer space, the deep sea, and the polar regions, where humans cannot efficiently operate. The militaries will seek to influence an adversary's perceptions through the denial, degradation, and manipulation of data and algorithms and the denial and degradation of computing systems. In addition, the increased effectiveness of AI and autonomy will enable rapid strike capabilities to initiate first strikes, including pre-emption.

China has meditatively banned global social media giants like Google and Facebook from operating on its soil, mainly due to their inherent AI capabilities. Instead, it has laid tremendous focus on developing its own AI capabilities in facial recognition, big-data analytics and behavioural assessment technologies. The success of its motives is evident in China managing the same application environment with its own 'UC Browser' and 'Weibo' platforms. Furthermore, the CCP is continuously enhancing its Targeted Population Program, which originated in the 1950s by heavily relying on commercial AI solutions to expand its reach and capabilities through AI applications.[19] The highlights are enumerated below:

- **Facial Recognition:** Megvii's 'Sharp Eyes' project utilises an algorithm, which claims to support networks of 50,000 to 100,000 cameras. This project is deployed across multiple Chinese provinces, including Xinjiang. These cameras work with the Integrated Platform for Joint Operations (IJOP).[20]
- **Emotion Recognition:** Development & exploitation of emotion recognition technology is rapidly rising across China. Not as well-known as facial recognition, the "emotion recognition technologies purport to infer an individual's inner affective state based on traits such as facial muscle movements, vocal tone, body movements, and other biometric

signals. It uses advanced ML to analyse facial expressions and other biometric data to infer a person's emotional state."[21]

- **Communication Monitoring:** Owing to monitoring susceptibility of both the voice and digital traffics, China continues to develop analytical tools. Chinese commercial firms like iFlytek are focusing on natural language processing (NLP) & voice recognition protocols in consultation with the Ministry of Public Security (MPS) to create a national speech pattern and voice database. Additionally, developing keyword-spotting technology to aid the national defence is also in progress.[22]

## Military-Civil Fusion

China's military-civil fusion (MCF) to seamlessly integrate its civilian and defence economies has received significant attention from Chinese leadership since the early 2010s and remains a top priority in Beijing's plans to restructure China's defence economy. A key MCF goal is to allow private civilian firms to provide material for the PLA. It helps China to leverage commercial innovations and resources for military applications. Chinese authorities have said that the beginning of the 2020s marks the transition of the MCF development strategy from a preparatory transition stage to 'deep implementation'. China plans to leverage its MCF capabilities to support the export of defence, dual-use and strategic high-technology products to its allied countries. The uninhabited aerial vehicle (UAV) and surveillance industry are already being promoted in this way. As a result, the Chinese Military's dual-use and commercial UAV exports have continuously risen since the early 2010s.

## New Developments

### *Quantum Computing*

From the smallest classical device to the most powerful supercomputers, the computers do their calculations through the binary manipulation of bits, which can be in only two states: on or off, 1 or 0. Quantum computers use the quantum state of an object to produce qubits. The complex math behind these qubits can be plugged into specialist algorithms to do calculations that would be practically impossible for a classical computer to perform—known as quantum advantage or supremacy. A quantum computer could theoretically break the internet's most secure cryptography, solve impossibly complex logistical and optimisation challenges, or simulate matter and chemistry on an incredibly precise scale.[23] Though a general-purpose quantum computer is likely still decades away, the first country to produce effective, working quantum computers will have a crucial advantage in economics, defence and cybersecurity—the US, China and Europe are all competing. [24]

Quantum computing, quantum communication, and quantum sensing—are the three significant subfields within quantum information science (QIS). QIS has the potential for revolutionary advances in science and technology involving large computations, much faster communication and precision measurement.

Quantum communications potentially have immense significance for ultra-secure communication networks. Quantum Cryptography can be used to transmit secret messages between two points by the 'Quantum Key Distribution' method, in which photons are used to transfer the data. China had established a 712 km Quantum communication link in November 2016 between Hefei and Shanghai.[25,26]

Quantum Radar uses quantum entanglement to detect active and passive stealth targets. The quantum Radar transmits in low frequencies, resolves small objects, has better range and cannot be jammed. The technology is under development in China, and a prototype is likely by 2025.

### *Drones*

Potential applications of AI in the PLA Combat force in the field of drones are—Intrusive' Lone-wolf operations', where a single unmanned system operates independently; 'Trojan horse operations', where an unmanned system covertly manoeuvres to a predetermined position to achieve surprise and 'Swarm operations', where a large number of low-cost unmanned platforms operate in coordination with a 'Mother ship'. In addition, there will be a larger platform to transport and command smaller assets in manned and unmanned combinations to conduct such saturation attacks.

To highlight the impact of Lone-Wolf operations, potential applications of AI will result in drones becoming increasingly autonomous. Commercial off-the-shelf drones are capable of basic waypoint autonomy.[27] That means they can be programmed to fly to particular points without a person moving the joystick.[28] That would allow the operator to create a crude "fire-and-forget" weapon; they could launch an attack, then run away before the first bomb explodes. Autonomy also poses a grand challenge for counter-drone systems because most counter-drone systems rely on jamming the signal between operator and drone. If the drone needs no signal, then those defences are obsolete.[29] Therefore, the critical infrastructure faces renewed and growing risks from such drones.

## Cruise Missiles

The Chinese Cruise missile programme has been a growing threat to both terrestrial and at-sea operations for a long time to come. With the relatively low-cost and ready availability of technology required to produce them, large-scale use of cruise missiles will remain highly probable.

Cruise missiles are far cheaper than heavy bombers, intercontinental ballistic missiles (ICBMs), or medium-range ballistic missiles. Their easy adaptability to multiple launching options makes them useful in principle to the strategic triad of Air-Ground and Sea launch capabilities. Cruise missiles are especially suitable for launch from bombers to avoid entering enemy radars' range by firing these missiles from a safe distance. The cruise missiles used for naval systems allow enhanced range and accuracy less expensively. Chinese cruise missiles of today can carry a large warhead over long distances with high accuracy and can fly from subsonic speeds to as much as Mach-5. Some examples are as under:

| Weapon | Type | Platform | Status |
|---|---|---|---|
| KD-20A | LACM | Bomber | Undergoing trials |
| KD-63A | LACM | Bomber | In service |
| YJ-18/18-A | ASCM | Ship, Submarine | In service |
| HD-1 | LACM/ASCM | Ship, Aircraft | Under Dev |
| PL-15/PL-21 | AAM | Fighter | In service |
| CJ-100/Df-100 | Cruise Missile | Vehicle | Under Dev |
| C-X1A/-X1B | ASCM | Ship, Vehicle | Under Dev |
| Future AI-equipped | Cruise Missile | Aircraft, Submarine, Ship, Vehicles | Concept stage |

## Hypersonic Weapons

While most traditional ballistic missiles fly hypersonic and most traditional cruise missiles fly within the subsonic to Mach-5 range, a hypersonic missile travels at least Mach-5. Hypersonic weapons generally fly at lower altitudes than ICBMs but greater altitudes than conventional cruise missiles. The objective is to attain unpredictable manoeuvrability at Mach-5 and render most air defence systems useless. Hypersonic weapons rely on kinetic energy to destroy targets; thus, these weapons require extreme precision to ensure target destruction. In addition, these weapons' capability to cover large distances at high speeds results in the shrinking of the shooter to target timelines. China is currently developing two types of hypersonic weapons—the Hypersonic Glide Vehicles (HGVs) and Hypersonic Cruise Missiles (HCMs).[30]

As reported by the *Financial Times* on October 17, 2021, "China tested a nuclear-capable hypersonic missile in August that circled the globe before speeding towards its target".[31] The report quoted five individuals familiar with the test stating, "the Chinese military launched a rocket that carried an HGV, which flew through low-orbit space before cruising down towards its target." In an interview on November 16, 2021, with CBS, Gen John Hyten, Vice Chief of Joint Chiefs of Staff, indicated it to be a Fractional Bombardment System (FOBS). The FOBS is a soviet-era orbital system that carried nuclear weapons; the twist with the Chinese system is that it carried a hypersonic glide vehicle (HGV). This hybrid FOBS-HGV system conducted by China was the first such test worldwide and was called "Sputnik moment", indicating the technological surprise.

China aims to have these systems with better penetration capability than any other Ballistic Missile Defence system in the world. In 2020, China had begun inducting the medium-range capable DF-17 fitted with DF-ZF HGV, possibly replacing older SRBM units. The DF-17 has passed the design stages in late 2018 and is primarily a platform for conventional warheads, but it is assessed that it can be equipped with nuclear warheads. In 2020, a PRC—based military expert described the primary purpose of the DF-17 as striking foreign military bases and fleets in the Western Pacific.[32] The 2021 Pentagon report tells that the DF-17 has been deployed.

In addition to DF-17, which ranges from 1600 to 2400 km, the PRC has developed DF-ZF HGV with a range of about 1950 km. China has also tested the Starry Sky-2 hypersonic vehicle prototype, which is expected to be operational by 2025. It is also expected to test its indigenous DF41 ICBM, DF-21 and DF-26 IRBM to carry an HGV.

## Electronic Sensors

China's decades-long campaign to become a semiconductor powerhouse has yielded significant results in recent years. The undeniable reality is that China's potential, based on the current trajectory, that President Xi will accomplish his goal of China becoming a top-tier player in the semiconductor industry by 2030.

**Photonic Radar**—In 2017, China announced a prototype microwave photonics-based Radar with a resolution of 30 times that of conventional radars. Silicon photonics is a chip-based technology using 'optical circuits' based on laser light guided in silicon optical nanowires, laying the framework of Photonic Integrated Circuits.[33]

**LiDAR**—Lasers operating in the blue-green region of the light spectrum could be used to detect and range submersible targets due to the relative low attenuation through water and good laser reflection. China is developing a space-based capability using LiDAR to detect underwater targets.

In **Electronic Warfare,** AI has a vital role to play. Unlike conventional signals detection techniques, AI in EW will assist in automating the detection and classification of the intercepted signals, thus relieving the tedious process of manual sorting of signals by the operators. The machine-learning feature will instantly characterise the threat based on its received parameters and automatically generate an appropriate response instantly.

## Nuclear Domain

On November 3, 2021, the United States Department of Defense (US DoD) released its annual report to Congress titled "Military and Security Developments Involving the People's Republic of China".[34] This report highlights the current trends in the growth of capabilities and shift in posture. China has made significant investments to improve its nuclear forces over the last few decades.[35] China's recent nuclear modernisation efforts are likely to affect the strategic balance with the United States. As a result, Beijing is improving and expanding its long-range nuclear forces without giving any indication of its intended endpoint. It is also modernising and enlarging its force of regional missiles, including dual-use weapons, in a likely effort to acquire more credible options for limited nuclear use. (Dual-use weapons can accommodate a nuclear or nonnuclear warhead).[36]

Like India, China's nuclear posture emphasises "assured retaliation", and both countries have committed themselves to a "No First Use" posture. China seems to be reacting to the technological advances in a range of areas from AI, robotics and quantum computing which could help the US develop capabilities to launch disarming conventional or nuclear first strikes that make retaliation impossible. Conventional technologies used in the swift & prompt global strike, and now hypersonic glide vehicles weapons, can quickly and accurately take out adversaries' nuclear weapons and missile systems.[37]

## Nuclear Posture

China has hardened its ICBM sites and is building at least three modern ICBM silo fields, dispersed its weapons, and has developed the capability to move its ICBMs around the country aboard trucks. Some of these ICBMs carry multiple warheads, making them difficult to intercept with missile defences. Though China's silos are ultimately very vulnerable to a US attack;[38] still, they significantly expand the number of targets the United States would have to hit for a first strike to disable China's nuclear retaliatory capability altogether.[39] Moreover, the new silos' locations and hardened construction will force the United States to use nuclear weapons to attack them. In essence, adding more ICBM silos raises the bar for the United States to attempt a counterforce strike successfully—a bar that China may believe was lowered in recent years given reported US advances that would significantly enhance the destructive power of nuclear warheads.[40]

ICBMs located in fixed silos are sitting ducks, so they are much more effective for a first strike than a response to the attack. Moreover, China's development of a strategic early-warning system that could enable it to launch its nuclear forces before they were destroyed in an incoming attack—thus enhancing their survivability—also creates the danger that it might mischaracterise a US' missile test' as an 'attack'.[41] All these developments have led the Pentagon to warn in 2021 report that Beijing likely intends to increase "the peacetime readiness of its nuclear forces by moving to a launch-on-warning (LOW) posture,[42] though PLA calls it "early warning counterstrike".

## PLA Rocket Force

The PLA Rocket Force (PLARF) organises, operates, trains, and equips the PRC's strategic land-based nuclear and conventional missile forces and associated support forces and missile bases. The PLARF is a critical component of the PRC's nuclear deterrence strategy to deter and counter third-party intervention in regional conflicts. The PLARF controls nine Corps or Corps Deputy Leader grade Bases, of which six Bases, viz. 61-66, are responsible for missile operations.[43]

The PLARF has advanced its long-term modernisation plans to enhance its "assured retaliation" capabilities. Though the Chinese have never publicly disclosed it, the US security establishment is increasingly making a realistic assessment regarding the Chinese nuclear arsenal, indicating that the Chinese intent is consistently battle-oriented. Though mobile launchers provide flexibility, the construction of silo's indicates the quest for increased survivability. In addition, nuclear-capable air-launched ballistic missiles would assign a nuclear role to PLAAF.

The PLARF has launched 250+ ballistic missiles for testing and training. This quantum is more than the rest of the world combined.[44] Although its arsenal remains far smaller and less sophisticated than those of the United States or Russia, China currently holds about 320-350 deliverable warheads and may have up to 700 by 2027 and at least 1,000 by 2030.

The modernisation plan of PLA RF can be summarised as under:

- **ICBMs.** The PRC is developing new ICBMs that will significantly improve its nuclear-capable missile forces and require increased nuclear warhead production, partially due to incorporating multiple independently targetable re-entry vehicles (MIRV) capabilities.[45] China's longest-range ICBM is the silo-based, liquid-fueled, two-stage Dong Feng-5 family of missiles. The road-mobile, solid-fuelled, three-stage DF-31A/AG ICBMs are the only operational missiles in China's arsenal to target the entire continental USA. In addition, PLA RF has been developing a longer-range ICBM, the road-mobile, solid-fuelled, three-stage DF-41, since the 1990s. There is speculation that the DF-41 might carry six to ten MIRV warheads.

- **Intermediate-Range Ballistic Missiles (IRBMs).** The PLARF continues to grow its inventory of road-mobile DF-26 IRBMs, capable of conducting both conventional and nuclear precision strikes against ground targets as well as conventional strikes against naval targets. It is estimated that the PLARF now has around 200 launchers for IRBMs, probably all for variants of the DF-26, which would give the design utility across the spectrum of PLARF mission types. This number is greater than the PLARF's total number of medium-range ballistic-missile launchers, which have traditionally formed the bulk of their nuclear and conventional theatre missile inventory, and likely reflects the growing emphasis the PLA places on being able to hold targets in the second island chain at risk. Two hundred launchers will allow the PLARF to equip 10 missile brigades (out of 39 in total) exclusively with IRBM variants, or more if they mix intermediate and medium-range ballistic missile systems within brigades. In addition, the PLA RF currently possesses one nuclear-capable medium-range ballistic missile (MRBM) DF-21, an upgraded variant, the DF-21 A, which was deployed in 1996 and an enhanced version in 2017. DF-21s have a reach up to New Delhi.
- **Anti-Ship Ballistic Missiles (ASBMs).** In 2020, The PLARF continued exercises, focusing on realistic training, enhancing combat readiness, rapidly mobilising, operating in complex electromagnetic environments, and integrating support elements. On August 26, 2020, the PLARF test-fired four medium-range ballistic missiles into the South China Sea, marking the second consecutive year that the PLA has conducted such a test. In July 2019, the PLARF had conducted its first-ever confirmed live-firing of six DF-21D ASBMs into the South China Sea, north of the Spratly Islands, in January 2019.[46] A variant of the DF-26 can also perform an anti-ship-attack strike role.
- **Nuclear Submarines** have the edge over conventional submarines in endurance, sustained speed, armaments, stealth, available power and

littoral operations (conducting operations close to coastlines). In the past year, China has deployed four nuclear-powered new-generation type-094 JIN-class submarines that carry a new class of ballistic missiles (JL-2s), a sea-based variant of DF-31. Two additional submarines are being outfitted in a shipyard in Huludao. In addition, PLAN is developing its next-generation SSBN, Type 096, which is expected to be larger and quieter than the Type 094 and might be equipped with more missile launch tubes. Type 096 submarine is expected to use DF-41 ICBM design, a MIRV capable ICBM incidentally.

- In the US DOD report of 2018, PLA AF has been assigned a nuclear mission. Until a new bomber is available, China currently possesses a small number of **H-6K bombers** that may have been given a nuclear weapon delivery role.[47] China is developing variants of DF-21 MRBM for delivery by a modified H-6N. China's H-20 capable air-to-air refuel-able stealth bomber with a range of 8500 km may be used for the 'nuclear weapon delivery' role.[48]

## PLA Army

China's Central Military Commission (CMC) is streamlining and modernising the People's Liberation Army (PLA) by deciding to regroup the PLA ground forces into 13 corps from the previous 18, the Ministry of National Defense (MND) in Beijing announced on April 27 2017.[49] The new formations will be the 71st, 72nd, 73rd, 74th, 75th, 76th, 77th, 78th, 79th, 80th, 81st, 82nd, and 83rd corps. The Central Military Commission (CMC) had directed the PLA to achieve "Full Mechanisation" by the end of the year 2020; the first of three military goals identified by President Xi Jinping in his October 2017 address to the 19th Congress of the Chinese Communist Party. The CMC focuses on improving the PLA's combat readiness. It is training to "fight and win" through increasingly realistic combat training. Despite initial delays due to the COVID-19 pandemic, the overall readiness target of the PLA remains undisturbed.[50]

- Although PLA has never publicly defined how it plans to judge the completion of the 'basic mechanisation' is complete by the end of 2020, it is highly probable that both the structural reorganisation for improved combined-arms operations, as well as the replacement of most of its ageing and obsolescent armoured vehicles and artillery systems, has been completed.

- The higher-level reorganisation of PLA after 2015 and PLA's combat and combat-support formations from 2017 is also complete, indicating that the structural aspect of the 2020 targets has been achieved. However, the army remains somewhat short of its goal in terms of modern equipment.
- About 66 to 75 per cent modernisation has been achieved in the PLA Group-Armies' combined arms brigades. By late 2020, 25 out of 32 heavy brigades were equipped with modern main battle tanks or light tanks, and additionally, 17 brigades had the ZBD-04/04A family of tracked infantry fighting vehicles. Similarly, at least 14 of the 18 Medium Brigades have the modern ZBL-08 family of wheeled armoured vehicles.
- PLA has focussed on acquiring wheeled artillery and air-defence systems in 2020. The PCL-181 (or PCL-18-1) 155 mm truck-mounted gun/howitzer, displayed in the 2019 parade, is now in service with five artillery brigades in the Eastern, Southern and Central theatre armies and artillery brigade Tibet. A new 122 mm truck-mounted system is also in service with a combined arms brigade in Tibet. Artillery systems on truck chassis enable faster movement by road than the towed systems and are easier to transport by air or rail than tracked systems. This enables these brigades to quickly re-deploy within and between theatre commands, which is a crucial objective of modernisation.
- Similarly, the PLA has adopted a new wheeled version of the HQ-17 (CH-SA—15) surface-to-air missile system (the HQ-17A) and a wheeled self-propelled anti-aircraft gun for a medium-weight combined arms brigade in the Northern Theatre Command. This modernisation shall enable Medium weight Brigades with better mobile air-defence capability.
- The PLA's aviation branch is modifying its WZ-10 attack-helicopter fleet and improving its land-attack capability with an improved missile design. Production of the Z-20 medium transport helicopter continues for the two dedicated air-assault brigades, and the PLA is now introducing a further upgraded variant of its Z-8 heavy-lift helicopter (reportedly designated Z-8L) into service.

- More realistic training is an additional critical component of the PLA's modernisation effort.

## PLA Air Force (PLA AF)

The People's Liberation Army Air Force (PLAAF) and People's Liberation Army Navy (PLAN) Aviation together constitute the most significant aviation force in the region and the third-largest in the world, with over 2,800 total aircraft (excluding trainer variants and UCAVs) of which, approximately 2,250 are combat aircraft (fighters, strategic bombers, tactical bombers, multi-mission tactical and attack aircraft). The remaining ones are in the transport role.

While PLA AF has around 157 fighters, including J-8F, J-8H, JH-7A, J-10, J-11, J-11A, J-11BS, Su-27UBK, Su-27SK, and J-7IIM, its UAV & drone inventory includes GJ-1/WD-1K precision strike UAVs, WD-1 ground attack and reconnaissance UAVs, WD-1 precision strike UAVs, and EA-03 reconnaissance and electronic warfare UAVs. As a part of its modernisation, PLAAF is continually inducting the trio of J-20, J-16 and J-10C fighters to replace the War-era J-7 and J-8 aircraft. As a result, it is estimated that over 75 per cent of its 1500 tactical-combat solid aircraft inventory now comprises modern fighters. The two-seater J-16 is a more capable multi-role platform than the single-seat J-10A Firebird and requires weapons-system officers to occupy the rear cockpit. An electronic-warfare derivative of the J-16, the J-16D, is also being developed and is being flight tested presently. An upgraded variant of the J-20—the J-20B—is also under development. This variant may be inducted in operationally significant numbers.

The PLAAF has also received the Y-9-based KJ-500 airborne early-warning and control aircraft with D band KLC-7 AEW radar, which has electronically scanning arrays and anti-jamming features with longer detection ranges. In addition, another improved endurance version of the aircraft fitted with an in-flight refuelling probe and CATOBAR-assisted system for possible use on Type-003 aircraft carriers is also being developed.

The Y-9 continues to be used in a variety of signals-intelligence roles. The PLAAF's fleet of the Xi'an Y-20 heavy-transport aircraft also has continued to grow and has outnumbered IL-76s. With this, the PLAAF has doubled its heavy-transport fleet in the last four years. In addition, the Y-20-based dedicated tanker and possibly an airborne early-warning and control platform are under development to replace the KJ-2000 Mainring.

PLAAF training is keeping pace with the improvements in the inventory and with the PLAAF's paradigm shift from "homeland defence" to the "regional power-projection" role.

## PLA Navy

The PLAN is the largest navy globally, with an overall battle force of approximately 355 ships and submarines, including approximately more than 145 major surface combat vessels. As of 2020, the PLAN was primarily composed of modern multi-role platforms. Shortly, the PLAN would have the capability to conduct long-range precision strikes against land targets from its submarine and surface combat ships using land-attack cruise missiles, notably enhancing the PRC's global power projection capabilities. The PRC enhances its anti-submarine warfare (ASW) capabilities and competencies to protect the PLAN's aircraft carriers and ballistic missile submarines. As China's military modernisation is shaping defence policies in the Asia-Pacific, Beijing's intent is on achieving primacy in its littoral areas.

The 2015 defence white paper candidly brings out the overseas interests, which are expanding and building up capabilities to conduct operations of "moderate-intensity". As a part of force projection, PLA Navy has been in Indian Ocean Region (IOR) since 2008 on anti-piracy patrols for three to six months. The 39th patrol is currently ongoing. These patrols also carry out exercises with different countries and have carried out one such exercise with Russia for the first time in 2021. China wants to be part of all mechanisms designed to carry out Ocean Governance in IOR. It also intends to dominate the IOR by creating a regional dialogue on the safety of its oil shipping lanes. Moreover, maritime domain awareness in the form of anti-piracy missions in the IOR will enable China to operate in this domain during crises.

The PLAN maintained an 'over-the-horizon' presence, with China's maritime paramilitary forces taking the lead and using facilities on Chinese-occupied features as forward-operating bases in the Spratly Islands in the South China Sea.

Naval shipbuilding continued at pace, with the launch of the 2nd of the new Type-075 amphibious, 8th Type-055 cruiser and 25th Type-052D destroyer ships. These ships should considerably add to the PLAN's ability to project power for a range of contingencies.

While the new PLA Marine Corps aviation brigade continues to work up, helicopters to support amphibious operations in China's littoral areas remain primarily responsible for army units.

China's second aircraft carrier, named Shandong, commissioned in December 2019, continued its trials, including operations with J-15 combat aircraft. In addition, China recently revealed an upgraded version of the J-15 ship-borne fighter jet with enhancements in its missile pylons, the infrared search and track system, the radar and the wings.[51] Meanwhile, the PLAN's third and more significant aircraft carrier is under construction. PLAN has also demonstrated the ability to deploy both the Shandong and the PLAN's first carrier, the Liaoning, at sea simultaneously, indicating that this might soon be translated into a true two-carrier operational capability.[52]

China has launched the 8th Type-055 (Renhai) cruiser and the 25th Type-052D/Type-052D mod (Luyang III/Luyang III mod) destroyer in mid-2020. Consequently, several legacy platforms, including the remaining two Type-051 mod (Luda IV) destroyers, have disappeared from the fleet. Now, only a handful of Type-053H1/H1G (Jianghu I/I Upgrade) frigates remain in service.[53]

## PLA SSF

"The Science of Military Strategy 2013", which is the most important PLA textbook of recent times, highlights China's strategic expansion in space and cyber and electronic warfare domains. The PLA Strategic Support Force (SSF) was formed in 2015 under CMC to create synergies in PLA's strategic cyber, electronics, information, communications, psychological warfare and space missions and capabilities. The PLA considers these domains critical for *"commanding strategic heights"*.[54]

The 2019 military white-paper[55] also describes the SSF's role comprising support for its military forces for battlefield environment, information, communications, information security, and new technology testing. Therefore, "*information support*" and "*information warfare*" could be inferred as the SSF's primary missions. The first information support broadly means collecting information, supporting theatre commands with information for joint operations, feeding information for strategic deterrence in space and nuclear domains, and enabling information to services for force development. The latter means conducting information operations like cyber espionage, countering space-cyber-electromagnetic missions, playing supporting roles to paralyse the enemy's joint operational capabilities, and blinding the enemy's war command system in the initial stages of the conflict.[56] Accordingly, the SSF oversees two deputy theatre command-level departments:

- the Network Systems Department, responsible for information operations (IO), which includes technical reconnaissance, EW, cyber warfare, and psychological operations; and
- the Space Systems Department is responsible for military space operations.

## PLASSF Leadership Structure

Senior PLASSF leaders, defined as Theatre Command (TC) leaders and TC deputy leader-grade officers, are responsible for military space operations, most national-level intelligence, surveillance, and reconnaissance (ISR), and strategic electronic countermeasures (ECM). The PLASSF is equal in grade to the PLA, PLAN, PLAAF, PLARF and the five Theatre Commands.[57] PLASSF leaders and supporting administrative staff presumably would facilitate "cross-domain fusion" of space and network operations.[58]

## Network Systems Department

The PLASSF Network systems Departments have integrated reconnaissance & electronic countermeasures missions, like those which were earlier under GSD; like Technical Reconnaissance Department (3 PLA), Electronic Countermeasures (ECM) and Radar Department (4 PLA). In addition, PLASSF may also integrate national-level technical reconnaissance assets (including cyberweapons) with ECM.[59]

Cyberweapons are computer codes that can infiltrate whole networks or infect individual computers. They rely on software vulnerabilities, poor cyber hygiene and people who inadvertently open attachments infected with malware. China's Military Strategy describes the primary objectives of

Cyber capabilities to include: "cyberspace situation awareness, cyber defence, support for the country's endeavours in cyberspace, and participation in international cyber cooperation." One of the objectives is national and social stability, and the other one is defending critical information infrastructure. Cyberattacks aim to destroy the infrastructure, whereas cyber espionage is used for intelligence collection, military, and economic.

Chinese government and military have been accused of cyberattacks in which intellectual property has been stolen. China has also hired a sophisticated network of private entities for hiring and training hackers as part of the civil-military integration model under PLA SSF.[60]

In February 2021, malware originating from China was found in an Indian power grid. Experts have suggested the malware may have shut off the lights of Mumbai city at the height of the border stand-off in Ladakh. Though the conflict at our Northern borders may have shaped 20th-century geopolitics, the growing cyber capabilities have added another dimension to conflict.[61]

## Space-Based Intelligence, Surveillance and Reconnaissance (ISR)

China has envisioned a robust space-based ISR capability to enhance its global situational awareness and is considered critical to China's power projection stand. It includes civil and military remote sensing and mapping as well as terrestrial and maritime surveillance. With the expansion of China's military deployment farther from the mainland, China aims to establish its dominance in space.[62] As the US military heavily relies on space technologies to project power globally, Russia and China are incentivised to develop capabilities to negate these advantages.[63]

- Using counter-space weapons, Russia and China can threaten American satellites, potentially deter American military action or deny the United States space-enabled advantages (i.e., communications, intelligence, reconnaissance and precision-guided munitions) in the event of a conflict. China and Russia share interests that will deepen their cooperation in space.
- Both Russia and China have agreed to carry out a joint robotic exploration of an asteroid in 2024, signed a memorandum of

understanding[64] to develop a lunar base together, and have established the China-Russia Consortium space weather centre in Beijing.

- China and Russia have also cooperated diplomatically, promoting the Treaty on the Prevention of the Placement of Weapons in Outer Space and on the Threat or Use of Force against Outer Space Objects.[65]

The conduct of Military Space operations by PLA can be summed up into the following significant operations:

- **Space Information Support.** It includes information from space-based sensors for air, ground and naval forces. The critical tasks performed are ISR, satellite communication, space communication, space-based position fixing, navigation and timing, weather sensing and early warning of ballistic missiles.[66]
- **Defensive Space Operations.** These operations are designed to defend their space assets and ground-based infrastructure from the attack, both active and passive measures. In the 'active defence', it is air defence cover for the ground-based assets, but in 'passive defence', it is electronic hardening and shielding from electromagnetic and LASER dazzling interference.
- **Offensive Space Operations.** These operations are intended to carry out softkills and hardkills onto the adversary's space assets.
- **Space Deterrence Operations.** These are intended to dissuade an adversary from acting against its space assets.[67]

China operates numerous military ISR satellites in an extensively integrated network.[68] Prominent satellite constellations for ISR applications have been enumerated below:

## Yaogan ISR Constellation

- Yaogan satellites form an essential component of China's Anti-Access Area Denial (A2AD) strategy. The constellation comprises satellites, which are a mix of Electronic Intelligence (ELINT) satellites, Broad area & High-resolution Electro-Optical (EO) satellites and Synthetic Aperture Radar (SAR) satellites.

## New Yaogan-30 Theatre ELINT Constellation

- Ten triplets of the ELINT constellation known as Yaogan-30 provide constant electronic surveillance over land and sea covering Taiwan, the Korean peninsula, Japan's southern waters, Guam, ASEAN countries and the Indian Ocean.

## Ludikancha Weixing (LKW ) Satellites

- The LKW series comprises four military satellites placed at an altitude of 500 km and are very similar to the Yaogan high-resolution EO satellites.

## Gaofen Satellites

- The Gaofen series, which comprises EO and SAR high-resolution satellites, provides imagery with sub-meter resolution and is a part of the China High-definition Earth Observation System (CHEOS) meant for civil use, but can be developed for military use also.[69]

## Jilin Satellites

- Jilin satellites are lightweight commercial remote sensing satellites with HD video and EO sensors of approximately metric resolution. Presently nineteen Jilin satellites are operational. With 60 satellites by 2020, a revisit of 30 minutes and with 138 satellites by 2030, a revisit of 10 minutes shall be achieved.

## Shijian Satellites

- The Shijian satellites have a variety of configurations and missions, like military ISR payloads due to their orbital characteristics, which can be used for Signal Intelligence (SIGINT), missile tracking payloads and counter space applications like Rendezvous and Proximity Operations (RPO).[70]

## Tongxin Jishu Shiyan (TJS) Early Warning Satellites

- China has launched five satellites of the TJS series in the Geostationary Orbit. These satellites provide early warning of the launch of ballistic missiles for their BMD programme.[71]

## Satellite Communication (SATCOM)

The development of China's communication satellites started at the beginning of the 1970s, and their first geostationary communication satellite was launched successfully in 1984. China's state-owned satellite operator 'China Satcom' currently operates a fleet of 10 GEO communication satellites. It has also been making considerable investments in developing high-throughput satellites (HTS) and LEO satellite constellations for communications.[72]

## China's Counter-Space Capabilities

The PRC continues to develop counter-space capabilities, including direct ascent, co-orbital anti-satellite systems, electronic warfare and directed energy capabilities, cyberattack capabilities and ground-based satellite jammers; that can contest or deny an adversary's access to and operations in the space domain during a crisis or conflict. The counter space developments are coherently and asymmetrically designed to counter a far more technologically advanced adversary's capability. China would employ a combination of 'hard attacks', which use kinetic methods to cause permanent and irreversible destruction of a satellite or ground support infrastructure and 'soft attacks', which use non-kinetic methods to affect the functionality of a satellite or ground systems temporarily.[73] These have been discussed in the succeeding paragraphs.

## Direct Ascent Anti-Satellite (ASAT) Missiles

In January 2007, China tested a direct ascent kinetic-kill missile (SC-19) against a defunct FY-1C weather satellite. The test demonstrated China's ability to strike satellites in LEO. Since then, China has conducted four anti-satellite tests for engaging targets in LEO (160-2000 km altitude) between 2010 and 2014. On May 13, 2013, China was reported to have tested a direct ascent ASAT weapon at an altitude of 10,000 km. It was a cold test with no impact or debris. It is expected that this rocket could be made to reach 30,000 km to threaten GEO satellites.[74]

## Co-orbital Anti-Satellite Systems

These systems consist of a satellite armed with a weapon such as an explosive charge, fragmentation device, kinetic energy weapon, laser, radiofrequency weapon, jammer or robotic arm. Once a co-orbital satellite is close enough to a target satellite, it can deploy its weapon to interfere with, disable, or destroy it. Co-orbital satellites also may intentionally crash into the target. These systems provide several advantages over direct ascent anti-satellite weapons, including their ability to target satellites in every orbital regime, generate less debris, conduct attacks without geographic limitations and limit escalation, as many co-orbital attack options are reversible and offer plausible deniability.[75]

Chinese satellites have conducted co-orbital manoeuvres in 2008, 2010 and 2013. On July 20, 2013, China launched three satellites: the Shiyan-7 (SY-7), Chuangxin (CX-3) and Shijian-15 (SJ-15). SY-7 initially flew close to SJ-15, then it changed orbit, coming closer to CX-3. SY-7 also carried a robotic arm which the Chinese claimed was for proving space manipulation technologies. However, in the anti-satellite role, it could also be utilised to alter the orbit of target satellites or cause damage to them.[76]

### Directed Energy Weapons (DEW)

Directed Energy Weapons can deliver concentrated energy along a line-of-sight trajectory at or near the speed of light to damage or destroy equipment, facilities and personnel. Since the 1990s, China has been committing substantial resources to research and development (R&D) for DEW, including those that could be used for anti-satellite missions. In 2006, China was suspected of firing a laser at a US satellite, resulting in a temporary degradation of its functionality.[77]

### Cyberattack

PLA during a conflict would attempt to conduct cyberattacks against satellites and ground-based facilities that interact with satellites. These cyberattack capabilities are an integral part of China's counter-space capabilities.[78]

### Ground-based Satellite Jammers

Since the mid-2000s, China has acquired several foreign and indigenous ground-based satellite jammers designed to disrupt an adversary's communications with a satellite by overpowering the signals being sent to or from it.[79]

## Conclusion

The PRC has achieved an extraordinary rise in power over the last two decades and has succeeded in multiple regional coercion actions. Still, its comprehensive national power is likely to peak between 2030 and 2035. Economic power is a fundamental prerequisite for military power. It is widely believed that China currently spends more on its armed forces.[80] Chinese writings on military-civil fusion (MCF) emphasise that comprehensive national power stems from economic and military power, both of which rely on the dominance of cutting-edge technologies within the technological revolution that is now underway. By this logic, as China dominates this technology revolution, it is poised to become a technologically-dominant economic and military power and would drive a revolution in its military affairs (RMA). This technology competition fuels Beijing's current sprint because whoever achieves dominance will enjoy tremendous economic and military advantages. Therefore, India also must closely watch the technological advances and brace up to face the challenges.

The PLARF has advanced its long-term modernisation plans to enhance its "assured retaliation" capabilities. But, the change in posture by China needs to be looked at from a different perspective. Keeping the increase in the holdings in view, China needs to be included in future Nuclear dialogues instead of just keeping them bi-lateral between the US & Russia. For India, China's increased inventory of intermediate, medium and short-range missiles is a serious matter of concern.

The changing Chinese nuclear policy may turn these missiles into better weapons to target the Indian facilities. Although, for example, HGVs travel fast in the atmosphere, they will travel slower by the time it reaches the target due to drag, thereby bettering the chances of success for point defences designed for a terminal stage intercept. While cruise missiles have agility, stealth and even loitering capability, ballistic missiles have the advantage of the speed and countering them is a challenging task for Air Defence systems.[81] Hence, our AD capabilities need to be continuously beefed up to face these challenges.

Cyberweapons combine three factors—vulnerability, exploitation and propagation method. The unique features of cyber weapons make it difficult for the instruments used to gather intelligence and inflict damage. The efficiency of a cyber weapon is a vital function of the target's characteristics, as even a tiny change can negate the effectiveness of a cyber weapon against it. Recently, NSCS has initiated coordinating cyber activities between all Indian cyber agencies and would help synergise the efforts to counter all threats.

China's journey toward becoming a space power has been a constant struggle since its inception. But its rapid success is attributable to political patronage and national vision. Chinese believe that as important as it is to possess advanced space-based ISR capabilities, it is equally important to deny these capabilities to their opponents in a combat situation.[82] Thus, China is developing systems and technologies that can interfere with or disable an adversary's vital space-based navigation, communication and intelligence satellites. Cross-domain integration of PLA SSF would enable the efficient launching of space and cyberattacks against political, economic, and civilian targets as a deterrent and poses a potential threat to India's national security.

## Notes

1. Economy, Elizabeth. "Xi Jinping's New World Order." *Foreign Affairs*, December 15, 2021, at https://www.foreignaffairs.com/articles/china/2021-12-09/xi-jinpings-new-world-order. Accessed on December 10, 2021.
2. Ibid.
3. Alvin Toffler and Heidi Toffler, *War and Anti-War: Making Sense of Today's Global Chaos*, Grand Central Publishing, 1995, at https://www.goodreads.com/book/show/67489.War_and_Anti_War. Accessed on November 28, 2021.
4. Boyd Henery, "China's army modernisation: progress, rhetoric and reality", August 21, 2019, at https://www.iiss.org/blogs/military-balance/2019/08/china-army-modernisation. Accessed on December 12, 2021.
5. Army Dreamers, *The Economist* (China) "Xi wants China's Armed forces to be 'World Class' by 2050", June 29, 2019, at https://www.economist.com/china/2019/06/27/xi-jinping-wants-chinas-armed-forces-to-be-world-class-by-2050, Accessed on December 26, 2021.
6. Economy, Elizabeth. "Xi Jinping's New World Order." *Foreign Affairs*, December 15, 2021, at https://www.foreignaffairs.com/articles/china/2021-12-09/xi-jinpings-new-world-order. Accessed on December 10, 2021.
7. "DPG China Monitor." *China Monitor*. Delhi Policy Group, November 11, 2021, at https://www.delhipolicygroup.org/publication/china-monitor/china-monitor-3455.html. Accessed on December 26, 2021.

8. Ibid.
9. Ibid.
10. Tian Nan, Kuimova Alexandra, Silva Diego Lopes Da, Wezeman, and Pieter D. Wezeman Siemon T, Trends in world military expenditure, 2019 April, 2020, at https://www.sipri.org/sites/default/files/2020-04/fs_2020_04_milex_0.pdf. Accessed on December 26, 2021.
11. Ibid.
12. Grosse Robert, Gamso Jonas, and Nelson Roy C, "China's Rise, World Order, and the Implications for International Business", Springer Link, March 3, 2021, at https://link.springer.com/article/10.1007/s11575-020-00433-8. Accessed on December 25, 2021.
13. Mazarr Michael J, "Understanding Perspective", Rand Corporation, April 15, 2020, at https://www.rand.org/content/dam/rand/pubs/perspectives/PE200/PE295/RAND_PE295.pdf. Accessed on December 25, 2021.
14. Richardson, John M. "A Design for Maintaining Maritime Superiority—NHHC." A Design for Maintaining Maritime Superiority, June 12, 2019, at https://www.history.navy.mil/content/dam/nhhc/get-involved/2019CNOContest/cno-stg.pdf. Accessed on December 20, 2021.
15. Finkelstein, David L. "CNA: The PLA's New Joint Doctrine." Concerning China. CNA, October 15, 2021, at https://concerningchina.com/cna-the-plas-new-joint-doctrine/. Accessed on December 20, 2021.
16. Office of the Defence Secretary. "Military and Security Developments Involving the PRC." Annual Report to Congress. DoD, USA, November 3, 2021, at https://media.defense.gov/2021/Nov/03/2002885874/-1/-1/0/2021-CMPR-FINAL.PDF?source=GovDelivery. Accessed on December 19, 2021.
17. Elsa Kania, "China's Artificial Intelligence Revolution." *The Diplomat*, July 27, 2017, at https://thediplomat.com/2017/07/chinas-artificial-intelligence-revolution/. Accessed on December 18, 2021.
18. Kania, Elsa B, and Ian Burns McCaslin. "Learning Warfare from the Laboratory—China's Progression in Wargaming and Opposing Force Training." Institute for the Study of War. ISW, September 21, 2021, at https://www.understandingwar.org/report/learning-warfare-laboratory-china%E2%80%99s-progression-wargaming-and-opposing-force-training. Accessed on December 19, 2021.
19. Sullivan, Ryan. "The U.S., China, and Artificial Intelligence Competition Factors." Air University (AU). China Aerospace Studies Institute, October 4, 2021, at https://www.airuniversity.af.edu/CASI/Display/Article/2793710/the-us-china-and-artificial-intelligence-competition-factors/. Accessed on December 17, 2021.
20. Ibid.
21. Ibid.
22. Ibid.

23. Walsh, Bryan. "Quantum Computers near a Quantum Leap." Axios, December 11, 2021, at https://www.axios.com/quantum-computers-ibm-google-57070e8c-8bf6-40fd-83f2-b493db52f11e.html. Accessed on December 19, 2021.
24. Ibid.
25. PTI. "China Launches World's Longest Quantum Communication Line." *The Economic Times*, November 20, 2016, at https://economictimes.indiatimes.com/news/science/china-launches-worlds-longest-quantum-communication-line/articleshow/55524536.cms. Accessed December 13, 2021.
26 Bath, Pushpinder. "Dragon's Space Arsenal: Dominating the Strategic High Ground." Vivekananda International Foundation, May 31, 2021, at https://www.vifindia.org/article/2021/may/31/dragon-s-space-arsenal-dominating-the-strategic-high-ground. Accessed on December 10, 2021.
27. Corrigan, Fintan. "Drone Waypoint GPS Navigation Technology and Uses Explained." DroneZon, July 14, 2020, at https://www.dronezon.com/learn-about-drones-quadcopters/drone-waypoint-gps-navigation-technology-explained/. Accessed on December 5, 2021.
28. Kallenborn, Zachary. "A Cascading Catastrophe: The Drone Threat to Critical Infrastructure." Bulletin of the Atomic Scientists, November 24, 2021, at https://thebulletin.org/2021/11/a-cascading-catastrophe-the-drone-threat-to-critical-infrastructure/. Accessed on November 29, 2021.
29. Ibid.
30. Joshi, Manoj. "The N-Challenge and Beyond." ORF, October 26, 2021, at https://www.orfonline.org/research/the-n-challenge-and-beyond/. Accessed on December 10, 2021.
31. Nambiar, Keerthana, Harini Madhusudan, and Joeana Cera Mathews. "China's Hypersonic Tests, Russia's Afghanistan Summit, and EU's Poland Challenge." Global Politics—China's hypersonic tests, Russia's Afghanistan summit, and EU's Poland challenge. NIAS, October 24, 2021, at https://globalpolitics.in/view_cir_articles.php?url=The+World+This+Week&recordNo=666. Accessed on November 15, 2021.
32. Osborn, Kris. "Beware: A China-U.S. Hypersonic Missile Showdown Has Begun." The National Interest. The Center for the National Interest, November 12, 2021, at https://nationalinterest.org/blog/buzz/beware-china-us-hypersonic-missile-showdown-has-begun-196200. Accessed on December 2, 2021.
33. Na, Chen. "China Develops Prototype of Microwave Photonics-Based Radar." China develops prototype of Microwave Photonics-Based Radar. Chinese Academy of Sciences, June 14, 2017, at https://english.cas.cn/newsroom/archive/news_archive/nu2017/201706/t20170614_178105.shtml. Accessed on December 1, 2021.
34. "What Does the Pentagon Say about China-India Conflicts?" Go News India, November 26, 2021, at https://www.gonewsindia.com/latest-news/international/

what-pentagon-says-about-china-india-conflicts-27005. Accessed on November 30, 2021.

35. Wbstadm. "Why China Wants More and Better Nukes." SmallArmsTactical. Gun Trade, November 20, 2021, at https://smallarmstactical.com/why-china-wants-more-and-better-nukes/. Accessed on December 1, 2021.
36 "Until 10:00 Reimagining Nuclear Arms Control—Politico.com." *Politico*, September 22, 2021, at https://www.politico.com/f/?id=0000017d-ba5f-dca7-a1fd-bb5f0cbe0000. Accessed on December 18, 2021.
37. Joshi, Manoj. "The N-Challenge and Beyond." ORF, October 26, 2021, at https://www.orfonline.org/research/the-n-challenge-and-beyond/. Accessed on December 22, 2021.
38. Ibid.
39. Wbstadm, n. 35.
40. Ibid.
41. Acton, James M, Thomas MacDonald, and Pranay Vaddi. "Reimagining Nuclear Arms Control: A Comprehensive Approach." *The Frontier Post*, December 16, 2021, at https://thefrontierpost.com/reimagining-nuclear-arms-control-a-comprehensive-approach/. Accessed on December 25, 2021.
42. Wbstadm, n. 35.
43. Xiu, Ma. "PLA ROCKET FORCE ORGANIZATION." China Aerospace Studies Institute, November 22, 2021, at https://www.airuniversity.af.edu/Portals/10/CASI/documents/Research/PLAAF/2021-04-12%20CASI_70%20Years%20of%20the%20PLAAF_FINAL%20ALL.pdf?ver=hTom1CXAjt0VTGTJzJBGAQ%3d%3d. Accessed on December 10, 2021.
44. Kris Osborn, "'In 2020, China Launched 250+ Ballistic Missiles, More than the Rest of the World Combined.'" Warrior Maven: Military and Defense News, November 15, 2021, at https://warriormaven.com/future-weapons/china-missiles-df-21d-df-17-df-26. Accessed on December 10, 2021.
45. Silver Stephen. "The U.S. Military Is Freaked out over China's Missiles and Submarines." 19FortyFive. 1945, November 7, 2021, at https://www.19fortyfive.com/2021/11/the-u-s-military-is-freaked-out-over-chinas-missiles-and-submarines/. Accessed on December 15, 2021.
46. Ibid.
47. Panda, Ankit. "Revealed: China's Nuclear-Capable Air-Launched Ballistic Missile." *The Diplomat*, April 18, 2018, at https://thediplomat.com/2018/04/revealed-chinas-nuclear-capable-air-launched-ballistic-missile/. Accessed on December 1, 2021.
48. Wbstadm. "Why China Wants More and Better Nukes." SmallArmsTactical. Gun Trade, November 20, 2021, at https://smallarmstactical.com/why-china-wants-more-and-better-nukes/. Accessed on December 1, 2021.

49. Chankalyee. "Pla Airborne Troops Conduct First Exercise with Y-20 Transport Aircraft", Tiananmen's Tremendous Achievements, May 11, 2018, at https://tiananmenstremendousachievements.wordpress.com/2018/05/11/30255. Accessed on December 10, 2021.
50. "Chapter Six: Asia, the Military Balance." T&F, February 24, 2021, at https://www.tandfonline.com/doi/abs/10.1080/04597222.2021.1868795?journalCode=tmib20. Accessed on November 27, 2021.
51. Anderson, Michael P. "China Reveals Upgraded J-15 Fighter Jet; Key Aircraft Carrier Roles Expected." Naval Open Source Intelligence, December 17, 2021, at https://nosi.org/2021/12/17/china-reveals-upgraded-j-15-fighter-jet-key-aircraft-carrier-roles-expected/. Accessed on December 20, 2021.
52. Rice, Jennifer and Eric Robb. "China Maritime Report No. 13: The Origins of 'Near Seas Defense and Far Seas Protection." U.S. Naval War College, February 2, 2021, at https://digital-commons.usnwc.edu/cgi/viewcontent.cgi?article=1012&context=cmsi-maritime-reports. Accessed on December 20, 2021.
53. Ibid.
54. Desai, Suyash. "PLA SSF: Why China Will Be Ahead of Everyone in Future Cyber, Space or Information Warfare." The Print, December 31, 2019, at https://theprint.in/opinion/pla-ssf-why-china-will-be-ahead-of-everyone-in-future-cyber-space-or-information-warfare/342772/. Accessed on December 27, 2021.
55. Xinhua, "China Issues White Paper on National Defense in New Era." China issues White Paper on National Defense in New Era. The State Council of the People's Republic of China, July 24, 2019, at https://english.www.gov.cn/statecouncil/ministries/201907/24/content_WS5d37ca73c6d00d362f668c58.html. Accessed on December 23, 2021.
56. Ibid.
57. Burton, Rache, and Mark Stokes. "The People's Liberation Army Strategic Support Force". Project 2049, September 25, 2018, at https://project2049.net/wp-content/uploads/2018/09/180925_PLA_SSF_Leadership-and-Structure_Stokes_Burton.pdf. Accessed on November 10, 2021.
58. Ibid.
59. Ibid.
60. Jinghua, Lyu. "What Are China's Cyber Capabilities and Intentions?" Carnegie Endowment for International Peace. Carnegie Endowment for International Peace, April 1, 2019, at https://carnegieendowment.org/2019/04/01/what-are-china-s-cyber-capabilities-and-intentions-pub-78734. Accessed on December 10, 2021.
61. Brar, Aadil. "China's Cyber Warfare Has Grown on the Back of Civilian Recruits." The Print. Eye on China, September 22, 2021, at https://theprint.in/opinion/eye-on-china/chinas-cyber-warfare-has-grown-on-the-back-of-civilian-recruits/737651/. Accessed on November 15, 2021.

62. Department of Defence, "DOD Releases 2021 Report on Military and Security Developments Involving the People's Repu." U.S. Department of Defense, November 3, 2021, at https://www.defense.gov/News/Releases/Release/Article/2831819/dod-releasesAccessed/. Accessed on December 20, 2021.
63. Department of Defence, "2020 Defense Space Strategy Summary." DEFENSE SPACE STRATEGY SUMMARY. DoD, June 1, 2021, at https://media.defense.gov/2020/Jun/17/2002317391/-1/-1/1/2020_DEFENSE_SPACE_STRATEGY_SUMMARY.PDF. Accessed on December 10, 2021.
64. Jones, Andrew. "China, Russia Enter MOU on International Lunar Research Station." Space News, March 9, 2021, at https://spacenews.com/china-russia-enter-mou-on-international-lunar-research-station/. Accessed on December 20, 2021.
65 Na, Chen. "China Develops Prototype of Microwave Photonics-Based Radar." China develops prototype of Microwave Photonics-Based Radar. Chinese Academy of Sciences, June 14, 2017, at https://english.cas.cn/newsroom/archive/news_archive/nu2017/201706/t20170614_178105.shtml. Accessed on December 16, 2021.
66 Bath, Pushpinder Singh. "China's Military Space Strategy". Vivekanananda International Foundation, June 15, 2021, at https://www.vifindia.org/article/2021/june/15/china-s-military-space-strategy. Accessed on December 10, 2021.
67. Ibid.
68. Ibid.
69. Bath, Pushpinder Singh. "Dragon's Space Arsenal: Dominating the Strategic High Grounds." Vivekanand Internationl Foundation, May 31, 2021, at https://www.vifindia.org/article/2021/may/31/dragon-s-space-arsenal-dominating-the-strategic-high-ground. Accessed on November 17, 2021.
70. Ibid.
71. Ibid.
72. Ibid.
73. Ibid.
74. Ibid.
75. Ibid.
76. Ibid.
77. Ibid.
78. Ibid.
79. Ibid.
80. Brown, David. "Why China Could Win the New Global Arms Race." BBC, December 21, 2021, at https://www.bbc.com/news/world-asia-china-59600475. Accessed on December 26, 2021.

81. Philip, Snehesh Alex and Simrin Sirur. "Why Pralay Quasi-Ballistic Missile, Tested by DRDO Today, Will Be a 'Game-Changer' for Army." The Print, December 22, 2021, at https://theprint.in/defence/why-pralay-quasi-ballistic-missile-tested-by-drdo-today-will-be-a-game-changer-for-army/785809/. Accessed on December 16, 2021.
82. Ibid.

# 4

# IAF as a Force Multiplier in Collaboration: The Quest for Dominance

ANIL GOLANI

*"The more you sweat in peace the less you bleed in war"*

—Norman Schwarzkopf

## Introduction

The complexity of the global security environment continues to challenge policy and decision-makers across the world. As new threats emanate, new alliances take shape. The enduring factor governing these strategies, however, remains national interest. Like all elements of national power, that must coalesce together to ensure national objectives and goals are met so must international and regional alliances collaborate to ensure the achievement of shared goals and mutual prosperity. Increasing strife and belligerence, natural and man-made disasters, and the ongoing covid pandemic, necessitate collaboration by nations to ensure safety and prosperity of its citizens. As the success of global institutions towards this endeavour remains circumspect, and would probably entail separate research, regional alliances have to come together cooperating with each other on trade, economy, diplomacy and humanitarian assistance and disaster relief.

Militaries need to understand each other before they can operate together against common foes or adversaries, both kinetic as well as non-kinetic, in the military and the humanitarian assistance roles. Post-Independence India maintained a strong non-aligned stand, with a pacifist outlook, concentrating on building national institutions, eradicating poverty and improving literacy and life expectancy. Unsettled borders and an unstable neighbourhood, with insurgencies in a few states, forced it to gradually modernise its military. With four conflicts since independence, and belligerent nuclear-armed neighbours the nation had no choice but to keep the powder dry. IAF remained inward-looking and refrained from participating in bilateral or multilateral exercises with other air forces. The contact remained only with the industry, and to a limited extent with the concerned air force for training, post-acquisition of the aircraft, radars and other electronic and weapon systems. Familiarity with the aircraft and associated systems accrued with this training, however operational concepts and the capability to jointly plan and carry out operations remained wanting. Demonstration of the capability of the Indian Air Force and the Indian Army remained largely confined to the international peacekeeping operations under the aegis of the United Nations, while the Indian Navy continued with their 'gunboat diplomacy' remaining to a large extent the sole face of India's Armed Forces. With the opening up of the Indian economy post the 1991 reforms, modernisation of the IAF, its performance during the 1999 Kargil conflict, and acknowledgement of its role in the United Nations Peacekeeping Operations, apart from increasing participation of its officers in courses abroad with friendly foreign countries, the IAF gained acknowledgement and an acceptance amongst the leading air forces of the world as a professional force to reckon with.

## Nascent Start

The Indian Air Force created history, when on July 2, 2004, six Jaguars of its fighter fleet, flew across the Atlantic, landing in Alaska, with mid-air refuelling being carried out by IL-78 tanker aircraft, to take part in Exercise Co-Operative Cope Thunder 2004, a multilateral exercise conducted by the United States Pacific Air Force. This was the first time that fighter aircraft of the IAF had operated outside Indian airspace in peacetime. Transport aircraft and helicopters of the IAF had hitherto been regularly participating in UN-led operations across the world. This exercise marked the beginning of a new era of the Indian Air Force's participation in multilateral exercises abroad. The IAF contingent consisted of six Jaguars, two IL-78 Flight Refuelling Aircraft (FRA), two IL-76 transport aircraft, and one flight of man-portable air defence systems (MANPADS) and two Forward Air Controllers (FAC). An approx distance of 20,000 km from Jamnagar to Alaska was covered with nine staging halts en route, with the most difficult and taxing stretch of over four hours across the Atlantic. The aircrew had to undergo extensive training in mid-air refuelling, long-duration sorties of more than double the duration that they were used to and flying with diapers and medication to overcome the physiological effects of changing time zones with lack of sleep. Flying over thirteen countries and landing in five, the route across the Arabian Sea, Red Sea, Mediterranean Sea and the Atlantic Ocean was indeed a giant leap for a fledgling fighter force in multilateral operations. This exercise marked the coming of age of the IAF's capacity and ability to make a mark amongst some of the most professional air forces in the world.

## The First Decade 2004-2014

The first decade saw India taking part in a number of bilateral and multilateral exercises. Some of these over the years progressed serially with mutual partners becoming adept and familiar with each other's concept of operations, areas of operation as well as shared mutual trust and bonding, which is an essential prerequisite for military operations to be successful. The NATO Air Forces and to a limited extent, those of the Warsaw Pact countries, before the collapse of the Soviet Union, had been used to conducting joint operations and exercises on a regular basis, unlike the IAF which had been operating in isolation in the region. Exercise Cope India with the USAF, Sindex with the Republic of Singapore Air Force, Garuda with the French Air Force, Indra Dhanush with the Royal Air Force UK, and Eastern Bridge with the Royal Air Force of Oman are some bilateral exercises that have matured to become a regular feature in the IAF's calendar. Exercise Co-Operative Cope Thunder, renamed as Red Flag is a premier multilateral exercise carried out by the Pacific Air Force, that simulates a realistic environment for combat operations during deployment with large force engagements taking place. Participation in Ex Red Flag, is an invaluable experience and an honour for military pilots the world over, a rare opportunity wherein apart from the pilots the aircraft maintenance engineers, technicians and combat support teams also get to experience operations in a realistic environment.

## Indo-US Exercises: Cope Thunder/Cope India/Red Flag

These are the series of exercises conducted between the US and India, with the Cope India series conducted on Indian soil and the Cope Thunder/Red Flag series in the United States. The first Cope India exercise between the USAF and IAF took place at Air Force Station Gwalior from February 16-27, 2004. This first Indo-US bilateral exercise focussed on cooperation through building upon mutual capabilities, aircrew tactics and force employment. Months of preparation went into the exercise with both sides gaining a better understanding of each other's capabilities and limitations. The IAF official statement at the end of the exercise indicated that, "the mutual respect and bonhomie that developed between the members of the two sides have cemented a firm foundation for moving ahead towards higher bilateralism."[1] The pilots of the USAF exercise, expecting the IAF pilots to use conventional cold war tactics were surprised by their 'unpredictability' and found it to be a positive experience that led to a re-think of some of their own assumptions of their tactics. The USAF took part with F 15 Eagles from Elmendorf Air Force Base Alaska, while the IAF participated with Mig 21 Bison, Mirage 2000 and Su 30K aircraft. The F-15 Eagles could not simulate the use of Beyond Visual Range (BVR) missiles because of the Indian request not to use the Advanced Medium Range Air to Air Missiles (AMRAAM). Both the F-15 Eagles and the IAF Su 30K were not equipped with the AESA radars and the Su 30K was the Russian aircraft, with the IAF yet to deploy the Su 30 MKI, made to Indian specifications. The IAF MiG 21 Bison, with low radar visibility, instantaneous turn rate, acceleration and equipped with helmet-mounted sight for off-boresight launch capable R 73 missiles, proved to be a formidable adversary to the F-15 Eagles of the USAF.

Cope India 2005 in the subsequent year had mixed teams of Indian and USAF pilots on both sides, with the USAF deploying its F-16 Falcons this time. Observers and participants during this exercise once again observed that the IAF pilots came out on top, especially in the encounters between the F-16 and the Su 30 MKI. This led the then Director-General of CAPS, Late Air Cmde Jasjit Singh to comment, "Since the Cold War, there has been the general assumption that India is a third world country with Soviet technology, and wherever Sovict-supported equipment went, it did not perform well. That myth has been blown away by the results."[2]

The next joint exercise on Indian soil, Cope India 2009 focussed on Humanitarian Assistance and Disaster Relief (HADR) operations. The US force consisted of C 130 H/J Hercules and C 17 Globemaster aircraft while the IAF was represented by IL 76 and AN 32 transport aircraft and Mi 17 and Chetak Alouette III helicopters. This was the first time that four US airmen and 12 Garud commandos of the IAF jointly carried out a High Altitude Low Opening (HALO) airdrop jointly over Indian territory. The exercise was carried out at Agra, one of the largest air bases in Asia and a premier transport base of the IAF, also home to the Para Brigade of the Indian Army. This exercise allowed both the countries to exchange humanitarian airlift, air land and airdrop delivery techniques.

After Exercise Co-Operative Cope Thunder 2004, the first exercise in which IAF fighters participated in a joint exercise overseas, the next multilateral exercise i.e Ex Red Flag took place in 2008. This was a multilateral joint combat training exercise organised at Nellis Air Force Base Nevada with the Nevada Test and Training Range, over 12,000 square miles of airspace and 2.9 million acres of land, in the premier military training area of the USAF. The IAF participated with 8 X SU 30 MKI, 2 X IL 78 tankers and 01 X IL 76 aircraft. This was the first time that the IAF pilots operated in a full network-centric environment and also in coordination with the USAF Airborne Warning and Control System (AWACS) aircraft. The Red Flag exercise which generally involves the NATO allies of the US is held on a regular basis and this was the first time that the IAF contingent participated along with the French and the Korean Air Force apart from the USAF. The IAF had earlier sent observers for this exercise. During the exercise, with as many as eighty aircraft participating at a given time the IAF pilots carried out Large Force Engagement, day and night Offensive Air Operations and Dynamic Targeting Missions. The exercise simulated a near realistic environment wherein the losses, by simulated kills with air-to-air and air-to-ground SAMs, were taken away from the combat zone, by the White Force armed with sophisticated debriefing tools and instruments, acting as umpires. The umpires rated the Indian pilots as among the best. IAF's Garud Commandos practised Combat Search and Rescue missions in urban warfare scenarios, winning laurels for their performance. They also practised neutralising an enemy radar site and capturing an airfield. The IAF gained invaluable experience and lessons operating in a network-centric environment that would enable it to integrate the AWACS in the Indian scenario.

## Indo-Singapore Exercises: Sindex

The first-ever bilateral exercise between the IAF and RSAF, Sindex 04, took place from October 11-27, 2004 at Air Force Station Gwalior. Six F-16 C/D Falcon aircraft of the RSAF participated in the exercise, with the IAF being represented by Su 30 MK, MiG 27, MiG 29 and Mirage 2000 aircraft. This exercise was a reflection of the growing defence engagement between the two countries, giving each other an opportunity to train and operate together in realistic conditions as also strengthen friendship and enhance interoperability between the two Air Forces.

The next in the series, Sindex 06 took place at Air Force Station Kalaikunda from January 3-20, 2006, with the RSAF participating with 08 X F-16 Falcon aircraft and the IAF with a squadron of MiG 27 aircraft. With an Air to Ground armament range in the near vicinity of the air base, the RSAF wanted to utilise the base and associated infrastructure for their training on a regular basis. The infrastructure at the base was upgraded to host foreign air forces for bilateral exercises and training. The RSAF entered into a Joint Military Training (JMT) under the ambit of the Air Force Bilateral Agreement, which was signed in 2007. Post this agreement bilateral exercises and exchange visits between the two Air Forces became a regular feature with both sides benefitting immensely while building friendships and bonds with each other in the process.

## Indo-French Exercises: Garuda

The Garuda series of exercises held between the IAF and the French Air Force started as an effort to enhance inter-operational capabilities between the two Air Forces. The IAF had been flying the French Mirage 2000 aircraft while the Rafale at that time had been under active consideration for the Medium Multi-Role Combat Aircraft (MMRCA) deal. The first edition of this exercise was held at Air Force Station Gwalior in 2003 with the participation of four Mirage 2000 RDI aircraft of the French Air Force. This was the first time that foreign combat aircraft exercised with IAF fighters on Indian soil. Garuda II, held at the Istres Air Base in France from June 15-30, 2005 was the first exercise in Europe for the fighter aircraft of the IAF. It was also the first occasion when Su 30MK aircraft participated in an exercise outside India. The Indian contingent consisted of six Su 30MK, two IL 78 refuellers and one IL 76 aircraft. The component from the French Air Force consisted of Mirage 2000-5, Mirage 2000 N, C 135, E-3F AWACS, and Tucano aircraft. This exercise gave the IAF an opportunity to familiarise themselves with NATO procedures, as well as testing the capability of the Su 30 against the latest versions of the Mirage 2000-5 of the French Air Force. The IAF aircraft participated in the coordination and control of the French E-3F AWACS, carrying out air defence missions and fighter sweeps. Air-to-air refuelling was carried out by both the forces from each other's tanker aircraft.

The third exercise in the Garuda series took place at Kalaikunda airbase from February 12-23, 2007 and it followed the signing of the Indo-French Defence Cooperation Agreement signed between the two countries in 2006. This was also the first occasion when the French AWACS operated from Indian soil. The fourth edition of Garuda took place at Istres Air Force Base in France from June 14-25, 2010. The IAF contingent consisted of 6 Su 30MKI and two IL 78 Flight refuelling Aircraft and this was the first occasion when cross-air to air refuelling took place by fighters from both the air forces from each other's tanker aircraft. This exercise for the first time included another country i.e., the Republic of Singapore Air Force, making it a trilateral effort.

Garuda V, which took place at Air Force Station Jodhpur from June 2-13, 2014 was the first occasion when the Rafale fighters of the French Air Force took part in an exercise with the IAF. Though the Rafale had demonstrated its capability at the Bengaluru Air Show in the past, this time the aircraft was doing tactical exercises with IAF Su MKIs, MiG 27 and MiG 21 Bison aircraft. IL 76 AWACS of the IAF also participated in the exercise along with its IL 78 refueller aircraft. During the exercise Chiefs' of both the Air Forces, i.e. Air Chief Marshal Arup Raha of the IAF and Gen Denis Mercier of the FAF flew in the Rafale and Su MKI respectively thereby making an upfront assessment of the capabilities of each other's fighter aircraft. The participation of the two Chiefs in the exercise along with their interaction with the technicians and pilots of both the air forces was an appropriate example of leading from the front and enhancing camaraderie and bonhomie amongst their personnel. The exercise also took place after the IAF had selected Rafale as their preferred choice for the MMRCA deal after protracted negotiations. This edition of the exercise, therefore, was a significant step toward taking the strategic partnership between the two countries to a different level altogether.

## Indo-UK Exercises: Indra Dhanush

'Indra Dhanush' which means rainbow in Hindi was planned as a bilateral exercise between IAF and RAF, to boost the ongoing Defence Cooperation between the two countries. The first edition of the exercise was held at Gwalior and Agra air bases of the IAF from October 2-13, 2006, with the RAF contingent consisting of six Tornado fighters, VC 10 tanker and E 3D AWACS aircraft. The IAF participated with Su 30MKI, MiG 27 and MiG 21 Bison aircraft. The joint operational exercise between the two air forces aimed to enhance operational understanding and familiarise each other with their training procedures. IAF pilots in the past had been trained in the UK on Canberras, Hunters, Gnat and Jaguar aircraft.

The second edition of the exercise Indra Dhanush-II was held at Waddington, the UK in June 2007 and was the first occasion when the IAF Su 30MKI flew over the European skies, evincing much interest in the UK. The RAF participated with Tornado and Typhoon and also Sea Harriers of the Royal Navy, carrying out aerial combat and LFE (Large Force Engagement) exercises under the cover of E3D Sentry AWACS of the RAF. The culmination of the exercise was witnessed by Air Chief Marshal F H Major of the IAF and Air Chief Marshal Sir Clive Loader of the RAF. Group Captain E Stringer, RAF Station Commander Leeming, while summing up the RAF experience stated that a major outcome of the exercise was the appreciation of the fact that the two Air Forces actually "see the world through similar eyes", and that there were many "commonalities" in the tactical procedures of the two air forces, thereby laying a foundation for further RAF-IAF interactions.[3] The exercise was followed by the Waddington air show where the IAF Su 30MKI were the star attraction having been judged the 'best static display' at the show.

The third edition of the exercise was held at Air Force Station Kalaikunda from October 18 to November 3, 2010. For the RAF contingent which participated with Eurofighter Typhoons, E3D Sentry AWACS and VC 10 tanker aircraft, it was a homecoming of sorts after more than six decades as the air base had been built by the British, serving a crucial role during the Second World War by carrying out missions against the Japanese forces along the Indo-Burma (Myanmar) border. This was the first time that the IAF AWACS participated in a joint air force exercise, as also the first occasion for the Eurofighter Typhoon in India, which at that time was under active consideration for the 126 aircraft MMRCA deal. The IAF participated with Su MKI, Mirage 2000 and MiG 27 aircraft with aim of giving exposure to maximum IAF aircrew and controllers in Large Force Engagement (LFE) exercises and protection of High-Value Aerial Assets (HVAA) as RAF had been doing these roles on a regular basis during their coalition/expeditionary deployments across the world.

## Indo-Oman Exercises: Eastern Bridge

Oman, geographically closest to India, featured as an important country in the Persian Gulf region for India which led to IAF-RAFO defence cooperation that was initiated in 2006. The country had been sending its officers for courses in India on a self-financing basis. The Royal Air Force of Oman (RAFO) also remained the only country apart from India that was still flying the Anglo-French Sepecat Jaguar aircraft. The first exercise between the two air forces, code-named Eastern Bridge, commenced on October 22, 2009, at Thumrait, the RAFO base in Oman. IAF participated with six Jaguars, one IL 78 refueller and an IL 76 aircraft, while the RAFO was represented by Jaguars and F 16 aircraft. The exercise aimed at enhancing understanding of operational, administrative and maintenance procedures between the two Air Forces also benefited the IAF in gaining operational experience in carrying out flying exercises over an unknown mix of land and desert terrain.

The second edition of the exercise took place at Air Force Station Jamnagar from October 17-21, 2011, with the RAFO bringing in six Jaguars while the IAF contingent was represented by Jaguars and MiG 29 aircraft. The exercise involved a variety of flying missions that included long-duration sorties with in-flight refuelling, large force strike packages, air-to-ground weapon firing and maritime strikes, giving exposure to the aircrew of both the air forces with each other's best practises. The interaction apart from being professionally enriching, forged social and cultural bonds between the two air forces as well, with an informal social evening and a football match played between the two sides.

Eastern Bridge III in October 2013 saw the deployment by six Jaguars of the Maritime Squadron of the IAF in Masirah where they exercised with the Jaguars, Hawk and F 16 aircraft of the RAFO. This was the first overseas deployment of the maritime strike Jaguars of the IAF. RAFO views Eastern Bridge as an important tool in maintaining its operational readiness and effectiveness.

## Indo-UAE Exercises: Desert Eagle

The strong bilateral relations between India and UAE going back to hundreds of years received a fresh impetus in defence cooperation after the signing of the 'Agreement for Defence Cooperation' during the visit of the Chief of Staff of the UAE Armed Forces to India in 2003. On the invitation of the UAE Air Force Chief, the IAF contingent of 8 Su 30MKi returning from Ex Red Flag in September 2008, stopped over at Al Dhafra air base in the UAE to participate in the first-ever bilateral exercise between the air forces of the two countries. A wide variety of missions were flown under the Beyond Visual Range (BVR) environment with the two sides drawing valuable operational lessons.

## Indo-Russia Exercise: Avia Indra

The first exercise between the IAF and the Russian Federation Aerospace Force (RSASF) started in August 2014 with Indian pilots flying joint sorties with their Russian counterparts in the Russian Air Force Su 30SM fighters and Mi 35 attack helicopters. The exercise took place over Russian test ranges near the Caspian Sea with the aircrew operating from Lipetsk. The exercise involved mid-air refuelling by Su 30SM and special helicopter operations. In addition, joint air defence crews at Ashuluk military ranges repulsed a simulated strike by firing anti-aircraft missile systems S-400, S-300, Buk M1 and anti-aircraft missile and gun system Pantsir-S1. The second phase of the exercise took place at Air Force Station Halwara in India from November 18-28, 2014. The 18-member Russian delegation consisted of fighter and helicopter aircrew apart from air defence crew and other members. The Russian aircrew carried out flying exercises with IAF aircrew on Su 30MKI, Mi 17V5 and Mi 35 helicopters that focussed on counter-terror operations, air defence and special heliborne operations.

## Enhanced Cooperation: 2015-2021

### *Indra Dhanush*

The fourth edition of IAF-RAF Exercise Indra Dhanush IV took place in July 2015 in the United Kingdom. The IAF Su 30MKIs operating from Coningsby were pitted against the Eurofighter Typhoons and combat support elements from Brize Norton. IAF Garud commandos also participated in the exercise carrying out drops from an RAF Hercules aircraft. This exercise created unwarranted controversy with the remarks of the IAF contingent commander claiming a 12-0 success by the IAF Su 30MKIs over the Eurofighter Typhoon in aerial combat owing to the "exceptional" performance of IAF pilots.[4] The RAF however was quick in rebutting these claims, stating "There must have been some clouded recollection on the flight back to India, as the headlines of the Indian press bear no relations to the results of the tactical scenarios completed on the exercise in any shape or form."[5] In matters that are professional in nature, scoring brownie points in the media defeat the very purpose of bilateral exercises that aim at fostering defence cooperation.

The fifth edition of Exercise Indra Dhanush commenced on February 24, 2020, at Air Force Station Hindan. This exercise focussed on "Base Defence and Force Protection" with 36 specialised combatants from the RAF regiment and 42 Garud commandos of the IAF participating. Combat Free Fall drops from C 130J Hercules aircraft and Special Heliborne Operations (SHBO) troop insertion by Mi 17 V5 helicopters were carried out with the utilisation of various airborne sensors. Both the elements of the special forces shared and validated tactics related to the terror threat to their installations, anti-terror operations in an urban scenario and practised airfield seizure operations. The theme of the exercise was topical and relevant considering the recent threats to military installations from terror elements.[6]

## Red Flag/Cope India

The first series of Red Flag exercises in 2016 was held at Eielson Air Force Base Alaska from April 28 to May 13, 2016. The IAF participated with Su 30MKI and Jaguar DARIN II aircraft. While referring to the overall exercise plan and its objectives the IAF Team Leader, Gp Capt H Assudani said, "the overall objective of this inter-continental deployment was not only to showcase IAF capability in undertaking Integrated Air Ops but also to imbibe operational lessons from the exercise engagements which will help us add more teeth to our overall war waging capabilities."[7] The exercise conducted under multiple scenarios simulating realistic settings had the IAF participate for the first time as a part of the 'Aggressors' comprising the 'Red Force.' There were three missions commanded by the IAF for which the mission commanders of both the Jaguars and the Su 30MKI were involved in the planning, execution and conduct of debrief. While talking about the IAF participation in the exercise Lt Col Brian Toth, Chief Operations Officer of 354 Operations Group said, "The IAF participation has been extremely good from my perspective. For most nations, it takes an exercise or two to step up to meet the requirements of a Mission Commander. The IAF has been mission commander three times and also performed the package commander roles and they have done a tremendous job."[8] The IAF contingent earned accolades for their exceptional standards displayed during the exercise and the 100 per cent serviceability achieved by its aircraft for the entire duration of the exercise. Lt Col Clarence McRae, the Red Flag Alaska 16-1 Expeditionary Forces Maintenance Group Commander said, " Red Flag Alaska provided all of the participants a fantastic opportunity to train with members of the Indian Air Force. The exchange of lessons learned and best practises with our partners in the Indo-Asia-Pacific region have enabled us to strengthen our partnership and signifies our commitment to this area of operations. The professionalism of the IAF airmen made bolstering our countries' relationship easy and helped provide realistic combat training for all participants."[9]

The fourth edition of the series of bilateral exercises between the IAF and USAF, in India was held from December 3-14, 2018. It was for the first time that the exercise was conducted from two bases, i.e. Kalaikunda and Panagarh. The USAF participated with 12 X F 15 C/D and 03 X C 130H aircraft while the IAF participated with Su 30MKI, Jaguar, M 2000, C 130J and AWACS.

## Desert Eagle II

The second in the series of bilateral exercises between the IAF and the UAE AF took place from May 23-June 3, 2016 when four Su 30MKI aircraft of the IAF stopped over at Al Dhafra on their way back from Ex Red Flag in Alaska, USA. The ten-day combat exercise saw the IAF Su 30MKI pitted against the Mirage 2000-9 and F 16 Block 60 of the UAE AF flying a variety of missions. The IAF Team Leader Gp Capt H Assudani said, "This was an excellent opportunity for both the Air Forces to learn from each other and exchange best practises which in turn would be mutually beneficial."[10]

## Eastern Bridge

The fourth edition of the exercise was held at Jamnagar airbase from January 14-20, 2017. This was the first time that the RAFO deployed its Block 50 F 16 C/D aircraft outside the Persian Gulf region and also the first time that the RAFO participated in an exercise outside the GCC countries. The IAF participated in the exercise with MiG 27, MiG 29 and Jaguar Maritime Strike aircraft. Eastern Bridge survived the retirement of Jaguars from the RAFO in August 2014. The culmination of the exercise saw an interaction between the RAFO Commander, Air Vice Marshal Mattar Bin Ali Al Ubaidani, a former Jaguar pilot and the IAF Chief, Air Chief Marshal BS Dhanoa.

Exercise Eastern Bridge V, which took place in Masirah, Oman from October 16-26, 2019 saw the IAF fielding its MiG 29 UPG (Upgrade) for the first time in an international exercise outside India. RAFO participated with Eurofighter Typhoon, F 16 and Hawk 200 aircraft. These biennial exercises between the IAF and the RAFO have helped to forge deep ties between the two Air Forces. The IAF Chief, Air Chief Marshal RKS Bhadauria visited Oman and met Air Vice Marshal Mattar Bin Ali Al Ubaidani, Commander RAFO at Masirah and interacted with the two contingents.

## Garuda VI and Desert Knight 2021

Garuda VI, the largest international air training exercise of 2019 took place from July 1-12, 2019 at Mont-de-Marsan, France. The IAF contingent consisted of four Su 30MKI, one IL 78 tanker and two C 17 aircraft which provided logistic support during induction and de-induction. Held in two phases the exercise saw both IAF and the FAF fly air combat exercises with LFE missions by both day and night in a near realistic environment. The IAF in an official statement at the end of the exercise said, "It was a unique, fascinating and timeless learning at the exercise for the IAF contingent. The operational lessons learnt by IAF during the exercise will assist IAF to add more teeth to its overall war waging capabilities and assist us in better jointmanship with the friendly forces."[11] There was excitement in the air as the IAF pilots were exercising with the Rafale which was soon to be inducted in the IAF. The exercise saw a pilot from each of the Air Forces flying in a Su 30MKI and Rafale respectively.

The IAF and the French Air and Space Force (FASF) participated in the first it's kind Exercise Desert Knight 21, at Air Force Station Jodhpur from January 20-24, 2021. This was the first international exercise with the IAF Rafale participating in the exercise with four Rafales of the FASF along with Airbus A 330 Multi-Role Tanker Transport (MRTT). The IAF component, apart from the Rafale consisted of Mirage 2000, Su 30MKI, IL 78 FRA, AWACS and AEW & C aircraft. This exercise marked an important milestone for the IAF, in the series of exercises held with their French counterparts. The exercise provided an opportunity to share best practises and evolve operational concepts, particularly for effective combat employment of the Rafale fleet. The IAF Chief, Air Chief Marshal RKS Bhadauria PVSM AVSM VM ADC visited Air Force Station Jodhpur along with the French Ambassador to India H.E. Mr Emmanuel Leanin on January 23, 2021, and interacted with the participants of both the contingents.

## Desert Flag

Exercise Desert Flag, an annual multilateral large force employment exercise hosted by UAE saw IAF participation for the first time in 2021. This was the sixth edition of the exercise conducted from March 4-21, 2021 at Al Dhafra Air Base, UAE. USA, UAE, France, Bahrain, Saudi Arabia and India participated with aerial assets, with India Fielding its Su 30MKI aircraft. Jordan, Greece, Qatar, Egypt and South Korea participated as observers. The objective of the exercise was to expose participating coalition forces to large force engagement (LFE), sharpen tactical capabilities and enhance interoperability along with fostering closer relations between the participating forces. The aim for the participating crew and specialist observers was to expose them to an operational environment in scenarios requiring multinational forces working together. This multinational exercise in UAE, with friendly forces, gave the IAF a unique opportunity to learn valuable lessons and forge a professional relationship with the participating forces based on mutual trust and understanding.

## Exercise Avia Indra

The first phase of the second edition of Exercise Avia Indra between the IAF and the RFASF took place in Lipetsk, as before, from September 17-28, 2018. The aim of the exercise was to formulate and validate the use of air power in anti-terrorist operations in a bilateral scenario. The IAF contingent for the exercise consisted of 30 officers from the Flying, Medical and Administrative branches of the IAF, including four women officers. The second leg of the exercise took place at Air Force Station Jodhpur in December 2018 with the RFASF officers flying alongside the IAF crew in Su 30MKI, Mi 17V5 and AN 32 aircraft. The participants of both the air forces gained valuable insights into each other's operational procedures, training philosophy and piloting procedures thereby increasing mutual understanding and cooperation between the two Air Forces.

## Exercise Blue Flag 2021

'Blue Flag' an international exercise hosting friendly Air Forces from around the world saw the participation of the Indian Air Force (IAF) by the host, i.e. another IAF (Israeli Air Force). The exercise took place in Israel from

October 13-28, 2021 and the IAF participated with 5 Mirage 2000, two IL 78 and two C 17 aircraft. Germany, Italy, the UK, France, Greece and the United States together with the IAF and the host IAF flexed their muscles in a volatile and troubled Mediterranean region to show their solidarity. The two IAFs were together in this exercise of many 'firsts'. It was the first-ever deployment of the IAF Mirage 2000 in Israel, the first deployment of the French Rafale in Israel as also the first-ever deployment of a British fighter squadron in Israel since the country gained independence in 1948. It was the largest and most advanced exercise ever held in Israel. Since the Air Forces came from different regions of the world with their own weapon systems, cultures, ethos and operating procedures, many of them operating together for the first time, the challenge was to get everyone on the same page and to facilitate this, all the participating forces stayed at one location. Flight Lieutenant Aakash, a Mirage 2000 pilot of the IAF, participating in the exercise had this to say to an Israeli website, "Each Air Force has its own culture both professionally and socially. Understanding how each force operates is a unique experience for us. We learn from other nations and they learn from us, that's how we manage to improve and become a better Air Force."[12]

The theme of the exercise was to integrate fourth and fifth-generation aircraft in complex operational scenarios. Air forces across the world cannot afford to use fifth-generation fighters only and therefore there would be a need to mix fourth and fifth-generation aircraft which would enhance the operational capability of the force being deployed. This was achieved during the exercise by combining the two from different Air Forces and utilising the relative advantages of each platform in heterogeneous scenarios. Maj Gen Amikam Norkin, the Commander of the Israeli Air Force said, "This exercise is groundbreaking in terms of technology, quality of training and the number of participating nations. It illustrates the partnership and strong bond between the nation's air forces and acts as a stepping stone towards regional and international cooperation."[13] The German Air Force Chief visited Israel for three days during the exercise and also took part in a flypast over Jerusalem along with the Israeli Chief, marking the first occasion for a German military aircraft to fly over Jerusalem after the First World War. The Commander of the UAE Air Force, Maj Gen Staff Pilot Ibrahim Nasser

Mohammed Al Alawi also paid a historic visit to Israel to witness the exercise even though the UAE Air Force was not participating, signalling the new-found bonhomie in Arab-Israel ties. The Indian External Affairs Minister S Jaishankar and the Indian Defence Secretary Dr Ajay Kumar visited Ovda Air Base in Israel and interacted with the IAF contingent. After meeting with the IAF contingent Dr Ajay Kumar said, "Great to visit Ovda Air Base Israel and meet with IAF contingent participating in multinational Exercise Blue Flag. Wonderful to see the professionalism and Josh of Indian Air Warriors, making India and IAF proud."[14] India and Israel have had a long and fruitful defence relationship with the IAF operating the Israeli Phalcon radar on its AWACS, apart from Israeli Heron, Searcher and Harop UAVs. The Indian Air Force recently inducted the Barak, Medium Range Surface to Air Missile (MRSAM) which has been jointly produced by the Israeli Aircraft Industry (IAI) and Defence Research and Development Organisation (DRDO).

## Exercise SIAM Bharat

This is a bilateral exercise between the IAF and Royal Thailand Air Force (RTAF) on Humanitarian Assistance and Disaster Relief. The second edition of this Table Top exercise took place from May 22-26, 2017 in Chiang Mai in which eleven members of the IAF participated. The aim of this exercise is to evolve Standard Operating Procedures (SOPs) for planning and executing relief missions during unforeseen natural calamities like tsunami, earthquakes, floods, cyclones, etc. The objective being to enhance interoperability between the two air forces in conducting joint operations triggered by a crisis. This exercise would help in laying down procedures and establishing decision support systems during the various stages of a natural calamity and its aftermath.

## Exercise Pitch Black

IAF for the first time participated in a large force multinational biennial exercise hosted by the Royal Australian Air Force (RAAF) from July 24 to August 18, 2018. The IAF participated with four Su MKI fighters, one IL 78 tanker, one C 130 Hercules and one C 17 Globemaster aircraft. The IAF contingent also included 45 Garud special forces commandos.

The exercise was conducted from RAAF bases in Darwin and Tindal in Australia's Northern Territory. With participants from Australia, Canada, France, Germany, Indonesia, Netherlands, New Zealand, Malaysia, Singapore, Indonesia, Thailand and the United States the exercise involved 4000 personnel and 140 aircraft. The RAAF in a statement said that, "Exercise Pitch Black features a range of realistic, simulated threats which can be found in a modern battle-space environment and is an opportunity to test and improve our force integration, utilising one of the largest training airspace areas in the world—Bradshaw Field Training Area and Delamere Air Weapons Range."[15] The IAF carried out day and night operations with the IAF Su 30MKI carrying out air-to-air refuelling for the first time from a RAAF KC 30A Multi-Role Tanker Transport (MRTT) aircraft. IAF pilots also flew exchange sorties on French Rafale and RAAF F-18 Hornet, with the RAAF and French Air Force crew flying in the IAF Su 30MKI. The IAF C 130J got an opportunity to carry out an assault landing at Dalmare, assault operations of dropping specialist vehicles in an op area and participation in Large Force Engagement (LFE) missions, both by day and night. Some maiden operations conducted by the IAF included its Garud commandos jumping from a C-27J Spartan in a foreign country, Container Delivery System (CDS) drop from a C 130J and Engine Running Ops (ERO) for dropping specialist op vehicles in a combat zone. The IAF maintenance crew ensured 100 per cent serviceability during the duration of the exercise.

India's participation in this multilateral exercise is significant considering its earlier refusal to the Australian Navy to participate in the Malabar Exercise hosted by the Indian Navy. This comes in the wake of India, Japan, Australia and the United States re-establishing the Quadrilateral Security Dialogue, now better known as QUAD, to ensure a free and open Indo-Pacific region.

## Exercise Shinyuu Maitri

IAF and Japanese Air and Self Defence Force (JASDF) carried out their first air exercise at Air Force Agra from December 3-7, 2018. The exercise code-named 'Shinyuu Maitri' means 'true or best friend.' According to Japan's Defence Minister Takeshi Iwaya, the goal of the exercise is to increase the air transport capabilities of the JASDF, and to enhance the "mutual understanding between Japan and India, and bolstering our relationship of trust."[16] The theme of the exercise was Joint Mobility and HADR on transport aircraft. JASDF Kawasaki C 2 and IAF An 32 and C 17 aircraft participated in the exercise with aircrew and observers.

The second edition of the exercise took place at Air Force Station Arjan Singh in Panagarh, West Bengal from October 17-23, 2019. C 130J of the IAF and C 130H of the JASDF participated in the exercise that focussed on joint mobility and tactical interoperability between the two air forces. This exercise was a precursor to Exercise Dharma Guardian 2019, a joint exercise of the JASDF with the Indian Army at the Counter Insurgency and Jungle Warfare School (CIJWS) in Mizoram. The exercise with the Indian Army involved platoon-level training on counter-terror operations in a jungle scenario.

## Exercise Desert Warrior

Increasing its engagement in the Middle East and the Mediterranean region, IAF first participated in a bilateral exercise with the Egyptian Air Force. IAF Mirage 2000 aircraft on their return from Ex Blue Flag in Israel, stopped over at El Berigat Air Base in Egypt on October 30-31, 2021. The exercise helped in developing mutual understanding and trust between the two air forces.

## Military Training vs Exercises

India's Armed Forces, trained professionally since inception has been involved in joint military training with a number of countries post-Independence. India assisted a number of countries in Africa in setting up their military training establishments, while the country was grappling with the after-effects of the 1962 Indo-China war and building its own capacity and capability. The professionalism and valour of the Indian soldiers was recognised by the world even before independence as Indian soldiers fought in various campaigns during the world wars under the British Flag. In fact, in recognition of the sacrifices of the Indian troops who fought for the liberation of Sudan in the East Africa campaign during World War II, the Sudanese government gave a substantial grant to build a memorial in India. This money was utilised to build 'Sudan Block' the administrative headquarters of the first tri-services training academy in the world, the National Defence Academy at Khadakwasla, Pune.

India has offered military training to a large number of personnel from friendly foreign countries since independence with the numbers and the demand for the same growing with each passing year. Similarly, a number of Indian Armed Forces personnel receive training abroad for a variety of courses across the three services. Training of military personnel underscores the importance of military diplomacy as an important cog in building strategic partnerships with other countries as it helps in mutual capacity building, learning from each other's experiences and facilitating a better understanding of each other's capabilities. Training courses give a theoretical knowledge of operations and technology while military exercises put this knowledge into practice. While operating together with other militaries it is essential to have a seamless understanding of operational procedures, communications, logistics, maintenance practises and each other's culture and ethos. Bilateral or multilateral exercises are an essential prerequisite for undertaking joint operations in collaboration. It is necessary to ensure interoperability because only then the effect of the sum would be larger than the whole. Joint military exercises facilitate ease in the relationship between the two air forces operating together and this cannot be achieved overnight. The threats that we face and the natural/humanitarian disasters that occur, often confront nations with hard choices, which become easier to implement and put into practice, provided the forces have trained together. The famous quote by Geroge Patton sums it up succinctly, "You fight like you train."

## Airshows

### *Surya Kiran*

The IAF aerobatic team 'Surya Kiran' which means 'rays of the sun' was formed in 1996. It is the youngest nine aircraft aerobatic team in the world and is recognised worldwide for its scintillating displays and performance. The team equipped with HAL HJT 16 MkII aircraft carried out its first display abroad in 2001, to mark the 50th-anniversary celebrations of the Sri Lankan Air Force (SLAF). The team performed again at the Asian Aerospace airshow in Singapore in 2004. The team subsequently made its debut at the

Langkawi International Maritime and Aerospace Exhibition (LIMA) in Malaysia from December 4-8, 2007, celebrating the 50th year of Malaysia's independence. The team also carried out a display at Subang airfield of Kaula Lampur on November 29, 2007. The team in coordination with the Royal Thai Air Force also carried out a nine aircraft display to commemorate the 80th birth anniversary of His Majesty the King of Thailand. On an invitation from China, the team performed at the Zhuhai Airshow in November 2008, where it was the only aerobatic team performing. On its return, the team also performed in Laos, Cambodia.

The team was resurrected in February 2015, after being disbanded in February 2011 when the IAF was facing a critical shortage of trainer aircraft. The team in its new 'avatar' was equipped with BAe Hawk Mk132 aircraft. The team, serendipitously, carried out its first display abroad in the Hawk aircraft once again in Sri Lanka, from March 3-5, 2021, this time to mark the 70th-anniversary celebrations of the SLAF. The event was also attended by the then IAF Chief, Air Chief Marshal RKS Bhadauria. The aerobatic team earned accolades for its performance, serving the role of IAF's goodwill ambassador and strengthening the strong bond in mutual ties between the IAF and the SLAF. The team also performed at the Dubai Air Show 2021 carrying out a synchronised display in coordination with UAE's Al Fursan display team over significant landmarks in Dubai like the Burj Khalifa, Burj Al Arab and Palm Jumeirah. The IAF in a statement called it "a display that signified the deep camaraderie and bonhomie between the two air forces.'[17]

### *Sarang*

The helicopter air display team of the IAF named 'Sarang' which means 'peacock' symbolising the national bird of India, was formed in 2003 on the modified Advanced Light Helicopter Dhruv, manufactured by HAL. The team carried out its first performance abroad at the Singapore Airshow in 2004. Performing at the Al Ain Aerobatic Show in UAE in 2005, the team earned its reputation as one of the best display teams of its kind in the world. With the unique distinction of being one of the only two helicopter air display teams in the world, it has performed at the Dubai Airshow 2021, MAKS International Airshow in Russia 2021, the 70th-anniversary celebrations of the SLAF in Sri Lanka in 2021 apart from other performances in Bahrain. Mauritius, Germany and the UK. Being an inherently unstable platform, synchronous manoeuvering by helicopters is inherently difficult and professionally challenging as compared to fixed-wing fighter aircraft. Constantly striving for excellence and innovating with signature manoeuvres like the 'Dolphin's Leap,' 'Crossover Break' and 'The Srang Split' the Sarang team with its 'symphony in the air' has won millions of hearts across the world, serving as a true ambassador of the IAF.

### *LCA Tejas*

The indigenously manufactured single-engine Light Combat Aircraft (LCA) Tejas of the IAF has showcased its skills in breathtaking displays carried out by IAF pilots. Perceived to be a high-performance reliable fighter aircraft and a flagship demonstration of India's Atma Nirbharta programme the aircraft has evinced interest in a number of countries in Southeast Asia. The aircraft performed in Sri Lanka commemorating the 70th-anniversary celebrations of the SLAF in 2021 and also in the Dubai Airshow the same year. Showcasing its superior manoeuvrability, flying ability and handling characteristics the aircraft enthralled spectators at both the venues.

## Conclusion

The Indian Air Force has come a long way from its first-ever bilateral exercise with the USAF in 2003. India, which is not a part of any military alliance values its strategic autonomy while making an effort to have a larger say in the region and the world. The increasing capacity and capability of the IAF with its recent inductions and the professionalism displayed by its personnel have made the IAF a much sought-after partner for multilateral exercises. The latest Global Firepower Index ranks India at number four in the world behind the USA, Russia and China. Countries that operated together as military alliances like NATO and the erstwhile Warsaw Pact regularly trained and operated together, which gave them a better understanding of each other's capabilities and facilitated joint operations. Training within the country has its limitations as both sides in any wargame have been trained together and know each other's capabilities well. Training with other's air forces enables a learning curve to develop as the training procedures, practises and the environment of each nation differs even though the purpose of armed forces the world over remains the same. Professional military interaction in live exercises differs significantly from training courses in each other's academies and institutions. These exercises help forge a bond between participating nations apart from learning from each other's operational capabilities and learning from operating in varied scenarios and regions of the world. The choice of partners is significant, because it builds a strategic relationship with the country not only in the military domain, but also by increasing diplomatic and economic cooperation. While bilateral exercises result in greater interaction between participating countries with its associated spin-offs, multilateral exercises enable a simultaneous engagement with many countries with its associated benefit of collective synergy.

The performance of the IAF aerobatic teams, Surya Kiran and Sarang have been important and significant in contributing to its outreach in the neighbourhood and beyond. Performances at international airshow abroad help in forging ties with teams from other countries and also display the professional acumen of the IAf air warriors. The IAF helicopter air display team, Sarang, being one of the only two in the world, is much sought after for its novel and scintillating displays. IAF's presence and engagement with the neighbourhood in Asia through its aerobatic display teams adds to its soft power projection in addition to its resolve to further strengthening its relationships with these countries through trade and diplomacy. LCA Tejas, having been inducted into active service in the IAF has been the show stopper at the Dubai Air show in 2021. The performance of the ALH Dhruv and LCA Tejas, both indigenously manufactured, have been appreciated by other countries and are likely to result in export orders in the near future. Defence exports would serve as a recognition of India's technological prowess in a sector which has been found wanting in the past. These exports as and when they fructify, would inevitably lead to a stronger strategic partnership between India and the other countries, for which the IAF would have played its role as the enabler.

With the country seeking to expand its sphere of influence in the region and the world, it is but natural for the Indian Air Force to not only exhibit its prowess but also collaborate with air forces across the world. Participation with other air forces in international exercises and its continued engagement in the bilateral as well as multilateral format has come to stay in an increasingly polarised, yet connected world. Even though India is not a part of any military alliance, it has been actively participating in operational exercises hosted by various countries wherein collaborative engagements have been undertaken with the best air forces in the world. The Garuda series of exercises with France, Red Flag/Cope India with USAF, Joint Military Training with Singapore. Avia Indra with Russia, Desert Eagle with UAE, Eastern Bridge with Oman and Indra Dhanush with the RAF, all constitute an important element of bilateral defence cooperation with these countries. It is through these relationships that strategic partnerships are built with the overall aim of keeping and maintaining peace while collaborating to help each other in times of crisis. The Indian Air Force forms the cornerstone of its military might, and acts as a force multiplier in collaboration in its quest for dominance.

| Name | Country | Aircraft / Units | Dates | Location |
|---|---|---|---|---|
| Garuda I | France | Mirage 2000 | Feb 03 | Air Force Stn Gwalior, India |
| Cope India | United States | Mirage 2000<br>Mig 21 Bison<br>Su 30K<br>F-15 | 14-27 Feb 04 | Air Force Stn Gwalior, India |
| Cope Thunder | United States | Jaguar<br>F-16 | 02-14 Jul 04 | Alaska, USA |
| Sindex 04 | Singapore | Su 30MK<br>MiG 27 / 29<br>Mirage 2000 | 11-27 Oct 04 | Air Force Stn Gwalior, India |
| Cope India | United States | Su 30MK<br>F -16 | Nov 05 | Air force Stn Gwalior, India |
| Garuda II | France | Mirage 2000-5 | 15-30 Jun 05 | Air Force Stn Gwalior, India |
| Sindex 06 | Singapore | F-16<br>MiG 27 | 03-20 Jan 06 | Air Force Stn Kalaikunda, India |
| Indra Dhanush I | United Kingdom | Su 30MK,<br>MiG 21,<br>MiG 27,<br>Tornado, VC 10<br>& E 3D | 13-20 Oct 06 | Air Force Stn Gwalior & Agra, India |

| | | | | |
|---|---|---|---|---|
| Garuda III | France | Su 30MKI<br>Mirage 2000 | 12-23 Feb 07 | Istres Air Base, France |
| Indra Dhanush II | United Kingdom | Su 30MKI<br>Typhoon<br>Tornado | Jun 07 | RAF Base Waddington, UK |
| Red Flag | United States<br>France<br>South Korea | Su 30MKI<br>F-16<br>F-15 | 09-23 Aug 08 | Nellis Air Force Base, Nevada USA |
| Desert Eagle I | UAE | Su 30MKI | Sep 08 | Al Dhafra, UAE |
| Eastern Bridge I | Oman | Jaguars | Oct 09 | Thumrait, Oman |
| Indra Dhanush III | United Kingdom | Su 30MKI,<br>MiG 27<br>Typhoon | 18 Oct-03 Nov 2010 | Kalaikunda, India |
| Eastern Bridge II | Oman | Jaguars<br>MiG 29 | 17-21 Oct 11 | Jamnagar, India |
| Eastern Bridge III | Oman | Jaguars<br>Hawk, F-16 | Oct 13 | Masirah, Oman |
| Avia Indra | Russia | Su 30SM / MKI<br>Mi 35, Mi 17 V5 | Aug 14<br>Nov 14 | Lipetsk. Russia<br>Halwara, India |
| Indra Dhanush IV | United Kingdom | Su 30MKI<br>Typhoon | Jul 15 | Coningsby, UK |
| Red Flag | United States | Jaguar<br>Su 30MKI | 28 Apr-13 May 2016 | Alaska, USA |
| Desert Eagle II | UAE | Su 30MKI<br>M 2000-9, F-16 | 28 May-03 Jun 16 | Al Dhafra, UAE |
| Eastern Bridge IV | Oman | MiG 21 / 27<br>Jaguar, F 16 | 14-20 Jan 17 | Jamnagar, India |
| SIAM Bharat | Thailand | HADR Tabletop Exercise | 22-26 May 17 | Chiang Mai, Thailand |
| SIAM Bharat | Thailand | HADR Tabletop Exercise | 03-14 Sep 18 | Agra, India |

| | | | | |
|---|---|---|---|---|
| Pitch Black | Australia, Canada, France, Germany, Indonesia, Netherlands, New Zealand, Malaysia | Su 30MKI F 18, C 130 J, C 17, E 7A, PC 9, KA 350 | 24 Jul-18 Aug18 | Darwin, Australia |
| Avia Indra | Russia | Su 30, Mi 17 V5, An 32 | 17-28 Sep 18<br>10-21 Dec 18 | Lipetsk, Russia<br>Jodhpur, India |
| Shinyuu Maitri | Japan | C 2, C 17 An 32 | 03-07 Dec 18 | Agra, India |
| Cope India | USA | Su 30MKI, Jaguar, M 2000, C 130 J, AWACS, F 15C/D | 03-14 Dec 18 | Kalaikunda & Panagarh, India |
| Garuda VI | France | Su 30MKI, Rafale | 01-12 Jul 19 | Mont de Marsan,France |
| Eastern Bridge V | Oman | MiG 29 UPG, Typhoon, F 16 | 16-26 Oct 19 | Masirah, Oman |
| Joint Military Training (JMT) | Singapore | Su 30MKI F 16 | 01 Nov-12 Dec 19 | Kalaikunda, India |
| Desert Knight | France | M 2000, Su 30 MKI, Rafale, A-330 MRTT | 20-24 Jan 21 | Jodhpur, India |
| Desert Flag VI | UAE, USA, France, Bahrain, Saudi Arabia | Su 30MKI | 04-21 Mar 21 | Al Dhafra, UAE |
| Blue Flag 21 | Israel, Germany, Italy, France, UK, USA, Greece | M 2000 Rafale, F-16, F-35, Typhoon | 13-28 Oct 21 | Ovda, Israel |

## Notes

1. https://en.wikipedia.org/wiki/Cope_India. Accessed on January 17, 2022.
2. https://www.rbth.com/blogs/2014/02/16/cope_india_how_the_iaf_rewrote_the_rules_of_air_combat_33111. Accessed on January 17, 2022.
3. https://www.livefistdefence.com/exercise-indradhanush-ends-a/. Accessed on January 21. 2022.
4. https://indianexpress.com/article/explained/why-iaf-vs-raf-is-a-dogfight-with-shadows/. Accessed on January 22, 2022.
5. Ibid.
6. https://pib.gov.in/PressReleseDetailm.aspx?PRID=1604402. Accessed on January 22, 2022.
7. https://pib.gov.in/newsite/PrintRelease.aspx?relid=145357. Accessed on January 22, 2022.
8. Ibid.
9. Ibid
10. https://www.netindian.in/news/international/india-uae-air-combat-exercise-desert-eagle-ii-concludes. Accessed on January 22, 2022.
11. https://forceindia.net/exercise-garuda-vi-ends-successfully/. Accessed on January 22, 2022.
12. https://www.aviation-defence-universe.com/exercise-blue-flag-2021-in-israel-showing-muscle-in-the-mediterranean-region/. Accessed on January 23, 2022.
13. Ibid.
14. Ibid.
15. https://thediplomat.com/2018/07/indias-air-force-to-participate-in-australias-pitch-black-air-combat-exercise/. Accessed on January 23, 2022.
16. https://thediplomat.com/2018/12/india-japan-air-forces-hold-first-joint-military-exercise/. Accessed on January 23, 2022.
17. https://www.republicworld.com/india-news/general-news/indian-air-forces-tejas-exhibits-versatility-and-agility-at-dubai-air-show-2021.html. Accessed on February 2, 2022.

# 5

# Geo-economics of Artificial Islands in the South China Sea: A China-Vietnam Case Study

NEHA MISHRA

## Introduction

With the rise of global capitalism, Artificial Islands or man-made islands have developed as the new strategic construction of cities being a 'new cultural icon' and representing the urban economy. The construction of these man-made islands expanded from the Persian Gulf and Black sea to the Caribbean and North Sea, with countries aspiring to expand their sea territory that established maritime as a new space of global anxiety and competition. The South China Sea (SCS) has developed one such region in the past decade, with China's increasing reclaims on the reefs or rocks of Spratly islands group by building artificial islands. These claims have been a perceived as a major threat by the Southeast Asian countries, most particularly by Vietnam who shares largest coastline in the South China Sea thus entitled to largest Exclusive Economic Zone (EEZ). China as the leading geo-economic player switching their geo-strategy from the logic of conflicts to the logic of commerce, initiated to construct artificial islands aims to restrict the EEZ power and control of countries that has been a cause of concern for SCS littorals.

In response to Chinese expansion, Vietnam also has been involved in the construction of these man-made islands in the past five years to sustain its control and sovereignty over the SCS resources. Vietnam has a strong position in the South China Sea that is even perceived as an obstacle/competition by China. Vietnam, with its sustained economic growth and significant role in ASEAN, keeps Southeast Asian countries united against China's illegal claims and emphasize on maintaining the code of conduct and frame ASEAN outlook for Indo-Pacific (AOIP).[1] The increasing Chinese aggressive activities motivated Vietnam to increase its effort to strengthen its maritime militia. Vietnam, with its large coastal area, shared high stakes in the South China Sea due to its geographic location that borders the Gulf of Tonkin, Gulf of Thailand, and the Pacific Ocean along with China, Laos and Cambodia. Vietnam shares 3,260 km long coastline that stretches from Mong Cai to Ha Tien. Vietnam has around 3,000 islets in the Tokin gulf, and claims on multiple islands in the Spratly and Paracel archipelagos.

The Chinese initiative and counter-initiatives by Vietnam reflects a growing shift from seeking military to economic opportunities in the SCS region. According to UNCLOS maritime laws, ownership of small rock type islands supporting no life gives entitlement to only 452 $nm^2$ of territorial sea, while a life sustaining island generates 125,664 $nm^2$ of EEZ. The entitlement to more territorial sea means ownership of more resources that has been the driving motivation for China, who has been extending historical claims of life and control on the reefs or rocks it occupies in the SCS region. This chapter is an attempt to analyse the shifting narrative from military conflict to economic opportunities in the South China Sea, through analysing geo-economic importance of islands that involves interest of China and Vietnam. The objective is to represent how the need to secure the access to resources have changed the approach from military to economic in SCS region, thus shaping the geo-economic competition between China and Vietnam.

## What is Geo-Economics of Resources: How Economics and Geography Interplay in IR?

The connection of Political Geography and International Relations goes back to the empires and kingdom times, which involved multifaceted political processes changing with the regime change. The major phases of Political Geography in International Relations have been developed in terms of conflict, followed by policy cooperation along with the logic of conflict, then economic and commercial based cooperation with limited or no logic of conflict, and now developing in form of energy geo-economics with the multifaceted mixture of conflict, strategies and competition, thus establishing as a new trend from the last decades. Sanjaya Baru defined Geo-economics as the mutual interplay of economics and geopolitics, as unless a country can't convert economic power into political power, it won't become a geo-economic power.[2] Most scholars consider geo-economics as the branch or revised version of geopolitics as both of them focus on the geographical factor, however, they are unique in themselves. Geo-economics, despite being called a new form of geopolitics, is unique with its narrow economic focus. It can replace firepower with capital, military advancement with civilian innovation and garrisons with market penetration.[3]

Geo-economics must rely on strategies, policies or agreements to ensure interconnectedness and interdependence, and the state dominant in these arrangements achieve its interests without using any coercion or force. Geo-economics requires a country to keep its economy under the condition of competition instead of isolating it and keep itself ready to counter the economic crisis and competitors by investing in strong and promising producing capacity.[4] Sanjaya Baru traced the intellectual history of the geo-economics concept that includes Classical economical ideas (Free trade, laissez-faire), Mercantilism, Capitalism and Liberalism. Cold war international economics and politics were driven by an ideological factor, not economic factors, but the three most defining ideas during the cold war define contemporary geo-economics—(a) Paul Kennedy's 'The Rise and Fall of the Great Powers' (1987)[5] emphasized on the fiscal and other economic limits on national power and its projection, and explained how all major shifts in the world's military have followed the alterations in the productive balance of states; (b) Edward Luttwak's 'From Geopolitics to Geo-economics: Logic of conflicts, Grammar of Commerce' (1990)[6] contributed the most in developing the understanding about methods of commerce displacing military methods.

Geo-economic does not mean reduced importance of boundaries and territories, but of their strict articulation. Michael Sparke suggested geostrategic discourses are recasting together, in the course of increasing globalised tension between territorial fixity and geographical expansion, as a disabling double vision—'a vision that maps the divergent economic imperatives towards territorial fixing and geographical expansion in a distorted way, which further divides the world into distinct zones of geopolitical conflict on the one side and spaces of geo-economic peace on the other'.[7] The Geo-economics of energy also involves the interconnection of the trends of political geography (geopolitics, geostrategy and geo-economics) as to secure the access to resources have become necessary to the functioning of modern economies, impacting their geopolitical equations and related geo-strategies.[8] The same geo-economics is happening in the South China Sea, due to the motivation of countries to secure the access to resources by increasing their territorial fixation and expand Exclusive Economic Zones (EEZ). Thus, besides military presence in the SCS region, China has been building its geo-economic presence through extending historical claims of its ownership on the occupied islands. This has been a cause of geopolitical conflict and competition with the other SCS littorals on the one hand and, the counter geo-economic cooperation among the SCS littorals on the other.

## Geo-economics of South China Sea

Territorial acquisition and claims is not a new development, as its foundation goes back to early 15th century when the claim to colonial territories was aiding the European industrialisation and colonisation in Asia, Africa, and North America. The territory reclamation has always been driven by two factors furthering anthropogenic advantage—(a) economic growth and (b) secure resource supply chain, thus reflected the presence of geo-economics way back even when the geopolitics was the preferable term.[9] The territorial claims have determined the balance of power both at global as well as regional level, in terms of leading conflict or competition among countries. While the traditional geopolitical balance of power guided by the ingredients of geography and ideology, the geo-economics balance of power, in contrast, determines by a nation's strategic autonomy link to three conditions—(a) Self-sufficiency in access to basic natural resources and energy; (b) Relative freedom from long-term dependency on overseas markets; and (c) An inexhaustible, inexpensive and relatively reliable control on the labour force. Unlike geopolitics game or conflict between states considering each other as threats, the geo-economics game remains between super-trading blocs considering each other as 'stakeholders' or 'competition' in terms of resource access.[10]

The geo-economic factors have also motivated China's reclamation in South China Sea (SCS) to achieve sustained economic growth with the access to resources reserves of gained sea territory. The geo-economic importance of South China Sea is connected to the availability of rich resources, multiple island groups, fisheries, shipping channels, and other. The region serves as an important trade route as 50 per cent of world's merchant fleet and one-third maritime traffic pass through SCS.[11] It stretches between China, Vietnam, Malaysia, Philippines and Brunei, being 3.5 million $km^2$ in size. It is the second most used sea lane in world and third most for shipping oil and gas reserves. China's stakes in the SCS goes back to 1940s with its 'nine-dash line' that represents a U-shape line in the sea between Vietnam and Philippines.[12] The maritime trade routes of SCS connects Indian Ocean Region (IOR) to the Western Pacific economies, and contributed to a significant rise in the seaborne trade. The presence of several chokepoints in the SCS region—the Straits of Malacca, Sunda and Lombok, adds to its geo-economic significance. All the East Asian economies have heavy reliance on the Sea Lines of Communication (SLOC) in the SCS for the import of oil and gas from the West Asian countries, most particularly Persian Gulf.[13]

The SCS region is also termed as the 'Second Persian Gulf', being rich in natural and oil resources. The geo-economic potential of SCS reflects in following features:

(a) The reserves of billion tons of crude oil and trillion cubic meters of natural gas.
(b) Around 48 Mesozoic and Cenozoic Sedimentary basins in SCS, and Nine Dash line (claimed territory of China) is 5,81,000 sq km in territory, with more than 350 proven oil and gas fields, as reported by China's Sea, oil and gas resources report by China Institute of International Studies (CIIS).

(c) The major undiscovered and unexploited resources are reported to be present in the Spratly and Paracel group of Islands of SCS region.[14]

The SCS's geo-economics can be traced to the 1970s when oil exploration began in the region due to the 1972 oil crisis caused by Middle East, and forced the Asian and Southeast Asian countries to seek alternative sources. This marked the rise of offshore drilling/exploring of oil and deep-water resources by the high importing countries like US and China, developing the energy geopolitics in SCS region. The SCS involve multiple disputes out of which the contestation over the Spratly islands, a group of 230 islands and reefs, has been rising in the past decade, to which six countries are claimant—China, Taiwan, Vietnam, Philippines, Brunei, and Malaysia. In fact, It was Philippines who found small quantities of natural gas near the Reed reef of Spratly island group for the first time in 1976, which however got acquired by US and UK in 2000s to explore the resources that sparked the opposition of China leading the beginning of geopolitics around these islands and SCS region. As per EIA estimates, these group of islands have around one million barrels of oil and 190 tcf gas reserves that are geographically closer to Vietnam and Phillippines, but have been claimed more by China.

China's economic interest in SCS resides in all the above-explained geo-economic aspects. It has already been engaged in the exploring and developing oil-gas assets from the offshores of SCS since 1980s through its state-owned enterprise—China's National Offshore Oil Corporation (CNOOC). Unlike other countries like United States supporting traditional 'freedom of the seas' in waters beyond limits of territorial seas including freedom of navigation, overflight and military activities including reconnaissance. China argued that the interest of a coastal state gets threaten by such Freedom of Navigation (FON) and even a violation of the international law, and with concerned about their own maritime security started building the Artificial Islands that itself threatening the FON and international law of SCS.[15] With concern for their EEZ rights, Malaysia and Indonesia agreed to the UNCLOS deal that gives exclusive offshore rights to countries in their EEZ and freedom of navigation through straits even though they were reluctant to approve the free trade through straits of SCS. Despite being signatory of the UNCLOS and supporter of EEZ rights, China stopped respecting them through its nine-dash line claims and constructing artificial islands that has been challenged by Vietnam, Philippines and Malaysia. China's desire to fortify its power and strategic autonomy in SCS has been driven by hunger for resources and fishing fleets that changed its approach towards EEZ and islands.[16] The need of expanding strategic control on the resources of SCS region increased Chinese territorial claims and counter-claims on the SCS region (see Map 5.1).

**Map 5.1: Territorial Claims in South China Sea**

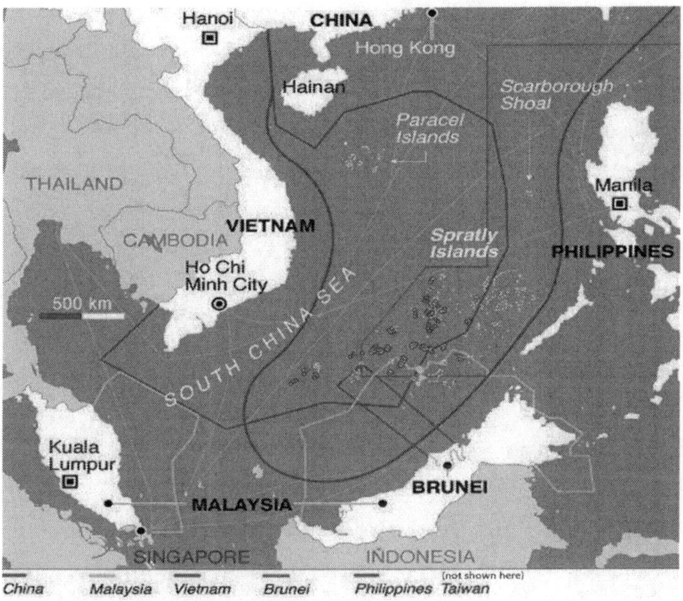


Source: VOA News. https://www.voanews.com/a/how-vietnam-quietly-built-up-10-islands-in-asia-most-disputed-sea/4882776.html. (Accessed on April 25, 2022).

## Artificial Islands: What and Why?

Resources are treasure for the human life and operation of global economies, which are majorly divided into natural and social resources. Maritime resources comes under the category of natural resources, and have different connotation than territorial resources, being of two kinds—nationalised (within the EEZ of a country), and internationalised (shared by international community). The nationalised maritime resources come under the absolute ownership or sovereignty within 200 sea miles EEZ of a particular country, such as seabed, territorial water, islands, and others. The nationalised resources remain exclusive means of a particular country for commercial purpose. While, internationalised resources are meant for shared ownership that gives equal right of freedom of navigation to all the littoral countries.[17]

The islands are perceived as such marine resources, acting as pawns in the game of regional as well as international game of territorial interest. They have been increasingly determining geopolitical and geo-economic games throughout the world due to two major factors: a) Resources to exploit and, b) Military and naval importance of the shipping channels.[18] The complexity of territorial sovereignty have also reached the South China Sea comprising, islets, shoals, reefs and other landforms, leading to dispute over their resources. China has been the leading claimer of these islands and their natural resources.[19] These islands are considered as possessive resources, involve four parts in SCS region—Pratas islands, Paracel islands, Macelesfield islands, and Spratly islands. The pratas islands comes under the sovereignty of Taiwan that has involved no dispute or concern for China, while Scarborough shoal of Macelesfield islands is the dispute area between China-Philippines. The Paracel and Spratly group of Islands are the major area of territorial dispute among SCS littorals, being claimed by six countries (see Map 5.2).[20]

The concept of Artificial Islands developed with the need to enhance the potential of port activities such as power generation, oil refining, residential developments, and ocean technological industry on these islands. The concept of man-made islands goes back to ancient Egyptian civilisation and, early 10th century when Venice began to build a city on the series of islands for its commercial and maritime growth. In 1636, Japan initiated the construction of artificial islands in Nagasaki for Dutch traders, and in 1891 for the coal mining operation penetrating to the ocean floor (which however ended up as a recreational facility by 1974). United States also developed New York Harbour's governor island. The major driving factors for construction of these man-made islands involve the need for larger public utilities, coal-fired or nuclear—powered generating plants, and efficient large scale industrial complexes. In other words, they have developed to accommodate the needs of residential and recreational activities.[21] The

Map 5.2: All Contested Islands of South China Sea

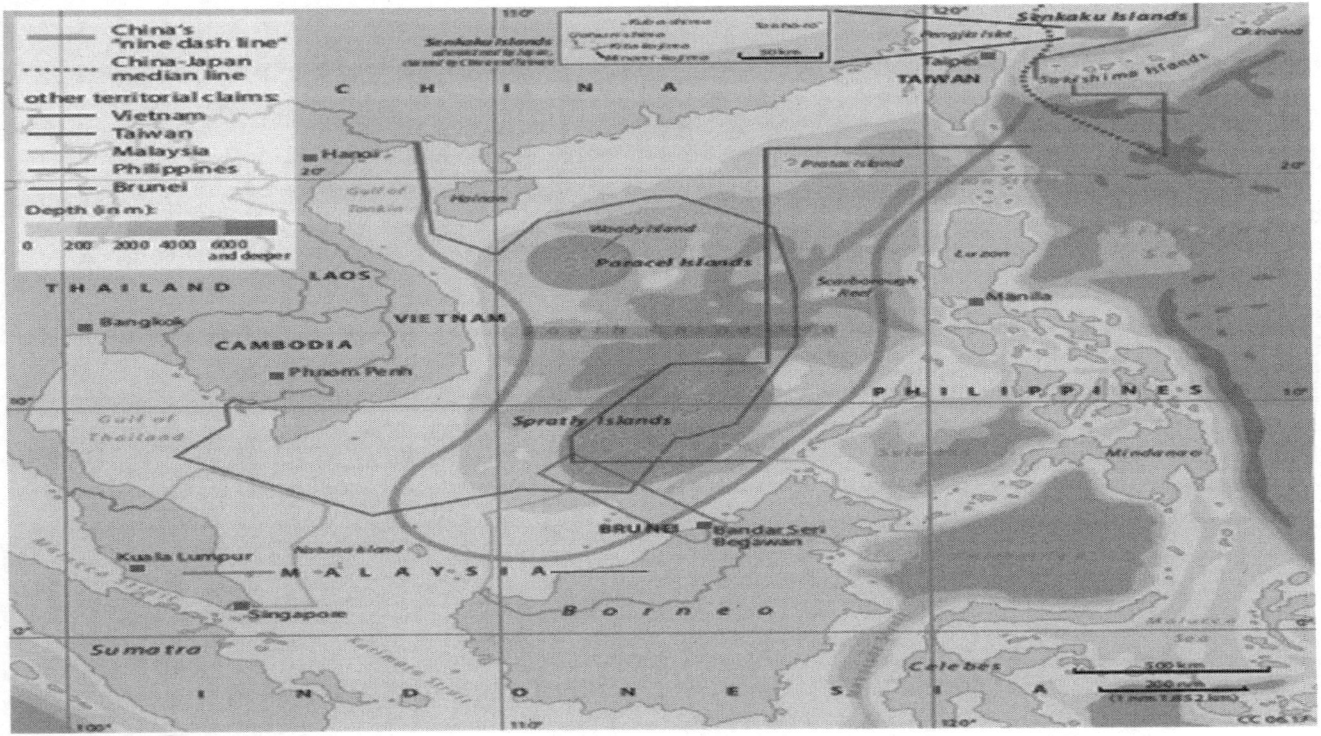


Source: Sreekumar, Kavya and Gazi Hassan, "A Study of Artificial Islands", Centre for Public Policy Research, 2020. https://www.vliz.be/imisdocs/publications/356482.pdf.

countries leading in the construction of artificial island are China, Japan, United, and the United Arab Emirates. Some famous Artificial islands constructed are—Palm Jumeirah Island, Danube Islands of Austria, Amwaj Islands of Baharain, Flevoland of Netherlands, and others. The successful operating artificial islands are—Upper Zakum oil field (Abu Dhabi), Forest city project (Malaysia), Kansai International Airport Island (Japan), South China's Artificial Islands (South China Sea).[22]

## China as the Leading Geo-economic Power

Economic development has been driving the rise of China since the launch of the 'Open Door Policy and the introduction of economic reforms by Chinese leader Deng Xiaoping in 1978. China is described as the world's leading practitioner of geo-economics to the extent that nations less fear China's military might, but its ability to give or withhold trade and investment.[23] Economic growth has been a strategic position in China since opening up to foreign trade and investment, and free-market reforms in 1979. China has transformed its foreign policy in different domains or regions to achieve its geo-economic goals and its geo-economics doesn't try to resist globalisation, but to bend flows of trade, capital to its advantage using export, credit, tax rebates and so forth.[24] The geo-economic era has been shaped by the elements of openness, cooperation, mutual benefits made the win-win cooperation among countries preferable. In the case of China's geo-economics, the focus remained on mutual benefits and asymmetric interdependence with neighbouring countries and regions thus driven by the key element of the geographical proximity that shaped its power discourse being dependent on the neighbouring countries as well as regions to change the geopolitical and geo-economic patterns.[25] The economic power model of China was constructed by Du[26] based on Keohane and Nye's theory and used the bilateral trade figures of China with other countries as the indexes to analyse the interdependence asymmetry. This economic model of China followed a new and distinctive path of capitalism, which experiments with the economic and political risks to accelerate its financial internationalisation.

The geo-economics involves the shifting meanings of economic interdependence across the world with re-definition of the existing "core-periphery relations" and Chinese geo-economic power has been attempting to re-define not only core-periphery but also the periphery-periphery relations using new institutional arrangements that would have multiple areas of regional interactions such as international trade, money, and finance. This reflects a first-ever non-Western attempt to restructure the international financial and monetary order since the Bretton Woods institutions (1948). Thus, the factors that drive the geo-economic projection of China ranges from strategic instrumental statecraft and domestic conditions to the policymaking and explorative approach towards the global market. The world can learn from the risk-averse strategies of China in its global financial engagement that involves the nesting and layering of newly established arrangements.[27]

These risk-averse strategies were reflected in the Chinese geo-economic experiments in three crucial policy fields:

(a) China's Mechanisms for the development of financing ranging from small and targeted investment fund institutions like China Development Bank (CDB) and Export and Import Bank of China (EXIM) to a full-fledged multilateral Asian Infrastructure Investment Bank. The main driving factor of these mechanism was China's focus on the Outbound Foreign Direct Investment (OFDI) with the 'Going Global' strategy set under the presidency of Hu Jintao in 1998. It got enhanced further after the financial crisis (2008-09) as China's capability to balance outbound and inward direct investment flows increased its global creditor and investor position.

(b) The Crisis Liquidity provision that involved bilateral currency swap arrangements even in renminbi and local currencies, for instance, the Chiang Mai Initiative (CMI) among the ASEAN plus three countries that were launched in 2000 and got 'multilateralised' after the 2008-09 global financial crisis: and the People's Bank of China (PBOC). These arrangements have been improving China's capability to protect other economies engaged in geo-economic independence from potential financial shocks, which is making it possible for China to establish 'Leadership-Followership' relations with the countries using its financial means.

(c) The Renminbi Internationalisation Project (RMI) using both domestic as well as cross border experimentation, which also introduced by China post-financial crisis of 2008-09 emphasizing the "Asian Regional Currency Development" as a crisis prevention mechanism. The crisis liquidity initiatives, Investment mechanisms and China International Payments System (CIPS) are contributing to the global infrastructure for RMB internationalisation as well.[28]

The 'Geo-economic roadmap' planned by China thus perceives as an arrangement including the nesting of new infrastructure investment instruments layered with regional as well as minilateral arrangements that minimise the potential economic risks. This reflects, in Wang words, that China is learning or know well "how to turn its new economic weight into legitimate and effective leadership".[29] Since 2015, China has been established as the world's largest trading nation, the second-largest source and destination of foreign direct investment (FDI) and the second-largest consumer market, which has progressively turned it into a hub of global commodity and capital flows. Although China has been in an advantageous position in the economic interdependence with the countries, absolute economic ties and common interests are becoming an increasing concern of the countries in their relations with China. In October 2017, President Xi Jinping in the report the Chinese Communist Party's 19th Congress stated that by 2050, China will have "become a global leader in terms of composite national strength and international influence."[30] The projects and routes announced under the BRI goals by Xi Jinping in 2013 have been expanding China's presence in the world not only through infrastructure construction but also through financial integration using yuan or renminbi currency and creation of Information Silk Road by nesting information and communication technology networks.[31]

## Geo-economics of China's Artificial Island: Claim to EEZ's resources

China began its claim to island in the Spratly group of islands in 1988 when it had conflict with Vietnam on Fiery reef. Since 2014, China begin the construction of artificial islands on the rocks or reefs of these islands as reported by the Asia Maritime Transparency Initiative (AMTI). These man-made or artificial islands are spread on almost 3200 acres of land being claimed by China, but don't qualify as territory under the international laws. Chinese began to increasingly announce its claims on the small and insightful islands of SCS from 2016 through positioning anti-aircraft missiles on Wooly and Paracel islands that were being claimed by Vietnam and Philippines. China aspire to use these islands to bolster its military dominance and capability as the satellite photographs revealed that China don't even allow space for a tree in these islands. The military bases of these islands host missile systems, radars, runways for heavy aircraft, fuel storage facilities, and others to supply the military and naval operations of China in SCS. The expanding control of China on the resources of these islands giving it a potential leverage over East Asian and South East Asian Economies.[32]

The major motivation to construct Artificial Island as a part of Chinese strategies in the SCS is to extend its territorial claims, control international waterway and maritime commerce. China is even seeking to develop air defence identification zone on the islands of Spratly and Paracel that will give it the control on the air of SCS and, make other countries to seek permission from China for all proposed air movements across the area.[33] In 2016, Philippines raised its maritime rights being exploited by China in the SCS that resulted into the 'Philippines versus China Arbitral Tribunal'. The tribunal ruled in favour of Philippines and held that China doesn't have historic rights in its Exclusive Economic Zone (EEZ), quoting the Article 121(3) of the United Nations Convention on the Law of the Sea (UNCLOS) that held two provisions:

(a) No Island is entitled to EEZ claim as supports no human habitation or economy.
(b) Low-tide elevation are not subject to sovereignty claims.

As per these UNCLOS rules, no territorials claims got accepted by any country if it comes in the EEZ of some other countries. For instance, in 1928, United States and Netherlands claimed on seminal islands of Palmas, that lies between Indonesia and Philippines, on the historic discovery basis but the arbitration awarded the island to Netherlands considering its presence on the territory with effective governance. In the same way, all claims of China have not been accepted on the reefs of Spratly islands as historic claims are not enough to get ownership approval, it also requires to increase official presence and activities in these claimed territory. According to UNCLOS maritime laws, ownership of small rock type islands supporting no life gives entitlement to only 452 $nm^2$ of territorial sea, while a life sustaining island generates 125,664 $nm^2$ of EEZ. A country like Vietnam with 2,200 km coastline in SCS gets hundred times greater EEZ than all the combined coastline of rocks and islands in SCS region.[34]

However, the tribunal did not take the man-made activities in the form of artificial island construction that brought the low tide elevation above water permanently. In SCS, China has occupied seven reefs and shoal of Spratly islands namely—Johnson, Cuarteron, Subi, Fiery Cross, Gaven, Mckennan, and Scarboroughre that are just rocks and cannot sustain human habitation or economic life of their own.[35] The UNCLOS rules motivated China to construct artificial island to make them capable to sustain human habitation or economic life, which begin in 2015 by pumping sand into the occupied reefs of Spratly islands. With high investment and advanced engineering, China turned these coral reefs into fully fledged islands having buildings, ports and runways in three years since 2015. Out of all, three are the most significantly advanced bases of China, called as 'Big Three' that are—the fiery cross, mischief and subi reef (see Figures 5.3, 5.4, 5.5, 5.6, and 5.7). In these three islands, China has constructed around 10,000-foot runways, deep water harbours and hangars to house bombers, tankers, airborne early warning aircraft, and other airfield support facilities. In addition, it constructed 400-metre running tracks, tennis and basketball courts, barracks, headquarters, workshops and warehouses. China even announced its plans to construct mobile nuclear power plants to provide electrical power to the islands. The regiment's fighters of China are planning to maintain indoors on each islands with set up of 24 hangars in each of the 'big three' bases. It has been assumed in some reports and analyses that China can deploy 'counter-intervention' anti-access/area denial ($A_2$/AD) systems on big three islands to counter US expansion in SCS and East Asian economies maritime territorial dominance in the region. China even deployed HQ-9 surface-to-air missiles, YJ-62 anti-ship cruise missiles, and J-11 fighters on woody islands in the Paracel islands.[36]

**Table 5.1: Islands Occupied by China and Vietnam in SCS region**

| Country | Occupied Island Name |
|---|---|
| China | Cuarteron Reef (Huayang Jiao)<br>Fiery Cross Reef (Yangshu Jiao)<br>Gaven Reefs (Nanxun Jiao)<br>Hughes Reef (Dongmen Jiao)<br>Johnson Reef (Chiguo Jiao)<br>Mischief Reef (Meiji Jiao)<br>Subi Reef (Zhubi Jiao)<br>Antelope Reef (Lingyang Jiao)<br>Bombay Reef (Langhua Jiao)<br>Drummond Island (Jinqing Dao) |
| Vietnam | Alison Reef (Bai Toc Tan)<br>Amboyna Cay (Dao An Bang)<br>Barque Canada Reef (Bai Thuyen Chai)<br>Central Reef (Dao Truong Sa Dong)<br>Collins Reef (Da Co Lin)<br>Cornwallis South Reef (Da Nui Le)<br>Discovery Great Reef (Da Lon)<br>East Reef (Da Dong)<br>Grierson Reef (Dao Sinh Ton Dong)<br>Ladd Reef (Da Lat)<br>Lansdowne Reef (Da Len Dao)<br>Namyit Island (Dao Nam Yet)<br>Pearson Reef (Dao Phan Vinh)<br>Petley Reef (Da Nui Thi)<br>Sand Cay (Dao Son Ca)<br>Sin Cowe Island (Dao Sinh Ton)<br>South Reef (Da Nam)<br>Southwest Cay (Dao Song Tu Tay)<br>Spratly Island (Dao Truong Sa)<br>Tennent Reef (Da Tien Nu)<br>West Reef ( Da Tay)<br>Alexandra Bank (Bai Huyen Tran)<br>Grainger Bank (Bai Que Duong)<br>Vanguard Bank (Bai Tu Chinh)<br>Rifleman Bank (Bai Vung May)<br>Prince of Wales Bank (Bai Phuc Tan)<br>Prince Consort Bank (Bai Phuc Nguyen) |

**Figure 5.1 and 5.2: Chinese Constructed Buildings and Pathways in Fiery Cross Reef (2015-17)**

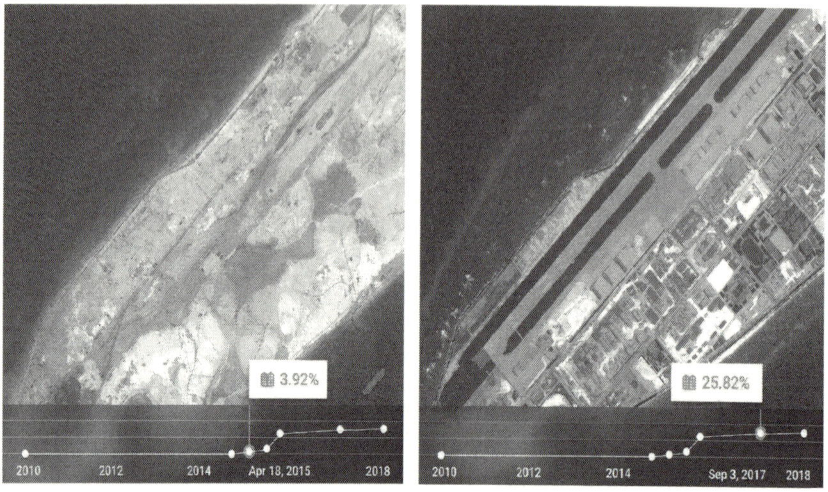


Source: SpaceKnow, "China's Island Build-Up: The View From Space", *The Diplomat*, July 11, 2018. https://thediplomat.com/2018/07/chinas-island-build-up-the-view-from-space/. Accessed on April 11, 2022.

**Figure 5.3: AI Construction on Johnson South Reef by China: Support Human Life**

Source: Comparing Aerial and Satellite Images of Chin's Spratly Outposts, Asia Maritime Transparency Initiative, at https://i1.wp.com/amti.csis.org/wp-content/uploads/2018/02/SubiD-Cargo2-10OCT17-Final-BOX.jpg?w=396&h=396&crop=1&ssl=1

**Figure 5.4: Chinese Cargo Vessels at Subi Reef: Enhancing Naval Facilities**

Source: Comparing Aerial and Satellite Images of Chin's Spratly Outposts, Asia Maritime Transparency Initiative, at https://i1.wp.com/amti.csis.org/wp-content/uploads/2018/02/SubiD-Cargo2-10OCT17-Final-BOX.jpg?w=396&h=396&crop=1&ssl=1

**Figure 5.5: Runway and Airfield in Mischief Reef: To Support China Air Power in SCS**

Source: Comparing Aerial and Satellite Images of Chin's Spratly Outposts, Asia Maritime Transparency Initiative, https://i1.wp.com/amti.csis.org/wp-content/uploads/2018/02/SubiD-Cargo2-10OCT17-Final-BOX.jpg?w=396&h=396&crop=1&ssl=1.

**Figure 5.6: Wind Turbines in Gaven Reef: To Support Renewable Energy Initiative of China**

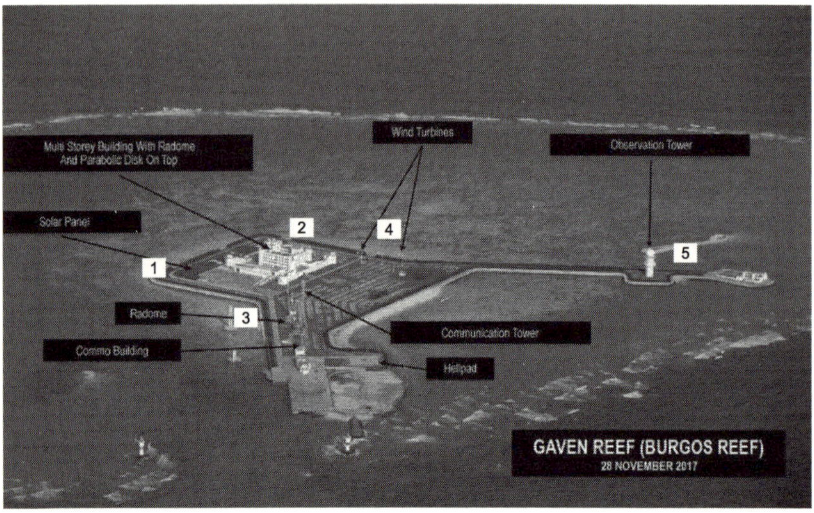


Source: Comparing Aerial and Satellite Images of Chin's Spratly Outposts, Asia Maritime Transparency Initiative, at https://i1.wp.com/amti.csis.org/wp-content/uploads/2018/02/SubiD-Cargo2-10OCT17-Final-BOX.jpg?w=396&h=396&crop=1&ssl=1

## Vietnam in South China Sea: Sustaining Sovereignty through Artificial Islands

Vietnam claims second largest maritime area in the South China Sea. Vietnam has a strong position in the South China Sea that is even perceived as an obstacle/competition by China. Vietnam, with its sustained economic growth and significant role in ASEAN, keeps Southeast Asian countries united against China's illegal claims and emphasize on maintaining the code of conduct and frame ASEAN outlook for Indo-Pacific (AOIP). Although Vietnam has no public opposition against China, but it oppose China's SCS claims through approaching UNSC.[37] The increasing Chinese aggressive activities motivated Vietnam to increase its effort to strengthen its maritime militia. Vietnam, with its large coastal area, shared high stakes in the South China Sea due to its geographic location that borders the Gulf of Tonkin, Gulf of Thailand, and the Pacific Ocean along with China, Laos and Cambodia. Vietnam shares 3,260 km long coastline that stretches from Mong Cai to Ha Tien. Vietnam has around 3,000 islets in the Tokin gulf, and claims on multiple islands in the Spratly and Paracel archipelagos. The claims of Vietnam to these islands derives from following concerns: (a) Existential issues of territorial and contiguous waters against nine-dash line claims of China; (b) Security of the Exclusive Economic Zone and its offshore resources; (c) Control over the maritime resources.[38]

Trung Nguyen, Dean of International Relations at the Ho Chi Minh University, said "In comparison to global criticism to China's islands construction, Vietnam's building of such islands got supported by the world considering it as a defensive strategy, not as expansion". As reports of AMTI mentioned, Vietnam slowly added buildings on some ten major islets since 2017 due to growing Chinese assertiveness in the SCS. It even reported the installation of solar panels, building, 25 pillbox forts on the reefs or islets claimed by Vietnam. Unlike Vietnam's quite development of islands, Chinese island construction drew attention of world due to the creation of infrastructure for military aircraft and radars that it was using to send bombers and naval vessels into the SCS to restrict the naval presence and passing of other countries.[39]

Vietnam began to reclaim the maritime territory in 2016 by quietly developing signal towers and administrative building in around 28.3 hectares (70 acres) of land at West reef. In 2019-20, Vietnam's work were evident in Pearson reef and Namyit islands through installation of radome, housing or communication system and several administrative buildings. Although the small size of these islands make it easy to quickly deploy and conceal for Vietnam, however they don't have the minimal support infrastructure.[40] By 2019, Vietnam occupied 49 outposts across 27 features in the vicinity of Spratly islands, out of which it developed 10 islets and rest remained underwater reefs. The expansion of islands allowed Vietnam to extend its runway to 1300 metres from just 750 metres, and completed two large sets of hangars at either end of runway which were planned to host PZL M28B maritime surveillance aircraft and CASA C-295 transport planes of Vietnam. It constructed a pair of large signals intelligence of communication facilities in 2018 that includes—solar panels, sports field, administrative buildings and others. Besides Spratly, It also occupied Pearson reef by constructing helipad, solar panels, vegetation planting, and greenery across the areas of artificial islands. Unlike China, Vietnam's occupied holdings are not on natural assets like Spratly or Pearson, but on small facilities perched on low-tide elevations and entirely submerged reefs or banks. Unlike China, Vietnam has not tried the large scale militarisation of its features. Six underwater banks of reefs/ islets of Spratly islands are claimed by Vietnam as its continental shelf (see Figure 5.8) that are being claimed as part of Nansha island by China and Taiwan thus leading to disputes in the SCS region. In these six underwater banks, Vietnam has constructed 14 outposts and calls them "Economic, Scientific, and Technological Service Stations or Dich Vu Khoa" (DK1). It has given licence for exploration of oil and gas blocks to foreign energy companies around the DK1 (see Figures 5.9, 5.10, and 5.11) which has been opposed and threaten by Chinese forces and even resulted in suspension of some contracts. Despite Chinese objection, Vietnam expanded four DK1 platforms on Prince of Wales and Grainger banks by installing second multi-story buildings and large helipads, which reflects the strategy of Vietnam to be committed towards a steady but modest expansion of its capabilities around the Spratly islands.[41]

**Figure 5.7: Vietnam's Occupied Spratly Islands**

Source: Asia Maritime Transparency Initiative, "Slow and Steady: Vietnam's Spratly Upgrades", at https://amti.csis.org/slow-and-steady-vietnams-spratly-upgrades/spratly_10_20_18_dgwm-north/.

**Figure 5.8: Vietnam's Occupied Pearson Reef**

Source: Asia Maritime Transparency Initiative, "Slow and Steady: Vietnam's Spratly Upgrades", at https://amti.csis.org/slow-and-steady-vietnams-spratly-upgrades/spratly_10_20_18_dgwm-north/.

**Figure 5.9: Vietnam's Pillbox Structures: Petley and South Reef**

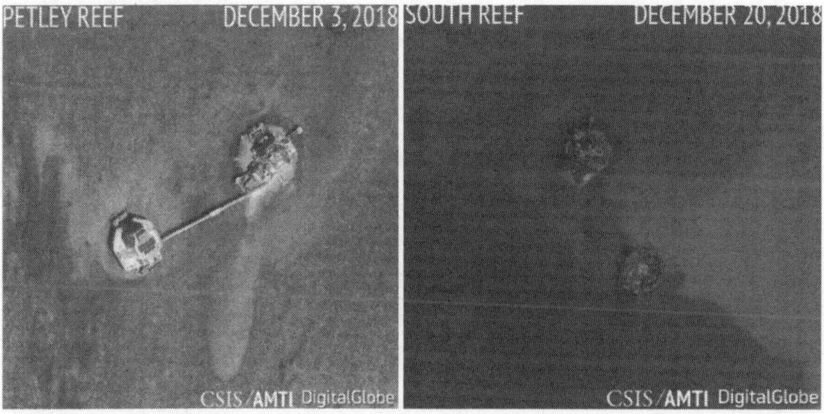


Source: Asia Maritime Transparency Initiative, "Slow and Steady: Vietnam's Spratly Upgrades", at https://amti.csis.org/slow-and-steady-vietnams-spratly-upgrades/spratly_10_20_18_dgwm-north/.

**Figure 5.10: Vietnam's Islets, Pillboxes and DK1 stations in South China Sea**

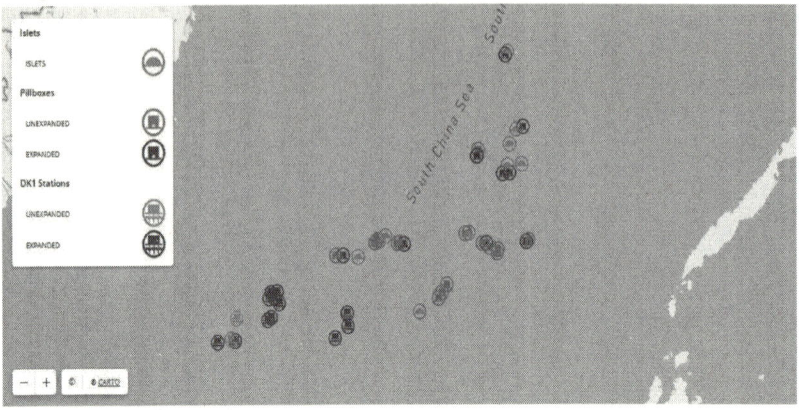


Source: Carto, at https://d.gusc.cartocdn.com/csis/api/v1/map/csis@e5c14609@9f6ddc6733eb1be45a0fc0b6a1b6336e:1614807856392/1,2,3/7/103/60.png

## Geo-economic Competition between China and Vietnam

The resources in South China Sea remained low profile until China began the exploration of them following its doctrine of 'uti possidetis', which supports the legitimacy of China's claim for SCS islands. Since announcing SCS region as a core interest, China has been claiming veto or considering any energy related project, for drilling of offshore oil and gas resources, as a challenge. For instance, China-Philippines standoff in 2012 when Chinese vessels took control of the Scarborough shoal of the Reed bank islands, on which Philippines' project was going on. Conflict remained a long preferred approach to expand its territory in the SCS, but its approach shifted to economic considering the regulations under UNCLOS maritime laws implying more EEZ entitlement for a life sustaining island (452 $nm^2$ for no life islands, while 125,664 $nm^2$ for life-sustaining islands). The conflict won't bring the desired maritime territory and exploration allowance for China, which the construction and management of artificial islands can do. With its shift to economic approach, China claims its intention of joint development but its definition of joint development involves more an intention to access the continental shelves of other claimants for producing of oil and gas fields.[42]

In the case of China versus Vietnam, their naval clash in 1974 was the first dispute in the South China Sea that initiated the conflicts in the SCS region taking multiple forms of disputes from state to state to multistate maritime clashes. Their conflict over the resource exploration in SCS begin to be evident in 2011, when Chinese marine surveillance vessel sabotaged an exploration vessel of Vietnam. This was followed by CNOOC inviting foreign oil companies in the bid to block the drilling of waters within EEZ of Vietnam. Vietnam has continued to prefer negotiation to oppose the growing assertiveness of China, but the growing threats by China to Vietnam's sovereignty over its maritime and continental shelf resources made it compulsory for Vietnam to go beyond the negotiation approach towards legal arbitration or unify with other countries.[43] The drilling and exploration operations by China have been continuously rising in the past years, since its unannounced drilling rig into the Vietnamese waters in 2011 and then May 2014, when China National Offshore Oil Corp's (CNOOC) began the drilling operations for natural gas within the 200 nm of Vietnam's EEZ that was close to Triton island claimed by Vietnam, China and Taiwan in the Paracel islands. This deployment of first deep-water semisubmersible for drilling reflected the value China attaches to the offshore oil, gas resources, and hydrocarbons.[44] In order to challenge, a maritime violation by a country like China, the filing country needs to initiate an arbitration under Article 287 (Annex VII) of UNCLOS that covers ruling regarding—(a) Entitlement to EEZ, continental shelf, and their living/non-living resources; (b) Legality of a country's claims and activities in the SCS.

Vietnam began its efforts to develop islands as counter-defence to Chinese activities in SCS in 2016, which picked pace in 2019 and increasingly get noticed since 2021. The state oil company of Vietnam has signed agreements with Eni SpA, Exxon Mobil, ONGC Videsh for deep-water shore exploration development.[45] Even the South China Morning Post said, by citing AMTI report, that Vietnam's emplacement of air and coastal defence system with upgradation of West reef and Sine Cowe islands reflects its stance against Chinese bases.[46] In 2016, Chinese media outlets, like its China's turn and China Youth Net, used satellite images to show the failure of Vietnam's Artificial Island and enjoy the schadenfreude of their loss. When the Vietnam's Artificial Island construction got washed away in Nanhua or Cornwallis South reef during the Typhone Jasmine, the Chinese media used the satellite images of them to prove Vietnam's illegal construction in these islands that were using only sand and low technological expertise. The China Youth net used the imaged to reflect the failure of Vietnam and technological superiority of China, and explained how Chinese methods works with sucking sand up to construct their island taller in comparison to Vietnam's old fashioned way of dredging sand from seafloor. In addition, the Chinese media bragged that 'Island building isn't as simple as it looks, it needs complicated and integrated engineering that depends on the national power of a country'.[47] Vietnam began dredging up the part of reefs and islets to create 40 acres of new land but the Vietnam's methods were more time-consuming and less environmentally disastrous than Chinese methods of industrial-scale dredging and landfill.[48]

## Shift from Military to Economic Opportunities: Implication for SCS

Besides being 'Third Golden Waterway' and economic lifeline of the world that connects East Asia, Africa and Europe for commercial shipping, South China Sea has established as a significant area of resource exploration.[49] The growing resource requirement of countries under their expanded urbanisation and technological goals makes every source as significant. In addition, the global commitment to clean energy transition adds magnetism to every new source of resource exploration, thus motivating geo-economic engagement as well as competition among countries. The countries seek to expand their control and preserve the supply chain of such resources as well as their source platforms. The case of China versus Vietnam represents how the maritime territorial expansion has been gaining weight not only for military but also economic opportunities. The resource geo-economics has also motivated their construction of the artificial islands to seek and secure the economic interest, as increased human life on the reef or shoals of island means more ownership on the resources of expanded maritime territory. The increasing shift toward geo-economics doesn't imply that there would be no conflict, however its nature will increasingly change turning more into competition. The future will unfold how much success Vietnam can get in its geo-economic exploration and man-made island construction to counter China's assertiveness, but the expanding strategies of China over SCS resources will definitely promote more competition as well as counter-alliance among SCS littorals.

## Notes

1. SD Pradhan, "Vietnam's Strategic Interests in the South China Sea: Challenges and Options", *Times of India*, June 27, 2021, at https://timesofindia.indiatimes.com/blogs/ChanakyaCode/vietnams-strategic-interests-in-the-south-china-sea-challenges-and-options/. Accessed on April 8, 2022.
2. Baru, Sanjaya, *India and the world: Essays on Geo-economics and Foreign Policy*, Academic Foundation, India, 2016.
3. Gady, Franz Stefan, "Geo-economics in East Asia." *The Diplomat*, March 31, 2020, at https://thediplomat.com/tag/geo-economics-in-east-asia/. Accessed on April 7, 2022.
4. Lachniniskii, S.S. and A.A. Anohin. "Evolution of the Ideas and Contents of Geoeconomic Studies." *Regional Research of Russia*, 2015, Vol. 5 (1): 90-95.
5. Paul Kennedy, *The Rise and fall of Great Powers*, HarperCollins Publishers, United States, 1987.
6. SP Huntington, "Why International Primacy Matters", *Journal of International Security*, Vol. 17 (4).
7 Sparke, Michael, I*ntroducing Globalization: Ties, Tensions, and uneven Development*, John Wiley & Sons, New Jersey, 2012.
8. Boulding, Kenneth, "The Economics of Energy." American Academy of Political and Social Science, 1973, pp, 120-126.
9. Danielson, Etta, "The New Geopolitics: A Comparative Analysis of Artificial Island Construction in China and Dubai", *Modus Vivendi Rhode College*, Vol. XXIII (2017): 40-55.
10. James C, Hsiung, "The Age of Geo-economics: China's Global Role, and Prospects of Cross-Strait Integration", *Journal of Chinese Political Science*. Vol. 14(2), 2009: 113-133.
11. Ibid.
12. Ratter, B.M.W., "Geopolitics of Small Islands", in *Geography of Small Islands*, Springer International Publishing, 2018: pp-93-131.
13. Bhatt, Pooja, "Economic Importance of the South China Sea" in *Nine Dash Line: Deciphering the South China Sea Conundrum*, KW Publishers, New Delhi, 2020: pp. 175-213.
14. Ibid.
15. Ibid.
16. James Kraska, "The Nine Ironies of South China Mess", *The Diplomat*, September 17, 2015, at https://thediplomat.com/2015/09/the-nine-ironies-of-the-south-china-sea-mess/. Accessed on April 24, 2022.
17. Su Hao, "Territorial Issues in Asia: Drivers, Instruments and Ways Forwards", Session II on 'Resources (Energy, Fishing) and Maritime Law' of the 7th Berlin Conference on Asian Security (BCAS), Konrad Adenauer Stiftung, July 2013.

18. Ratter, B.M.W., "Geopolitics of Small Islands", in *Geography of Small Islands,* Springer International Publishing, 2018, pp. 93-131.
19. Bhatt, Pooja, n. 13.
20. Su Hao, n. 17.
21. Muller, Gerhardt, "Ports and Artificial Islands: Development of a New Relationship", Port Authority of New York and New Jersey, One World Trade Center, New York, at http://ieeexplore.ieee.org/abstract/document/1160816/similar.
22. Sreekumar, Kavya and Gazi Hassan, "A Study of Artificial Islands", Centre for Public Policy Research, 2020, at https://www.vliz.be/imisdocs/publications/356482.pdf.
23. M. Harris, Robert D. Blackwill and Jennifer. 2016. *War by other Means: Geo-economics and Statecraft.* Cambridge: Harvard University Press.
24. Holslag, Jonathan. 2016. "Geoeconomics in a Globalized World: The Case of China's Export Policy", *Asia Europe Journal,* pp. 173-84.
25. Yi Lang, Mingxing Chen, Dadao Lu, Zijin Ding, and Zhi Zheng. 2019. "The Spatial Evolution of Geo-economic Pattern among China and Neighboring Countries since the Reform and Opening-Up", at www.mdpi.com *Sustainability Journal* Vol. 11 (2168).
26. D.B. Du, D.Z. Duan, and W.L. Yang., "Spatial Evolution Pattern of Chinese Economic Power based on the sensitivity and vulnerability of states interdependence", *Acta Geographica Sinica,* 2016: 1741-1751.
27. Mikko Huotar, Sandra Heep. 2015. "Learning Geoeconomics: China's experimental financial and monetary initiatives", *Asia European Journal,* 14 (2): 153-171.
28. Ibid.
29. Honying Wang, "From "Taoguang Yanghui" to "Yousuo Zuowei": China's Engagement in Financial Minilateralism", Centre for International Governance Innovation, December 12, 2014, at https://www.cigionline.org/publications/taoguang-yanghui-yousuo-zuowei-chinas-engagement-financial-minilateralism/. Accessed on March 23, 2022.
30. Xi Jinping's report at the 19th Chinese Communist Party National Congress, Secure a decisive victory in building a moderately prosperous society in all respects and strive for the great success of socialism with Chinese characteristics for a new era, October 18, 2017.
31. Corre, Philippe Le, "China's Rise as a Geoeconomic Influencer: Four European Case Studies", Carnegie Endowment for International Peace, 2018: Washington.
32. Serena Seyfort, "What are China's Artificial Islands and why are there concerns about them", 9News.com, November 26, 2021, at https://www.9news.com.au/world/what-are-chinas-artificial-islands-in-the-south-china-sea-and-why-are-there-concerns-about-them/3f0d47ab-1b3a-4a8a-bfc6-7350c5267308. Accessed on April 18, 2022.
33. Ibid.

34. James Kraska, "The Nine Ironies of South China Mess", *The Diplomat*, September 17, 2015, at https://thediplomat.com/2015/09/the-nine-ironics-of-the-south-china-sea-mess/. Accessed on April 24, 2022.
35. Robert Bekman, "China Island Building in the South China Sea: Implication for Regional Security", Council for Security Cooperation in the Asia Pacific Regional Security Outlook Report, 2017, pp. 40-42.
36. Thomas Shugart, "China's Artificial Islands are Bigger (And a Bigger Deal) than ou think", War on Rocks, Texas National Security Review, September 21 2016. https://warontherocks.com/2016/09/chinas-artificial-islands-are-bigger-and-a-bigger-deal-than-you-think/. Accessed on April 21, 2022.
37. SD Pradhan, "Vietnam's Strategic Interests in the South China Sea: Challenges and Options", *Times of India*, June 27, 2021, at https://timesofindia.indiatimes.com/blogs/ChanakyaCode/vietnams-strategic-interests-in-the-south-china-sea-challenges-and-options/. Accessed on April 8, 2022.
38. Ibid.
39. Ralph Jennings, "How Vietnam quietly built up 10 islands in Asia's most disputed Sea", East Asia VOA News, April 19, 2019, at https://www.voanews.com/a/how-vietnam-quietly-built-up-10-islands-in-asia-most-disputed-sea/4882776.html. Accessed on April 17, 2022.
40. The Economic Times, "Vietnam builds up defences against China in Spratly islands", February 24, 2021, at https://m.economictimes.com/news/defence/vietnam-builds-up-defences-against-china-in-spratly-islands/articleshow/81190247.cms. Accessed on April 8, 2022.
41. Asia Maritime Transparency Initiative, "Slow and Steady: Vietnam's Spratly Upgrades", April 8, 2019, at https://amti.csis.org/slow-and-steady-vietnams-spratly-upgrades/. Accessed on April 11, 2022.
42. John R. Weinberger, "China Seeks to Dominate Off-Shore Energy Resources in the South and East China Seas", International Association for Energy Economics, 2015, pp. 17-21.
43. Hong Kong To Nguyen, Manh Tung Ho, Quan-Hoang Vuong, "Probing Vietnam's Legal Prospects in the South China Dispute", National Bureau of Asian Research Project Muse, Vol. 16(3). July 2021, pp. 105-131.
44. John R. Weinberger, n. 42.
45. Ibid.
46. *The Economic Times,* "Vietnam builds up defences against China in Spratly islands", February 24, 2021, at https://m.economictimes.com/news/defence/vietnam-builds-up-defences-against-china-in-spratly-islands/articleshow/81190247.cms. Accessed on April 8, 2022.
47. Shannon Tiezzi, "Chinese Media: Our Artificial Islands are better than Vietnam's", *The Diplomat*, February 5, 2016, at https://thediplomat.com/2016/02/chinese-media-our-artificial-islands-are-better-than-vietnams/. Accessed on April 10, 2022.

48. Asia Maritime Transparency Initiative, "Slow and Steady: Vietnam's Spratly Upgrades", April 8, 2019, at https://amti.csis.org/slow-and-steady-vietnams-spratly-upgrades/. Accessed on April 11, 2022.
49. Ibid.

# 6

# Health Diplomacy Amid the Pandemic Crisis: India 's Opportunity for Leadership

MAHIMA DUGGAL

The first COVID-19 case recorded was in December 2019 in China's Wuhan province; merely months later, in March 2020, the World Health Organization (WHO) declared the coronavirus a full-blown global pandemic. Since then, as of February 2, 2022, COVID-19 has resulted in a massive 5.67 million deaths (see Figure 6.1), with over 391 million in total infections (see Figure 6.2). Apart from thoroughly challenging health systems across the world, the pandemic has proved to be a transnational and international crisis—exacerbating geopolitical, geo-economic, and geostrategic tensions across the world. Two years after its onset, the effects of the pandemic are only just becoming evident; COVID-19 has not only caused devastating social disruption with massive loss of life worldwide, but also colossal economic repercussions with both national and internal borders becoming more restrictive. It has resulted in serious consequences for the livelihoods and human security of individuals and communities. The SARS-CoV-2 virus has surpassed borders, nationalities, and political affiliations and presented a tremendous challenge for all alike, and has become a 'black elephant' event for international politics that has stressed fault lines and caused divisions" to "politics, stressing fault lines and amplifying existing divisions. In other words, the pandemic was an external shock to the global economy, and its impact is not limited to first-order (or direct) effects, but includes a profound impact on domestic politics and international affairs. By acting as a catalyst, COVID-19 has contributed significantly (and continues to do so) to a change in the international rules-based order.

**Figure 6.1: Total Confirmed Deaths by COVID-19**
(January 22, 2020-February 2, 2022)

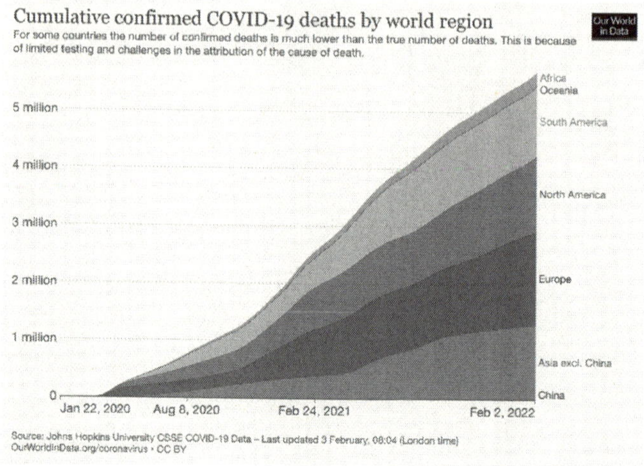


Source: Raw data sourced from the COVID-19 Data Repository by the Center for Systems Science and Engineering (CSSE) at Johns Hopkins University. Compiled by Our World in Data (University of Oxford).[1]

Global issues often present an opportunity for the international community to band together and work cohesively and collaboratively to tackle the onslaught of the pandemic, and prepare for similar future disruptions. However, rather than being a uniting episode, the COVID-19 pandemic proved to be a divisive event that threw international politics, particularly in the Indo-Pacific region, into flux. While the long-term implications of the pandemic on the international order can only be speculated at this point, what COVID-19 did was strip a lot of illusions of the existing international and regional orders as well as the balance of power and state of geopolitics. For one, the already heated debate on globalisation has seen a surge of anti-globalisation sentiments, a return of nationalism and identity politics, and a rapid rise of protectionist tendencies as national borders become shrouded by a vaccine curtain. In essence, COVID-19 has caused a pivot in the political ecology or fabric of several countries.

**Figure 6.2: Cumulative Confirmed COVID-19 Cases**
**(January 22, 2020-February 5, 2022)**

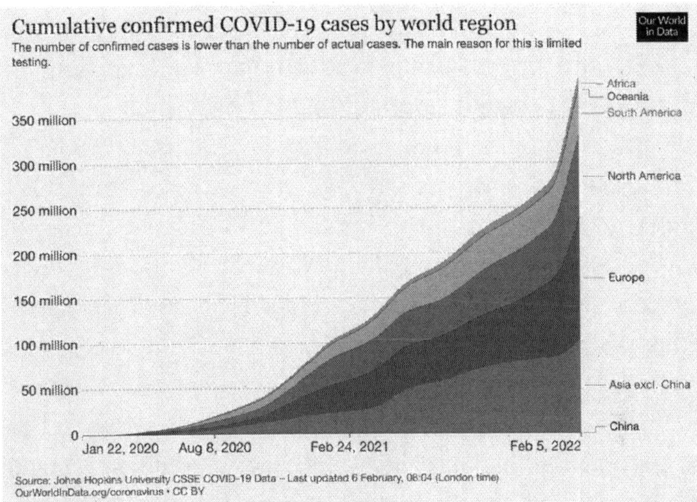


Source: Raw data sourced from the COVID-19 Data Repository by the Center for Systems Science and Engineering (CSSE) at Johns Hopkins University. Compiled by Our World in Data (University of Oxford).[2]

As the pandemic (and its impacts) cause immense shifts in bilateral relationships and regional and global power dynamics, and usher in a new era in international politics, it is critical to understand how India has responded to the challenge. This paper traces India's foreign policy amidst the pandemic to understand New Delhi's health diplomacy outlook since the onset of COVID-19. Through a discussion on international governance and a reimagining of multilateralism amid the pandemic, the paper argues that notwithstanding its obvious negative impacts, the COVID-19 pandemic has presented India with a window of opportunity to assert itself on the global stage as a leader. To make this case, the paper examines the rationale and impact of India's '*vaccine maitri*' (meaning, vaccine friendship) program in its neighbourhood and beyond. It advances the claim that as small and middle-income states in the region struggle to achieve their vaccination targets, India can employ its strengths through deft health diplomacy to lead a vaccine initiative in the region in collaboration with other like-minded players, such as India's Quadrilateral

Security Dialogue (Quad) partners—the United States (US), Japan, and Australia.

## COVID-19 and International Governance: Reimagining Multilateralism through Global Health Diplomacy

To study and explore the health diplomacy and the foreign policy of any state during the pandemic crisis, it must first be noted that COVID-19 marked the first such global crisis since the 1930s—almost a century ago—when there existed no substantial international governance mechanism. Multilateral governance institutions and mechanisms have been in crisis since well before the pandemic hit. Factors such as the steadily rising US-China rivalry and the threat of a new Cold War; the emergence of technological competition; the race to dominate cyberspace and outer space; and growing political discontent owing to economic inequality, social fragmentation and job insecurity have all led to a multilateral order in crisis. Over the past few years, the international governance system has seen increasing calls for structural reforms within bodies like the United Nations (UN), the World Trade Organisation (WTO) and the WHO among others. In this context, the COVID-19 pandemic has only further exacerbated such existing geo-economic, geopolitical, and strategic faultlines.[3]

In their book *Aftershocks,* American national security experts Colin Kahl and Thomas Wright claim that the COVID-19 crisis is in fact the greatest shock to the international system and world order since the Second World War.[5] Not only have millions of people been infected and killed, but the economic crash caused by COVID-19—which will amount to over USD 9 trillion over the coming years according to estimates by the International Monetary Fund[6]—was arguably one of the worst since the Great Depression, and perhaps more severe than the Global Financial Crisis of 2008-2009 (see Figure 6.3).[7] More importantly, COVID-19 has exposed the already prevalent vulnerabilities in the global financial system and the global supply chain nexus that is inherently designed to "maximize short-term efficiency at the expense of robustness and resilience".[8] In this context alone, COVID-19 has presented a gross challenge to international governance and international relations that is unprecedented in recent times. The secondary human impact of the pandemic, already visible to some extent, on the international order is also set to be immense. As inequalities rise globally, weak and fragile states in the Global South face the maximum downturn, creating conditions that make conflict likely. Additionally, the world also witnessed trends of growing nationalism and isolationism, increased inequality, and the widening of a global governance gap that will add to the likelihood of conflict.[9]

**Figure 6.3: Consensus Forecasts of Global GDP (per cent)**

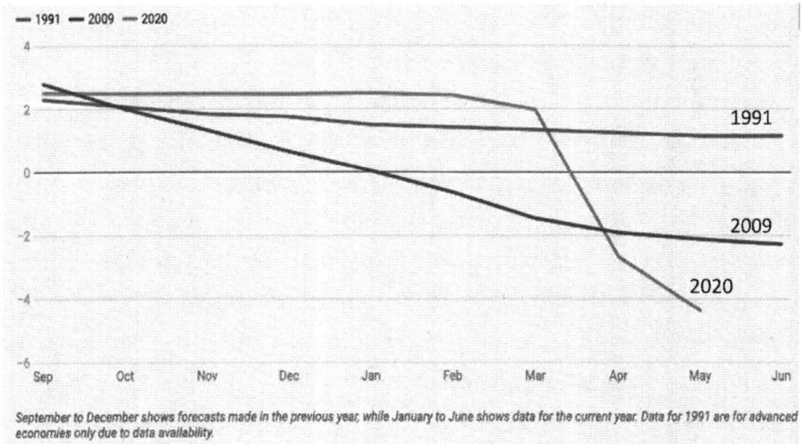


Source: World Bank.[4] The recession induced by COVID-19 saw the fastest and steepest downgrades in consensus growth projections among all global recessions since 1990.

As international institutions and alliances staggered under the weight of the pandemic, China and the US were pushed further towards a new Cold War. China's belligerence amid the pandemic, its secrecy and lack of transparency, its disinformation campaigns, and its aggressive wolf warrior form of diplomacy shattered hopes that it will become a "responsible stakeholder in the international order".[10] This has forced states to rethink and recalibrate their threat perceptions and security calculus to account for future disruptions, caused by both events like pandemics and geopolitical tensions and conflicts.

In brief, multilateralism was already under siege and global governance facing massive challenges; COVID-19 only amplified these issues. However, at the same time, it has also generated new thinking on multilateralism and the new international order. While any black swan event like the pandemic certainly leads to an intensification of geopolitical tensions and exacerbation of regional fault lines, it also opens doors for greater cooperation and collaborations—at least amongst like-minded states. Despite the challenges it presented and the vulnerabilities it revealed, COVID-19 has also changed the orientation of global politics, bringing to the forefront global health diplomacy as a way of tackling the declining multilateralism. It has, in other words, brought to prominence 'health diplomacy' as a pathway for states to enhance their regional and global outreach.

Simply defined, global health diplomacy is the intersection of "public health, law, international affairs, management, and economics, concentrating on negotiations and shaping the global policy climate for health".[11] It is built on the premise that—given the international community's limited knowledge on how to respond to a pandemic that threatens global health and economic security—countries must cooperate and engage in a continuous dialogue. This allows for sharing of experiences and information, formulating and enforcing policies and therefore, successfully managing the pandemic. No country is entirely immune from the magnitude of challenges brought on by the pandemic. It, therefore, becomes pertinent that countries render the highest levels of political and diplomatic support to reach a peaceful solution. In other words, "the importance of global solidarity as the health threats transcend the borders in no time in this globalized world" makes health diplomacy a critical tool in the foreign policy tool belts of states across the region.[12] In other words, at a time of declining multilateralism amid the pandemic, the focus on global health diplomacy can help states reimagine multilateralism to build a more sustainable future.[13]

In many ways, COVID-19 forced a change in the orientation of global politics, and by extension, the very manner in which diplomacy is conducted. For example, at a time when face-to-face interactions were crucial to conduct complex negotiations and manage heightening tensions, countries were forced to adapt to a digital age with virtual diplomacy—creating both opportunities and challenges. In fact, even as traditional diplomacy returns, governments and international organisations have continued to employ online diplomacy, with the UN Security Council using Virtual Reality (VR) technology for 3-D virtual field trips to Colombia.[14] Under such conditions, global health diplomacy has emerged as an added way to conduct more holistic, inclusive and comprehensive engagement between like-minded states to address global challenges, both health and non-health related, by emphasizing greater bilateral partnerships, peace, prosperity and development. To put it another way, the pandemic has created an opportunity for states to practice health diplomacy to achieve their ambitions, strengthen global cooperation, solidarity amongst the international community, global health security, and sustainable and resilient trade and development.

Successful global health diplomacy can help states bolster their health systems and invest more in their science and technology infrastructure. It sensitizes states to the importance of the health sector for the security and prosperity of their nations, and gives them incentives to work more closely with the global community and contribute more to the development of novel technologies and medical innovations so as to prepare better for such future events. Through global health diplomacy, states can frame health security as a priority; they can come together on global platforms to highlight "the strategy of Health in All Policies" for better outcomes in the post-pandemic world.[15] This would involve recalibration of global trade, development, security, peace and other geo-socio-economic policies to incorporate health-related global targets.

In 2003, the SARS epidemic provided a similar opportunity for affected states to work together to address the vulnerabilities in their healthcare systems and respond effectively to the outbreak.[16] Unlike SARS, however, COVID-19 has seen a global spread. Here, global health diplomacy is crucial to enabling international cooperation to resolve challenges like the bottlenecks in pandemic control regulations and cracks in multilateralism.[17] Nevertheless, with COVID-19, we witnessed several indications of the failure of such coordination and a lack of global leadership by any state or international institution.[18] In the earlier months of the COVID-19 outbreak, for instance, the lack of transparency on China's part prevented the global community from working together to stop the spread of the disease. Over time, however, despite growing geopolitical tensions, like-minded states have gradually begun coming together under global health diplomacy to enhance their outreach and engagement and emerge as responsible regional and global leaders.

## Vaccine Maitri: India's Window of Opportunity?

### *Vaccine Nationalism*

As COVID-19 highlighted the importance of global health security and global health diplomacy, India stood out as a leader in the region and a major and reputed global supplier of COVID-19 vaccines. As countries across the world struggled to secure coveted vaccine supplies and become the first to inoculate their populations so as to resume regular economic activity, they entered into what can only be described as a 'vaccine race'. The buzzword of the day became 'vaccine nationalism', that is, a "my country first" attitude to the allocation of vaccines,[19] which has seen governments sign agreements with vaccine manufacturers to secure supplies for their own populations ahead of those of other countries. The rise of nationalistic movements has seen several countries try to hoard up drugs, vaccines and essential personal protection equipment, thus stressing the already fragile healthcare systems in disadvantaged countries (and communities).

Even before the vaccinations developed for COVID-19 underwent the requisite clinical trials and were approved by various national regulatory agencies, several wealthy nations—including the US, Britain, Japan and the European Union—quickly procured millions of doses in advance.[20] In some cases, the number of doses procured was far more than that needed by their populations. A report published in 2020 revealed that in total, wealthy countries had made an agreement to purchase over two billion vaccine doses, which were sure to have a significant impact on limiting available supplies for low—and middle-income countries.[21] By August 2020—well before vaccines had undergone the critical phase III large-scale clinical trials to assess their safety and efficacy—the US secured 800 million doses of at least six different types of vaccines under development, with an agreement to purchase an additional billion. The UK too concluded deals for 340 million vaccine doses—about five doses per citizen.

At the same time, even as they virtually bought up a majority of the potential supply, the wealthy nations overtly argued for "equitable access" in a plainly hypocritical move.[22] It should also be noted that most of the deals lacked transparency; very little information was made public about what was bought via pre-order and at what price, and who would have access. While vaccine supplies remained limited in the early months of the pandemic, the reservation of millions of doses naturally delays access for others. In other words, in the early months, vaccine allocation was akin to the classic game theory problem (or the prisoner's dilemma),[23] meaning that as wealthy and vaccine-manufacturing countries shorten the queue, it comes at the expense of other poorer-resourced, non-vaccine manufacturing countries. Therefore, vaccine nationalism emerged as an ethically deplorable and rather shortsighted trend during the pandemic, that made the pandemic a matter for individual countries rather than the international community as a collective and made it a divisive factor between the rich and poor countries.

### *India's Vaccine Diplomacy*

Against such a trend of vaccine nationalism, India—a major global supplier of COVID-19 vaccines—emerged as a shining example of a state employing health diplomacy, and particularly vaccine diplomacy, for common good. Instead of resorting to vaccine nationalism, on January 20, 2021, India launched a 'Vaccine Maitri' (or Friendship) campaign, which is essentially a diplomatic mission to supply vaccines to low-income countries in the neighbourhood and key partner states.[24] In a speech in the Rajya Sabha, India's External Affairs Minister (EAM) S. Jaishankar elaborated the thinking behind it was built on the Indian philosophy of '*Vasudhaiva Kutumbakam*', translated as the belief that 'the world is one family'.

> "... as Indians, we are all naturally internationalist by virtue of our culture, traditions, heritage and history. We have never seen a contradiction between this internationalism and the nationalism that was the driver of our independence struggle and subsequent endeavours at nation building. Indeed, this experience of the freedom movement has even further reinforced our internationalism, by creating a strong solidarity

> with other nations who similarly struggled for their freedom. In recent years, as democracy struck deeper roots, we have found our own cultural expressions and identities that define us in a diverse world. In fact, drawing from our heritage, we have become even stronger voices for international cooperation and solidarity. That, of course, is most in demand at times of global stress, such as the Covid pandemic."[25]

Such rationale was given practical shape through the Vaccine Maitri policy. In other words, India's vaccine (and health) diplomacy became a way to actualise its goodwill, much like New Delhi does with its humanitarian assistance and disaster response programmes, which have given the country recognition as a reliable first responder. Over the past two decades, India has built itself into a pharmaceutical powerhouse and has been popularly hailed as the "pharmacy of the world".[26] Based on its low-cost skilled manpower and well-established manufacturing base, India has a booming pharmaceutical industry. It is known as one of the largest global suppliers of low-priced generic versions of drugs, as well as critical medicines or vaccines for HIV/AIDS, Tuberculosis, Malaria, Hepatitis C and other non-communicable diseases at an affordable price.[27] The turnover from such exports is well over US$ 20 billion. The Indian pharmaceutical industry's provision of low-cost antiretroviral medicines for HIV/AIDS struck African countries—at a time when Western pharmaceutical companies demanded exorbitant prices from poor states suffering from HIV epidemic—only enhanced India's reputation.[28] India's Vaccine Maitri followed in such footsteps.

As the supplier of 60 per cent of the world's vaccines, India quickly developed the capacity to produce over three billion COVID-19 vaccines on an annual basis.[29] Most of these were the Covishield vaccine, made possible through a tie-up between the Serum Institute of India (SII) and the Oxford University-AstraZeneca. This positioned India perfectly to grant complimentary and low-cost vaccines to low-income countries, especially in its neighbourhood.[30] Within a month of the initiative's inception, India had sent over 5.6 million vaccine doses to states in its neighbourhood as grants, and another 10 million doses to 17 states in its neighbourhood, West Asia, Africa and South America in commercial deals.[31] By November 2021, this figure had grown to over 65 million Covid vaccine doses to almost 100 countries, and other critical medicines and medical equipment to more than 150 countries.[32] See Table 6.1 for a list of India's vaccine supplies—including grants, commercial deals, and doses donated to the global COVAX program—to some of its top recipients.

**Table 6.1: India's Vaccine Supply (as of April 27, 2022) in Lakhs**

| Country | Grant | Commercial | COVAX | Total Supplies |
|---|---|---|---|---|
| Bangladesh | 33.000 | 150.008 | 42.920 | 225.928 |
| Myanmar | 37.000 | 175.000 | - | 212.000 |
| Nepal | 11.120 | 20.000 | 63.870 | 94.990 |
| Afghanistan | 10.000 | - | 4.680 | 14.680 |
| Iran | 10.000 | 1.250 | - | 11.250 |
| Bhutan | 5.500 | - | - | 5.500 |
| Sri Lanka | 5.000 | 5.000 | 2.640 | 12.640 |
| Cambodia | 3.250 | 0.100 | 3.240 | 6.590 |
| Maldives | 2.000 | 1.000 | 0.120 | 3.120 |
| Paraguay | 2.000 | 4.000 | - | 6.000 |
| Nicaragua | 2.000 | - | 1.350 | 3.350 |
| Thailand | 2.000 | - | - | 2.000 |
| Guatemala | 2.000 | - | - | 2.000 |
| UN Peacekeepers | 2.000 | - | - | 2.000 |
| Mongolia | 1.500 | - | - | 1.500 |
| Nigeria | 1.000 | - | 96.660 | 97.660 |
| Mozambique | 1.000 | - | 11.040 | 12.040 |
| Kenya | 1.000 | - | 10.200 | 11.200 |
| Uganda | 1.000 | - | 8.640 | 9.640 |
| Mauritius | 1.000 | 3.000 | - | 4.000 |
| Bahrain | 1.000 | - | - | 1.000 |
| Oman | 1.000 | - | - | 1.000 |
| Fiji | 1.000 | - | - | 1.000 |
| Guyana | 0.800 | - | - | 0.800 |
| Zimbabwe | 0.750 | - | - | 0.750 |

| Dominica | 0.700 | - | - | 0.700 |
|---|---|---|---|---|
| Ivory Coast | 0.500 | 12.000 | 5.040 | 17.540 |
| Ghana | 0.500 | 0.020 | 26.520 | 27.040 |
| Rwanda | 0.500 | 5.000 | 2.400 | 7.900 |
| Malawi | 0.500 | - | 3.600 | 4.100 |
| Jamaica | 0.500 | - | - | 0.500 |
| Suriname | 0.500 | - | - | 0.500 |
| Albania | 0.500 | - | - | 0.500 |
| Netherlands | - | 451.112 | - | 451.112 |
| Australia | - | 93.121 | - | 93.121 |
| Indonesia | - | 90.080 | - | 90.080 |
| Saudi Arabia | - | 45.000 | - | 45.000 |
| Mexico | - | 20.300 | - | 20.300 |
| Syria | - | - | 12.573 | 12.573 |
| South Africa | - | 10.000 | - | 10.000 |

Source: Based on the COVID-19 Update, Ministry of External Affairs website[33]

It should be noted here that vaccine diplomacy is not a new phenomenon, but has been a part of international relations and the advancement of science and health throughout history.[34] For example, when a British scientist discovered the smallpox vaccine in 1798, he offered critical advice to other countries like Russia, Turkey, Spain, Canada and Mexico. In the 1800s, Francophone, Indochina and North African countries worked together to create a network of laboratories that collaborated to produce and administer the French-developed rabies vaccine. Another example is the eradication of the poliovirus which was made possible by international and intersectoral cooperation on vaccines. In the case of COVID-19, however, collaborations were hindered by not only the lack of reliable information from China (which was critical considering that its Wuhan province was ground zero for the pandemic), but also the rise of nationalism on a global scale (that created a vaccine race). Under such conditions, India's pursuit of vaccine diplomacy, which allowed states access to life-saving medication without the added economic burden at a time of intense economic recession, gave the country recognition as a regional and global leader.

### *Situating Vaccine Maitri in India's Foreign Policy*

At the same time, the provision of complimentary vaccines as gifts to India's immediate neighbours opened doors for New Delhi to strengthen partnerships, achieve greater equitable access to vaccines and project itself as a trusted and responsible actor in the region. India's Vaccine Maitri towards the region was rooted in its 'Neighbourhood First' policy, which commits India to forging friendly and mutually beneficial partnerships with its neighbours through joint projects. New Delhi's engagement with its neighbours is based on a "consultative, non-reciprocal and outcome-oriented approach, which focuses on delivering benefits like greater connectivity, improved infrastructure, stronger development cooperation in various sectors area, security and broader people-to-people contacts".[35] Coming as an extension to this, the provision of vaccines further cemented India's position as a net security provider and reaffirmed its status as the 'pharmacy of the world'.

In Bangladesh, public opinion on India had deteriorated owing to New Delhi adopting controversial policies like the Citizenship Amendment Act (CAA), the revocation of the special status granted to Jammu and Kashmir in 2019 and imposition of a communication blackout in the region. Yet, both countries share an all-weather-friendship, built on their historical and civilisational links. For India, Bangladesh is a vital ally in the region; therefore, India's willingness to come to Bangladesh's aid in response to Prime Minister Sheikh Hasina's request was aimed at protecting and bolstering their bilateral strategic partnership by improving India's image amongst the Bangladeshi people. Interestingly, Dhaka's request came after it refused Beijing's offer to purchase the Chinese vaccine, which included a cost-sharing clause.[36] India's massive vaccine supplies to Bangladesh as gifts, therefore, came as an opportunity to regain some goodwill and set the foundations for a solid partnership in the uncertain geopolitical circumstances with China's rise and expanding power.

Similarly, both Nepal and Bhutan were granted a significant number of vaccine doses under India's diplomatic outreach. As India-China relations became increasingly fraught, India-Nepal dynamics also changed and became more complex. Misunderstandings between Delhi and Kathmandu have been accompanied by China's subtle moves to gain greater political sway in the country.[37] India's image in Nepal thus deteriorated rapidly[38] and became one of a self-declared 'superior' power with a "suzerain mentality".[39] Their frictions over the map of the disputed Kalapani region only stirred tensions further.[40] Against this background, India's vaccine diplomacy with Nepal came as a show of good faith to sway negative sentiments and restore New Delhi's image as a responsible and reliable partner, instead of a 'superior' one. To some extent, India's focus on Nepal via its health diplomacy has already resulted in a visible uptick in their relations and an effort from both sides to bring their relations back on track. In April 2022, Nepalese Prime Minister Sher Bahadur Deuba visited India for a three-day trip, along with his spouse and a 50-member delegation, in his first official foreign visit post his election to office for the fifth term.[41] This was also the first visit by a Nepalese leader in over four years (with the last coming in August 2017). Both leaders launched a host of new initiatives, ranging from a cross-border railway network, power transmission line, expanding India's RuPay payment card in Nepal, and Indian private sector's participation in Nepal's hydropower development.[42] Therefore, while 2020 saw one of the lowest points in India-Nepal relations on the boundary issue, and the spread of COVID-19 only led to a hardening of bilateral ties, the post-pandemic period has been characterised by normalisation and drive to uplift their partnership.[43] India's Vaccine Maitri was certainly one factor contributing to this.

Apart from such bilateral outreach, India's health diplomacy in its neighbourhood also extended via regional bodies like the South Asian Association for Regional Cooperation (SAARC). As early as March 2020, Prime Minister Narendra Modi had mobilised SAARC to fashion a regional response; this included New Delhi instituting early exchanges of information and conducting workshops and training courses to bolster capacities. In regular meetings of senior health officials of the SAARC nations, they further "shared the outcome of their deliberations with Prime Minister, who urged a special visa scheme for doctors and nurses, coordinating a regional air ambulance agreement, a platform for studying data on the effectiveness of vaccines and a network for technology-assisted epidemiology for preventing future pandemics."[44]

Strategically, India's leadership moment to coordinate a South Asian response to the pandemic was a way to effectively counter China's own actions in the region, which included tactics like charm offensive (that is, the provision of critical medicines and medical equipment, albeit with strings attached). The India-China rivalry aid their Galwan Valley clash and thus became an important sub-text in India's health diplomacy and regional and global pandemic response. In the earlier months of COVID-19, India overshadowed China as a provider of cheap and accessible drugs, medical equipment and vaccines to the Global South, as well as several richer Western states. India's exchanges with Brazil, Canada, UK, Cambodia and Afghanistan (alongside countries in India's neighbourhood) offered further examples of India's successful health diplomacy. While Indian vaccines beat the Chinese in Cambodia and Afghanistan; countries like Brazil, Canada and the UK, turned to India as China's credibility crisis worsened.[45] As polls showed a majority of Brazilians were unwilling to take China's Sinovac vaccine, President Bolsonaro appealed to India, which responded promptly to the request. He expressed his appreciation by likening India's actions to the Hindu god, Lord Hanuman, delivering *Sanjeevani Booti* (a life-saving herb) to Lanka in Hindu mythology.[46] Similarly, when Canadian Prime Minister Justin Trudeau's appeal for two million doses was delivered within days, he gushed that a global victory over the pandemic would be "because of India's tremendous pharmaceutical capacity, and Prime Minister Modi's leadership in sharing this capacity with the world".[47] Such comments demonstrated how India's vaccine diplomacy had proved to be a resounding strategic success. Most importantly perhaps, India's Vaccine Maitri became a tool to export soft power, as well as a signal that India held the potential to stand as an alternative to China's dominance.

## China's Diplomacy Game Amid the Pandemic

For India, China's rise and growing influence and dominance in India's backyard formed major elements to be factored in considering New Delhi's response, foreign policy and global health diplomacy efforts. Therefore, any discussion on global health diplomacy and India's vaccine diplomacy amid the pandemic necessitates a closer examination of China, not only because it was the epicentre of the health crisis, but also because its tactics and behaviour as the world battled the virus proved to be telling signs of its global designs.

### *The Rise and Fall of China's Wolf Warrior Diplomacy*

While Vaccine Maitri began with the best of intentions, it came to an abrupt pause in late April 2021 when India was struck by the particularly devastating second wave of COVID-19. As the excess death toll rose to over 49 lakh in a matter of months—making the second wave the country's "worst human tragedy since Partition"[48]—the Indian government was forced to prioritise its national health emergency. Several pending orders to countries in the neighbourhood were hence delayed, and a significant number of vaccine doses were imported, as India scrambled to inoculate its own population.[49] This in fact gave Beijing an opportune moment to expand its own vaccine diplomacy efforts and attempt to fill the gap left by India when it was forced to stop deliveries. China has delivered over 183 million doses (compared to India's 201 million doses).[50] Although India's pause led to swift and harsh criticism claiming that the halt displayed India's limited bandwidth, and gave rise to worries that China would gain even greater influence in the region,[51] New Delhi swiftly resumed the Vaccine Maitri program and has continued to provide immense amounts of doses (refer Table 6.1) to countries in its neighbourhood and beyond.

One reason that India sustained its initiative was the utter failure of China's own diplomatic tactics, like 'wolf warrior' diplomacy. In recent years, several countries have borne the brunt of a new type of Chinese diplomacy. Rather than adhering to Deng Xiaoping's 'low profile' doctrine, Xi Jinping's second term in office (since 2017) witnessed a gradual shift to a much more strident, controversial and assertive stance; during COVID-19, this behaviour was termed as 'wolf warrior diplomacy'.[52] The tactics were most apparent on online platforms like Twitter, where Chinese diplomats, led by Ministry of Foreign Affairs spokesperson Zhao Lijian, have dramatically increased their presence and began using as a means to directly engage with the Western governments and the publics. Their messaging included criticism of the US and EU's pandemic policies while praising China's own successful response—which proved to be in particularly bad taste as these countries were ravaged by pandemics and suffering from high death rates. Using clickbait content, viral memes and even panda videos to build a following, Chinese diplomats (or 'wolf warriors') have employed provocation, confrontation and manipulation rather than diplomacy in their online interactions.[53]

However, China's propaganda efforts have received very little traction with Western audiences, which have not found its messaging compelling but have been grossly offended by it. Even as it became a hallmark of China's grand strategy, most countries subject to such tactics have in fact recognised wolf warrior diplomacy as a "belligerent, defensive nationalism that lashes out without heed of consequences".[54] Beijing's adoption of wolf warrior tactics, therefore, came at a cost, as it only served to damage China's reputation and detract from its potential as a global leader, making it more difficult to manage its rise. In fact, by June 2021, President Xi Jinping had already given indications that China was looking to tone down this aggressive approach, even if not entirely abandon it. Calling for better communication, he stated that "[China] should make friends, unite and win the majority, and continuously expand the circle of international public opinion friends who know China and are friendly to China."[55] Nonetheless, despite its attempt to course-correct and moderate its tone, wolf warrior behaviour did considerable and lasting damage to China's standing among even the friendlier European states as well as regional partners (including Australia and New Zealand). Notably, India's vaccine diplomacy was based on the belief that the pandemic was a global problem requiring a collective response, and a sign that New Delhi was prepared to take on greater responsibility as a prominent state in the emerging multipolar world. In stark contrast, China's COVID-19 policy was calculated and self-serving, aimed primarily at expanding its soft power and influence.

### *Xi's Health Silk Road Post-Pandemic*

China's health diplomacy in the region was conducted primarily via its Health Silk Road (HSR), which has long been a part of its Belt and Road Initiative (BRI). Especially prominent in the Mekong and Southeast Asian region, the HSR primarily involves bilateral and multilateral cooperation in the healthcare sector. While most of Beijing's (and indeed the BRI recipient countries') focus was directed toward the development of physical connectivity infrastructure pre-pandemic, COVID-19 kickstarted intensive focus on HSR. Beijing began viewing it as a tool to strengthen its health diplomacy with strategic regional partners, and bolster its role in medical supply chains and regional and global health governance frameworks.[56] In other words, the pandemic has brought about an expansion of the HSR, which is likely aimed at improving the damage caused to the country's reputation by the wolf warrior diplomatic tactics and thereby demonstrating its capacity to become a global leader. As vaccine diplomacy gradually becomes an instituted part of HSR, India and its like-minded partner countries must recalculate their own regional strategies to ensure they can balance China's health diplomacy.

## India's Leadership Opportunity in the Indo-Pacific

In recognition of China's ardent efforts to gain ground in the region, India has quickly expanded its own collaboration with Quad partners US, Japan and Australia. The Quad was borne out of the 2004 tsunami in South Asia, when the four countries came together in an ad hoc setting to display excellent cooperation in helping crisis-struck states. In March 2021, the Quad held its first virtual leaders' summit, which resulted in their first joint statement and the launch of three initiatives—foremost among them a Vaccine Expert Working Group. They pledged to join hands to expand "safe, affordable, and effective vaccine production and equitable access" in the Indo-Pacific.[57] This would be in close cooperation with the WHO and the COVAX program. The vaccine expert group was practical pathway to implement this effective and equitable vaccine distribution goal.

Within just a year, the Quad programme has already demonstrated success. In February 2022, a Quad joint statement announced that under their vaccine partnership, the four states had already delivered 500 million (of a total of 1.3 billion pledged) vaccine doses collectively.[58] As of mid-May 2022, the partnership has delivered 79 million doses and US$ 894 million in financial and technical support.[59] Notably, India stands as an integral part of this Quad endeavour as a major producer and contributor to the COVAX programme. Working with its partner states, New Delhi is now focusing on expanding production at its Biological E Ltd facility, with the goal of manufacturing 1 billion doses by 2022 end. In addition to vaccine production, the partnership also involves training of healthcare personnel, information campaigns to tackle the growing problem of vaccine hesitancy, bolstering public healthcare infrastructure (including cold chain systems), as well as last-mile vaccine delivery to ensure coverage of hard-to-reach states and communities in the Indo-Pacific.[60] In this context, a major part of the Quad partnership is to 'Build Back Better Health Security'—which follows the G-7's 'Build Back Better World' initiative—as it looks to bolster health security coordination in the Indo-Pacific. This includes organising Quad pandemic preparedness exercises, improving science and technology collaborations to ensure future diagnostics and vaccines within 100 days, launching additional centres for vaccine trials, enhancing viral genomic surveillance by working with WHO, and supporting regional states in their augmenting their capacity to undertake sound research.[61]

While obviously massively useful, the global COVAX programme has proved to be insufficient in its goal of ensuring equitable access to vaccines, especially for low to middle-income states. During the COVID-19 pandemic, vaccine nationalism displayed just how complicated it was to achieve vaccine equity when rich countries were hoarding doses, often in excess of their immediate needs. This has translated to a vast gap in vaccination rates by country income level. While approximately 80 per cent of the populations in high and upper-middle-income countries have received at least one vaccination dose, in low-income countries this number stands at only 17 per cent.[62] In some poor states, this number is astonishingly low, like Burundi (0.1 per cent), Democratic Republic of Congo (0.9 per cent), Haiti (1.6 per cent), and Yemen (2.3 per cent).[63]

In taking the onus to export millions of vaccine doses against the vaccine nationalism trend, India clearly established itself as a leader. Now, to capitalise on the goodwill that India earned and to balance China's HSR, it is critical that New Delhi continue its health diplomacy in the region. The Quad Vaccine (and Health) Partnership is one format for this. The Indo-Pacific region is home to low to middle-income countries. Through the support of its Quad partners—such as with the ongoing project in which Quad states are supporting India's efforts to significantly expand its vaccine production capacity—India can continue to grow its health diplomacy outreach. Such outreach would focus on not only equitable and last-mile vaccine delivery but also on supporting public healthcare infrastructures and science and technology cooperation with small states in the Indo-Pacific. The aim will be to ensure India (in cooperation with the Quad) can establish itself as a leader and responsible power in the emerging multipolar world order. In other words, the pandemic was an inflexion point for India to consider its leadership potential. The challenge now is to sustain and expand such outreach to realise this potential and rebrand India as a global leader.

## Notes

1. Ensheng Dong, Hongru Du and Lauren Gardner, "An Interactive web-based dashboard to track COVID-19 in real time," *The Lancet Infectious Diseases* 20, no. 5 (2020): 533-534, at https://doi.org/10.1016/S1473-3099(20)30120-1 [at https://ourworldindata.org/grapher/cumulative-covid-deaths-region.] Accessed on February 3, 2022.
2. Ibid.
3. See Rajesh Bansal, et al., "Recovery, Resilience and Adaptation: India From 2020 to 2030," working paper, New Delhi: Carnegie India, September 2020, at https://carnegieendowment.org/files/Chaudhuri_et_al_-_Recovery_Resilience_and_Adaptation_v2.pdf. Accessed on February 3, 2022.
4. Paul Blake and Divyanshi Wadhwa, "2020 Year in Review: The impact of COVID-19 in 12 charts," World Bank, at https://blogs.worldbank.org/voices/2020-year-review-impact-covid-19-12-charts. Accessed on February 4, 2022.
5. Colin Kahl and Thomas Wright, *Aftershocks: Pandemic Politics and the End of the Old International Order* United Kingdom: St. Martin's Publishing Group, 2021.
6. Gita Gopinath, "The Great Lockdown: Worst Economic Downturn Since the Great Depression," IMF Blog, April 14, 2020, at https://blogs.imf.org/2020/04/14/the-great-lockdown-worst-economic-downturn-since-the-great-depression/. Accessed on February 4, 2022.
7. Zongyun Li, Panteha Farmanesh, Dervis Kirikkaleli and Rania Itani, "A comparative analysis of COVID-19 and global financial crises: evidence from US economy," *Economic Research-Ekonomska Istraživanja* (2021): 1-15, at https://doi.org/10.1080/1331677X.2021.1952640. Accessed on February 7, 2022.
8. Kemal Dervis and Sebastian Strauss, *Global governance after COVID-19: Survey report.* Washington DC: Brookings Institution, July 2021, at https://www.brookings.edu/research/global-governance-after-covid-19/. Accessed on February 7, 2022.
9. Manqing Cheng, "The Impact of COVID-19 on Patterns of International Relations and the World Order," *The Dig*, accessed May 4, 2022, at https://thedig.nz/transitional-diplomacy/the-impact-of-covid-19-on-patterns-of-international-relations-and-the-world-order/.

10. Kahl and Wright, *Aftershocks,* n. 5.
11. Sanaz Taghizade, Vijay Kumar Chattu, Ebrahim Jaafaripooyan and Sebastian Kevany, "COVID-19 Pandemic as an Excellent Opportunity for Global Health Diplomacy," *Frontier Public Health,* July 12, 2021, at https://doi.org/10.3389/fpubh.2021.655021. Accessed on May 2, 2022. Also see WHO, *Policy Brief Health Diplomacy,* policy brief, World Health Organization, 2014, at https://applications.emro.who.int/docs/Policy_Brief_2014_EN_15340.pdf?ua=1&ua=1&ua=1&ua=1&ua=1&ua=1. Accessed on May 2, 2022.
12. Ibid.
13. See Nippun Gupta, Bawa Singh, Jaspal Kaur, Sandeep Singh, and Vijay K. Chattu, "COVID-19 Pandemic and Reimagination of Multilateralism through Global Health Diplomacy," Sustainability 13, no. 20 (2021): 11551, at https://doi.org/10.3390/su132011551. Accessed on May 2, 2022.
14. ANI, "UNSC uses 3-D virtual diplomacy for the first time, says report," *Business Standard,* January 22, 2022, at https://www.business-standard.com/article/news-ani/unsc-uses-3-d-virtual-diplomacy-for-the-first-time-122012100219_1.html. Accessed on May 2, 2022.
15. Taghizade, Chattu, Jaafaripooyan and Kevany, n. 11.
16. Ibid.
17. Ibid.
18. See Ahmed Abdelnaby Diab, Abdelmonem Metwally and Mostafa Mohamed, "The Failure of Global Leadership and Accountability Problems during the COVID-19 Pandemic," *Academy of Strategic Management Journal* 20, no. 3 (May 2021): 1-8, at https://www.researchgate.net/publication/351849394_The_failure_of_global_leadership_and_accountability_problems_during_the_covid-19_pandemic. Accessed on May 2, 2022; Tom Wilson and David Pilling, "WHO chief says lack of global leadership has prolonged pandemic," *Financial Times,* October 12, 2020, at https://www.ft.com/content/972b3194-45fc-4635-bb42-39ac9f3d1616. Accessed on May 2, 2022; David Miliband, interview by Scott Simon, "WHO Report Calls Pandemic 'Preventable Disaster,' Calls Out Lack of Global Leadership," NPR, May 15, 2021, at https://www.npr.org/2021/05/15/997105728/who-report-calls-pandemic-preventable-disaster-calls-out-lack-of-global-leadersh. Accessed on May 2, 2022. For research on the importance of political leadership to mitigate the impact of COVID-19, see Ziad A. Memish, Shahul H. Ebrahim, Rana F. Kattan, Abdulrahman Alharthy, Saleh A. Alqahtani and Dimitrios Karakitsos, "Leadership to prevent COVID-19: is it the most important mitigation factor?," *Travel Medicine and Infectious Disease,* no. 38 (November-December 2020), at https://doi.org/10.1016/j.tmaid.2020.101925. Accessed on May 2, 2022.
19. Thomas J. Bollyky and Chad P. Bown, "The Tragedy of Vaccine Nationalism: Only Cooperation Can End the Pandemic," *Foreign Affairs* 99, no. 5 (September/October

2020): 97, at https://www.wto.org/english/tratop_e/trips_e/techsymp_290621/bown_pres2.pdf. Accessed on May 3, 2022.

20. Amir Khan, "What is 'vaccine nationalism' and why is it so harmful?," *Al Jazeera,* February 7, 2021, at https://www.aljazeera.com/features/2021/2/7/what-is-vaccine-nationalism-and-why-is-it-so-harmful. Accessed on May 3, 2022.
21. Ewen Callaway, "The unequal scramble for coronavirus vaccines—by the numbers," *Nature* 584 (2020): 506-507, at https://doi.org/10.1038/d41586-020-02450-x. Accessed on May 3, 2022.
22. Ibid.
23. Bollyky and Bown, n. 18.
24. Ministry of External Affairs, "Supply of Indian manufactured vaccines to neighbouring countries and key parnters," press release, Government of India, January 19, 2021, at https://www.mea.gov.in/press-releases.htm?dtl/33399/Supply_of_Indian_manufactured_vaccines_to_neighbouring_and_key_partner_countries. Accessed on May 3, 2022.
25. S. Jaishankar, "Statement by External Affairs Minister in Rajya Sabha on the Vaccine Maitri Initiative," speech, Ministry of External Affairs, Government of India, March 17, 2021, at https://www.mea.gov.in/Speeches-Statements.htm?dtl/33653/. Accessed on May 3, 2022.
26. See IANS, "India is now being called 'pharmacy of the world', says PM Modi," *Business Standard,* November 18, 2021, at https://www.business-standard.com/article/current-affairs/india-is-now-being-called-pharmacy-of-the-world-says-pm-modi-121111801288_1.html. Accessed on May 3, 2022.
27. "Why is India the Pharmacy of the World?," *Financial Express,* September 25, 2021, at https://www.financialexpress.com/lifestyle/health/why-is-india-the-pharmacy-of-the-world/2337554/. Accessed on May 3, 2022.
28. Biswajit Dhar, "India's Vaccine Diplomacy," *Global Policy,* April 8, 2021, at https://www.globalpolicyjournal.com/blog/08/04/2021/indias-vaccine-diplomacy. Accessed on May 4, 2022.
29. Abdulkader Puranwala, "Covid-19 vaccine update," *India Equities, Bloomberg Quint,* December 3, 2020, at https://images.assettype.com/bloombergquint/2020-12/c8d891f5-e8b7-4ae3-acbd-e6697bcf70a4/Anand_Rathi_Covid_19_Vaccine_Update.pdf. Accessed on May 4, 2022.
30. See Khan Sharun and Kuldeep Dham, "India's role in COVID-19 vaccine diplomacy," *Journal of Travel Medicine* 28, no. 7 (2021), at https://doi.org/10.1093/jtm/taab064. Accessed on May 4, 2022.
31. Jyoti Sharma and S K Varshney, "India's vaccine diplomacy aids global access to COVID-19 jabs," *Nature India,* February 17, 2021, at https://doi.org/10.1038/nindia.2021.31. Accessed on May 4, 2022.

32. IANS, "India is now being called 'pharmacy of the world', says PM Modi," n. 25.
33. "COVID-19 Updates: Vaccine Supply," Ministry of External Affairs, Government of India, updated April 27, 2022, at https://www.mea.gov.in/vaccine-supply.htm. Accessed on May 4, 2022.
34. Sharma and Varshney, n. 31.
35. V. Muraleedharan, "Question No. 3692 Neighbourhood First Policy," answer of the Minister of State in the Ministry to External Affairs to Rajya Sabha unstarred Question No. 3692, Ministry of External Affairs, Government of India, July 25, 2019, at https://mea.gov.in/rajya-sabha.htm?dtl/31673/QUESTION+NO3692+NEIGHBOURHOOD+FIRST+POLICY. Accessed on May 4, 2022.
36. Sohini Bose, "Bangladesh: Navigating Diplomacy Challenges in Search for Vaccines," ORF, June 15, 2021, at https://www.orfonline.org/research/the-dynamics-of-vaccine-diplomacy-in-indias-neighbourhood/. Accessed on May 4, 2022.
37. Vijay Gokhle, "India's Fog of Misunderstanding Surrounding Nepal-China Relations," Carnegie India, October 4, 2021, at https://carnegieindia.org/2021/10/04/india-s-fog-of-misunderstanding-surrounding-nepal-china-relations-pub-85416. Accessed on May 4, 2022.
38. Wu Zhaoli, "India's Promotion of BBIN Sub-Regional Cooperation: Aspirations and Challenges," *China International Studies* 64 (2017): 96, at https://heinonline.org/HOL/LandingPage?handle=hein.journals/chintersd64&div=8&id=&page=. Accessed on May 5, 2022.
39. Buddhi Prasad Sharma, "China-Nepal Relations: A Cooperative Partnership in Slow Motion," *China Quarterly of International Strategic Studies* 4, no. 3 (2018): 439-445, at https://doi.org/10.1142/S2377740018500239. Accessed on May 5, 2022.
40. See Sohini Nayak, "India and Nepal's Kalapani border dispute: An explainer," issue brief no. 356, ORF, April 2020, at https://www.orfonline.org/wp-content/uploads/2020/04/ORF_IssueBrief_356_India-Nepal-Kalapani.pdf. Accessed on May 10, 2022.
41. ANI, "Nepal PM Deuba embarks on first official visit to India," *The Print,* April 1, 2022, at https://theprint.in/world/nepal-pm-deuba-embarks-on-first-official-visit-to-india/898063/. Accessed on May 10, 2022.
42. PTI, "India-Nepal sign four pacts to expand cooperation, vow to strengthen bilateral ties," *The Print,* April 2, 2022, at https://theprint.in/india/india-nepal-sign-four-pacts-to-expand-cooperation-vow-to-strengthen-bilateral-ties/899169/. Accessed on May 10, 2022.
43. Hari Bansh Jha, "Nepal-India relations in post-COVID-19 period," Observer Research Foundation, January 10, 2022, at https://www.orfonline.org/expert-speak/nepal-india-relations-in-post-covid-19-period/. Accessed on May 10, 2022.

44. S. Jaishankar, "Statement by External Affairs Minister in Rajya Sabha on the Vaccine Maitri Initiative," Ministry of External Affairs, Government of India, March 17, 2021, at https://www.mea.gov.in/Speeches-Statements.htm?dtl/33653/. Accessed on May 10, 2022.
45. Shashi Tharoor, "India's Smart Vaccine Diplomacy," Project Syndicate, March 11, 2021, at https://www.project-syndicate.org/commentary/india-covid19-vaccine-diplomacy-by-shashi-tharoor-2021-03.
46. "Covid-19: Brazil president thanks India for 'sanjeevani booti' vaccines, tweets image of Hanuman," Scroll, January 2021, at https://scroll.in/latest/984892/coronavirus-brazilian-president-thanks-india-for-vaccines-pm-modi-says-honour-is-ours.
47. Prime Minister's Office, "PM receives a telephone call from H.E. Justin Trudeau, Prime Minister of Canada," press release ID 1696957, Press Information Bureau, February 10, 2021, at https://pib.gov.in/PressReleasePage.aspx?PRID=1696957. Accessed on May 10, 2022.
48. Sneha Mordani, "2nd Covid wave was India's worst tragedy since Partition, saw up to 49 lakh excess deaths: Report," *India Today,* July 21, 2021, at https://www.indiatoday.in/coronavirus-outbreak/story/2nd-covid-wave-was-india-worst-tragedy-since-partition-saw-up-to-49-lakh-excess-deaths-1830894-2021-07-21. Accessed on May 11, 2022.
49. Krishna Das and Neha Arora, "India Shifts From Mass Vaccine Exporter to Importer, Worrying the World," *The Wire,* April 14, 2021, at https://science.thewire.in/health/india-shifts-from-mass-vaccine-exporter-to-importer-worrying-the-world/. Accessed on May 11, 2022.
50. For data on China's vaccine diplomacy, see "China COVID-19 Vaccine Tracker," Bridge Beijing, accessed May 14, 2022, at https://bridgebeijing.com/our-publications/our-publications-1/china-covid-19-vaccines-tracker/.
51. Anuttama Banerji, "India's Flawed Vaccine Diplomacy," South Asian Voices Project, Stimson Centre, June 25, 2021, at https://www.stimson.org/2021/indias-flawed-vaccine-diplomacy/. Accessed on May 12, 2022.
52. See Peter Martin, "Understanding Chinese 'Wolf Warrior Diplomacy'," interview by Joanna Nawrotkiewicz, The National Bureau of Asian Research, October 22, 2021, at https://www.nbr.org/publication/understanding-chinese-wolf-warrior-diplomacy/. Accessed on May 12, 2022.
53. Jessica Brandt and Bret Schafer, "How China's 'wolf warrior' diplomats use and abuse Twitter," Brookings, October 28, 2020, at https://www.brookings.edu/techstream/how-chinas-wolf-warrior-diplomats-use-and-abuse-twitter/. Accessed on May 12, 2022.
54. Sulmaan Wasif Khan, "Wolf Warriors Killed China's Grand Strategy," *Foreign Policy,* May 28, 2021, at https://foreignpolicy.com/2021/05/28/china-grand-strategy-wolf-warrior-nationalism/. Accessed on May 12, 2022.

55. Shi Jiangtao and Laura Zhou, "Xi Jinping wants isolated China to 'make friends and win over the majority'," *South China Morning Post,* June 2, 2021, at https://www.scmp.com/news/china/diplomacy/article/3135672/xi-jinping-wants-isolated-china-make-friends-and-win-over. Accessed on May 13, 2022.
56. Atmaja Gohain Baruah, "China's Health Diplomacy: Taking Forward the Health Silk Road," Institute for Security and Development Policy, September 2021, at https://isdp.eu/content/uploads/2021/09/Chinas-Health-Diplomacy-Taking-Forward-the-Health-Silk-Road-in-Southeast-Asia-FA-03.09.21.pdf. Accessed on May 13, 2022.
57. "Quad Leaders' Joint Statement: "The Spirit of the Quad"," press release, The White House, March 12, 2021, at https://www.whitehouse.gov/briefing-room/statements-releases/2021/03/12/quad-leaders-joint-statement-the-spirit-of-the-quad/. Accessed on May 13, 2022.
58. "Joint statement by the Foreign Ministers of Australia, India and Japan and the Secretary of State of the United States following the 4th Quad Foreign Ministers' Meeting," press release, Ministry of External Affairs, Government of India, February 11, 2022, at https://mea.gov.in/bilateral-documents.htm?dtl/34854/Joint+statement+by+the+Foreign+Ministers+of+Australia+India+and+Japan+and+the+Secretary+of+State+of+the+United+States+following+the+4th+Quad+Foreign+Ministers+Meeting. Accessed on May 13, 2022.
59. "Quad Country COVID-19 Response in Indo-Pacific Region—Beta Dashboard," US Aid, accessed May 14, 2022, at https://share.usaid.gov/views/QUADCountryCOVID-19ResponseDashboard/Indo-PacificRegionOverview?%3AshowAppBanner=false&%3Adisplay_count=n&%3AshowVizHome=n&%3Aorigin=viz_share_link&%3AisGuestRedirectFromVizportal=y&%3Aembed=y. Accessed on May 13, 2022.
60. "Joint statement by the Foreign Ministers of Australia, India and Japan and the Secretary of State of the United States following the 4th Quad Foreign Ministers' Meeting," n. 58.
61. "Fact Sheet: Quad Leaders' Summit," press release, The White House, September 24, 2021, at https://www.whitehouse.gov/briefing-room/statements-releases/2021/09/24/fact-sheet-quad-leaders-summit/. Accessed on May 13, 2022.
63. Josh Holder, "Tracking Coronavirus Vaccinations Around the World," *The New York Times,* May 11, 2022, at https://www.nytimes.com/interactive/2021/world/covid-vaccinations-tracker.html. Accessed on May 13, 2022.
63. Ibid.

# 7

# On the Fly: Israeli Air Power and India's Options

ANU SHARMA

## Introduction

The West Asian security scenario is changing and with it, there are emerging new alliances between old adversaries and new partners. However, the persisting threats and challenges in the region have forced Israel to develop its military-industrial complex to an unbeatable capacity not only in West Asia but also globally. In all of this Israeli Air Force's role and responsibility becomes prominent to protect the parameters of the nation threatened for its existence and survival. Since its conception, the Israeli Air Force has fought overwhelming odds to protect the state of Israel from its many adversaries in the West Asian region. In assessing the role of Israeli defence and air strategies Israeli Defence Force's (IDF) becomes quite significant. In the initial years after the formation of the Israeli state, IDF's operational doctrine assigned a limited role to air power. At that time, the scarce resources and abilities raised the issues of utilisation of air power and the role it should play in its operational doctrine. Israel's new doctrine further enhances the role of its air power with the aim to maintain its air superiority. The purpose for this has been to have a much greater impact on the land battle than in the past. Keeping this in mind, the Israeli Defence Forces (IDF) through its various doctrines has been trying to bolster Israeli air superiority. In this context, the aim of this paper is to assess the role of Israeli air power in the context of IDF and further speculate and understand the performance of its air power and whether the emerging scenarios has resulted in the shift in

Israeli air strategies in the past few years. It should be kept in my that Israel's possible involvement in nuclear, biological or chemical warfare scenarios have been kept out of the scope of this research and therefore this paper largely discusses conventional battlefield.

In all of Israel's defence and military superiority role of the United States cannot be ignored. Israel's alliance with the United States is one of the mainstays of former's national security and in this scenario, diminishing influence and engagement of the United States in the West Asian region could result in weakened Israel—and unlikely but probable scenario. This is significant in context of American support to maintain Israel's qualitative military edge in a way assuring access to the cutting-edge American industries and technologies. So, Israel's advanced defense force, well-established deterrence capabilities and American strategic support reinforce its security posture in the West Asian region.[1] Added to this is the digital transformation of the IDF with respect to Artificial Intelligence (AI) in its divisions and commands. This will be the nascent step taken by the IDF by drawing up a multifaceted plan through the utilisation of AI. This is due to IDF's belief mechanism wherein data and AI play a crucial role in winning future conflicts. This they plan to go through processing the massive data being generated by countless sensors and converting it into comprehensible information in the requisite departments and divisions.[2] In this context the sections below will discuss in detail Israeli threat perception, and its air power capabilities with detailed discussions related to its missile and drone inventories. One of the sections also discusses India-Israel defence trade specifically in terms of aircraft and munitions.

## Israeli Threat Perception

The threats faced by Israel have made a significant impact on conscripting and conduct of its national security policy in the West Asian region. The historical factors, along with religio-political ideology have had a profound effect on Israel's security policy. For this reason, there remain minimal alterations and variations in its security policy vis-à-vis its internal, regional or international changes. Nonetheless, there can be shifts in threats and threat perceptions. These can include regime changes, conception of new alliances, alterations in the international system, and treaties signed during war and peace times wherein all these factors can alter the regional balance. This all seems very plausible in the case of West Asia which is also considered as one of the most volatile regions of the world. These changes in threats and threat perceptions reflect on the national security policies and the strategic doctrine of any nation-state. It can be said that in the West Asian region, Israel can be considered to be a small nation within the large group of hostile neighbours of this region till the past few years which has become the primary factor of Israel's post-conflictual regional security perceptions. Furthermore, this threat perception of the Israelis is not only related to Arab hostility but also the vulnerability of the Israeli society to these threat perceptions. The ideas related to their disadvantage vis-à-vis their strategic depth in the West Asian North African (WANA) region, comparative low population, perils of being continuously being engaged in wars, global dependence for their energy security and sustain its economy through these also factor in Israeli strategic doctrine. Therefore, these issues related to Israeli vulnerability have had considerable direct repercussions on their security perceptions.

Threat perception can be defined as a situation or circumstance in which an actor or a group has either the ability or purpose to inflict negative consequences on another actor or the group. In international relations, threats can be from collectives also in the form of (1) military threats, (2) economic threats, or (3) cultural threats.[3] Both classical realists such as Gulick and structural realists such as Kenneth Waltz argue that threats result due to power asymmetries. In case, the neighbouring nation is comparatively more powerful there are chances that the smaller or less powerful nation might feel threatened due to the risk factor. This is because in the anarchical international system there is not anything that restrains any nation from using force against the other nation in order to resolve a conflict.[4] This seems true in the case of Israel's struggle with its neighbours in the WANA region. This results in nations to depend on their domestic military expenditure and international alliances to counterbalance the power of other nations. Another theoretical concept which defines the concepts of threat perceptions is the realistic conflict theory. It is corresponding to realism in international relations wherein the power (or resource) asymmetries are often the underlying reason for conflict amongst nations or groups of nations. The theory argues that the "real" conflicts are related to material resources. In this theory, it is often argued that when power amongst the group of nations is disproportionate then both the actors in the asymmetric association may result in uncertainty and vulnerability. In such circumstances, there are chances that the weaker nation can become anxious about their exploitation and in such a scenario the weaker nation may become aggrieved about their inferiority. However, opposite to that, the stronger nation may feel apprehension about the unavoidable shift in the balance of power in the long term which might result in challenging the status quo.[5]

According to Raymond Cohen, the notion of threat should be comprehended as the anticipation by the leader/decision-maker—of looming risks (generally military, strategic or economic threats) for a nation.[6] However, theorist Dean G Pruitt argues that the threat perception is influenced "mostly" by "predispositions" which are derived from such sources as distrust, past experiences, contingency planning and personal anxiety.[7] However, there have been new inclusions of in this paradigm of security threats in the recent years which are mainly non-military threats such as threats from the non-state actors (such as international terrorism) organised crime, pandemics, natural disasters, drug and human trafficking, etc. all these non-traditional security threats have made the nations to take steps to counter these new forms of challenges.[8] All these factors included have increased the threat perceptions of the Israeli state adding to the threats and challenges that this nation faces. If globalisation has been responsible for the changing role of the nation-state which in turn has been responsible for the shift in the conceptualisation of national security. Therefore, these kinds of non-state threats have driven the nations to look for options in order to defend themselves from these existing transnational threats.[9] In this aspect, theorist Keith Krause contends that there is no denying the fact that the role of the state has expanded due to various securitisation issues as well as looming non-traditional threats.

In case of Israel, the majority of its threat perception is also related to its geographical positioning in the region. Israel shares several kilometres of land borders with Lebanon, Syria, Jordan and Egypt (Maps 7.1 & 7.2). Israel also shares its borders with the West Bank and Gaza Strip. However, most of these boundaries are disputed by Israel. Israel's perceived threat also emanates from being surrounded by the Arab neighbours. So, as mentioned above, Israel's security perception is not restricted to the threats to its peoples, territory and assets; however, it is also related to its existence as a nation-state. Even though Israel had formalised its borders with Egypt and Jordan following the peace treaties in 1979 and 1994 respectively; but its border dispute with Syria is complex due to various past events. In case of Israel's geographical positioning, the significance of Golan Heights and other disputed territories is enhanced as it acts as a buffer zone for Israel (Map 7.1). However, the most complex and persisting border dispute of Israel is with Palestine which is mostly related to the Jewish settlements. There are approximately 1,90,000 Jewish settlers (242 settlements) in the West Bank, almost 5,000 (25 settlements) in the Gaza Strip and around 1,80,000 (29 settlements) in East Jerusalem (Map 7.1).[10]

**Map 7.1: Map of Israel**

Source: https://www.nationsonline.org/oneworld/map/israel_map2.htm. Accessed on November 28, 2021.

There is an issue of strategic depth that Israel faces in terms of geography which can become more challenging in case of war on its own territories having pernicious repercussions. In this context, Israeli war doctrine has been more focussed on pre-emptive actions and fighting war in the territory of the aggressor. Furthermore, Israeli war doctrine underlines the removal of the potential causes of war. In this list, included are the blockade of Israeli freedom of navigation in the Strait of Tiran, procurement or manufacture of a nuclear bomb by any West Asian nation and the militarisation of the Sinai Peninsula (Map 7.2). Even though Israel boasts of a strong military capability; still the collective strength of its existing and potential adversaries in the region cannot be ignored. In all of this, it definitely enjoys the qualitative military edge vis-à-vis its neighbours; however, the acquisition of modern arms and strategic weapon systems like long-range ballistic missiles by various West Asian nations can become an unending challenge for Israel.[11]

**Map 7.2: Israel and the Sinai Peninsula**

Source: https://worldview.stratfor.com/article/egypt-israel-and-sinai-peninsula. Accessed on November 29, 2021.

There are some emerging threats to Israel arising from the shifting global geopolitical changes and long-term changes of the major powers (such as the United States, Russia, China and the United Kingdom) in the West Asian region. Russian manoeuvrings in West Asia along with the rising economic power of China is concurring with the American reticence to engage in the region. This, in turn, is upending the structure of regional and global politics in Israel's neighbourhood. With the Obama administration's move to reduce the American commitments in the region has become a challenge for Israel, wherein the United States can be regarded as the top security and armament supplier to Israel. The declining interests of the United States in the West Asian region has, in turn, become an opportunity for both China and Russia in the region.[12] Many analysts claim that Israeli threat perception emanates not only from its immediate neighbours but also from other West Asian nations, for instance, Iraq. Iraq once posed a grave threat to not only Israel but other nations in the region also; however, in case of Israel, the long-standing threat from Iran is a bigger one, especially in terms of its long-range missile capabilities and clandestine nuclear weapons programme.

So, it can be said that till the past few years, the spectre of acquisition of nuclear, biological and chemical weapons by Israel's adversaries was not implausible, bearing in mind their easy availability since the disintegration of the Soviet Union.[13] So in the tumultuous West Asian region, even though there are visibly several pillars of Israel's successes. However, the change of leadership in Israel, the United States and Israel's prime adversary in the region i.e., Iran, has resulted in shifts in the regional and global scenarios with the culmination of new alliances in the region along with the emergence of new threats and risks which can become impending challenges for Israel's security in the near future. In some instances, swift and decisive changes in policy are in order. To discuss this in detail, the following sections will discuss Israeli strategic doctrine along with its contemporary military capabilities. Any nation-state including Israel faces threats to its civilian infrastructure vulnerable to precision-guided attacks. These include civilian ports, power plants, desalination plants, offshore drilling facilities, gas terminals at the coast, etc. In case of Israel, it can also include its major water supply pipelines, canals and tributaries as well as major storage facilities for harmful materials. Furthermore, military installations are also susceptible to similar attacks including major airbases, naval facilities, major personnel staging grounds, and particularly nuclear facilities. In such a scenario, nations develop and acquire technologies to counter these emerging threats. In case of Israel in West Asia, it is altering the region in ways that hasn't been witnessed in the past.

***Israel-Hamas-Hezbollah Conflict:*** Israel faces considerable threats to its security from Hamas and Hezbollah. Israel is fighting a multi-dimensional war in the region with Hezbollah in Lebanon and with Palestinian-backed Hamas in Gaza strip. However, the alleged support of Iran and Syria to Hezbollah has added another complexity to the conflict. This has also indicated the rising influence of the non-state actors through political movements/ terrorist organisations in a way affecting the internal and external security of Israel. Neither of these organisations recognises Israel's right to exist as a nation-state.[14] Hamas[15] was formed at the beginning of the first Palestinian *Intifada* (or uprising), against Israel's annexation of the West Bank and Gaza Strip. Since then, it has been carrying out its attacks against Israeli targets. Eventually, Hamas started acting independently of the Palestinian organisations leading to hostility between Hamas and its secular nationalist counterparts. A few years later after its formation, Hamas experienced restructuring to strengthen its command structure and position its key leaders beyond Israel's clutches. Since its formation, Hamas had rejected peace negotiations between Israel and Palestine rejecting that it would cede any land. In 2007, Hamas gained control of the Gaza Strip leading Israel to declare the Gaza Strip a hostile region. Following this, Israel initiated sanctions on Gaza Strip which included power cuts, heavily restricted trade and border restrictions. Hamas attacks on Israel have been continuing as did Israeli attacks on the Gaza Strip. In the past few years, the tensions between Hamas and the Palestinian Authority are rising with Palestinian Authority's diminishing control in the West Bank. On the other hand, Hamas and another organization known as Islamic Jihad are intensifying their attacks against Israelis. These attacks are destroying Palestinian Authority's control there along with mounting public discontentment with the latter. It appears that the internal politics between Hamas and other non-state actors in the West Bank region have increased the tension within Hamas, resulting in stiffening its violent actions towards Israel.[16]

Another significant of Israel's non-state adversaries is Hezbollah. Hezbollah is a Shi'ite Muslim political party and militant group based in Lebanon. The organisation was formed during the fifteen yearlong Lebanese civil war, this group is motivated by its hostility towards Israel and its resistance to the Western influence in the West Asian region. In the past, due to its long-standing alliances with Iran and Syria have transformed it into an effective military force.[17] Israel is Hezbollah's major enemy owing to Israeli occupation of Southern Lebanon in 1978. In August 2021, Hezbollah had fired several rockets in retaliation to Israeli air strikes in Lebanon. This was also the first time that Hezbollah claimed responsibility for any such attack on Israel since the Israel-Hezbollah War in 2006.[18] In the few years, Hezbollah has used sophisticated anti-ship and anti-armour weapons in its attacks on Israel. More often than not, it was stated in Western sources that these modern arms and ammunitions and sophisticated weaponry were supplied by Iran to Hezbollah. Hezbollah is now in quest of converting its huge reserve of rockets and missiles as precision weapons with greater capability. In fact, it is being purported that precision weaponry is being supplied to Hezbollah by Iran with the aim of it becoming an increasingly dangerous threat to Israel.[19] Hezbollah already has an estimated 150,000 rockets and missiles in its stockpile. All these weapon systems are intended for attacks on Israel. Hezbollah accreted valuable tactical experience in Syrian war which it is utilising against Israel.[20] The conversion of Hezbollah's rocket and missile stocks indicates an unprecedented threat to Israel.

## Israeli Air Power Capabilities

The initial years after the conception of the Israeli state saw the confusion related to the role of the Israeli Air Force in its doctrine and strategy. It will be correct to say that Israel acquired air superiority in the intermittent Arab-Israeli wars fought since the six-day war it fought in 1967. However, since then Israel has acquired air superiority through its wide-ranging defence manufacturing and acquisitions. This has also immensely contributed to nation's national security architecture which even the air powers of major Arab nations have been able to impede. In the past two decades, Israel's air superiority as compared to other adversaries in the West Asian region or adjacent regions has increased considerably. It already boasts of its massive edge in air-to-air combat capabilities with introduction of better intelligence and battel management systems further strengthened by inclusion of aircraft, missiles and missile defence systems. The latter has been upgraded considerably in the past decade eventually providing Israel with a security cover from enemy aircraft.

Also known as *Hel Avir* in Hebrew which means meaning "Air Corps" is considered as one of the most powerful air forces globally. Israeli Air Force has played a significant role in achieving major military victories for Israel since its creation. It will right to say that in the present circumstances, Israeli Air Force is the key component of IDF playing a substantial role in deterring threats and ensuring Israel's strategic advantage during conflicts. Israeli Air Force is made up of squadrons and commands that play a variety of roles in defending both Israel's borders as well as home front. The selected few pilots graduate from the Israeli Air Force's flight academy twice every ycar. Israel is in possession of space assets, advanced fighter jets, sophisticated armed drones and nuclear weapons. Its air force also has incredibly difficult entry and training criteria. It will be correct to say that in the past four decades Israeli Air Force has progressed from being a purely reactive and defensive force developed to fulfil strategic military objectives both at home and abroad. So, it can be said that Israel's Air Force has developed as one IDF's most significant strategic tools.

In the past decades, Israeli Air Force has considered that almost all of its procurements and operational priorities should accomplish its key missions. These include attaining air superiority, steering long-range strikes and execution of surface support operations related to its large-scale warfare against its conventional adversaries in the West Asian region. During various missions carried on by Israeli Air Force, it foresaw the Air Force to act as a barrier around Israel in air and its ground forces all along taking fight to enemy territory.[21] In the more contemporary conflicts, its newly emerging alliances and engagements with Arab nations include intelligence sharing and the joint participation of the UAE and Israeli air forces in an air combat exercise in Greece in 2021.[22] Such acts even though are unprecedented in the history of the West Asian region, however, could pave the way for Israel's acceptance by its Arab neighbours eventually reducing its threat perception in a hostile region. In November 2021, the Israeli and UAE air forces participated for the first time in the Blue Flag, the American Air Force's key air-to-air combat training exercise.[23] The Israeli Air Force has at least 684 fighter jets. Along with it, Israeli Air Force has approximately 34,000 active personnel along with 10,000 active-duty personnel.[24] In terms of force concentration, Israel has 251 attack units, 176 support units, 154 training units and 68 future units. The sections below discuss in detail Israel's missile and drone inventories followed by a section on Israel's prep technological and transformative warfare.

***Israeli Missile Arsenal:*** Israel is technologically the most advanced nation in the West Asian region to have an advanced missile arsenal majorly funded by foreign assistance in the span of more than six decades. Israel's missile arsenal represents its contingency planning considering the adversaries it faces in the region. In addition to several cruise-missile systems, Israel has ballistic missiles with short, medium and, reportedly, intermediate ranges, which contribute to the state's strategic deterrence.[25] Even though Israel's acquisition of these weapons' technology is mainly for strategic deterrence purposes—the maximum of Israel's missile forces comprises of shorter range, tactical systems. It also has a company of long-range ballistic missiles of the Jericho family.[26] Israel has not signed the Nuclear Non-Proliferation Treaty (NPT) and it is not a member of the Missile Technology Control Regime (MTCR). However, Israel has unilaterally committed to follow the MTCR's restrictions on the export of missiles, it has adhered to the group's guidelines since 1992. Its sales of Unmanned Aerial Vehicles (UAVs) to several nations around the world are consistent with MTCR guidelines.[27]

Along with the strike systems Israel has also positioned its sophisticated, layered missile defence shield—popularly known as the Iron Dome—which is jointly developed with the United States.[28] This partnership between the Israeli missile and space industries has also enabled the domestic production of satellite launch vehicles. Israeli missile capabilities point towards its possession of nuclear-capable medium-range ballistic missiles (MRBM). It also has short-range sub-sonic cruise missiles with advanced capabilities such as Non-Line of Sight Targeting (NLOS) and mid-flight manoeuvrability. Further Israel also has significant defensive missile capabilities.[29] Israel's missile Jericho-2 claims to have an estimated 1,500 km range with a 1,000 km payload. With this range, it becomes easier for Israel to reach entire Egypt, Syria and Iraq but only the border areas of western Iran. However, there have been speculations that this missile system possesses a range of 3,500 km which can make it easy for it to reach the whole of Iran.[30] Mentioned below is the list of missiles of Israel, along with their class and range and their present status in the Israeli armed forces.

**Table 7.1: Missiles of Israel**

| Missile Name | Class[31] | Range | Status |
|---|---|---|---|
| Delilah | ALCM/Loitering Munition | 250-300 KM | Operational |
| Gabriel | ASCM | 34-400 KM | Operational |
| Extra | Artillery Rocket | 150 KM | Operational |
| Harpoon | ASCM | 90-240 KM | Operational |
| Jericho 1 | SRBM | 500 KM | Obsolete |
| Jericho 2 | MRBM | 1500-3500 KM | Operational |
| Jericho 3 | IRBM | 4800-6500 KM | Operational |
| LORA | SRBM | 280 KM | Operational |
| Popeye | ALCM | 75-100 KM | Operational |

Source: https://missilethreat.csis.org/country/israel/. Accessed on January 16, 2022.

Israel adopted the new defence doctrine in the late 2000s which was considered as both proactive and multitiered. One of the reasons for this can be the proliferation of rockets and ballistic missiles across the West Asian region, especially in Iran, Syria, Lebanon and Palestine. This has also resulted in the development of active anti-missile technology by Israel. So, the idea of active missile defence related to the development of advanced anti-missile systems as well as the assemblage of air, rocket and missile defence capabilities quite clearly reinforces Israeli defence doctrine. This is also supported by the early-warning, passive defence and counter-strike capabilities.[32] Israel in partnership with the United States, has established a multi-tiered missile defence system to counter Israel's perceived threats in the region through this world-class advanced systems. The Patriot missile system was initially used in Israel during the Gulf War I (1990-1991) in retaliation to the Scud missiles used by Saddam Hussein on Israel. The upgraded versions—PAC-2 & PAC-3—are considerably advanced, consistent and destructive with the ability to counter advanced threats such as aircraft, tactical ballistic missiles, cruise missiles and UAVs. The state-of-the-art Israeli version of this has replaced the previously used four-missile stationary launcher with a 16-missile launcher. This version is improved and equipped to resist the protracted barrage of missiles.[33]

Israel has a missile defence system to protect against cruise missiles. The Barak-8ER system developed by Israel Aerospace Industries (IAI) possesses the improved anti-tactical ballistic missile capabilities with the ability to destroy missiles as well as has protection against electronic countermeasures. It has three variants: (1) the Barak 8AMD/LRSAM is a naval air defence system which was originally designed for Israeli Navy. This is currently being used by several nations including India. (2) The Medium Range, Land-Based Missile Systems (MRSAM) are equipped with tracking radar, command and control systems and mobile launcher systems. (3) Barak MX has the dual-use option which can be useful both in naval and land missions.[34] The ship-based Barak-8 has an approximate range of 50 miles.[35]

David's Sling is an air and missile defence system designed to counter aircraft, cruise missiles, ballistic and guided missiles. Developed in partnership with the United States, its Stunner interceptor missile is created for land-based, maritime and aerial applications. It is equipped with a dual-band imaging infrared and radio-frequency seeker, as well as a multi-pulse rocket motor which allows it to carry out all-weather operations. Unlike the Iron Dome, Stunner has no warhead and defeats targets by striking them directly.[36] David's Sling is the middle tier in Israeli missile defence systems.[37] On the other hand, Iron Dome is its mobile missile defence system created to intercept short-range rockets and artilleries. Iron Dome forms the part of Israel's lowest tier of missile defence system envisioned to defend Israel against the unguided rocket and drone attacks.[38] Often lauded as the "game changer" by the Israeli defence forces, Iron Dome has been further upgraded to its naval variant known as the C-dome. In March 2021, it was announced by Israel that it has completed upgrades to Iron Dome to facilitate its engagement of missiles and UAVs.[39] Below listed is the Israel's Air Defence Systems (Table 7.2).

**Table 7.2: Israeli Air Defence Systems**

| Name | Type | Number | Origin | Status |
|---|---|---|---|---|
| MIM-104 Patriot | Surface to Air missile | NA | United States | Upgraded to the GM+ "Yahalom" standard |
| Iron Dome | Air defence missile battery/ Anti-rockets missile | 9+ | Israel | Has intercepted several artillery attacks since it became operational in 2011 |
| David's Sling | Medium—to long-range anti-ballistic missile/ surface-to-air missile | NA | Israel | Medium—to long-range anti-ballistic missile with surface-to-air missile capability |
| Arrow | Anti-ballistic missile | NA | Israel | Out of the atmosphere anti-ballistic missile series |
| Barak-8ER | Anti-cruise and ballistic missile system | NA | Israel | Anti-cruise and ballistic missile systems with vertical launch capabilities |

Nevertheless, the logic behind Israel's development of its IRBM range of missiles is still obscure as most of Israel's adversaries in the West Asian region including Iran are well within the range of its short-range missiles. One of the plausible reasons for this can be related to Israeli threat perception as a nation in a region hostile to its existence. Through these air and missile defence capabilities, Israel has been able to maintain military supremacy over its neighbours. All these indicate that Israel has effective anti-missile defence systems even though they have weighty price tags has resulted in limited number of these systems around the world. In case of Israel, it is essential to acquire or develop top-grade precision missiles which could strengthen its security. Israel has also tested the laser technologies and other preventive strategies to deal with emerging threats which include drone attacks.[40]

***Israel's Drone Inventory:*** As one of the world's foremost UAV users and manufacturers, Israel can easily be considered as one of the highest operators of armed UAVs in the West Asian region. In mid-2017, it was assessed that in the past three decades Israel has accounted for almost 60 per cent of global UAV exports.[41] All known exports of drones during 2011-2014 all the supplies were of unarmed drones. The major portion of IDF's UAV inventory is also unarmed. This is also due to Israeli doctrine in which their primary function is to provide real-time situational awareness for ground forces.[42] However, even though not part of official declarations, it is anticipated that Israel operates three types of UAVs which can be armed if required. These UAVs have been used to carry out consistent strikes against its threats. The drones are namely the Heron TP, the Hermes 450 and the Hermes 900 (Table 7.3).[43] Israel is also a significant pacesetter in anti-drone systems. Drone Dome is a radar-based system[44] which can detect targets and can neutralise them through lasers.[45] In terms of proliferation, there are more than 50 nations that utilise Israeli reconnaissance UAVs, however in the West Asian region but mostly unarmed.[46] Furthermore, Israel is not part of MTCR but has unilaterally agreed to abide by its principles and rules. However, Israel's readings of MTCR provisions have allowed it to carry out sales of UAVs around the world. These drones can theoretically be armed and fitted as per the MTCR criteria. One of the favourable aspects of Israeli UAVs is that its payload is significantly lower than the American Predator/Reaper family or Chinese Wing Loong and CH-5 offerings.[47]

**Table 7.3: Drone Capabilities of Israel[48]**

| Drones | Range | Type | Manufacturer | Weaponry |
|---|---|---|---|---|
| Heron TP UAV | 1000+ km | Medium Altitude Long Range (MALE) UAV | Israel Aerospace Industry | Potential capability of carrying Rafael Spike anti-Tank missiles or other weaponry |
| Hermes 450 UAV | 300 km (ltd by line of sight to ground control station) | MALE UAV | Elbit Systems | Option for 4 Rafael Spike anti-Tank guided missiles |
| Hermes | 1000+ km | MALE UAV | Elbit Systems | Internal bay & with hard point options including 4 Rafael Spike anti-Tank guided missiles |

*Technology and Transformation of Warfare:* Israel has military superiority as compared to its regional adversaries—both nations and non-state actors. These include indigenously produced or acquired drones, missiles and cyber capabilities, amongst other defence technologies. However, with the changing scenario of warfare and the altering geopolitical dynamics might alter Israel's consideration of a few Arab nations as adversaries, still, the revamping of military arsenal of many West Asian nations is a matter of concern for Israel. With several West Asian nations acquiring newer weapons technologies could, in turn threaten Israeli targets due to these technological innovations. One such arena is the cyber warfare which opens up new avenues for attacking targets with greater anonymity than any overt military action. For nations of this unstable region and the various non-state actors operable in West Asia, such kinds of attacks are fast becoming attractive options due to their low-cost and large destruction capabilities. Furthermore, the number of attacks and intensity is unlimited until a weak point is discovered. A series of precision attacks on a tiny nation like Israel could cripple its infrastructure. For example in July 2014, a rocket launched from Gaza hit a house in the town of Yehud, in close proximity to Israeli main international airport, eventually resulting in ceasing flights for a few hours.[49] These kinds of incidents in future might become an issue of economic distress if sustained over an extended period of time. Furthermore, the easy accessibility of cheap, destructive technologies in the hands of non-state actors like Hamas could threaten Israeli security. There have emerged new weapons of warfare which included cyber hacking and surveillance of not only the domestic populations as well as the various military installations. There has already emerged as a sustained asymmetrical arms race in new technology that increases the stakes in these areas. Nations might gain superiority as well as be exposed to new vulnerabilities. As these factors can act as instigators of future crises and the emerging trends in technology could provide the non-state actors or terrorist organisations with an enhanced ability to challenge their adversaries which also holds true in case of Israel—which has considerable military advantage.[50]

## India-Israel Defence Trade

The pillar of India-Israel bilateral relations remains the defence trade which is further deepened with the Israeli companies seeking to develop long-term partnerships through New Delhi's 'Make in India' efforts to encourage indigenously produced arms and ammunitions under joint ventures. Being one of India's topmost arms suppliers, the Israeli arms sales to India amount to more than $1 billion annually. This raises the significance of India as a consumer of Israeli defence industry as well as strengthening the strategic ties between the two nations. One of the factors for New Delhi's push to establish a self-reliant defence industry is the swift rise in the security challenges faced by India which demands constant availability of military equipment for its all three services as well as other associated law enforcement agencies. This is also due to the escalation of threats due to cross-border terrorism and the aggressive and expansionist behaviour of its neighbouring nations eventually increasing New Delhi's threat perceptions. Another factor is particularly similar to the Israeli case, wherein economic motivations of having a robust defence industry are quite prominent as the transfers of indigenously developed weapon systems will help in earning foreign currency and considerably reduce the import bills. This in turn could initiate the subsidisation of the nation's annual defence budget. In the past few years, India's defence cooperation with Israel is the major factor in the growing strategic partnership between two nations. The defence cooperation between India and Israel in terms of arms trade in addition to technology transfer and licensed production has become an important dimension of this strategic partnership. In the past eight years, Israel's share in the Indian defence sector has increased swiftly with Indian arms imports from Israel increasing by almost 175 per cent from 2015-2019. This eventually makes Israel second largest supplier of major arms to India.[51] In 2017, for the first time, the Indian Air Force had participated in the Blue Flag exercise in *Uvda* air force base in southern Israel where elite Garud Commandos and Hercules C-130J-30 of Indian Air Force were deployed. The growth of defence cooperation is signalled by utilising Israeli technology in the field of missiles, air defence systems, UAVs and more.

One such example of this is when Israeli high technology company *Elbit systems* dealing in wide-ranging defence, homeland and security programs initiated a joint venture with Adani Defence in Hyderabad for the production of Hermes drones in 2018.[52] The 50,000-sq ft. state-of-the-art facility is the first venture outside Israel for manufacturing the Hermes 900 MALE UAV. Elbit System's another joint venture with Alpha Design Technologies was also launched and this Israeli enterprise is also associated with Bharat Electronics for developments in the domains of electronic warfare and electro-optics.[53] Israel's *UVision*, responsible for manufacturing of loitering munitions, has also signed a deal with Indian company *Aditya Precitech* via a joint venture known as *Avision* to manufacture the PALM (Precision Attack Loitering Munition) Hero system. So, Israel's state-of-the-art defence and technological expertise can become the main pillars for India's drive for a self-reliant defence industry. Indian Defence Research and Development Organisation (DRDO) and Israeli Directorate of Defense Research and Development has also signed a bilateral agreement to promote the development of technologies for both military and commercial usage. As part of this agreement, the Indian and Israeli startup companies will work together on technologies such as small UAVs and artificial intelligence.[54] Furthermore, India and Israel have jointly developed Barak 8 (MRSAM) air defence system. The missile is driven by an indigenously developed rocket motor and control system for high manoeuvrability in the terminal phase. This is jointly developed by the Israel Aerospace Industries and DRDO. Several other Indian and Israeli companies are involved in this project such as Rafael, Bharat Electronics Limited, Bharat Dynamics Limited and Larsen & Toubro.[55]

India needs to support in specialised avionics, airborne radars, electronic warfare equipment, SAMs, UAVs, etc. apart from other equipment in which Israel can be helpful to India. Israel has also supported India in its ballistic missile defence (BMD) and space satellite programs.[56] There has been cooperation between India and Israel in terms of various targeting and intelligence, surveillance and reconnaissance (ISR) systems. For instance, the Indian Air Force has procured Litening 2 and Litening 4 advanced targeting pods to be installed on Mirage 2000s, Su 30s, Jaguars and LCA Mk 1A. Furthermore, this system is also consistent with India's newest acquisitions

Rafale fighters. Another significant acquisition of the Indian Air Force from Israel is the Software Defined Radios supplied by Rafael (Israel) for IAF's network-centric operations.[57] Rafael has also invested in Astra Rafael Company as JV, based in Hyderabad. In 2020, Israel Aerospace Industry (IAI) and Indian Bharat Electronics Limited (BEL) signed an MoU to launch a new technical and maintenance support centre for India's air defence systems. IAI has also signed an MoU as part of strategic collaboration with Indian Hindustan Aeronautics Limited (HAL) and Dynamatic Technologies Limited for its 'Make-in-India' UAVs.[58] Furthermore, an MoU was also signed between HAL and Elbit Systems for joint development of a Vertical Take-off and Landing (VTOL) Rotary UAV of 2,000 kg class.[59] HAL and Elbit have also signed an MoU for Digital Head-Up Displays. These systems will integrate new features such as 'Wide Instantaneous' and 'Total Field of View' with negligible binocular disproportions.[60] So, it is clear that the partnership between India and Israel is quite crucial for India's future security and success of its 'Make in India' initiative in terms of defence production; and it is also crucial for the prosperity of both nations as well as maximising the military and commercial engagements which can further strengthen India-Israel strategic partnership in defence domain.

## Conclusion

Israel's constant existential threat, necessity for securing its borders and lack of strategic depth in the first few years of its formation had considerable influence over the evolution of the Israel's Air Force. In the scenarios when Israel was faced with threats from its immediate geographic neighbours led to the urgency of modernising and strengthening its air power transforming it into its air superiority. The fundamental understanding of the potential of air power led to a vision of the basic requirements to maximise the potential of its air power. As mentioned in the paper above that Israel is a small nation with little strategic depth geographically, demographically and economically. Thus, its air force had to be strategic in terms of its future inventory and capability plans. The role of Israeli air power in the IDF is in convergent with its aims and motives however differing in its approach and tactics. Even though the threat perception of Israel in the West Asian region persists, still the new emergence of new partners and alliances have changed the course of politics in the region also affecting the IDF's plans and visions. Still, Israeli Air Force's primary task remains to gain air superiority over its adversaries—both nations and non-state actors in the region. In this context, there exists a continuity in Israeli air power's role in terms of its past and present operational doctrines. However, its role is much more enhanced under the IDF's new operational doctrine.

A closer look, however, reveals that the Israeli Air Force has become gradually unwilling to accept the human costs of war, relying to a greater extent on a "force multiplier" such as its air superiority. However, at the same, there needs to be a realisation that it should not become too dependent on its air power to win wars. Leaders of Israel—both political and Air Force have realised the emerging challenges in attaining air superiority due to evolving techniques and technologies. In this scenario, the challenge posed by a new generation of missile systems, UAVs and cyber warfare, the dilemmas faced by the Israeli Air Force are rising; however, it still remains a preferable tool as compared to the ground forces. Today, air power plays a fundamental role in every Israeli aggressive action. Since the end of the First Lebanon War in 1982, ground forces have remained the last tool in Israel's strategic toolbox with air power gaining superiority in conflicts. In the contemporary scenario, India and Israel strategic partnership with the pillars of it being defence trade. The two nations further began cooperation in a wide array of issues including cultural, political, and economic fields beyond strategic. This is further advanced by India's balancing act, highlighted by its de-hyphenation strategy—between Israel and Palestine definitely earned a few brownie points for policymakers in New Delhi. In such a scenario, India and Israel's partnership in terms of defence trade further solidifies this relationship eventually profiting both the nations.

## Notes

1. Amos Yadlin and Assaf Orion, "Israel's New Strategy", *Foreign Affairs*, February 18, 2022, at https://www.foreignaffairs.com/articles/middle-east/2022-02-18/israels-new-strategy. Accessed on February 19, 2022.
2. Seth J. Frantzman, "Israel Unveils Artificial Intelligence Strategy for Armed Forces", Defence News, February 11, 2022, at https://www.defensenews.com/artificial-intelligence/2022/02/11/israel-unveils-artificial-intelligence-strategy-for-armed-forces/. Accessed on February 18, 2022.

3. David L. Rousseau and Rocio Garcia-Retamero, "Identity, Power, and Threat Perception: A Cross-National Experimental Study", *Journal of Conflict Resolution*, volume 51, number 5, October 2007, pp. 744-771, at https://www.albany.edu/~dr967231/articles/RousseauJCROct2007.pdf. Accessed on November 28, 2021.
4. Ibid., p. 746.
5. Ibid., p. 747.
6. Raymond Cohen, *Threat perception in International Crisis*, The University of Wisconsin Press, 1979, p. 5.
7. Raymond Cohen, "Threat Perception in International Crisis", *Political Science Quarterly*, volume 93, number 1, Spring 1978, pp. 93-107.
8. Christian Fjäder, "The Nation-state, National Security and Resilience in the Age of Globalisation", *Resilience: International Policies, Practices and Discourse*, volume 2, issue 2, 2014, pp. 114-129, at https://www.tandfonline.com/doi/full/10.1080/21693293.2014.914771. Accessed on November 28, 2021.
9. Ibid.
10. RSN Singh, "Israel's Threat Perception", *Indian Defence Review*, September 10, 2014, at http://www.indiandefencereview.com/spotlights/israels-threat-perception/. Accessed on November 28, 2021.
11. Ibid.
12. Matthew Rojansky, et al., "Russia in the Middle East: National Security Challenges for the United States and Israel in the Biden Era", *Kennan Institute, Institute for Policy And Strategy (IPS), IDC Herzliya*, 2020, at https://www.wilsoncenter.org/publication/report-russia-middle-east-national-security-challenges-united-states-and-israel-biden; Marc Lynch, "Does the Decline of U.S. Power Matter for the Middle East?", *Carnegie Endowment for International Peace*, March 2019, at https://carnegieendowment.org/2019/03/19/does-decline-of-u.s.-power-matter-for-middle-east-pub-78645. Accessed on November 29, 2021.
13. RSN Singh, "Israel's Threat Perception", *Indian Defence Review*, September 10, 2014, at http://www.indiandefencereview.com/spotlights/israels-threat-perception/. Accessed on November 28, 2021.
14. "Lebanon: The Israel-Hamas-Hezbollah Conflict" *Congressional Research Service Report*, September 15, 2006, at https://www.everycrsreport.com/reports/RL33566.html. Accessed on January 23, 2022.
15. Hamas—Ḥarakat al-Muqāwamah al-Islāmiyyah.
16. Amos Harel, "Hamas is Back to Threatening Israel, but that Doesn't Mean its in Control", *Haaretz*, December 26, 2021, at https://www.haaretz.com/israel-news/does-hamas-want-quiet-or-another-war-with-israel-1.10491236. Accessed on January 23, 2022.

17. Kali Robinson, "What is Hezbollah", *CFR*, Updated October 26, 2021, at https://www.cfr.org/backgrounder/what-hezbollah. Accessed on January 21, 2022.
18. Ibid.
19. Ibid.; "Israel Imperiled: Threats to The Jewish State", *Joint Hearing before the Subcommittee on Terrorism, Non-proliferation and Trade; Subcommittee on the Middle East & North Africa,* Committee on Foreign Affairs, House of Representatives, 114th Congress, 2nd Session, April 19, 2016, at https://www.govinfo.gov/content/pkg/CHRG-114hhrg99849/html/CHRG-114hhrg99849.htm. Accessed on January 12, 2022.
20. Ibid.
21. Matthew M. Hurley, "On the Fly: Israeli Airpower Against the Al-Aqsa Intifada, 2000-2005", *Air Force Research Institute Papers*, June 2010, at https://media.defense.gov/2017/Jun/19/2001765136/-1/-1/0/AP_HURLEY_ON_THE_FLY.PDF. Accessed on January 14, 2022.
22. Judah Ari Gross, "Israeli, UAE Fighter Jets Fly Together in Large International Exercise in Greece", *Times of Israel*, April 21, 2021, at https://www.timesofisrael.com/israeli-uae-fighter-jets-fly-together-in-large-international-exercise-in-greece/. Accessed on February 13, 2022.
23. Bradley Bowman, Jacob Nagel and Ryan Brobst, "Blue Flag Exercise has Israel's Enemies Seeing Red", *Defence News*, November 21, 2021, at https://www.defensenews.com/opinion/commentary/2021/11/03/blue-flag-exercise-has-israels-enemies-seeing-red/. Accessed on February 11, 2022.
24. "This is the Imbalance of Power between Israel and Palestine in the Real Terms", *TRT World*, May 12, 2021, at https://www.trtworld.com/magazine/this-is-the-imbalance-of-power-between-israel-and-palestine-in-real-terms-46651. Accessed on January 28, 2022.
25. Mark Fitzpatrick, "Israel's Ballistic Missile Programme: An Overview", *IISS-Analysis*, August 25, 2021, at https://www.iiss.org/blogs/analysis/2021/08/israel-ballistic-missile-programme. Accessed on January 16, 2022.
26. "Missiles of Israel", *CSIS Missile Defence Project*, updated August 10, 2021, at https://missilethreat.csis.org/country/israel/. Accessed on January 16, 2022.
27. Mark Fitzpatrick, "Israel's Ballistic Missile Programme: An Overview", *IISS-Analysis*, August 25, 2021, at https://www.iiss.org/blogs/analysis/2021/08/israel-ballistic-missile-programme. Accessed on January 16, 2022.
28. Undated, "US-Israel Missile Defense Cooperation", *The Embassy of Israel to the United States*, at https://embassies.gov.il/washington/Obama_in_Israel/Pages/US-Israel-Missile-Defense-Cooperation.aspx. Accessed on January 17, 2022.
29. "This is the Imbalance of Power between Israel and Palestine in the Real Terms", *TRT World*, May 12, 2021, at https://www.trtworld.com/magazine/this-is-the-

imbalance-of-power-between-israel-and-palestine-in-real-terms-46651. Accessed on January 28, 2022.

30. Ibid.
31. ALCM—Air Launched Cruise Missile; ASCM—Anti Ship Missile; IRBM—Intermediate Range Ballistic Missile; MRBM—Medium Range Ballistic Missile; SRBM—Short Range Ballistic Missile.
32. "Israel's Missile Defence Systems", *Jewish Virtual Library*, at https://www.jewishvirtuallibrary.org/israel-missile-defense-systems. Accessed on February 10, 2022.
33. Ibid.
34. "Barak-8 Missile: A Strategically Vital and Lethal weapon for the Forces", *The Economic Times*, February 15, 2021, at https://economictimes.indiatimes.com/news/defence/barak-8-missile-a-strategically-vital-and-lethal-weapon/articleshow/72474051.cms?from=mdr. Accessed on February 14, 2022.
35. Arie Egozi, "Israel Boasts New Operational Cruise Missile Defense," *Breaking Defense*, October 4, 2019, at https://breakingdefense.com/2019/10/israel-boasts-new-operational-cruise-missile-defense/. Accessed on February 10, 2022.
36. "Israel's Missile Defence Systems", *Jewish Virtual Library*, at https://www.jewishvirtuallibrary.org/israel-missile-defense-systems. Accessed on February 10, 2022.
37. "David's Sling", *Rafael*, at https://www.rafael.co.il/worlds/air-missile-defense/long-range-air-missile-defense/; Missile Defense Project, "David's Sling (Israel)," *Missile Threat*, Center for Strategic and International Studies, April 14, 2016, at https://missilethreat.csis.org/defsys/davids-sling/. Accessed on February 13, 2022.
38. "Iron Dome (Israel)", *Missile Threat*, Center for Strategic and International Studies, Updated July 13, 2021, at https://missilethreat.csis.org/defsys/iron-dome/; Undated, "How Israel's Iron Dome Missile Defence System Intercepts Rockets fired by Hamas," *WION*, at https://www.wionews.com/photos/how-israels-iron-dome-missile-defence-system-intercepts-rockets-fired-by-hamas-384586#israels-defence-shield-384563. Accessed on January 20, 2022.
39. Ibid.
40. Anupama Ghosh, "Israel becomes the 'first country' to use Aerial Laser Weapons to Shoot Down Hostile Drones," *Eurasian Times*, June 22, 2021, at https://eurasiantimes.com/watch-israel-becomes-the-first-country-to-use-laser-weapons-to-shoot-down-hostile-drones/; Seth J. Frantzman, "Israel is Developing Lasers to Kill Drones and Rockets", Defence News, January 9, 2020, at https://www.defensenews.com/industry/techwatch/2020/01/09/israel-is-developing-lasers-to-kill-drones-and-rockets/. Accessed on January 23, 2022.

41. Elisa Catalano Ewers, et al., "Drone Proliferation: Policy Choices for the Trump Administration", *Papers for the President—Center for a New American Security (CNAS)*, June 2017, at https://drones.cnas.org/wp-content/uploads/2017/06/CNASReport-DroneProliferation-Final.pdf. Accessed on February 4, 2022.
42. Uri Sadot, "Proliferated Drones: A Perspective on Israel", *Center for a New American Security (CNAS)*, at http://drones.cnas.org/reports/a-perspective-on-israel/#1460581134371-761437b9-c370. Accessed on February 4, 2022.
43. Elisa Catalano Ewers et al., "Drone Proliferation: Policy Choices for the Trump Administration", *Papers for the President—Center for a New American Security (CNAS)*, June 2017, at https://drones.cnas.org/wp-content/uploads/2017/06/CNASReport-DroneProliferation-Final.pdf; "Israel", RUSI—Armed Drones in the Middle East, https://drones.rusi.org/countries/israel/#_ftn1. Accessed on February 4, 2022.
44. Drone Dome is anti-drone system with soft kill and hard-kill with a quick response time and a high success rate while inflicting minimal collateral damage. "Drone Dome C-UAS", at https://www.rafael.co.il/worlds/air-missile-defense/c-uas-counter-unmanned-aircraft-systems/. Accessed on February 3, 2022.
45. Richard Tomkins, "Rafael Unveils Drone Dome Anti-Drone System", *United Press International (UPI)*, June 23, 2017, at https://www.upi.com/Defense-News/2017/06/23/Rafael-unveils-Drone-Dome-anti-drone-system/9161498239207/. Accessed on February 3, 2022.
46. Rob O'Gorman and Chris Abbott, 'Remote Control War: Unmanned Combat Air Vehicles in China, India, Iran, Israel, Russia and Turkey', Open Briefing, September 2013, p. 11.
47. George Nacouzi, et al., "Assessment of the Proliferation of certain Remotely Piloted Aircraft Systems", RAND Report, 2018, at https://www.rand.org/content/dam/rand/pubs/research_reports/RR2300/RR2369/RAND_RR2369.pdf. Accessed on February 4, 2022.
48. "Israel", RUSI—Armed Drones in the Middle East, at https://drones.rusi.org/countries/israel/#_ftn1; "Middle East and North Africa", *Military Balance*, 2021, pp. 354-357.
49. Ben Hartman, "Rocket Damages Yehud House in First Direct Hit in Tel Aviv Area", *The Jerusalem Post*, July 22, 2014, at https://www.jpost.com/operation-protective-edge/rocket-damages-tel-aviv-region-house-in-first-direct-hit-in-area-since-start-of-gaza-op-368444; "Operation Protective Edge: A Detailed Summary of Events", *IDC Herzliya*, July 12, 2014, at https://www.ict.org.il/Article/1262/Operation-Protective-Edge-A-Detailed-Summary-of-Events#gsc.tab=0. Accessed on January 20, 2022.
50. Natan Sachs and Kevin Huggard, "Israel in the Middle East: The Next Two Decades", *Foreign Policy at Brookings*, November 2020, at https://www.brookings.

edu/wp-content/uploads/2020/11/FP_20201120_israel_me_sachs_huggard-1.pdf. Accessed on January 15, 2022.

51. Pieter D. Wezeman and et al., "Trends In International Arms Transfers, 2019", SIPRI, March 2020, at https://www.sipri.org/publications/2020/sipri-fact-sheets/trends-international-arms-transfers-2019#:~:text=The%20volume%20of%20international%20transfers,%2C%20France%2C%20Germany%20and%20China. Accessed on February 11, 2022.
52. "Adani Defence and Aerospace and Elbit Systems Inaugurate India First Private Unmanned", *Adani Defence and Aerospace*, December 14, 2018, at https://www.adanidefence.com/newsroom/media-release/Adani-Defence-and-Aerospace-and-Elbit-Systems-inaugurate-India-first-private-Unmanned. Accessed on February 12, 2022.
53. Seth J. Frantzman, "New Joint Ventures hint at 'burgeoning relationship' between Israel and India", Defence News, February 18, 2020, at https://www.defensenews.com/industry/2020/02/18/new-joint-ventures-hint-at-burgeoning-relationship-between-israel-and-india/; "Israel India's Natural Airspace Partner", *Air Asia*, May 6, 2020, at https://airpowerasia.com/2020/05/06/israel-indias-natural-aerospace-partner/. Accessed on February 11, 2022.
54. Moyoru Baba and Takeshi Kumon, "India. Israel Aim to Boost Ties through Defence Tech and Trade", *Nikkei Asia*, November 28, 2021, at https://asia.nikkei.com/Politics/International-relations/India-Israel-aim-to-boost-ties-through-defense-tech-and-trade#:~:text=That%20follows%20an%20October%20agreement,bilateral%20FTA%20by%20June%202022. Accessed on February 13, 2022.
55. Rahul Singh, "IAF Inducts BARAK 8 Air Defence system that can Hit Multiple Targets 70 km Away", *Hindustan Times*, September 9, 2021, at https://www.hindustantimes.com/india-news/iaf-inducts-barak-8-air-defence-system-that-can-hit-multiple-targets-70km-away-101631198455089.html. Accessed on February 14, 2022.
56. "Israel India's Natural Airspace Partner", *Air Asia*, May 6, 2020, at https://airpowerasia.com/2020/05/06/israel-indias-natural-aerospace-partner/. Accessed on February 11, 2022.
57. Ibid.
58. "IAI Enters Strategic UAV Collaboration with HAL and DTL at DefExpo", *Israel Aerospace Industries*, February 5, 2020, at https://www.iai.co.il/iai-strategic-uav-collaboration-with-hal-and-dtl. Accessed on February 11, 2022.
59. "MoU Between HAL and Elbit Systems ISTAR Division, Israel Signed", *Hindustan Aeronautics Limited*, February 5, 2020, at https://hal-india.co.in/MoU%20Between%20HAL%20and%20Elbit%20Systems%20ISTAR%20Division,%20Israel%20Signed/ND__290. Accessed on February 12, 2022.

60. "HAL signs MoU with Elbit Systems for digital head-up displays for fighter planes", *The Economic Times*, February 6, 2020, at https://economictimes.indiatimes.com/news/defence/hal-signs-mou-with-elbit-systems-for-digital-head-up-displays-for-fighter-planes/articleshow/73981655.cms. Accessed on February 12, 2022.

# 8

# China's Nuclear Missile Modernisation from 2010 to 2020 and Implications for India

NASIMA KHATOON

## Introduction

Over the last decade, China's People's Liberation Army (PLA) has been steadily developing and modernising its strategic weapons and armed forces. China initiated a reform in its armed forces primarily since 2013 to "fully transform the people's armed forces into world-class forces by the mid-21st century".[1] The modernisation aims of the PLA are to greatly improve strategic capability, military organisational structure, weaponry and comprehensive reform of national defence to transform it into a world-class force in the coming decades.

A significant part of this transformation is China's nuclear missile force which has undergone numerous technological advancements and organisational and operational changes over the past decade. These changes essentially reflect China's shifting priorities and national security and defence strategies in the East Asian and Western Pacific and Indo-Pacific region that impacts the larger geopolitics of the region. Though China's nuclear policy and strategies are essentially US-centric, the development of its strategic missile programme with varied range and capability of nuclear-capable missiles also impacts India's threat perceptions. These advances in China's nuclear missile programme make the study of missile development in the last decade crucial.

In the past one decade, China has worked on a range of technologies to attempt to counter its threat perception. Most significant technological developments include Multiple Independently-Targetable Re-entry Vehicles (MIRVs), Manoeuvrable re-entry vehicles (MaRVs), successful development of submarine-launched ballistic missile capability and solid fuelled ICBM capability. Apart from this China is possibly also developing an air-launched dual-capable ballistic missile. It is estimated that China has a stockpile of approximately 320 nuclear warheads (according to the 2020 US DoD report 200 warheads) and 180 to 190 land-based ballistic missiles.[2] Whereas, in 2011 the country had an estimated nuclear weapon stockpile of 240 nuclear warheads. The 2020 US DoD report has estimated that with the present rate of development and modernisation China might double the number of nuclear warheads over the next decade.

The chapter starts with a brief mention of the PLA rocket force—the primary military organisation of China responsible for operating nuclear missiles follows by the identification of the nuclear missiles of China as provided in Table 8.1. The subsequent sections analyse trends in missile testing from 2010 to the present time, capability assessment of nuclear missiles, analysis of China's defence white papers, implications for India and future trajectories of its missile development are analysed in detail.

## PLARF

The People's Liberation Army Rocket Force (PLARF) is the primary military organisation responsible for operating and maintaining the conventional and nuclear missile forces of China. It was formerly known as Second Artillery Force that was created in 1966, two years after China's first nuclear test at Lop Nor. The PLA Second Artillery Force (PLASAF) or Second Artillery Corps (SAC) was renamed as PLA Rocket Force (PLARF) in December 2015, as part of China's ongoing military reforms.[3] PLARF is under the direct command of the Chinese Central Military Commission (CMC). Since 2016, China is undergoing major military reforms. According to the 2019 Defence White Paper, the PLARF comprises of nuclear missiles, conventional missiles and subordinate missile bases. The White Paper further states that the PLARF is responsible for enhancing the credibility and reliability of the country's nuclear deterrence and counterattack, strengthening precision strike forces and enhancing strategic counter-balance capability to modernise the PLA Rocket Force.[4]

To further highlight the significance of the PLARF, during its inauguration in December 2015, Chinese President Xi Jinping stated that the Rocket Force is "core force of strategic deterrence, a strategic buttress to the country's position as a major power, and an important building block in upholding national security."[5] China also elevated the PLARF to service-level status as part of the reform and established it as the fourth service in China's armed forces. An article published in *Science and Technology Daily* by a political instructor of the Rocket Army, reflecting on this advancement of the force stated that "The Rocket Army is no longer a paper tiger that puts missiles on the launcher to scare opponents, but is a strategic iron fist ready to launch missiles to frighten opponents at any time".[6] As the core force of strategic deterrence, the PLARF is responsible for the command of China's nuclear forces and exercises custodial and operational control over China's nuclear warheads.[7]

## Nuclear Missiles of China

Presently, China has eight types of nuclear-capable ballistic missiles, i.e., DF-5, DF-41, DF-4, DF-21, DF-26, DF-31, DF-15 and JL-2. Based on the launch platform, these missiles are divided into two types—land-based and sea-based ballistic missiles. JL-2 is a submarine-launched ballistic missile (SLBM), a sea-based variant of DF-31. Three of these land-based ballistic missiles—DF-5, DF-31 and DF-21 have variants, of which China is yet to complete the development of the DF-5C and DF-41 land-based ballistic missiles.

Various US military publications from time to time have speculated that some of China's cruise missiles might have nuclear capability, although a high degree of uncertainty remains in this regard.

The Table 8.1 summarises China's nuclear missiles with specific details. The missiles are listed based on their range, starting from the longest to the shortest range.

**Table 8.1: Nuclear Missiles of China**

| Missile Name | Range | Type of the Missile | First test | Remarks |
|---|---|---|---|---|
| **Ballistic Missiles** | | | | |
| Dong Feng-5A / CSS-4 Mod 1 | 13,000 km | Liquid-fuelled, two-stage, silo-based ICBM | May 1980 | It is an upgraded version of the earlier first-generation liquid-fuelled ballistic missile DF-5 The missiles entered service in 1981 and were deployed in hardened silos in central China. |
| Dong Feng-5B / CSS-4 Mod 2 | 13,000 km | Liquid fuelled, two-stage, silo-based ICBM | | The missile is identical to DF—5A but upgraded to carry MIRV warheads.<br>The missile was first displayed in 2015. |
| Dong Feng-5C / CSS-4 Mod 3 | Not available | Upgraded version of DF-5B | First known flight test in February 2017 | China's Ministry of National Defence acknowledged the test launch of the missile in February 2017, and cited the US media report (Washington Free Beacon) that the missile carried 10 MIRVs.[8] However, it did not confirm the report.<br>The missile is presently under development. |
| Dong Feng-41 / CSS-X-20 | >12000[9] km | Solid fuelled, three-stage, silo/road-mobile ICBM. | 24 July 2012 | DF-41 was first time showcased at China's National Day parade on October1 1, 2019.<br>Chinese analysts have speculated that the |

| | | | | |
|---|---|---|---|---|
| | | | | DF-41 can carry 6-10 MIRVed warheads, although there is significant uncertainty about the actual capability[10]. The missile is presently under development. The DF-41 is expected to replace aging and liquid-fuelled DF-5 ICBM |
| Dong Feng-31A/ AG / CSS-10 Mod 2 | 11,200 km | Solid-fuelled, three-stage, road-mobile ICBM. | Deployed in 2007 | An extended range version of the DF-31. According to the 2020 US DoD report the missile has the capability to reach almost all locations within the continental US |
| Dong Feng-31 / CSS-10 Mod 1 | 7,200 km | Solid-fuelled, three-stage, road-mobile ICBM. | August 1999 | DF-31 (CSS-10 Mod 1) was the first solid fuelled ICBM developed by China It is predicted that the missile will eventually replace the liquid-fuelled ballistic missile DF-4. |
| Dong Feng-4 / CSS-3 | 5,500 km | Liquid fuelled, two-stage ICBM. | Not available | The missile reportedly has the capability to reach Moscow and Guam DF-4 is predicted to be replaced by DF-31 ICBM |

| | | | | |
|---|---|---|---|---|
| Dong Feng-26 | 4,000 km | Solid fuelled, two-stage, road-mobile ballistic missile | 24 January 2019 | The missile is known as "Guam Killer" or "aircraft carrier killer" owing to its range which gives it ability to reach US military base on the Pacific island of Guam. According to a report by Chinese state-controlled media Global Times, the weapon can strike a moving aircraft carrier. The missile is capable of precision conventional or nuclear strikes against ground targets, as well as conventional strikes against naval targets. |
| Dong Feng-21 & DF-21A/ CSS-5 Mod 2&6 | 1750 km to 2,150 km | Solid fuelled, two-stage, road-mobile ballistic missile | May 1985 | The missile is capable of hitting targets in the Indo-Pacific region, this suggests that with limited range the missile serves a regional deterrent role. The new variant DF-21A (CSS-5 Mod 2) was first deployed in 1996 |
| Dong Feng-15/ CSS-6 Mod 1 | 600 km | Solid fuelled, land-based, road-mobile ballistic missile | First deployed in 1994 | China's only nuclear-capable land-based short-range ballistic missile. The US DoD report 2020 termed the missile as a conventional missile. |

| Julang-2[11] (JL-2)/ CSS-NX-14 | More than 7,000 km | Solid fuelled, Submarine-launched ballistic missile (SLBM) | 2002. First successful test in August 2012 | The missile was first time showcased at China's National Day parade on October 1, 2019. Launch platform—Jin-class nuclear-powered ballistic missile submarines (SSBN). China has four SSBNs with two more under construction. Each SSBN can carry up to 12, JL-2 missiles. The range of the missile enables China to target Alaska, Guam, Hawaii, India and Russia from Chinese waters. |
|---|---|---|---|---|

## Trends in Missile Testing: 2010 to 2020

In the last decade, China has added two new types and two new variants of land-based ballistic missiles to its inventory. This addition includes—DF-5B, DF-5C, DF-26, DF-41. While development and test of a few of these missiles were initiated before 2010, these missiles were either deployed or introduced publicly post 2010. Based on available data, ICBM DF-41 has been tested ten times since 2012. The DF-26 has been tested twice since January 2019; submarine-launched ballistic missile JL-2 has also been tested twice in the last ten years.

While analysing the trend of China's missile modernisation over the period of the last 10 years, the following significant developments can be observed that likely indicate China's nuclear strategy and its future trajectories.

A recent estimate shows that as of January 2020, China maintained a stockpile of approximately 320 nuclear warheads, compared to an estimated stockpile of 240 nuclear warheads in 2011.[12] US DoD report 2020 estimates the number of warheads is likely to increase at least double over the next decade. However, considering the actual estimated increase in past one decade and past estimates of US DoD report that claimed a sharp increase in numbers over the years, such increase is not likely to take place. Instead, an interesting trend can be observed regarding the number of land-based and sea-based ballistic missiles.

According to the estimate of the *Bulletin of Atomic Scientists,* presently China has approximately 190 nuclear-capable land-based ballistic missiles and 48 sea-based ballistic missiles.[13] The US DoD report, 2020 estimates that of these missiles, around 100 missiles are ICBMs. With the operationalisation of ICBM DF-5C and DF-41, this number is likely to grow further. Whereas, the estimated number of missiles (land-based ballistic missiles) till 2011 was nearly 140. These estimates do not include conventional missiles which have also increased significantly over the years. Considering the fact that few of these missiles are dual-capable in nature, this growth impacts the overall capability of the missile force.

Therefore, a trend can be observed where increasing the numbers and improving the technological variants of missiles are preferred over the sole increase in the number of warheads to defeat the US missile defence system and at the same time to increase the survivability of its missiles. This tendency likely indicates towards Chinese perception of a nuclear weapon as "political tool of deterrence, which obviates the need for nuclear superiority".[14]

Reportedly, China has many missiles including cruise missiles that are speculated to be dual-capable, i.e., capable of carrying both nuclear and conventional warheads. China's land-based ballistic missile DF-15 has been declared as nuclear-capable many times in the past, though the 2020 US DoD report lists it as a conventional missile. Some of its cruise missiles are also likely to have nuclear capability but China has always maintained ambiguity in this matter in order to add to its deterrent value. The 2020 US DoD report confirms that the solid fuelled DF-26 is designed to rapidly swap conventional and nuclear warheads and is capable of conducting precision strikes against ground targets, as well as conventional strikes against naval targets. While this ambiguity is inherent part of China's nuclear policy this might invite complex challenges for countries with nuclear first use doctrine as in the presence of ambiguity related to the nature of payload might led to miscalculations and nuclear escalation.[15]

Another trend in China's missile modernisation is increasing the penetrability of its missiles to build an effective deterrence posture. China perceives US missile defence architecture as a major challenge to its missile operations. As a result, China resorted to improve the penetrability of its missiles against adversary missile defences by investing in development measures such as multiple independently-targetable re-entry vehicles (MIRVs), manoeuvrable re-entry vehicles (MaRVs) and hypersonic glide vehicles (HGV).

Presently, China's DF-5B ICBMs have MIRV capability. A MIRVed missile can carry several miniaturised warheads, each of which can be targeted independently, which provides it a greater advantage over a missile containing a single warhead. The DF-5B ICBM is liquid-fuelled and silo-based with a range of 13, 000 km that can reach the continental US. While the long time required for fuelling the missile makes it more susceptible to adversary attack, the missiles intercontinental range with greater throw weight and most significant capability to carry MIRVed warhead increases its ability to penetrate missile defence and enhances the capability of China's missile force with more survivable delivery systems. In addition to this, a new generation of silo-based/road-mobile, solid fuelled ICBM—DF-41 is undergoing development in China that reportedly has a greater number of MIRVed warhead carrying capabilities. The missile has been tested many times as recently as in May 2018. Another ICBM, upgraded version of DF-5B—ICBM DF-5C with stated capability of carrying 10 MIRVs is in development and flight-tested in February 2017. These developments specify China's greater importance towards developing MIRVed missiles with improved warheads and a prominent inclination towards building more solid fuelled missiles besides maintaining a limited number of liquid-fuelled missiles to increase the credibility of its deterrence.

According to 2020 US DoD report, China's conventionally armed DF-21D is fitted with a MaRV warhead, and is capable of rapidly reloading in the field. MaRVed warheads are capable of performing pre-programmed flight manoeuvres during the atmospheric re-entry phase, they are also difficult to intercept and therefore better able to engage adversary missile defence systems.[16] Though China's ability to successfully develop this technology is uncertain, the development suggests China's continued quest towards enhancing the capability of its missile force by developing manoeuvrable warhead technology.

Another recent addition to China's missile technology is hypersonic weapon programme. China's hypersonic weapon programme is rapidly advancing and it has operationalised the DF-17 solid fuelled missile equipped with a hypersonic glide vehicle (HGV) DF-ZF that can reach speeds of Mach 5 to Mach 10 (approximately 6174 to 12,348 km per hour) in its glide phase that is far greater than the speeds missile defences are built to counter.[17] It reportedly conducted nine tests of the hypersonic glide vehicle between January 2014 and November 2017 and the missile has demonstrated a high degree of accuracy.[18] While Chinese media stated DF-17's conventional role the missile may have nuclear warhead carrying capability. The missile was first time showcased in China's October 2019 military parade. The very high speed of the weapon combined with extreme manoeuvres, evasive nature and ability to fly at low altitudes and to maintain a flat trajectory makes it far less vulnerable to area missile defences as interception becomes extremely difficult.[19] While hypersonic weapons are effective against ballistic missile defence systems, China is yet to fully develop this technology and has intensified research on developing and testing HGVs in recent times.

Besides, road-mobile ICBMs and strategic nuclear submarines, China is also building a large number of missile silos. Recent evidence indicates that China is constructing more than 200 missile silos for its silo-based ICBMs.[20] Reportedly, these silos are being constructed in two silo fields near Yumen in Gansu province in north-central China and another one near Hami city in eastern Xinjiang. Regardless of the number of silos China intends to fill with its ICBMs, the development indicates the possibility of a significant increase in the Chinese nuclear arsenal.

## Capability Assessment

### *Land-Based Ballistic Missile Capability*

As mentioned in the previous section, presently China's ballistic missile inventory contains eight operational nuclear-capable ballistic missile types, this includes DF-4, DF-5A, DF-5B, DF-21, DF-26, DF-31, DF-31A/AG, DF-41, JL-2 and DF-15. In this, the DF-4, DF-5A and DF-5B are only liquid-fuelled missile systems; all other ballistic missiles are solid propellant systems.

In the last 10 years China has added four land-based (mention of DF-5B and DF-26 are only found post-2011 reports of SIPRI database and US DoD report, although the development of these missiles *began* before 2010) ballistic missiles to its existing missile inventory. This includes, addition of DF-5B, DF-5C, DF-26 and DF-41, of these missiles DF-5C and DF-41 are under development. With this China's land-based ballistic missile inventory contains seven types of intercontinental-range ballistic missiles (ICBM), i.e. DF-4, DF-5A, DF-5B, DF-5C, DF-31, DF-31A, DF-41; one intermediate-range ballistic missile (IRBM), i.e. DF-26; and two types of medium-range ballistic missile, i.e. DF-21 (1750 km) and DF-15 with a range of 600 km. From this database, it can be observed that China has a combination of missiles with varied ranges and capabilities with two (DF-5B and DF-41) of these missiles having the capability of carrying MIRVed warheads.

Several flight tests of these missile systems have been conducted over the past ten years to achieve improved performance, targeting and accuracy parameters. According to the 2019 US DoD report "in 2019, the PRC launched more ballistic missiles for testing and training than the rest of the world combined." To comprehend these developments in the past one decade, the following is a detailed analysis of some significant and recently developed missiles in China's missile inventory.

**DF-41**—DF-41 (CSS-X-20) is an intercontinental-range, road-mobile, three-stage, MIRV-capable, solid-fuelled ballistic missile. PLARF is developing the missile since the late 1990s.[21] The range of this missile is estimated to be more than 12,000 km. Reportedly, the missile is able to carry six to ten MIRVed warheads, however, uncertainty remains regarding the actual capability of the missile. Also, according to some reports China is considering rail-mobile and silo-based deployment for the DF-41.[22] As the missile becomes larger, rail-mobile deployment offers certain advantages, which allow effective concealment and reduce the challenges of road mobility both for the transporter and supporting network of roads and bridges.

Based on the limited public information about the test of the missile, the missile was last tested in May 2018 and there have been ten flight tests of the missile since 2012, with an increase in the pace of testing since 2015.[23] DF-41 was first officially revealed at China's National Day parade on October 1, 2019. According to US DoD 2019 report, at least, 16 road-mobile DF-41 launchers were paraded at the parade in October 2019 that belong to two PLARF brigades. The DF-41 is expected to replace aging and liquid-fuelled DF-5 ICBM.

According to a report in the Washington Free Beacon "DF-41 is assessed by US intelligence agencies to be powerful enough to deliver ... warheads up to 7456 miles—far enough to reach every corner of the United States from launch areas in eastern China".[24] For China, deployment of the DF-41 ICBM is one of the ways to counter the US missile defence that might negatively impact the credibility of China's second-strike capability. For them, it is one of the most advanced ICBMs that can survive the first strike and effectively counter US missile defence.

A brief background on China's ICBM development would help to comprehend the evolution of the DF-41. By mid-1980s China successfully developed ICBMs that could be launched from silos. This led to the development of ICBM DF-31 in the mid-1980s and the flight test of the missile began in August 1999.[25] The DF-41 was supposed to debut in 1999 military parade but was cancelled and development of DF-31 continued. Eventually, after a decade in 2010, DF-41 was handed over to PLARF (at that time PLA second artillery force) and the flight test began in 2012. The first flight test was conducted on July 24, 2012, followed by two more tests on December 13, 2013 and December 13, 2014, respectively. The frequency of tests increased thereafter, two more tests were conducted on August 6 and December 4, 2015, two tests in 2016 on April 12 and December 12, one test on November 6, 2017 and two more tests on January 30 and May 27, 2018.[26] According to some Chinese media reports, the DF-41 has reached service standard and ready for commissioning.[27]

**DF-31 and DF-31A**—DF-31 (CSS-10 Mod 1) were the first solid-fuelled ICBM developed by China. China's first generation of ballistic missiles were liquid-fuelled, including the ICBM DF-5. The DF-31 is solid-fuelled, road-mobile, three-stage ICBM with a range of 7,200 km. The flight test of this missile started in August 1999 and was probably completed by the mid-2000s.[28] The DF-31 is known to be first deployed in 2006. But the deployment of the missile appears to have been terminated with fewer than ten launchers presently fielded.[29] In the recent issues of US DoD reports, hardly any mention of the missile has been found. The 2020 US DoD also did not mention the missile. It can be inferred that the DF-31 might get replaced by its upgraded version DF-31A. Some analysts predict that the missile will eventually replace the liquid-fuelled ballistic missile DF-4 with almost same range.

An extended range version of the DF-31 known as DF-31A/AG (CSS-10 Mod 2) is developed and deployed by China in 2007. The DF-31A is a road-mobile, solid-fuelled, three-stage ICBM with a range of 11,200 km that has the capability to reach almost all locations within the continental US.[30] According to some media report another variant of the missile, DF-31B might also undergoing development by China.[31]

**DF-4, DF-5A & DF-5B**—DF-4 (CSS-3) and DF-5 are China's first-generation liquid-fuelled ballistic missile. The DF-4 is a two-stage, liquid-fuelled ballistic missile with a range of at least 5,500 km that has the capability to reach Moscow and Guam. Being one of the oldest and first developed liquid-fuelled ICBMs, DF-4 is predicted to be replaced by DF-31 ICBM. DF-4 was expected to be decommissioned by 2005, but reportedly one brigade remains operational near Lingbao, Henan province.[32]

The silo-based, liquid-fuelled, two-stage intercontinental-range ballistic missile DF-5A (CSS-4 Mod 1) is an upgraded version of the earlier first-generation liquid-fuelled ballistic missile DF-5, that was first deployed in 1981. DF-5 was first tested in 1971. In September 2015, China first time displayed the DF-5B (CSS-4 Mod 2) missile that can carry multiple independently targetable re-entry vehicles (MIRVs). Another variant of the missile, DF-5C is reportedly under development by China that was flight tested in 2017 with MIRVs.[33] Both the DF-5A and DF-5B have a minimum range of 13,000 km and these missiles are presently China's longest-range ICBMs. According to some estimate China has approximately 20 DF-5A and DF-5B and half of these missiles are equipped with MIRVs.[34] It is predicted that China has started to deploy DF-5B with multiple warheads in response to the US deployment of ballistic missile defence system to improve the capability of its missile force with more survivable delivery systems.

**DF-21 & DF-21A**—In January 1985, the Chinese government approved a plan in China's missile programme to develop solid fuelled nuclear-capable missiles to replace the earlier version of liquid-fuelled nuclear missile of the *banian sidan* plan of 1965. According to this plan, China adopted a programme to build "four missiles in eight years".[35] China's current generation of solid fuelled strategic missile-like DF-21 (CSS-5) was developed as a part of this plan and first deployed in 1996 after it was first tested in May 1985.[36] DF-21 is a solid fuelled, two-stage, road-mobile ballistic missile and has a range of at least 1750 km.

Research on an upgraded variant of the missile began in August 1995 and the new variant DF-21A (CSS-5 Mod 2) was first deployed in 1996. An enhanced range (2150 km) version, possibly known as DF-21E (CSS-5 Mod 6) of the missile was deployed in 2017.[37] According to the US Department of Defense report 2020, the missile is capable of hitting targets in the Indo-Pacific region, this suggests that with limited range the missile serves a regional deterrent role contrary to the ICBMs which are primarily built to deter US missile defence system. According to a report by the Federation of American scientists, DF-21 can hit targets throughout Northern India, the Republics of Central Asia, and most of Vietnam and Southeast Asia from China's southern and north-west border.[38]

**DF-26**—DF-26 is a road-mobile, solid-fuelled, two-stage, dual-capable ballistic missile and has a range of approximately 4000 km. The missile is capable of delivering nuclear warheads to ground targets in the Western Pacific and can also be used for conventional strikes against ships in the same region.[39] The PLARF first revealed the missile in August 2015 and it was deployed in 2017, although according to the 2020 US DoD report, the missile was deployed in 2016. Also, the report claims that the missile is "capable of conducting both conventional and nuclear precision strikes against ground targets as well as conventional strikes against naval targets". First known flight test of the DF-26 was carried out on January 24, 2019.[40] Another possible test launch of the long-range anti-ship missile was carried out in August 2020 as part of a military exercise. Though China's Defence Ministry has not confirmed the missile test, China's government-controlled media Global Times claimed that the launch was carried out in a response to a US joint naval exercise with Japan, India and Australia.[41] As part of the exercise, two US aircraft carrier was sent to South China Sea in July 2020, after which the exercises were carried out in the Indian Ocean and the Philippine Sea. Chinese experts perceived the exercise in the South China Sea as an act of containment by the US against China and claimed that the precision strike "aircraft carrier killer,"—DF-26 has given "the PLA the ability to effectively attack aircraft carriers at far ... ranges".[42] It was also reported by the Chinese media that the missile is capable of striking a vast region in the West Pacific and the Indian Ocean and US military bases in Guam, Darwin and Diego Garcia. Although, China has other missiles that have the capability to strike Guam, the DF-26's capability to strike aircraft carriers with precision strike makes it a significant addition in the PLARF. According to a former director of operations at the US Pacific Command's Joint Intelligence Center, the August 2020 "missile tests showed a high level of sophistication ... China has or is very close to establishing procedures for coordinated fleet-SRF anti-ship ballistic missile attacks". Earlier in a report, Chinese state media claimed that Beijing had developed a "complete system" that includes aircraft, satellites and ships to monitor the movements of enemy vessels and relay information to the missile so that it can adjust its trajectory during the final attack.[43] The recent tests and media reports of the DF-26 missile indicate towards this development. The weapon essentially represents China's strategic advancement in the recent time which is focused on expanding Beijing's reach in the Western Pacific Ocean to challenge US military dominance in the region.

### *Sea-Based Ballistic Missile Capability*

JL-2—The JL-2 (CSS-NX-14) is a solid fuelled, intercontinental range, three-stage submarine-launched ballistic missile (SLBM) with a minimum range of 7000 km. The missile was first time showcased at China's National Day parade on October 1, 2019. JL-2 was first to test-launched in 2002 and subsequent test launch was reported in 2003, 2004, 2005, 2012 and 2015.[44] It suffered series of testing failures until its apparent successful test in August 2012.[45] The missile is a sea-based variant of the DF-31 ICBM and it has been deployed on China's four operational *Jin*-class SSBNs which are equipped to carry up to 12 JL-2 SLBM based at Yulin Naval base of Hainan island in the South China Sea.[46] The missile may bring Hawaii and Alaska (not continental US) within its reach if it is launched from Chinese territorial water. But until the missile is positioned significantly eastward in areas near north and east of Hawaii, it could not target the continental US and stationing the missile well within the Pacific Ocean would make it vulnerable to hostile attack.[47] According to US DoD report 2020, a longer-ranged, more capable variant—JL-3 is presently under development and that will likely be deployed on China's next-generation 096 SSBN.

With the development of the JL-2, China acquired its first credible sea-based nuclear deterrent that would enable it for viable sea-based second-strike capability. Similarly, owing to the limited range of the ICBM it can be inferred that China has developed the missile primarily to reduce its threat perception and to assert Beijing's territorial claim in the South China Sea area by stationing its attack submarines.

## An Analysis of China's Defence White Papers

The reflection of China's nuclear missile modernisation over the decade can be observed in the 2013 defence white paper and two subsequent defence white papers. The following section traces these developments in China's defence white paper post-2010.

Even as China continues to maintain ambiguity and secrecy regarding its nuclear and missile programme, however, it shares limited information related to nuclear strategy and policy by issuing the defence white paper, typically published biennially. Since 2011, China has published defence white papers three times in 2013, 2015 and most recently in 2019. An analysis of these documents would help to trace any changes and/or features of China's official outlook on the nuclear and missile programme and its nuclear policy from time to time.

As stated by the 2019 China defence white paper, China's main strategic goal is to "maintain national strategic security by deterring other countries from using or threatening to use nuclear weapons against China by keeping its nuclear capabilities at the minimum level required for national security". The paper states that "China is always committed to a nuclear policy of no first use of nuclear weapons at any time and under any circumstances, and not using or threatening to use nuclear weapons against non-nuclear-weapon states or nuclear-weapon-free zones unconditionally". The white paper also states that "China advocates the ultimate complete prohibition and thorough destruction of nuclear weapons" and that "China does not engage in any nuclear arms race with any other country". Therefore, China asserts its commitment to complete nuclear disarmament. Though, steady and continuous development of nuclear arsenal throughout the past years along with incessant development and modernisation of nuclear-capable missile technologies by China likely suggest a different reality that makes such claims difficult to substantiate.

China's 2013 defence white paper did not specifically use the word "no first use", while describing its nuclear posture. The white paper (2013) rather stated that in the event of a nuclear threat, China's nuclear force will act upon the order of the Central Military Commission (CMC) and get ready for "a nuclear counterattack to deter the enemy from using nuclear weapons against China" and in the event of a nuclear attack "nuclear missile force of the PLASAF (now PLARF) will use nuclear missiles to launch a resolute counterattack".

However, the 2015 defence white paper reconfirmed China's nuclear posture of "no first use" and stated that "China has always pursued the policy of no first use of nuclear weapons and adhered to a self-defensive nuclear strategy" and further declared its commitment towards non-use of nuclear weapon against non-nuclear-weapon states and nuclear weapon-free zone. These views of China's nuclear strategy remained largely similar in the 2019 defence white paper except for some changes related to modernisation of nuclear force and capability building.

In the 2015 white paper, China indicated towards optimising its nuclear force structure, improved "strategic early warning, command and control, missile penetration, rapid reaction, and survivability and protection". While, in the 2019 defence white paper apart from strengthening "the safety management of nuclear weapons and facilities" Beijing emphasised on maintaining the "appropriate level of readiness of its nuclear weapon". It further stated that the PLA has "moderately increased the active force" of the PLA rocket force (PLARF) and PLA Navy while maintaining the active force of the Air Force and significantly downsizing that of PLA army.

These developments highlight primarily two priorities of China—enhancing its sea-based deterrent, specifically in the Western Pacific Ocean and the South China Sea to essentially deter US presence and to assert its disputed claim in the region; and to enhance strategic deterrence capability by modernising the PLA rocket force.

The 2019 Defence White Paper has repeatedly mentioned and blamed the US for increasing regional and global tension and described US pursuit as "absolute military" supremacy.[48] China has specifically held responsible for US dominance in the Asia-Pacific region for creating complexities and stated that "the US is strengthening its Asia-Pacific military alliances and reinforcing military deployment and intervention, adding complexity to regional security." And it continues to assert its territorial claim on the South China Sea by adding that "the South China Sea islands and Diaoyu Islands are inalienable parts of the Chinese territory. China exercises its national sovereignty to build infrastructure and deploy necessary defensive capabilities on the islands and reefs in the South China Sea". This differs from the 2015 white paper where China vaguely addressed these issues and stated, "some external countries are also busy meddling in South China Sea affairs". The recent deployment of "aircraft-carrier killer" missile DF-26 and submarine-launched ballistic missile JL-2 along with the public display of the JL-2 as recently as in October 2019 specify China's priority to proclaim dominance in the Western Pacific and South China Sea islands to deter primarily US "intervention".[49]

Another significant development related to China's nuclear force that can be found in 2019 defence white paper is the transformation of the PLA second artillery force (PLASAF) to the PLA rocket force (PLARF). In 2015 defence white paper it had been stated that "the PLA Second Artillery Force (PLASAF) will strive to transform itself in the direction of informationization … the PLASAF will strengthen its capabilities for strategic deterrence and nuclear counterattack, and medium—and long-range precision strikes". As mentioned in the previous section, the renaming took place in December 2015 and PLARF was established as fourth branch of China's armed forces. To underscore PLARF's advanced role in the "new era" in the 2019 defence white paper it was stated that "the PLARF is enhancing its credible and reliable capabilities of nuclear deterrence and counterattack, strengthening intermediate and long-range precision strike forces, and enhancing strategic counter-balance capability, so as to build a strong and modernized rocket force". Likewise, it was mentioned that while the active force of the PLAA, PLAAF has remained same or trimmed significantly, the active force of PLARF has moderately increased and optimised. In this regard, the 2020 US DoD report found China's claim of keeping its "nuclear capabilities at the minimum level required for national security" contradictory, as seemingly China's nuclear force is on a trajectory to exceed the "minimum deterrent" level as evident from the latest white paper.

## Implications for India

Principles of India's nuclear force are clearly articulated in India's nuclear doctrine, unlike its nuclear-armed neighbours. The draft report of NSAB on the Indian Nuclear Doctrine specified that the Indian nuclear force would be "effective, enduring, diverse, flexible, and responsive to the requirements in accordance with the concept of credible minimum deterrence".[50]

The objectives behind these principles were to enhance the credibility, effectiveness and survivability of the nuclear force against a first strike and to retaliate efficiently. Accordingly, India has resolved to keep the nuclear arsenal at a minimum level and purely for deterrence purposes.

Both of India's nuclear neighbours, China and Pakistan continue to have a larger number of nuclear warheads compared to India.[51] Pakistan follows an aggressive nuclear first-use posture. Apart from the large stockpile of nuclear warheads, China has qualitatively superior nuclear missiles. While India still faces challenges regarding the size, scope and qualitative superiority of its arsenals vis-à-vis China.

Also, since India follows NFU policy, it is crucial to ensure the survivability of its nuclear forces. This implies the need to develop and maintain a reliable and effective nuclear force by investing in emerging nuclear technologies that include MIRVs, hypersonic weapon capability, Ballistic missile defence systems, artificial intelligence, missile launcher and R&D. Last few year's trends of India's nuclear modernisation show India has been developing these technologies and conducts regular missile tests.

One of the most significant of this modernisation is the development of India's sea-based deterrence capability. India will have to contribute significantly to strengthen its sea-based leg of deterrence and thus the nuclear triad. An effective sea-based leg of nuclear deterrence enhances survivability. Due to its stealth capability, the survivability of nuclear-powered submarines as a platform for SLBMs makes them the most reliable of the nuclear triad. As mentioned before, China has four Jin-class SSBNs with two more under construction. Each SSBN can carry up to 12, JL-2 missiles. The range of the missile enables China to target Alaska, Guam, Hawaii, India and Russia from Chinese waters. Whereas, India's only SSBN INS Arihant became operational in November 2018. Therefore, there is a compelling need for India to further strengthen its nuclear submarine fleet to provide adequate platforms for its SLBMs.

Similarly, as previously mentioned, China is actively developing and modernising its MIRV and hypersonic weapon capabilities besides the development of its dual-capable missiles.

To reduce vulnerabilities, apart from developing long range nuclear missiles, reportedly, India is also focusing on developing effective hypersonic weapon capability and MIRV technology.[52]

In September 2020, the DRDO test-fired a Hypersonic Technology Demonstrator Vehicle (HSTDV) using a solid rocket motor that will lead to the development of a hypersonic cruise missile system[53] in the future. Similarly, it is reported that India's Agni-V and Agni-VI are MIRV-capable nuclear missiles.[54] Although there are no government reports available that confirm this. Some analysts argue that there is no need for MIRVs on Indian missiles.[55] Without clear insights into China's operationalisation of a prospective BMD system, developing MIRVed missiles by India might not provide any cost-effective tactical utility.[56]

While not every capability build-up needs to be addressed by similar development, a close insight into these developments is required to focus on the actual prerequisite of India's nuclear force and to avoid wasteful expenditure of resources.

As Beijing continues to improve on the quality and number of the nuclear arsenal, it refuses to be part of any negotiation with the US and Russia that might restrict the expansion of PRC's nuclear arsenal. In the absence of any arms control measure that limits the scope of China's arsenal, it is predicted to continue the expansion of its nuclear capabilities. Since Beijing argues its nuclear arsenal is too small to enter a trilateral arms control agreement with Russia and United States.

Similarly, the recent development that shows China is likely to construct a large number of new nuclear missile silos indicates the rapid pace of modernisation of its nuclear arsenal. While it is predicted by some analysts that China is building up its strategic capabilities in response to US hostility. The absence of dialogue might lead to wrong assumptions regarding the use of nuclear weapons in future conflict and this will potentially generate new threat perceptions.[57] This ambiguity and capability build-up by Beijing also adds up to New Delhi's threat perception, risking degradation of overall security relations.

## Future Trajectories and Conclusion

From the above analysis, it can be observed that in the last decade China's missile development programme has grown significantly and new missile systems have been added to mitigate China's national security risk. Missiles like DF-26, JL-2, DF-41 have undergone significant development over the last ten years. Enhancement of sea-based deterrent reflects China's increasing priority to deter the US and its military alliance dominance or presence in the South China Sea and western pacific region. It has been enhanced by addition and further development of solid-fuelled, silo-based ICBMs and MIRV capable-nuclear missiles like DF-41 and the "aircraft-carrier killer" DF-26 to deter the US missile defence system. The US missile defence system poses a significant threat to China that is prominent from its 2019 defence white paper, which stated: "it (US) has provoked and intensified competition among major countries, significantly increased its defense expenditure, pushed for additional capacity in nuclear ... and missile defense, and undermined global strategic stability." The development of China's sea-based nuclear deterrent would provide China with viable second-strike capability and also a nuclear triad of delivery systems that would be completed with development of nuclear-capable air-launched ballistic missile (ALBM) that is predicted to be undergoing development by China.

Moreover, the transformation of PLA second artillery force to PLA rocket force and giving it full-service status, apart from increasing the active force number of PLARF, reflects China's strategic goal of "enhancing its credible and reliable capabilities of nuclear deterrence and counterattack, strengthening intermediate and long-range precision strike forces". Although China has repeatedly asserted a minimum nuclear deterrence posture and might not be seeking numerical parity of nuclear warheads with the US or Russia, reported open-ended growth of the Chinese nuclear arsenal and nuclear forces is deepening uncertainty and anxiety in neighbouring countries and other nuclear-armed states about China's long-term intentions.[58] Similarly, China has also invested in a range of technologies including MaRVs, MIRVs, hypersonic glide vehicles and conducted numerous training exercises to increase its force survivability and operational readiness.

Likewise, there is an ongoing effort to shift towards solid fuelled missiles while maintaining a limited number of liquid-fuelled missiles. China's first-generation missiles like DF-3, DF-4 and DF-5 were liquid-fuelled and in 1985, Central Military Commission restructured China's missile programs to develop a new generation of solid-fuelled missiles. Although MIRV capable, liquid-fuelled ICBM DF-5C is undergoing development, variants of DF-5 are the only liquid-fuelled system in China's nuclear inventory. As mentioned earlier, another liquid-fuelled missile DF-4—one of the earliest developed liquid-fuelled missiles is expected to be replaced by DF-31 solid-fuelled ICBM. China has also continued to diversify, improve and increased the number of nuclear missile launch platforms and launch sites with a seeming increase in developing silo-based nuclear missiles that provide increased readiness to its nuclear force.

Finally, over the next decade China's nuclear capability is likely to grow, but whether it will double as predicted by the US estimates remains unclear. China is predicted to have enough nuclear material to double the stockpile without producing new fissile material. But, will it continue to be guided by the philosophy of minimalism?

In any case, as China moves ahead with its current pace of modernisation to improve the capability and readiness of its rocket force, it is likely that China will continue to be a potential threat to the neighbouring countries and US. Although China views development in the US posture as a serious challenge to its deterrent based on a minimal missile force, at the same time China seeks to avoid a nuclear arms race with the US, a lesson that many analysts claim China had learnt from the Soviet experience of the Cold War.[59] As a result, while maintaining the posture of assured retaliation, China is likely to alter how it implements the assured retaliation by allowing ambiguity regarding its missile force and expanding the size and sophistication of its arsenal to ensure survivability.[60] These developments coupled with lack of transparency of its missile force raises a serious question regarding its minimum deterrent posture and increase in its active missile forces. What is minimal for China might not be perceived as same by its neighbouring countries and the rest of the world.

## Notes

1. "China's National Defence in the New Era", 2019 Defence white paper, The State Council Information Office of the People's Republic of China, July 2019.
2. Hans M. Kristensen and Matt Korda, "Chinese nuclear forces 2019", *Bulletin of the Atomic Scientists*, 75:4, pp. 171-178.
3. "China inaugurates PLA Rocket Force as military reform deepens (2)", Xinhua, January 2, 2016, at http://en.people.cn/n3/2016/0102/c90786-8998406-2.html. Accessed on June 15, 2020.
4. Li Jiayao (Editor), "China's National Defense in the New Era", Xinhuanet, July 24, 2019, at http://eng.mod.gov.cn/publications/2019-07/24/content_4846452.htm. Accessed on May 23, 2020.
5. n. 3.
6. Li Xuan, "From "soldiers" to "army", the Rocket Army has to take up the historical mission", *Science and Technology Daily,* February 23, 2016, at http://www.81.cn/depb/2016-02/23/content_6923516.htm. David C. Logan, "Making Sense of China's Missile Forces," in Phillip C. Saunders and Joel Wuthnow (eds), *Chairman Xi Remakes the PLA: Assessing Chinese Military Reforms,* NDU Press, Washington D.C., 2019. Accessed on June 17, 2020.
7. World Nuclear Forces, SIPRI yearbook 2020.
8. "China says its trial launch of DF-5C missile normal", Ministry of National Defense the People's Republic of China, press release February 6, 2017.
9. The range is an uncertain figure. For more information refer to Shannon N. Kile and Hans M. Kristensen, Chinese nuclear forces, World nuclear forces, *SIPRI Yearbook 2018.*
10. Ibid.
11. Submarine-launched ballistic missile JL-1, which dates from the 1980s, is no longer considered to be operational. China's Type 092/Xia-class nuclear powered ballistic

missile submarine (SSBN) was the launch platform for SLBM JL-1. The Xia-class submarines were replaced by Jin-class submarines launched in the 2004-2012 timeframe. For more information check https://missiledefenseadvocacy.org/missile-threat-and-proliferation/missilewwwwwwww-proliferation/china/jl-1/

12. Chinese nuclear forces 2019, *Bulletin of Atomic Scientists.*
13. Ibid.
14. Manpreet Sethi, "China's Ballistic Missile Capability and India's Preparedness", *Scholar Warrior,* Autumn 2015, Centre for Land Warfare Studies.
15. Ibid.
16. U.S.-China Economic and Security Review Commission, *China's Offensive Missile Forces,* Chapter 2 Section 3, annual report 2015, at https://www.uscc.gov/annual-report/2015-annual-report-congress. Accessed on October 15, 2020.
17. Missile Defense Project, "DF-17," Missile Threat, Center for Strategic and International Studies, February 19, 2020, last modified June 23, 2020, at https://missilethreat.csis.org/missile/df-17/. Accessed on October 15, 2020.
18. Ibid.
19. Zachary Keck, "Will Hypersonic Capabilities Render Missile Defense Obsolete?", *The Diplomat,* February 7, 2014, at https://thediplomat.com/2014/02/will-hypersonic-capabilities-render-missile-defense-obsolete/; and James M. Acton, "China's Offensive Missile Forces", Testimony: U.S.-China Economic And Security Review Commission, Carnegie Endowment for International Peace, April 1, 2015, at https://carnegieendowment.org/2015/04/01/china-s-offensive-missile-forces-pub-59613. Accessed on October 15, 2020.
20. Matt Korda and Hans Kristensen, "China Is Building A Second Nuclear Missile Silo Field", Federation of American scientist, July 26, 2021, at https://fas.org/blogs/security/2021/07/china-is-building-a-second-nuclear-missile-silo-field/. Accessed on October 16, 2021.
21. Shannon N. Kile and Hans M. Kristensen, n. 9.
22. Ibid.
23. Ibid
24. Hans M. Kristensen & Robert S. Norris, "Chinese nuclear forces 2016", *Bulletin of the Atomic Scientists,* 72:4, pp. 205-211.
25. David C. Logan, n. 6.
26. M. S. Prathibha, "China's DF-41 Ballistic Missile Deployment and the Impact on its Nuclear Deterrence", *Journal of Defence Studies,* Vol. 13, No. 4, October-December 2019, pp. 51-69.
27. Qiu Yue, "Expert: Dongfeng-41 has reached service standards and ranks among the world's most advanced missiles", *People's Daily,* June 9, 2018, at http://military.people.com.cn/n1/2018/0609/c1011-30047293.html. Accessed on July 9, 2020.
28. Logan, 2019, n. 5.

29. Hans M. Kristensen and Matt Korda, "Chinese nuclear forces 2019", *Bulletin of the Atomic Scientists*, 75:4, pp. 171-178.
30. Military and Security Developments Involving the People's Republic of China 2020, Office of the Secretary of Defense, Department of Defense, USA.
31. Ibid.
32. Missile Defense Project, "DF-4 (Dong Feng-4 / CSS-3), "Missile Threat", Center for Strategic and International Studies, October 26, 2017, last modified November 26, 2019, at https://missilethreat.csis.org/missile/df-4/. Accessed on August 13, 2020.
33. Kristensen and Korda, n. 29.
34. Ibid.
35 John Wilson Lewis and Xue Litai. "Strategic Weapons and Chinese Power: The Formative Years." *The China Quarterly*, no. 112 (1987): 541-54, at http://www.jstor.org/stable/653778. Accessed on September 19, 2020.
36. John Wilson Lewis and Xue Litai, *China's Strategic Seapower: The Politics of Force Modernization in the Nuclear Age*, Stanford University Press, Stanford, 1996. Also, see Logan 2019, n. 5, p. 398.
37. Chinese nuclear forces, *SIPRI yearbook 2020* n. 1.
38. DF-21 / CSS-5, *Federation of American scientists,* at https://fas.org/nuke/guide/china/theater/df-21.htm. Accessed on August 15, 2020.
39. Brendan Scott, "China missiles able to send nukes to Western Pacific, US says", *Stars and Stripes,* June 7, 2017, at https://www.stripes.com/news/pacific/china-missiles-able-to-send-nukes-to-western-pacific-us-says-1.472424. Accessed on August 20, 2020.
40. Caitlin Doornbos, "China tests 'Guam killer' missile, claims weapon could strike moving aircraft carrier", *Stars and Stripes,* January 29, 2019, at https://www.stripes.com/news/china-tests-guam-killer-missile-claims-weapon-could-strike-moving-aircraft-carrier-1.566456. Accessed on August 15, 2020.
41. Liu Xuanzun, "PLA Rocket Force launches DF-26 'aircraft carrier killer' missile in fast-reaction drills", *Global Times,* August 6, 2020.
42. Ibid.
43. Brad Lendon, "China test fires so-called 'carrier killer' missiles into South China Sea", CNN, August 29, 2020, at https://edition.cnn.com/2020/08/28/asia/china-missile-tests-exercises-intl-hnk-scli/index.html. Accessed on September 5, 2020.
44. Missile Defense Project, "JL-2 (Ju Lang-2/CSS-NX-14)," Missile Threat, Center for Strategic and International Studies, August 12, 2016, last modified October 7, 2019, at https://missilethreat.csis.org/missile/jl-2/. Accessed on September 10, 2020.
45. Hans M. Kristensen and Robert S. Norris, Chinese nuclear forces, 2011, *Bulletin of the Atomic Scientists,* 67(6), pp. 81–87. *Also see,* Annual Report to Congress: Military

and Security Developments Involving the People's Republic of China 2013, at www.defense.gov/pubs/2013_china_report_final.pdf. Also see n. 5.

46. Chinese nuclear forces, *SIPRI Yearbook 2020* n. 1.
47. US DoD report 2020.
48. Ibid.
49. "China's National Defence in the New Era", 2019 Defence white paper, The State Council Information Office of the People's Republic of China, July 2019.
50. Government of India "Draft Report of National Security Advisory Board on Indian Nuclear Doctrine", August 17, 1999.
51. World Nuclear Forces, *SIPRI Yearbook 2020.*
52. "Shaurya Missile Test this week", *The New Indian Express,* September 20, 2011, at https://www.newindianexpress.com/states/odisha/2011/sep/20/shaurya-missile-test-this-week-292787.html and Ministry of Defence, "Year End Review-2020", Government of India, at https://pib.gov.in/PressReleaseIframePage.aspx?PRID=1685437
53. ANI, "India can have complete hypersonic cruise system in 4-5 years: DRDO", *The Economic Times,* October 14, 2020, at https://economictimes.indiatimes.com/news/defence/india-can-have-complete-hypersonic-cruise-missile-system-in-4-5-years.
54. India's Nuclear Forces 2020 and PTI, "India developing Agni-VI missile capable of carrying multiple warheads: DRDO chief", *Business Line,* March 9, 2018, at https://www.thehindubusinessline.com/news/india-developing-agni-vi-missile-capable-of-carrying-multiple-warheads-drdo-chief/article20575500.ece1.
55. H M Kristensen, "India's Missile Modernization Beyond Minimum Deterrence." FAS Strategic Security Blog, October 4, 2013 as noted in India's Missile Capability 2020, *Bulletin of Atomic Scientist.*
56. Rajesh Basrur and Jaganath Sankaran, "India's Slow and Unstoppable Move to MIRV", *The Lure and Pitfalls of MIRVs,* ed. Michael Krepon, Travis Wheeler and Shane Mason. Stimson, May 2016.
57. Tong Zhao, "What's Driving China's Nuclear Buildup?", Carnegie Endowment for International Peace, August 5, 2021, at https://carnegieendowment.org/2021/08/05/what-s-driving-china-s-nuclear-buildup-pub-85106.
58. US DoD report 2020.
59. Fiona S. Cunningham and M. Taylor Fravel, "Assuring Assured Retaliation: China's Nuclear Posture and U.S.-China Strategic Stability", *International Security,* Vol. 40, No. 2 (Fall 2015), pp. 7-50, at doi:10.1162/ISEC_a_00215. Accessed on October 12, 2020.
60. Ibid.

# 9

# OTH Radar: A Necessity for the Indian Skies

SWAIM PRAKASH SINGH

> Lord Wellington always dreamt of how he could see over the hill to deploy his forces and so is our concern today to look beyond Himalayas.

The government of India has put the arduous task of safeguarding and securing the Indian skies from any external intrusion to the Indian Air Force (IAF) as mandated in the Union War Book of India. This task is a mammoth challenge for the IAF as India has vast and varied territory to defend. The geographical dimensions in thousands of kilometres include a variety of terrain, including high mountains, arid deserts, plateaus, and peninsular coastlines. India has moved quite significantly in protecting its skies to a considerable extent through the medium of sensors. These include High and Medium Powered Radars with versions of both static and transportable ones and Low-Level Transportable Radars (LLTR). IAF, as the lead service and organisation, has effectively integrated sensors of all kinds, be it military or civil, static or mobile, integrated into its network-centric operations. In a nutshell, the Air Defence of IAF has grown leaps and bounds in ensuring gap-free coverage of the majority of its skies.

A few years now, India has started concentrating away from the western axis to the Northern front. Particularly of concern to India is the massive development of China's Logistics infrastructure in the TAR that enables rapid build-up of PLA along the Sino-India border area. From present indications, China will require another couple of years for its military modernisation programme to produce a modern force capable of defeating a moderate size adversary. Our concerns have enhanced, and so is the preparedness in this theatre. Union war book of India entrusts the responsibility of safeguarding the Indian Airspace to IAF. And northern and eastern India and a credible adversary opposite have maximum to detect and defend. It may be appreciated that technological advancements worldwide have forced us to look beyond conventional surveillance measures. Therefore, it is imperative that unconventional measures may also be explored for better and more effective surveillance set up in India.

## Sensors Deployment in India

**Military Sensors.** IAF has a well-institutionalised mechanism of control and reporting of aerial objects flying in the Indian skies. The Air Defence stream of IAF has been proficiently monitoring the skies through a time-tested network of a plethora of radars stitched together in a system called Air Defence Ground Environmental System (ADGES). The flying objects from ground level upwards are mainly detected by High Powered Radars (HPR) and Medium Powered Radars (MPR) located at vantage locations spread all over the country, especially in the border areas. Sighting and finding these radars is an arduous task for the planners as radars are required to be positioned in an obstruction-free area for an adequate formation of radar beam pattern to detect all flying objects. Typically, these radars operate on S and L band frequencies. Indian airspace is well covered in the desert areas and plains as there are few restrictions on its placement. However, hilly areas and mountainous regions do not have such luxury due to inherent loss of line of sight. It, therefore, gives rise to areas where flying objects cannot be detected adequately, thus creating a difficult proposition for the Air Defence operators to ensure foolproof coverage of the entire Indian airspace.

The Air Defence network of radars is a mix of Soviet, Israeli and French-origin sensors. The backbone of medium and high-level detection of flying objects is through the workhorse of rugged THD 1955 radars of French origin and the low-level coverage is through a variety of LLTRs spread across the country. The Indian airspace covers a neighbourhood of roughly 3,290,000 sq km over its landmass alone. To provide desirable early warning capability, the airspace would almost double to 7,000,000 sq km.[1] As per the conventional concept of airspace management, gap-free radar overlap over the intended area and built-in redundancy are the prime requirements for ensuring effective surveillance. This task would require pooling sensors from all national resources and bring in under the ambit of network-centric operations for timely decision-making through centralised command and decentralised execution. The IAF sensors alone would not suffice to ensure the prime requirements, thus stitching in of multiple sensors of varied origins of sister services and civil radars of Airports Authority of India (AAI) is necessitated beyond any doubt.

**Airports Authority of India (AAI).** IAF and AAI are the two critical organisations from the military and civil sectors respectively to ensure the monitoring and surveillance of air traffic in the Indian skies. IAF as 'guardian of Skies' would fall short in its expectations of safeguarding the Indian skies if the procedural and networked architecture of an all-inclusive surveillance system of the Indian airspace along with AAI is not ensured. The technological, architectural networking and Standard Operating Procedures (SOP) are currently well placed, practised, time tested, and fully operational. Website of AAI updated as of 18 August 2017 showcases its operational might in civil traffic management as "AAI manages 137 airports, which include 24 International Airports including three International Civil Enclaves, 10 Customs Airports including four Customs Civil Enclaves, 80 Domestic Airports and 23 Domestic Civil Enclaves at Defence airfields". AAI is also responsible for providing Air Traffic Management Services (ATMS) over the entire Indian Air Space and adjoining oceanic areas with ground installations at all airports and 25 other locations to ensure the safety of aircraft operations. All major air routes over Indian landmass are radar covered (29 Radar installations at 11 locations) along with VOR/DVOR coverage (89 installations) co-located with Distance Measuring Equipment (90 installations). The website also showcases its achievements as "AAI's successful implementation of Automatic Dependence Surveillance System (ADSS), using indigenous technology, at Calcutta and Chennai Air Traffic Control Centres, gave India the distinction of being the first country to use this advanced technology in the South East Asian region, thus enabling effective Air Traffic Control over oceanic areas using satellite mode of communication".[2]

**Civil Sensors.** Airports Authority of India (AAI) is the single nodal agency and Air Navigation Service Provider (ANSP) responsible for the entire traffic management of civil airlines and operators throughout the breadth and length of the country. Till a decade back, the surveillance system of AAI was mainly dependent on the radars of Raytheon origin. However, AAI has been on the upgradation spree to modernise its airspace control to reinforce safety, efficiency and increase airport and airspace capacity, which is a challenging task for India, the seventh-largest country by area in the world.[3]

**Spanish Indra System.** In 2009, Indra, a Spanish company was awarded several significant contracts to enhance air traffic management in India. The installation of nine Monopulse Secondary Surveillance Radars (MSSR) deployed all over the country will improve the overall radar coverage as part of the ATM system upgradation. These radars will feed air traffic data to main ATCs at Chennai, Mumbai, Kolkata, Delhi, Hyderabad, Ahmedabad, Guwahati Nagpur and Varanasi. Spanish Indra system includes installing 38 tower automation systems for 38 different airports in three different configurations. This contract is for the supply of the highest number of Automation Systems globally in recent years. The Original Equipment Manufacturers (OEM) claims that "It will meet all requirements concerning air traffic safety and high reliability of the equipment by the innovative use of the state-of-the-art technology, with a system that is safe, reliable, user-friendly, and easy to maintain". Additionally, it will cover more than 80 per cent of the Indian Airspace with the most crucial number of flight movements bringing significant improvements in ensuring Air Traffic Operations.[4]

**Czech ELDIS System.** In 2012, a new service centre for radars made by ELDIS Pardubice, a member of the industrial group Czechoslovak Group (CSG), was opened in the presence of the Chairman of AAI and Ambassador of the Czech Republic to India in New Delhi. As part of the contract total of 17 secondary surveillance radars (MSSR-1) will be installed at various airports covering almost 90 per cent of Indian airspace under its radar cover. The further acquisition of another four radars will protect nearly the whole Indian airspace by Czech radar systems for civil aviation transport.[5] These radars will be sharing the radar information with all other radars controlling the airspace of the country.[6]

**Map 9.1: Radar Coverage of** Spanish Indra System

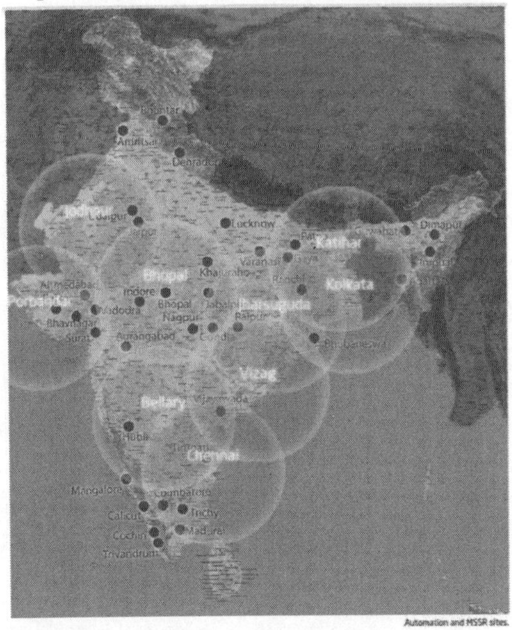


Source: https://www.indracompany.com

**Map 9.2: Radar Coverage of Czech ELDIS System**

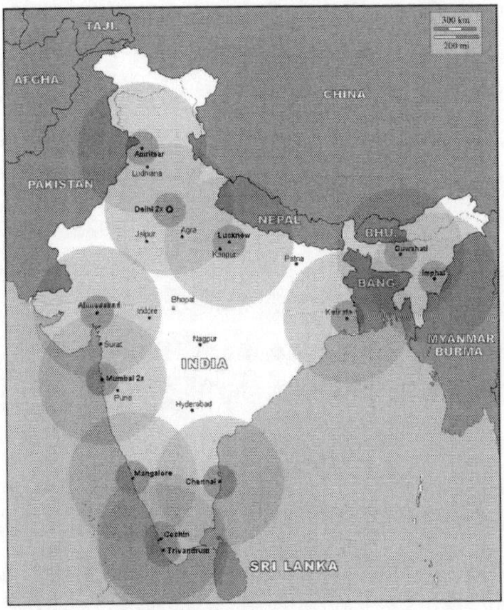


Source: Embassy of the Czech Republic.

## Radar Coverage in India

**Radar Coverage in Peninsular India.** The radar coverage in peninsular India has significant gaps all over the coastline on both eastern and western sides. It has been understood that the threat would hardly ever emanate from the seaside as the immediate border with China and Pakistan is on the land at northern and western sides, respectively. With this premise, the deployment of HPRs, MPRs, and LLTRs has been almost negligible. Also, no major airbase in the peninsular region has been the reason for not having any worthwhile radar in southern India. Vast swathes of airspace in central and peninsular India are "quite bereft" of surveillance, especially in the arena of medium-level and low-level radar coverage. IAF also wants to induct static phased array radars, coastal radars, and over-the-horizon radars, with corresponding anti-ballistic missile systems capable of neutralising missiles with a range up to 2,500 km.[7] It was only in 2009, IAF came alive to the situation after the incident of an airstrike by LTTE in Colombo in 2007. The unprecedented action by LTTE forced the government to step up radar vigil in peninsular India as the threat could emanate from the high seas, unlike in the past. It resulted in the deployment of Transportable Radar Units (TRU), which could undertake surveillance tasks at medium and high levels up to nearly 300 km into the sea to detect any intrusion into the Indian airspace.[8] Through secondary surveillance radars, AAI radars are the saving grace in the peninsular region for ensuring timely and near effective surveillance of the Indian skies. With China's growing influence in the Indo-Pacific and India's concern to tackle it through various military-diplomatic efforts and associations such as QUAD, SAGAR, IONS, etc., it becomes more critical to strengthen the number of sensors in the region.

**Radar Coverage in Mountainous Region.** The effectiveness of any radar in the mountains is adversely affected due to terrain masking. This, irrespective of whether it is a ground-based radar system or an airborne radar system. As all radars work on the line of sight principle, they are prone to radar shadows due to the mountains.[9] These problems have been overcome to a minimal extent by using mountain radars and their sitting's. However, they too have their share of issues like beam pattern of radar, extreme weather conditions affecting performance, frequency of operation, atmospheric conditions and clutter pattern. With technological developments, these factors have been reduced, yet they cannot be totally eliminated.

The sighting of radars in the hilly or mountainous region has its peculiarity and inherent limitations in detecting flying objects as described earlier. Due to the break-in Line of Sight (LOS), adversary aircraft may utilise the radar shadows to meet their intended objectives. India has got entire northern and eastern borders along with China at higher altitudes in the Himalayan ranges. It is considered a significant challenge to detect every aircraft in such areas along the edges. IAF has a few mountain radars deployed at high altitudes and in challenging climatic conditions, looking at Pakistan and China. These specialised and rugged mountain radars have played a vital role in monitoring and preventing any air intrusions by adversaries. However, there is a need to plug the existing gaps to timely detect fixed and rotary wing aircraft and drones in real-time. Due to the harsh terrain, IAF has explored the possibility of placing Low-Level Light Weight Radars (LLLWR) especially designed and manufactured for the landscape of Ladakh and the Sikkim area. These indigenous radars clubbed together are expected to pick up even small aircraft from a distance of 300 to 400 km away.[10]

## Threat Perception

**The Threat Emanating Across the Himalayas from China.** India is an emerging regional power that has been very effectively-acknowledged by most countries globally after a vigorous and well-calculated drive by Prime Minister Modi since 2014. Mr Modi has risen to greater heights in his stature the world over, and so is India as a nation. The continuing rise of India despite numerous internal challenges and economic slowdown has proven its commitment and character to the world. Such rise has irked China in all possible fields, and thus, the Modi-Xi ping duo photo ops have not yielded much in our favour for a couple of years. Pakistan, as usual, has been a constant nuisance in the region, and the recent fall of Afghanistan has been added to its accomplishment list.

India surrounded by such neighbours has always kept the nation's security apparatus on toes as the trust deficit from these countries is always on the rise. Incidents like Uri, Pulwama, Galwan, Doklam, etc., have started becoming a norm in the relations of India with the team of the Sino-Pak nexus. Post-Galwan clash, the Indian armed forces have revisited the op preparedness in the sectors along with the Himalayan ranges and have arrived at various loopholes which are being filled adequately with a firm military stance. Strengthening the radar e-Orbat in the region is one of the foremost tasks being undertaken. Mr Jayadeva Ranade quite explicitly narrates the Sino-Pak nexus as "China clearly sets the agenda. It probably views Pakistan as a junior partner, but certainly, one that is important enough for its strategic ambitions to make huge investments and secure its enduring influence". He further states that "As China's strategic and financial investments in Pakistan have grown, so too has its influence and interest. Having staked his prestige on the BRI and CPEC, Xi Jinping will not allow Pakistan to sink beyond a point".[11]

He further comments on the increasing military conniving between them as "While close Sino-Pak ties in the diplomatic, economic, military and nuclear fields and the development of weapons systems are fairly well documented, their cooperation in the maritime domain is becoming a greater and lethal concern. In addition to collaborating in building frigates, collaboration on submarines and Unmanned Underwater Vessels (UUVs) is now mentioned. If China supplies these to Pakistan, they will be based at Gwadar, Karachi, and Jiwani, increasing the vulnerability of India's western coast and the Arabian Sea. Reflecting official level thinking, China's military media in 2019 mentioned that China might sell its first aircraft carrier, Liaoning, to Pakistan once its fourth aircraft carrier is ready. They have also mentioned that Chinese air force fighter aircraft could be given to Pakistan in the event of the outbreak of hostilities with India."[12]

**Latest Acquisitions by China.** China has made remarkable progress in building up its military might. PLAAF has developed or acquired most of the sophisticated aircraft and missile technology and infrastructure. The airfields available in TAR do provide an additional advantage to her. The ROA of a few fighters and bomber covers our entire mainland VA/VPs in central India. The newly developed Gargunza airfield has become an essential launchpad for PLAAF to cover our strategic airbases. Missiles like DF 3 & DF 3 A can cover the entire country; however, we need to be concerned that SRBM such as DF 11, DF 11A and DF 15 itself are good enough to destroy the prominent targets on our side. Therefore, to minimise or neutralise the threat, our strategy to counter it would be through effective surveillance and detection of Aerial objects at all levels, including detection of SSMs. It will at least strengthen the sensor element of *'Sensor to shooter'* cycle. The present capability of PLAAF can be summarized in the following pictorial depiction.

**Map 9.3: Airfields in Tibet Autonomous Region (TAR)**

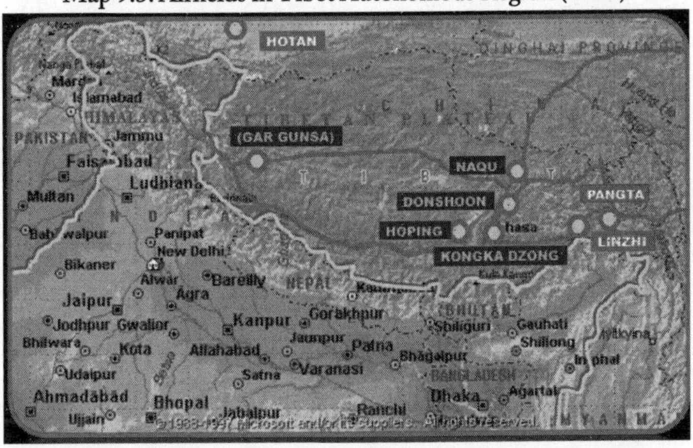


Source: Author

**Map 9.4: Radius of Action of PLAAF Aircraft from North Eastern Area**

Source: Author

### Map 9.5: Radius of Action of PLAAF Aircraft from Northern Area

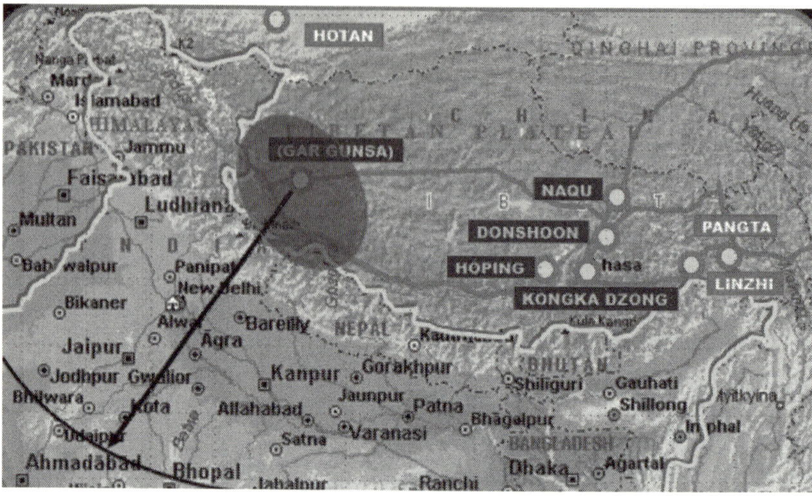


Source: Author

### Map 9.6: Coverage of Chinese IRBM

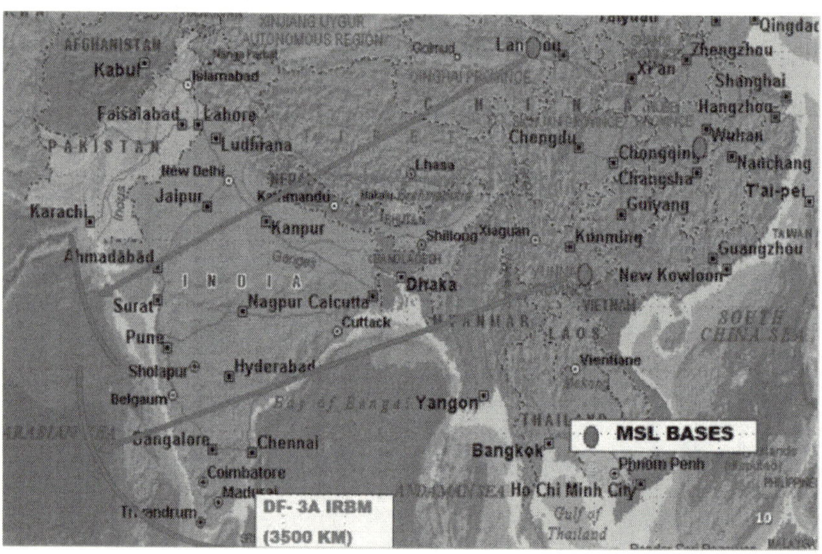


Source: Author

**Map 9.7: Radius of Action of PLAAF SRBM**

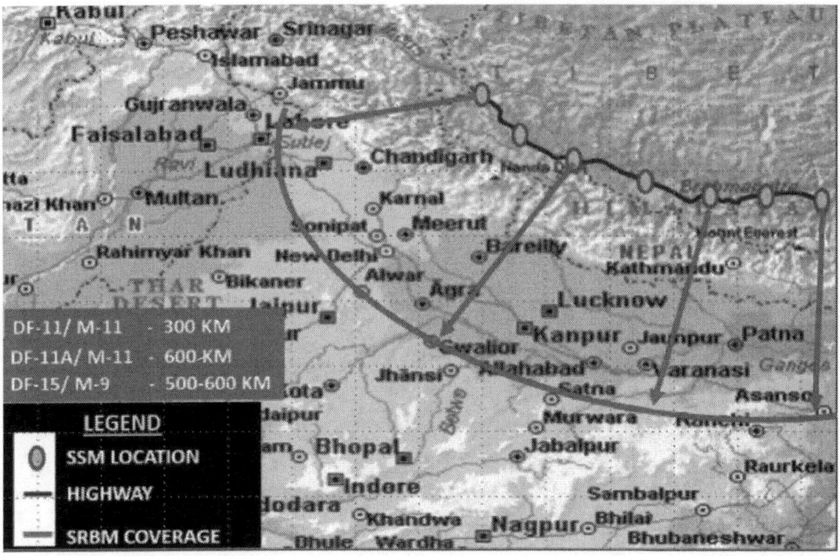


Source: Author

After having reorganised its military into regions, China must become a more firm, aggressive and capable army in the world. It has an enormous technological and numerical advantage over India at any time. Moreover, pooling the assets of PLAAF and PLAN makes it further highly potent and effective militaries. It has got a significant upper hand in both areas across the Himalayas and the Indian Ocean. Future wars will be initiated and mostly fought through the medium of air, be it through manned or unmanned aircraft, missiles or space. Land or sea will eventually come into the picture only on the culmination stage of war or the impact of the weaponry. Therefore, once again, it becomes the necessity to *catch the adversary weaponry the fastest and farthest*. Thus, India must build up or possess the capability of having entire airspace over the mainland, the Himalayas and on the high seas under its sensor cover at all times through conventional radars, OTH radars and space surveillance.

## Need for OTH Radar

Having analysed the threat looming large on the immediate bordering areas in India, it is considered essential to move beyond the dependence on the conventional static and mobile radars for the mountainous regions to counter simultaneous emerging aerial threats from China and Pakistan. India and IAF, in particular, may think of exploring the possibility of exploiting the space resources and Over the Horizon Radars (OTH) to counter threats in both Himalayan ranges and the Indo-Pacific regions. Both space resources of satellites and OTH have inherent limitations in terms of revisit time, swath, pinpointing the targets, etc. However, it is time for India must invest in these resources vigorously for safeguarding the skies. At least in the near future, there are pretty higher chances that India will have to face a few more embarrassing situations like Uri, Pulwama and Galwan.

As the seventh-largest country in its size, India would require an unprecedented number of radars in the mainland, coastline, mountainous regions, and deserts. Apart from the conventional high, medium powered radars, India may look ahead with the OTH radars in the gamut of its radar detection envelope for the entire country. India has thus far not oriented itself for this kind of Radar as the necessity was not felt so much as the condition exists today. Threats from high seas and across the Himalayas need to be detected well in time for an effective neutralisation. Thus, OTH radar could be one of the solutions to plug gaps for achieving gap-free radar coverage over the Indian skies.

**Basic Radars.** Radar basics are nothing but the essential characteristics of the travel of electromagnetic waves once encountered with any object. One of the most uncomplicated narratives of it written by Md Waqar Haider can be summed up as "Radar is a detection system that uses radio waves to determine objects' range, angle, or velocity. It can be used to detect aircraft, ships, spacecraft, guided missiles, motor vehicles, weather formations, and terrain. The RADAR system generally consists of a transmitter that produces an electromagnetic signal radiated into space by an antenna. When this signal strikes an object, it gets reflected or re-radiated in many directions. This reflected signal is received by the radar antenna, which delivers it to the receiver, where it is processed to determine the geographical statistics of the object. Radar is still most familiar as a military technology. Radar antennas mounted at airports or other ground stations can be used to detect approaching enemy aeroplanes or missiles".[13]

**Why OTH Radar?** OTH, a well-known radar technique that lost its relevance in the past due to inherent limitations and problems, has proved to be a very effective early warning and surveillance tool due to rapid technological advancements in digital signal processing. OTH radar system with the ability to detect targets at very long ranges and 'over the horizon, typically up to thousands of kilometres, will be a boost in the surveillance setup of India. Such radars are operational with the US, Russia, China, Australia and France.

Radar word stands for Radio detection and ranging. It is mainly influenced by the line of sight (LoS) the radar beam travels to the flying object in the sky. The curvature of the earth highly dictates this LoS. Any entity beyond the LoS and below the curvature of the earth is not likely to be picked up by the radar, thus creating a radar shadow. Such challenges of an object not getting detected by the radar can be overcome by raising the platform of the stationary radars; thus, the requirement of airborne radars came into being. But is it neither humanly nor technically possible to monitor the entire airspace through the airborne radars? Therefore, technology was invented in the 1960s where a radar beam was sent through the Ionosphere to detect the objects hidden in the radar shadow area. This technological invention was termed Beyond the Horizon or Over the Horizon Radars. The literal meaning or definition of OTH Radar, as quoted in the tutorial, is "A radar system that makes use of the atmospheric reflection and refraction phenomena to extend its range of detection beyond the line of sight. Over the horizon radars may be either forward scattered or backscatter systems".[14]

Conventional microwave radars propagate in a straight line and cannot detect objects beyond their line of sight. OTH radars overcome this limitation by 'bouncing' High Frequency (HF) radio waves off the Ionosphere. With such radars, the problem of looking across the hill at more extensive ranges can be overcome. Therefore, the deployment of OTH against China can be thought of. However, the deployment location will be dictated by the distance at which EM waves start being reflected from the Ionosphere, known as the skip zone. OTH radars are typically made up of huge fixed transmitters and receiver antennas.

**Figure 9.1: Principle of OTH Radar**[15]

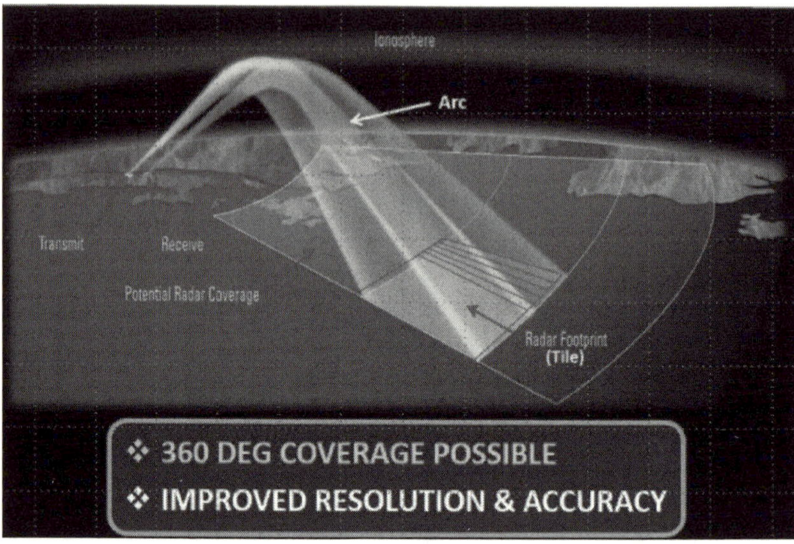


Source: *Journal of Physics*: Conference Series

The position and alignment of these arrays determine the lateral confines or arc of radar's coverage. The extent of OTH coverage in range within this arc is variable and primarily dependent on the state of the Ionosphere. Unlike conventional radars that continuously 'sweep' an area, the OTH radars 'dwell' by focusing the radar's energy on a particular area within the coverage area. In case of operational tasking, the transmitted HF energy can be electronically steered to illuminate another area of interest within the radar's coverage area. However, with advancements in technology, few OTH radars can also cover 360 degrees with improved resolution and accuracy.

## OTH Radars in the World

**Chinese OTH Radar.** The last decade has witnessed significant progress in developing OTH radar in China. These radars can look at longer ranges due to operating at high frequency (HF) radio frequencies of 15 to 30 MHz. As the received signals comprise the back-scatter reflections from the ionosphere, they are also commonly known as OTH-B radars. China has a number of OTH-Surface Wave and OTH-B radars, both onshore as well as inland, of which at least one operational radar is located in the coastal area of Shencheng in Zhejiang province.[16]

**Figure 9.2: Seaward Coverage of Chinese OTH Radar**

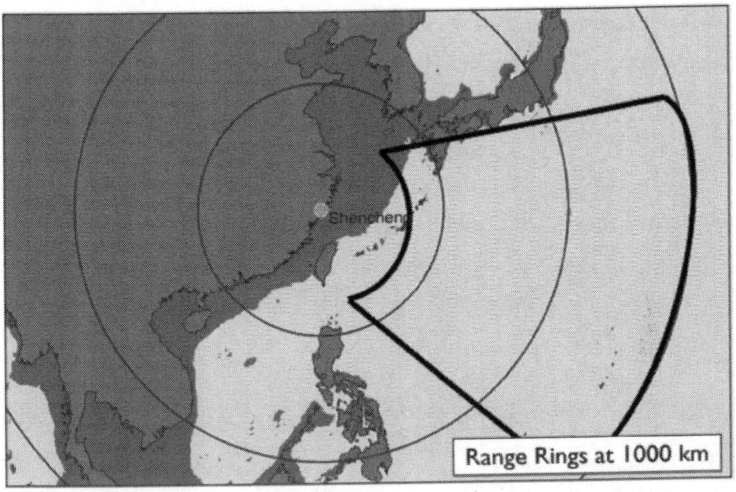


Source: *IDSA Journal of Defence Studies*, Vol. 7, Issue 1, 2013, p. 21.

**Assessment of Deployment of Chinese OTH Radars.** A Research Fellow with the China Cell of the National Maritime Foundation, New Delhi, Commander Kamlesh Kumar Agnihotri in his assessment brought out the impact of OTH radar coverage of India on the mainland and on the high seas quite aptly. Excerpts from his study are "The current known deployment of OTH Radar is on the Chinese east coast. However, the deployment of other radars under speculation remains unknown. Though the OTH radars are capable of all-around radiation, practical considerations dictate the radiation pattern. Consequently, the coverage sector of OTH radars would generally extend in a semi-circle of interest. Going by this consideration, an OTH radar meant for Indian Ocean coverage would probably be facing the Sino-Indian land border in Tibet. It would, of course, be located well inland, given the coverage range of up to 3,000 km, thus providing it with the advantage of security in-depth. The accurate ionospheric behaviour prediction system and advanced digital processing techniques will enable the OTH Radar to function quite effectively at long distances. Even the rugged

Himalayan Mountain range, comprising high peaks and deep valleys, will not affect the radar's performance. The HF radiation and reception follow the 'sky wave' principle of reflection from the Ionosphere, rendering their propagation independent of terrestrial obstructions. When coupled with the Doppler frequency shift techniques to differentiate moving targets from stationary ones, including interference from the land, these facilities would enable such radars to detect moving ships and aircraft in the Indian Ocean. For instance, an OTH Radar placed near Lhasa would virtually cover the entire Bay of Bengal and most of the Arabian Sea abutting India. If located in northern Tibet (Ali District), the same would provide comprehensive coverage of the Arabian Sea maritime space, extending from the horn of Africa till well beyond the southern tip of India and the Bay of Bengal."[17] The area so covered is shown in Figure 9.3.

**Figure 9.3: Chinese OTH Radar Coverage from two Locations in Tibet**

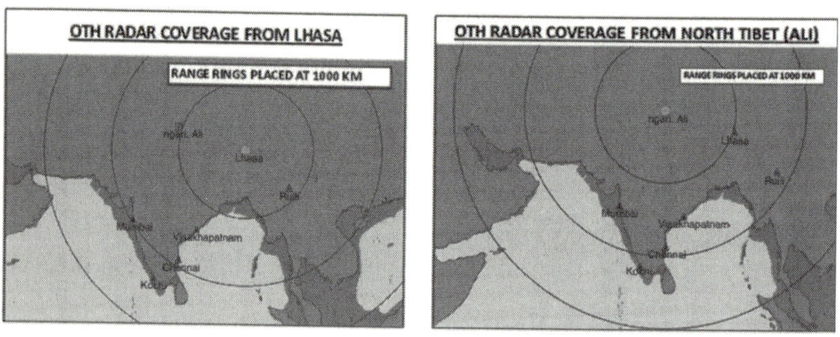


Source: *IDSA Journal of Defence Studies*, Vol. 7, Issue 1. 2013, p. 21.

The brief overview of OTH radars in use globally signifies that major economic and military powers have been successfully using and further innovating the technological advancements in maintaining and sustaining the OTH radars to keep their airspace safe and secured. Therefore, it would be pertinent to have a look at various advanced OTH radars briefly.

(a) **AN/FPS-118 (OTH-B) & ROTHR (US).** The US Air Force developed the AN/FPS-118 in 1970, known as Continental United States OTH Backscatter (CONUS-OTH-B). It was further refined in the form of a Re-locatable OTH radar. It operates in the HF band (5-28 MHz) and is designed for over-the-horizon detection and tracking of aircraft and cruise missiles flying at any altitude at extended ranges of 1000 to 3,000 km. The radar is a bistatic system with a separation of 100-200 km between transmitter and receiver. The coverage of ROTHR is as shown. The radar was initially deployed against the erstwhile USSR, which was redeployed towards South America after the end of the Cold War.

**Figure 9.4: US OTH Radar**[18]

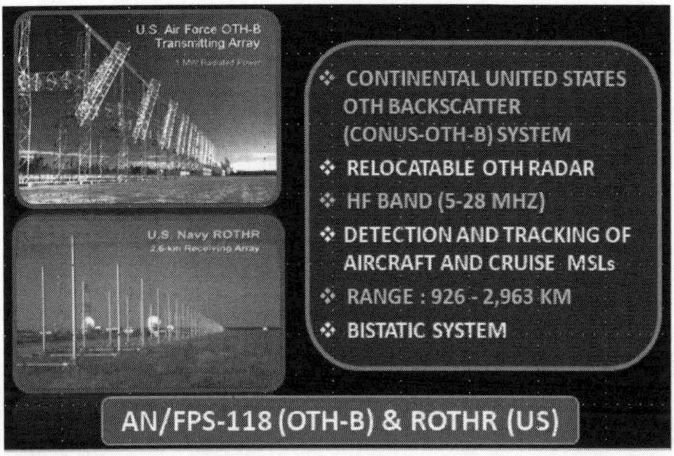


Source: globalsecurity.org

**Figure 9.5: Coverage of Bistatic OTH Radar of USA**[19]

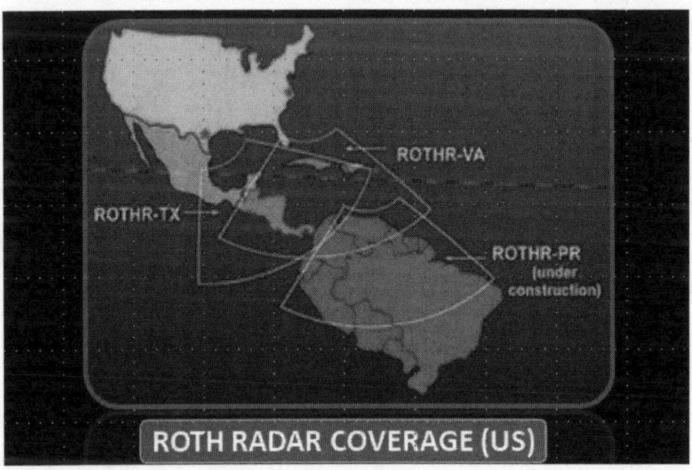


Source: wikiwand.com

(b) **STEEL YARD (Russia). The** Russian used the backscatter principle in the OTH radar in the early 1970s. It aimed to detect missile launches by detecting the disturbances in the Ionosphere caused by missile exhaust plumes. Four OTH-B systems were deployed for the early warning surveillance. In addition, Russia had used four such OTH-B radars for enhanced early warning and surveillance. Two were deployed towards the West against the USA and two in the east against China and Japan. It operates in the HF band (4-30 MHz).

(c) **TYPE 110 OTH Radar (China).** China is improving its ISR capabilities to detect, monitor and target naval air activities in the Western Pacific Ocean. The open-source intelligence indicates that China may have three OTH-B radar systems and at least one surface wave OTH radar for early warning. The Chinese OTH radar is to provide surveillance of the South China Sea. It operates in the HF band (6-22 MHz) and has an extended range of 700 to 3,500 km.

**Figure 9.6: Chinese OTH Radar**[20]

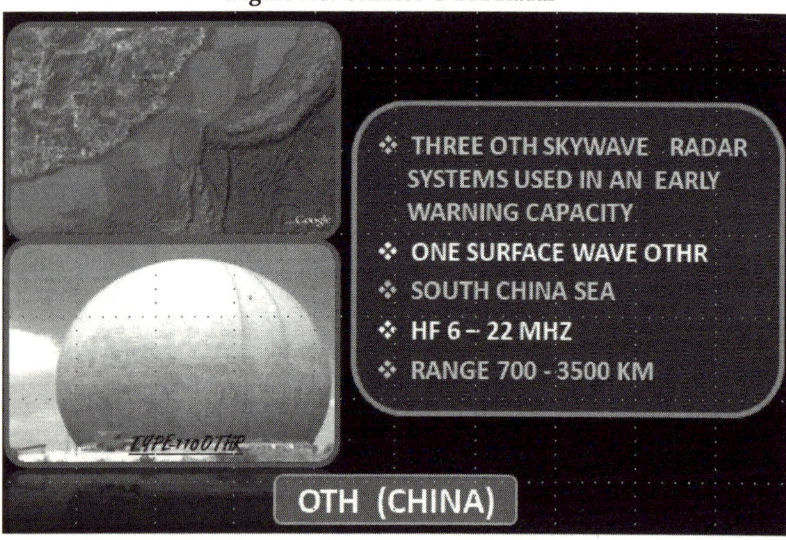


Source: Over-The-Horizon Radar.

(d) **NOSTRADAMUS (France). During the 1990s, France undertook research and development of OTH radar with a term coined as**

**NOSTRADAMUS,** the acronym of New Trans horizon Decametric System Applying Studio Methods. Eventually, the study fructified in the induction into French Army in 2005. This radar operates in the HF band (3-30 MHz). It consists of 288 emitting and receiving antennas placed in a star pattern with three equally spaced arms with a detection range between 800 and 3,000 km. The French military applied the Nostradamus OTHR to detect stealth aircraft, and cruise missiles with low Radar and infrared signatures. The Nostradamus OTH radar is relatively economical since it uses commercial off-the-shelf components. First, built by France, the Nostradamus OTH radar has two distinct advantages. First, it is monostatic, i.e., the signal is transmitted and received at the exact location; secondly, the star-shaped antenna structure provides 360°coverage. The pictorial representation of French sky wave HF OTH radars and their location is shown.

**Figure 9.7: France Nostradamus OTH Radar[21]**

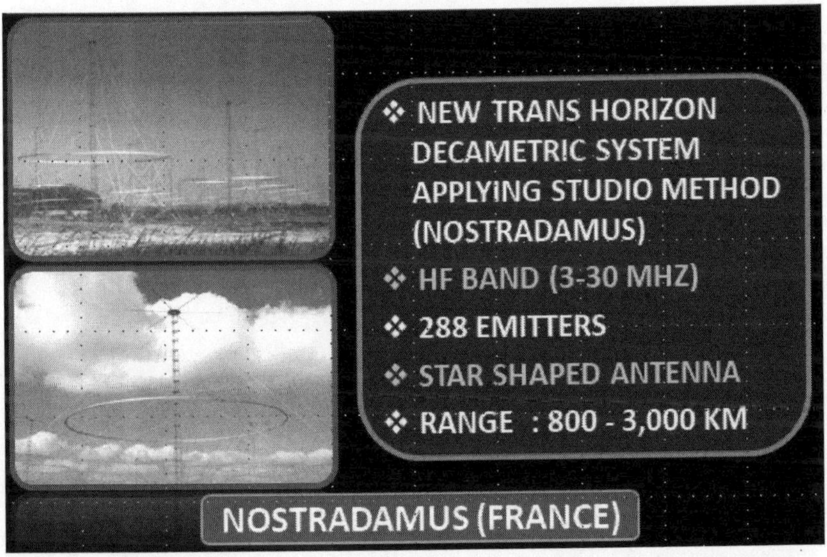


Source: radartutorial.eu

**Figure 9.8: Coverage of French Nostradamus OTH Radar**

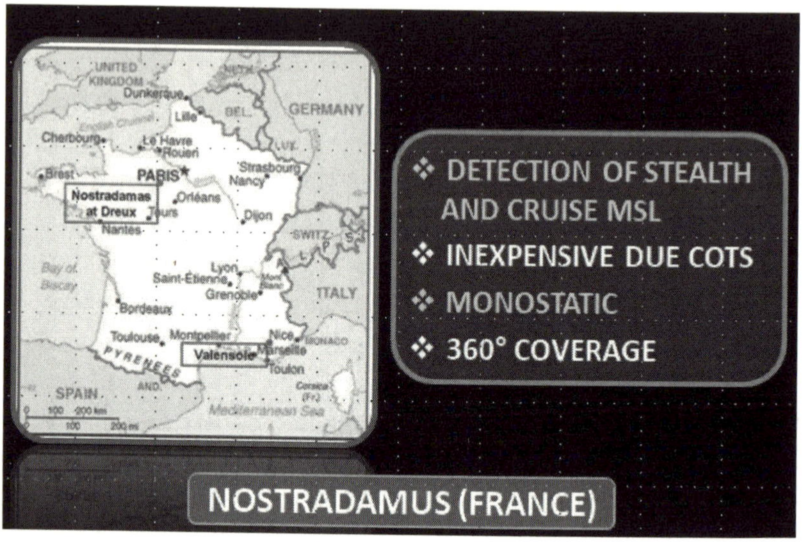


Source: Key Publications Ltd Aviation Forum

(e) **JORN (Australia).** The Jindalee project started in the 1960s but effectively took off only in the late 1970s. This project was initially called the "bare bone". It is a multistatic radar system using OTH-B, with Tx and Rx separated by 160 km. It has both long-range as well as anti-stealth capabilities. It has an official range of 3,000 km, but in 1997 the prototype was able to detect missile launches by China over 5,500 km away. The system operates on HF Band (5-30 M Hz). Jindalee radar was further integrated with two more OTH radars and became a Jindalee Operational Radar Network (JORN) network. To have deeper electronic visibility in the Pacific Ocean and the Indian archipelago, radars were set up at Laverton, Western Australia, and Longreach, Queensland, in eastern Australia. JORN ensures a surveillance area with an arc of almost 180° wide. The cost incurred for the JORN project was approximately $1.8 billion. The coverage of JORN is as shown.

Figure 9.9: Jindalee Operational Radar Network (JORN) OTH Radar of Australia[22]

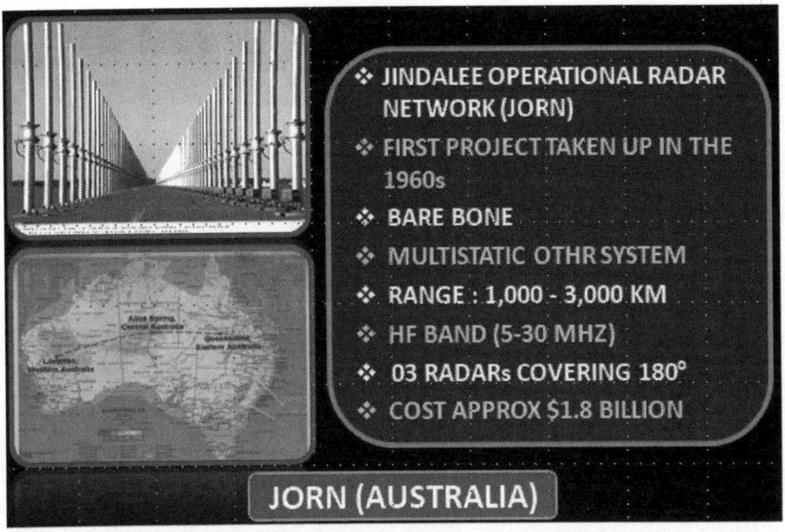


Source: Key Publications Ltd Aviation Forum

Figure 9.10: Coverage of Australian Jindalee OTH Radar[23]

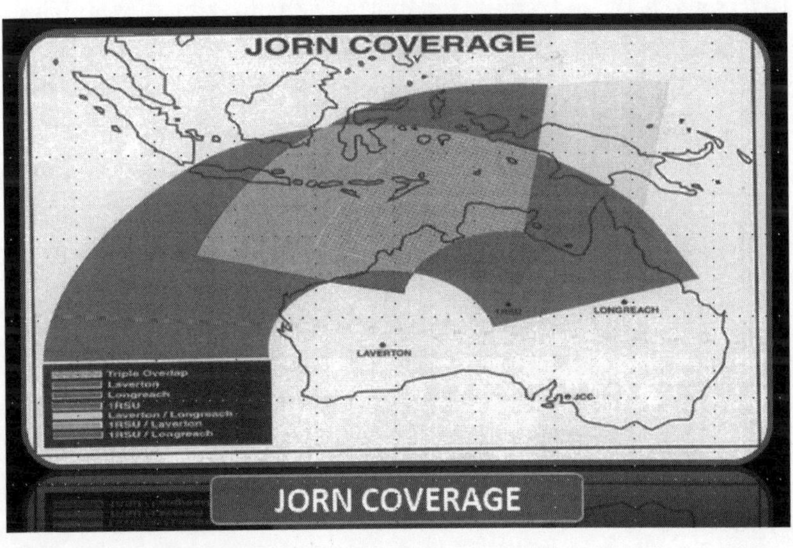


Source: Key Publications Ltd Aviation Forum

Advantages of OTH in Indian Scenario. The chapter brings out the inadequacy of radar cover over peninsular India, into high seas and across the Himalayas throughout the width of India. OTH radar coupled with other HPRs/MPRs and LLTRs and long-range radars of the Ballistic Missile Defence (BMD) System of India can make a formidable radar e-Orbat throughout the country. One main driver for early research into OTH radar was detection of ICBM launches, although satellite-based systems have largely supplanted OTH radars in this role. Other applications include surveillance for ships or aircraft, remote sensing, ocean wave detection and ionospheric sounding.[24] The following could be the unambiguous advantages India would accrue with the installation of OTH in central India:

(a) It will provide India deeper electronic visibility inside China and Pakistan, thus catering well for detecting aerial objects simultaneously from two fronts.
(b) India may successfully achieve and clear visibility across the Himalayas.
(c) It could be very effective for hilly terrain in all directions.
(d) It would cover and sanitise the Indian Ocean for targets over high seas assuring gap-free coverage in the EEZ.
(e) Early detection of SSM would be feasible.
(f) The OTH could be deployed outside the range of SRBM.
(g) Very long-range and Multi-level area scan may be feasible with the integrated network of all kinds of sensors in the country.
(h) The French Nostradamus OTH radar with 360-degree coverage and Australian Jindalee OTH radar (JORN) is the most advanced of all the systems. They are also cost-effective and technologically impressive.
(i) India has come closer to France and Australia in recent times. Thus, procurement of OTH from any of these countries will further solidify military, diplomatic and economic fronts and human resource exchange.
(j) DRDO/ISRO or any other private company may attempt to develop this technology under the *Atmanirbhar Bharat* drive.

**Figure 9.11: Proposed OTH Coverage in India**

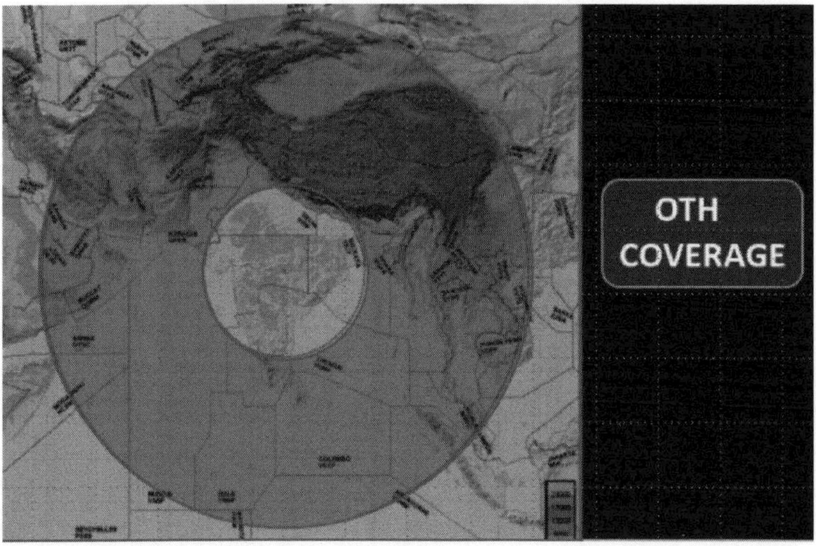


Source: Author

## Limitations of OTH Radars

OTHR technology has been pursued by other countries for approximately 50 years with varying degrees of success. The successful approaches have generally involved a carefully staged succession of development. These experiences suggest that planning for acquisitions will also have to consider infrastructure requirements, including land preparation for the large antenna arrays, communications to support the coordination of separate transmit and receive sites, spectrum monitoring to determine the background electromagnetic environment, and HF sounding to estimate the ionospheric propagation paths.[25]

**Massive Land Requirement.** The idea of having an OTH radar for India is very little taken in the proper stride mainly because of primarily two factors, i.e., it requires a considerable land in hectares and its accuracy of detecting targets. Despite having the best of everything, India cannot meet the necessary facts and figures of progress due to the apprehension of moving away from the status quo approach and outlook. If OTH radar requires having a massive piece of land, so be it. Why leave the installation part but do not encourage to discuss it just because of the enormous land requirement appears to be absurd. The OTH radar can be best placed in the general region of the Nagpur axis, which an ideal location is keeping the range of OTH radar and its skip distance in the centre in mind.

**Networking of Sensors.** An optimistic picture of fusing the tracks picked up by ground-based HPRs/MPRs/LRTRs/LLLTRs/Civil radars and AWACS is available in the Integrated Air Command and Control Centre (IACCS). The optimistic picture would be to integrate further the radar tracks picked up by OTH radars and Maritime Domain Awareness (MDA) of the Navy for a Recognised Air Situation Picture (RASP) stitched at the IACCS. It can be achieved by using the AWACS and OTH radars in conjunction with the other smaller, ground-based radars like the Low-Level Transportable Radars (LLTR) and Low-Level Light Weight Radar (LLLWR).[26] Having integrated these radars, a composite air picture could be formed. This would be possible in future with the activation of the IACCS, ODL, AWACS and the OTH, all working in good coordination. The enemy aircraft will use terrain masking and the valleys to avoid detection and give as little early warning as possible. However, the disadvantages of such ingress are that the approach routes are predictable and the entry and exit points from and to the valley are well known. These can be covered by the effective deployment of mobile observation posts and radars. Also, the use of Remotely Piloted Aircraft (RPA) can increase surveillance activities.

## Procurement of OTH Radar

At present, only a few countries US, Russia, China, France and Australia, are a few countries that are operating OTH radar alongside its production primarily for them. Since its inception, the technology in signal processing, resolution, and determining exact target location has improved manifold. However, very little has been done so far to procure such radar for the country. Not much of the official stance is available on the subject. However, in 2009, some efforts were made to study this system in the Indian context. Companies like Russian JSC Rosoboronexport have been trying to sell their OTH radars consisting of triplanar array supposedly covering 360 degrees and have emerged in specific discussions. However, it has not seen the light of the day since then.

India has maintained a cordial relationship with France throughout. Recent procurement of Rafael aircraft to the IAF has given further Philip to the association. IAF has been procuring radars and sensors technology from Thales France for its air defence Ground Environmental systems (ADGES). The defence cooperation between India and France have always resulted in the best of the bargain and defence assets worth its mettle. The Nostradamus OTH radar looks quite promising in its capability, and it may be a good bet for the Indian scenario. The most significant advantage of this system is its 360-degree coverage which may have the upper hand with the OTH radars of other countries.

There has been recent speeding up of bilateral relations between India and Australia, especially in the backdrop of QUAD in the Indo-Pacific. Bilateral engagements in the past six months included meeting Heads of the States, 2+2 dialogue, defence cooperation and exchanges of viewpoints between the think tanks Centre for Air Power Studies (CAPS) and Air and Space Power Centre (ASPC) of Australia under a Memorandum of Understanding (MoU). Both think tanks conducted the first-ever international bilateral webinar on Aerospace Power in September 2021, followed by a seminar in Australia in March 2022. Australia has an effective Jindalee Operational radar Network (JORN), another OTH radar India may procure to keep the defence diplomacy alive with both Air Forces.

In an attempt at indegenisation, the premier radar development laboratory at DRDO is working on the Indian model of OTH radar. The reports from Alpha Defence India, indicate that development is aimed to keep a close watch on Chinese movements in the Indian Ocean region. The report states that "The system design has already been completed and the next step is the realisation of a prototype. The radar prototype is to have two different types of radar arrays of a log-periodic wire antenna array and a broadband monopole antenna array. The monopole antenna array is to consist of an array of 32 elements. The existing system is to be developed later after extensive testing and evaluation".[27] The deadlines of all major projects such as AEW&C and ODL can be taken as a template wherein the prototype was developed quite early. Still, its integration and reaching even the Initial Operational Configuration (IOC) took time beyond explanation and operational need. ODL is yet to see its fate for operational use by the IAF. Therefore, India must promote the Atmanirbhar concept to the maximum but keep the deadlines realistic and operational worthy. In an interview with Deccan Herald reporter Kalyan Ray, DRDO chairman G Satheesh Reddy shared the details of futuristic technologies on which DRDO is working and the areas in which India will become self-reliant in the next five years. India will become self-reliant on radars and sonar in the next five years (2024). It is time for DRDO to carry out the mid-course assessment to honour the deadlines.[28]

## Conclusion

Securing the national airspace comes dearly, and no government can achieve this without being considerate enough to release funds for meeting the national and political objectives. Procuring OTH radar may cost handsome money, but it will be worth it once dividends are reaped. The current procurement approach of hundreds of radars of varied ranges and power output may not suffice the actual requirement of sensors to ensure gap-free coverage in India. While various sensors have their advantages and limitations, it is imperative that a wholesome system like OTH radar must be part of the inventory of the Indian sensors grid. Discussion about OTH radar in the Indian context requires a change of mindset and unlearning of the indoctrination of requirement of sensors for many who are designing the qualifying requirements and analysing it with operational requirements.

India has a culture of having an effective working ethos in crisis and achieving success after that to culminate in weaving rhetoric for generations to follow and imbibe upon. However, many wasteful efforts can be easily avoided if the situation's gravity and need were thought on time. India has a few glaring examples in the recent past where we reacted in the procurement of items and assets on the wish list for ages. However, the concern was not given adequate due when required. Similarly, a thought of requirement of OTH radar in the Indian context is not syncing into the overall gambit of procurement of assets reflecting the deep-rooted indoctrination of remaining in the 'status-quo' regime. The procurement of OTH radar for India is getting delayed without any doubt. The timely procurement is the key to ensuring its populace's safety, security, and national integrity. In 2015, then Defence Minister Late Mr Arun Jaitley while addressing the military commanders in the Naval Commanders' Conference said, *"Effort needs to be strengthened for timely induction of platforms in our armed forces"* The statement holds relevance today as well and will remain so forever.

## Notes

1. Air Marshal (Retd) V.K. Bhatia. "Defending The Airspace" SP Aviation Issue: 08-2010, at https://www.sps-aviation.com/story/?id=539. Accessed on November 6, 2021.
2. https://www.aai.aero/en/corporate/aai-today. Accessed on November 8, 2021.
3. Context. "Most Extensive Presence In India Thanks To Customer Confidence", at https://www.indracompany.com/en/extensive-presence-india-thanks-customer-confidence. Accessed on November 6, 2021.
4. "Indra Gains Major ATM presence in India", at https://www.indracompany.com/sites/default/files/indra_gains_major_atm_presence_in_india.pdf. Accessed on November 8, 2021.
5. Newsletter of the Embassy of the Czech Republic "Czech Radars ELDIS will Cover 90% of Indian Airspace" 22.08.2019 / 05:06, at https://www.mzv.cz/newdelhi/en/economy/ceske_radary_eldis_pokryji_90_vzdusneho.html. Accessed on November 8, 2021.
6. "Three secondary radars MSSR-1 for India" 12/05/2018, at https://www.eldis.cz/en/three-secondary-radars-mssr-1-india. Accessed on November 8, 2021.
7. Rajat Pandit. "Unsafe! India's airspace has many gaping holes". May 24, 2005, at https://timesofindia.indiatimes.com/india/unsafe-indias-airspace-has-many-gaping-holes/articleshow/1120669.cms. Accessed on November 8, 2021.
8. TNN New Report, "Armed forces continue to maintain vigil over peninsular India", February 22, 2009, at https://timesofindia.indiatimes.com/india/armed-forces-continue-to-maintain-vigil-over-peninsular-india/articleshow/4166885.cms. Accessed on November 8, 2021.
9. Atul Kumar Singh, *Transformation of Air Defence in Asia*. KW Publishers Pvt Ltd, New Delhi, Ch 3, p. 73. Accessed on November 6, 2021.
10. Rajat Pandit. "India to now procure special mountain radars for borders with China" July 21, 2010, at https://timesofindia.indiatimes.com/india/india-to-now-procure-special-mountain-radars-for-borders-with-china/articleshow/6192599.cms. Accessed on November 9, 2021.
11. Jayadeva Ranade. "China-Pakistan Strategic Nexus: Implications for India". April 16, 2021, at https://www.vifindia.org/article/2021/april/16/china-pakistan-strategic-nexus-implications-for-india. Accessed on November 9, 2021.

12. Ibid.
13. Newsletter from globalsecurity.org. "India—Radars", at https://www.globalsecurity.org/military/world/india/radars.htm, Accessed on November 8, 2021.
14. https://www.thefreedictionary.com/OTH+radar. Accessed on December 6, 2021.
15. S Litvinov. "Over-the-horizon detection radar ionosphere support system" *J. Phys2020.: Conf. Ser.* 1632 012021. Accessed on December 6, 2021.
16. Chandrashekar, S., R.N. Ganesh, C.R. Raghunath, Rajaram Nagappa, N. Ramani and Lalitha Sundaresan, China's Anti-Ship Ballistic Missile: Game Changer in the Pacific Ocean, NIAS Report No. R5-2011, Bangalore: National Institute of Advanced Studies, November 2011, pp. 8-9. Accessed on November 21, 2021.
17. Commander Kamlesh Kumar Agnihotri. "China's 'Anti-ship Ballistic Missile' based Anti-access Concept Implications of a Southward Re-orientation" Journal of Defence Studies, Vol. 7, Issue 1, 2013, pp. 21, at http://www.idsa.in/jds/7_1_2013_ChinasAnti-shipBallisticMissile_KamleshKAgnihotri. Accessed on November 20, 2021.
18. Weapons of Mass Destruction (WMD). https://www.globalsecurity.org/wmd/systems/an-fps-118.htm. Accessed on December 6, 2021.
19. Coverage of the three U.S. Navy ROTHR stations in Texas, Virginia, and Puerto Rico, at https://www.wikiwand.com/en/Over-the-horizon_radar. Accessed on December 6, 2021.
20. Over-The-Horizon Radar, at https://stationhypo.com/2017/09/27/over-the-horizon-radar/. Accessed on December 6, 2021.
21. Nostradamus, at https://www.radartutorial.eu/19.kartei/01.oth/karte020.en.html. Accessed on December 6, 2021.
22. Locations of the JORN Radar Stations and the areas covered based on a nominal range of 3000 km. Jindalee Over-the-horizon Radar Nomination for Heritage Recognition, Image: Key Publications Ltd Aviation Forum. May 2016, p. 11. Accessed on December 6, 2021.
23. Ibid.
24. Cameron, Alex. "The Jindalee Operational Radar Network: Its Architecture and Surveillance Capability", *IEEE International Radar Conference 1995*. 692-697. Institute of Electrical and Electronic Engineers, 1995. Accessed on December 2, 2021.
25. RJ Riddolls. "A Canadian Perspective on High-Frequency Over-the-Horizon Radar" DRDC Ottawa TM 2006-285; Defence R&D Canada—Ottawa; December 2006. P3. Accessed on December 2, 2021.
26. Neelam Mathews, "Indian Radar Buys Prompt Thales Joint Venture", at the webpage of ainonline.com, New Delhi, November 26, 2014.
27. "Is India building its own over-the-horizon radar (OTHR)?" International Amateur Radio Union Working for the Future of Amateur Radio November

25, 2021, at https://www.iaru-r1.org/2021/is-india-building-its-own-over-the-horizon-radar-othr/. Accessed on November 30, 2021.

28. Kalyan Ray, "We'll become self-reliant in radars, sonars in 5 yrs" Deccan herald News Service, September 9, 2019, at https://www.deccanherald.com/national/we-ll-become-self-reliant-in-radars-sonars-in-5-yrs-760227.html. Accessed on November 30, 2021.

# 10

# Democracy—At the Crossroads

SANU KAINIKARA

The dictionary defines democracy as a system of government by the whole population, usually through elected representatives; a nation so governed; and a classless tolerant form of society.[1] Another more generic definition is that democracy is a theory of government which, in its purest form, holds that the state should be controlled by all the people, each sharing equally in privileges, duties and responsibilities and each participating in person in the government, as in the city-states of ancient Greece. It also denotes political, legal and social equality.[2] The term itself was derived in the 5th century BC in Greece from the Greek 'democratia', coined from the words 'demos' (people) and 'kratos' (rule).

## Introduction

Since the time of the ancient Greeks, the theory and practice of democracy has undergone profound changes. For thousands of years, the unit to be ruled, normally a tribe and later a city-state, was small enough to practice the concept of direct democracy. It was only in the 18th century when this unit became a nation-state or a country that representative democracy was established.[3] This was a step-change transformation from well-established norms and in turn, necessitated the creation of several associated political institutions that were either not available previously or needed to be radically different to existing ones. The introduction of representative democracy brought out one potent question—who had the right to participate in government? This is a question that has not been fully answered even today and continues to rage across many debates in most democracies.

Initially, the right was restricted to a small minority of the adult population. Only in the 20th century was this right extended to a majority of the adult population. By today's standards, ancient Athens where the term itself originated, would not qualify as a democracy since participation was limited to a minority of the elite. Therefore, the fundamental requirement in any democratic process would be to define who constitutes the 'demos', the people. Once again, this raises more questions than answers. Assuming that children, as defined by society, should not participate, the questions that emerge are—should all adults be participants in government, or should they be only a sub-set of the adult population? If only a sub-set should participate, what should be the constitution of this sub-set and its size?[4] The limitations of who and size must be balanced with the requirement to ensure that the 'unit' being governed still qualifies as a democracy. This dividing line between a democracy and an aristocracy (rule by the best—'aristos') and an oligarchy (rule by the few 'oligos') is very thin and cannot be drawn arbitrarily.

In the past decade or so, populist leaders with authoritarian trends have made inroads into power in several democracies, propelling illiberal politicians to leadership roles. Analysts are unable to find a common thread in the rise of such leaders in Europe, the United States, Latin America as well as in South and South-East Asia. However, the accompanying erosion of democratic values has been caused mainly by economic grievances and a cultural backlash brought on by divergence.[5] Economic upheavals in the wake of globalisation has led to rising income inequality in many democracies. Industrial workers, especially in the more developed nations of the world, have been left behind in the rapid economic progress of the nation. As a result, they have turned their support to more extremist political parties and ideologies.[6] Culturally, the more developed democracies have witnessed divergence of values and beliefs between the conservative small towns, which were the dominant cultural force even a decade ago and the socially progressive policies that are being conceived and formulated in metropolitical cities. The divergence is not relished by the conservatives who tend to gravitate toward extreme right-wing political parties and to support such ideologies.[7]

## Brief History of the Development of Democracy

The creation of fixed communities, from the natural human instinct of being hunter-gatherers in prehistoric times, initiated the beginning of entrenched inequalities in wealth and power in the society. The spread of inequalities encouraged the spread of hierarchical societal organisations. For thousands of years, governments were based on the concepts of monarchy, despotism, aristocracy or oligarchy which were considered the most natural forms of governance.[8] Around 500 B.C. a few small groups of people started to create 'popular' governments that gradually became primitive democracies and the harbingers of people's involvement in governance. Crucial developments took place in the Mediterranean Basin, Greece and Rome, during the Classical Period, corresponding to 5th and 4th centuries BC. Greece at that time was not a country in the modern sense but a collection of many 'city-states'. Among them, Athens could be considered one of the most advanced and studied as an example.

Athens defined the 'people' who were permitted to participate in the government as all male citizens above the age of 18 years—which was later, around 400 BCE, revised to 20 years. In this case, citizenship was hereditary, meaning all persons were born to Athenian citizens. From the scanty data that is available, it would appear that of the total population that included slaves and resident foreigners, only about 10-15 per cent could participate in the government.[9] Around the same timeframe, Rome in the Italian Peninsula was introducing a system, initially called 'respublica' from the Latin 'res', meaning thing or affair and 'publica' or public. It came to be called republic—a thing that belonged to the 'populus romanus', the Roman People. The rapid territorial expansion of Rome and the liberal rules regarding citizenship combined to develop a somewhat adapted democracy with the concept of a powerful senate and some other political structures being introduced.[10]

Around the 12th century AD, Italy developed a system of popular governments with the election of leaders for limited tenures. These were called 'republics', but the 'public', the people who could participate remained a small fraction of the total population, being restricted to rich landowners and the hereditary nobility. These republics could not be called democracies;

they were more accurately described as 'constitutional oligarchies'.[11] As a natural progression of the non-viability of this form of government and buffeted by economic decline and civil wars, these weakened republics were eventually replaced by monarchs and princes.

The English Civil Wars (1642–51) expanded the powers of the Parliament and ensured broader representation, more as a practical than a philosophical solution to emerging challenges to the government. Thereafter, representation became a part of the theory and practice of democracy within the next century. By the end of the 15th century, the basic features of a modern parliamentary system of government had evolved primarily in England. By the early 1800s, significant powers of governance had been shifted to the Parliament. Even so, this was not a fully democratic system. Franchise and voting rights, were given only to about 5 per cent of the population above 20 years of age and the reform Act of 1832 extended suffrage to about 7 per cent of adults.[12] Further acts of Parliament—in 1867, 1884 and 1918—achieved universal male suffrage and a law enacted in 1928 secured the same right for adult women.

The United States of America (USA), often touted as the leading democracy of the current era, took a slightly different route after the War of Independence, adopting representative democracy through elections at the federal and state levels that also brought about the need to create political parties. Unfortunately, in the US the answer to who the 'people' would be was never answered satisfactorily and continues to remain an enigma even today. Suffrage was broadly extended to white male adults, while completely excluding women, slaves, freedmen of African descent and Native Americans.[13] In the USA, adult white women would be granted voting rights in 1920, whereas African Americans were admitted into the political process and given suffrage only after the passage, and more importantly enforcement, of the Civil Rights Act of 1964.[14] For a nation that claims to be the bastion of democracy, this is not a proud record.

By the end of the 18th century, the idea and practice of democracy had been profoundly transformed. In the 20th century, in the wake of the decolonisation drive, the number of countries adopting democracy and building the necessary institutions had increased significantly. In the early decades of the 21st century more than one-third of the independent countries of the world possessed institutions that support and are essential for the practice of democracy and, taken globally, there is a historic high in the number of democratic governments. Today, almost half the population of the world are being governed by some form of democratic government.

## An 'Ideal' Democracy

Considering the many conceptual variables involved in creating a democratic government, is it possible to define an ideal democracy? The description of an ideal system can be used as a benchmark to identify the critical and essential elements within the system; to delineate the underlying laws that are crucial to ensuring the robustness of a democratic system; and to measure the efficiency and efficacy of a 'practising' democracy. The description of an ideal democracy does not prescribe any definitive political system but elaborates on the minimum critical components necessary to ensure a reasonably well-functioning democracy.

## Minimum Critical Components

There is no doubt that some basic, minimum requirements must be satisfied before democracy can be considered the ideal. Four such components are of such importance that the absence of even one of them at the requisite level of integrity would deny the government any claim to being democratic.[15]

**Equal Opportunity to Vote.** All citizens above a minimum prescribed age must be eligible to vote; should be given opportunities to vote; and each vote must have the same weightage.

**Information to the Electorate.** All the people must be provided truthful information regarding government policies as well as the alternatives, with sufficient time to understand them. They must be made aware of the consequences if the suggested policies are enacted so that an informed decision can be made by individual voters.

**Opportunity to Participate.** The system must provide a clear opportunity for every person to make known his/her opinions about the policy being debated or discussed with others. At the same time, it must be ensured that each person is permitted to participate equally in the discussion, and if necessary to influence others.

**Ensuring Individual Rights.** The government process must be able to ensure and if necessary, protect, the right of each person to communicate with others; the right to gather and disseminate information; and the right to participate in all these processes on an equal footing with everyone else. In other words, democracy is not only a political process but a system of fundamental rights.

Democracies ensure the efficacy of these critical components through establishing a variety of political processes, which are in themselves crucial to ensuring that democracies are moved as much as possible towards the ideal position. The four components that are essential for the viability of democracy as enumerated above, will only function when the following three activities are plainly made possible. One, elections are free, fair and frequent with all eligible persons able to participate openly without fear or favour and the results are valid and legal; two, all citizens have the opportunity to indulge in the right to express themselves on all politically relevant subjects freely without fear of negative repercussions; and three, information about policies and other political processes are made available outside the control of the government or any single controlling authority.[16] Further, the information made available must be devoid of inaccuracies and verifiable, while people must have the freedom to form and associate with political organisations of their choice.

In 2004, the UN General Assembly adopted a resolution that lays out seven 'essential elements' of democracy, which include: separation and balance of power; independence of the judiciary; a pluralistic system of political parties and organisations; respect for the rule of law; accountability and transparency; free, independent and pluralistic media; and respect for human and political rights, for example, freedoms of association and expression, the right to vote and to stand in elections.[17] Even though the components and criteria vary, essentially a democratic political order must be characterised by fairness, equality and individual rights for all citizens.

After World War I, the legacy systems of monarchy, aristocracy and oligarchy fell by the wayside as being ineffective with no chance of revival. Similarly, World War II discredited the lure of fascism that had been proposed as an alternative to democracy in the inter-war years. In the post-war years, several non-democratic governments suffered political, economic, military and diplomatic failures and the appeal of such systems diminished in direct proportion. Democracy adopted by the major nations became the default position because of the failure of non-democratic governments. The economic and political failure of the Soviet Union ended the forced ascendancy of the Soviet-style communism, leaving no other viable alternative to democracy, which was already tried and tested. However, this situation does not indicate that democracy is a flawless process, far from it. There are a large number of challenges to be addressed and failure to do so will gradually diminish the veracity and status of democracy.

## On-going Challenges

As early as the 17th century when democratic norms of governance was being developed, established and fine-tuned, academics and thinkers had already started to express their fears of the challenges that the system would face as it started to get implemented. Some of the major challenges are enumerated below.

**Tyranny of the Majority.** The first challenge to be avoided is what has been termed by thinkers as the 'tyranny of the majority'. The fear is that the majority, once established as the ruling bloc, would deny the legitimate rights of the minority.[18] This deprivation would be particularly applicable to the distribution of wealth, which in any case is never equitable in a capitalist economy. This challenge can be overcome by establishing checks and balances on the system through political institutions crafted to ensure a balanced approach to 'majority rule'.[19] The will of the majority can be tempered with the aspirations of the minority.

**Inequality of Income.** In the late 20th and early 21st centuries, the global economy rapidly became decentralised, and market controlled. Even though restrictive regulations were applied, this model of the economy produced large inequalities in income generation that in turn led to great disparities in social and educational status.[20] In states where regulations were lax or non-existent, the gap became almost unbridgeable fairly quickly. The gradual erosion of the influence of the poorer sections of society thereafter led to the 'haves' being able to turn the political system to their advantage, making the concept of political equality for all people an impossibility to put into practice.[21] Income inequality creates a vicious and self-perpetuating cycle of events—increasing income and social disparity feeds into increasing poverty and unemployment for a section of the population, normally at the lower end of the socio-economic scale, who are already politically disenfranchised.

**Domestic Security.** Democratic societies are by definition and necessity open with limited government control over personal freedoms. The emphasis on individual freedoms spawned an increasing number of acts of terrorism in democratic nations, starting from the 1970s. As a response to such events, democratic governments have been forced to enact laws that have given increased arbitrary powers to the policing and law enforcement authorities, broadly to protect the nation.[22] In turn, the civil and political liberties of the citizens have had to be curtailed, eliciting criticism that these measures go contrary to democratic principles.[23] The challenge that faces real democracies is to strike the correct balance between the conflicting requirements of curtailing freedoms to ensure the security of the people and the nation and preserving the fundamentals of democracy.[24]

**Less Mature Democracies.** In the post-colonial world of the late 20th century, several newly independent nations embraced democratic ideology as their preferred form of government. However, they faced a large number of challenges in embedding the concepts of democracy such as: less than optimum education level of the broader population; the absence of an entrenched middle-class; implementation of flawed economic policies that led to inflation and even negative rates of growth; widespread poverty and unemployment; increasing disparity between the rich and the poor; and the lack of an effective legal system that in turn does not assure civil rights.[25] In most cases 'independence' from colonial rule was achieved after civil wars and long years of authoritarian rule. Therefore, in many of these countries, the newly 'elected' leaders were not able to fully establish the rule of law, leading to a lack of belief among the broader population in the values that support democratic governance.[26] A large number succumbed to becoming autocratic dictatorships.

By the early 21st century, the pace of democratisation had already slowed visibly, and the rapidity of its spread seen in the mid-20th century is unlikely to be rekindled. Democratic institutions across the world have weakened and in some newer democracies are ill-formed. Both these factors tend to support the trend towards the creation of authoritarian rule with popular approval, which is increasingly becoming a distinct possibility in several nations.

## The Erosion and Decline of Democracy

The past decade has witnessed the visible decline of traditional democratic norms across the world. Europe, long-held as the bastion of democratic governments and protector of individual freedoms, has seen even centre-left parties struggle to garner 25-30 per cent of the popular vote.[27] This move away from the social-democratic parties manifested itself in the loss of 32 of the 185 seats that centre-left Socialists and Democrats had held in the 751-member European Parliament, in the May 2019 elections.[28] This trend is not peculiar, or limited, to Europe but is noticeable globally.

The sharp decline in the democratic norms in countries as far apart as Hungary, Venezuela, Russia and Turkey prompt the necessity to investigate the phenomena. Understanding and analysing the decline in democratic norms in a nation is a complex undertaking for the following reasons. One, all variants that are considered for study offer different lenses to view them, increasing the complexities and complications by a quantum jump. Two, any deduction that is drawn is prone to become inaccurate with even the smallest change in the 'quality' of the democracy being investigated—democracy itself being a Utopian concept. Three, the critical elements of a democratic system are sensitive to even subtle alterations in the overall political system and processes.

Is a democratic recession taking place across the world? If so, what is the magnitude and the impact that can be expected?[29] Further, it becomes necessary to look at successful democracies to garner a robust understanding of the reasons for the failure of less mature democracies. What social, economic and political factors combine to increase their chances of survival in some cases and their back-slide in others? In either case, the fact remains that the survival or diminishing relevance of democracies are the results of actions by persons with vested interests and not a natural process of evolution. Analysis indicates that groups or persons who want to sabotage democracy prefer a graded approach to ensure its erosion rather than a surprise, direct frontal attack.[30] There are two basic advantages to adopting the gradual and indirect approach. First is that the gradual process can be couched in legalese and defended if questioned but yields the same result of destabilising the democratic institutions and processes with minimal risk of repercussions. Second, a gradual approach tends to diffuse the focal points which would otherwise be identified as critical to democracies, thereby denying defenders of democracy the ability to organise effective responses in a timely manner.[31]

The corollary to this situation is that the gradual erosion of democratic norms, because of the long incubation period, could also provide opportunities for some institutions and political forces to stop the trend and maybe even reverse it. On the other hand, a sudden collapse, for example through a military coup d'état does not provide such windows of opportunities to save democracy. For the same reason, institutions and pro-democracy forces that could combine to withstand gradual erosion have almost no influence or relevance in the case of a coup d'état. Military takeovers are fait accompli and reclaiming democracy from such a situation normally follows the path of civil war and conflict.[32] The gradual erosion is characterised by a calculated degradation of democratic institutions that uphold the rule of law such as courts of justice and law-enforcement agencies. Normally, these activities are accompanied by nepotism and corruption that dilutes economic stability. Invariably, the next stage is an attack on the media, especially on independent journalists who are incarcerated or even murdered.

The questions to be answered are: how can the deterioration of democratic norms be detected, identified and measured? What evidence can be considered irrevocable signs of the erosion of democracy, if this is at all possible? The answers can be gleaned from case studies of democratic decline in different regions, at different times or periods and in different circumstances. These case studies assist in delineating the elements of the democratic system that matter most in times of crisis when the repudiation of democratic norms through erosion is being attempted.[33] These elements have to function before the erosion of democracy reaches a critical point and crosses an invisible point into authoritarianism that could generate its own momentum.

**Party Elite.** First is the role of the party elite who are aligned with the potential authoritarian leader. They can forestall the move towards authoritarian erosion of democratic norms by visibly opposing such moves before they become irrevocable and starts to gather their own momentum.

**Non-elected and Minority Institutions.** Democratic erosion can be staved off by non-elected and minority institutions such as the military forces and the bureaucracy. A strong and independent judiciary tends to play a pivotal role at times during the process of dilution of democratic norms.[34] The judiciary could also form the basis for the creation of independent bodies that act as checks and balances to curtail anti-democratic tendencies that manifest themselves in the executive branch. An independent and robust judiciary is vital to check the erosion of democracy and to keep the elected representatives accountable to the people.[35] The surprising finding in the case studies was that it is the unelected and unrepresentative 'elites' who come out in defence of democratic norms and not the elected representatives, who owe their position to the practice of democracy. This is one of the main reasons for the judiciary, lawyers and other 'intelligentsia' being targeted by would be autocrats, as a first measure when they decide to start the destabilisation process.

**Political Process as a Deterrent.** The political process itself could create new movements with ideological differences that act as a deterrent to either proposed or the ongoing erosion of democratic systems, thereby challenging the status quo of the prevailing political system and marginalising the anti-democratic political movement.[36] A new movement could also provide an opportunity for the political elite to make a prudent choice of leadership to side-line the one's with authoritarian streaks and reinstitute full democratic norms. A new movement in combination with judicial intervention could provide the 'breathing space' needed for the political process to start a push-back against undemocratic activities in the executive branch.

**Effective Election Machinery.** Even when the above three elements are available and functioning well, a piece of neutral and effective election machinery is a vital cog in ensuring that democracies do not fail. Free and fair elections are a foundational component of democracies and broader political freedom.[37] The electoral machinery must also be staffed by neutral officials capable of withstanding very high levels of political pressure. Officials of high professional competence, personal courage and impeccable integrity are worth their weight in gold to prevent the subversion of the electoral process.[38] They form an essential and unavoidable part of the 'elite' that safeguards democracies from decline, decay and eventual fall.

The case studies referred to in this chapter also prove that popular sentiment can, at best, play only a distant secondary role in stemming the slide to authoritarianism, even though mass politics can become the tipping element in some rare cases. The fact is that there is no single magical bullet, in the form of an institution or process, that can prevent or arrest the erosion of democracy even after it has been clearly identified. It is necessary to have a combination of functioning democratic processes, supported by a non-elected judiciary, military forces and government officials who have sufficient integrity to repudiate elected authoritarian leadership to stem the slide into non-democratic activities by the executive. Timely intervention by the political elite will become a catalyst to provide public movements and the time for democratic institutions to regroup and reorganise.

It must be recognised that sustained and prolonged assault on democratic norms—irrespective of whether the assault is by a person in power or out of power—is hard to defend against and defeat. Safeguarding democracy requires concerted efforts by judges, civil officials and in extremis even by military officers. Well-timed action is the only way to restore democracy in these cases.

## Populism—The 21st Century Challenge to Democracy

The events of the decade of the 1990s seemed to vindicate the concept of liberal democracy with the breakup of the Soviet Union and the brief move of Russia to adopt some form of democracy. It appeared that liberal democracy, as a concept of governance, had triumphed over all obstacles and opposition, both in practice and in principle.[39] The US, self-declared champion of liberal democracy, revelled in the belief that it had proven once and for all that democracy was the only legitimate form of government. The hypocrisy of this self-congratulatory pose was immediately visible as the US continued to support the theocratic autocracies and monarchies of the Middle-East, while at the same time continuing to shun the theocratic 'democracy' of Iran.[40] However, there is no doubt that even at the point of self-declared triumph, democracies were faced with multiple external challenges.

More limiting to the concept is the internal challenge of populism, which attempts to delineate democracy and liberalism. Starting from the Brexit (Britain's exit from the European Union) debate that started in the early 2010s, the liberal democracies of the world, most of them located in the 'West', have been forced to content with moves by traditional right-leaning parties to encompass and champion far-right policies to ensure electoral victories. The reasons for this somewhat involuntary shift are complex and some of them are co-joined. At the core of the issue is the ongoing economic changes that are particularly noticeable in democracies. In the democracies of the post-World War II era, there was a tacit covenant between the people, the elected representatives and the unelected 'experts' that promised to create sustained prosperity and deliver a steadily improving standard of living to the common people.[41] As long as this covenant was held, the people deferred to the experts.

Globalisation weakened this covenant with the growing competition from developing countries, which upset the somewhat lopsided global status quo that had existed between the 'developed', 'less developed' and 'developing' nations. The experts were now unable to manage the 'developed' economies as well as to be expected and the promise of improving standards of living started to falter in many nations.[42] Two trends took centre stage in the developed economies. First, economic activities started to become concentrated in a few metropolitan areas, which led to increasing income inequality vis-à-vis the rural areas. Second, globalisation assisted the already 'rich' in the developed nations at the cost of the working and middle classes who saw a deterioration in their income status.[43]

The economic recession that hit the developed world in 2007 was the result of the failure of economic and political leadership and irrevocably sundered the existing covenant between the people and the government that had so far held the fragile balance together. The general public lost faith in both mainstream political parties and the established institutions as unemployment and accompanying financial hardships became unavoidable.[44] Inevitably this led to populist upsurges in most democratic nations that stood the US political process on its head and continue to threaten the European Union. In general, the situation endangers liberal governments across the world.

While the economy is at the foundation of challenges to democracies, other factors of more recent origins have added to the complexity of the situation. The Western nations considered matured democracies and developed nations, could not deal effectively with the waves of immigrants who gate-crashed across their borders in large numbers. These immigrants endangered not only the reducing number of available jobs, but more importantly, threatened to overwhelm the long-established cultural ethos of the notions and concepts of public safety.[45] Unfortunately, the liberal democratic governments of the time did not react in the manner that people wanted them to, and concerns regarding immigration and refugees influenced people to support far-right political stances and parties. This was also a distinctive factor of influence in the 2016 US Presidential elections.[46]

At about the same time, there was a class divide becoming apparent in the developed nations of the world. The decline of manufacturing industries in these countries and the accompanying lowering of the workers' status while the 'educated, urban citizens' prospered, created a new class of affluent people, and entrenched a hitherto not seen class divide.[47] The emergence of an education-based meritocracy left behind the working and middle class who automatically turned to the far-right parties as to the hard-working people with the grievance that they had been relegated to the 'have-nots' status. Unfortunately for the concept of democracy, most democratic nations have been unable or unwilling to address this mounting challenge comprehensively, further exacerbating the class divide and the flock to right-wing extremism.[48]

The longstanding covenant has been broken, a new class-divide has been established and for the newly disenfranchised in this upheaval, the familiar comfort of culture and societal ethos are under attack and fast receding. Under these circumstances, people automatically swing towards strong leadership and tend to question the veracity of, and need for, key liberal democratic values such as freedom of the press, minority rights and even the rule of law.[49] The people give priority to supporting an authoritarian government that promises to return the situation to 'normal'—the status quo ante—an imagined past of prosperity.[50]

For a nation to claim its government as a liberal democracy it must meet five requirements based on the fundamental principles of freedom. First, the legitimacy of all kinds of government is vested in the people, i.e., all powers of the government are derived from the consent of the people to be governed.[51] Second, all citizens of the state are equal and citizenship itself is broadly inclusive, which means that almost all adults of the nation are its citizens, and their votes have equal weightage.[52] It also means that majority rule prevails. Third, it needs a basic structure that formalises institutional power, which is normally written down and accepted as the basis for governance. These 'constitutions' establish the boundaries for the institutions that wield power, both vertically and horizontally.[53] Fourth is the ability of the people to select representatives who would govern for a stipulated period of time through free, fair and regular elections with voting rights being made available to all citizens above a minimum laid down age.[54] Fifth, people must be able to enjoy a peaceful 'individual independence', which means that individuals must be able to conduct economic, social, cultural and religious activities without state interference. This is the core of 'liberalism'—protecting the individual bubble, beyond which the government does not have the legitimate power to intervene.[55]

## What is Populism?

So, what is populism and how does it impact a functioning liberal democracy? In its purest form, populism is the process by which an individual or political party seeks support from the ordinary people to accept the principle of democracy as the exercise of majority rule.[56] The issue is that populism does not accept the structure that institutionalises the application of majority decisions and is disdainful of minority rights and individual freedoms.[57] In other words, populism practices the 'tyranny of the majority'. Populism strives to translate popular—meaning majority—preferences into policy while ignoring any institutional checks and balances, thereby threatening the true meaning and practice of liberal democracy.

The challenge of understanding populism stems from the fact that it is difficult to define 'the people', whose majority view determines national policy-at-large. More importantly, who or what determines and defines 'the people', considering that in all democracies it has always been difficult to do so to the satisfaction of all. Historically, the right-leaning populists have claimed shared ethnicity, common heritage and culture, while the left-leaning ones are more class-ridden and tend to exclude the rich and powerful. Of late in the US, populists have started to divide the people into the 'real people', the working-class Americans, and the elites who they dub the 'globalists'.[58] The common thread in all three is that each group considers itself to be homogenous with an opposing and different set of values to those that they consider the 'others'. This division is pushed to an extreme position by populist leaders who claim that they alone represent the people.[59] Therefore, they alone have the legitimate right to rule and can push aside all institutional restraint that is imposed.

## What is the Impact of Populism

An essential, even critical, element of democracies is the necessary inclusion of all the people into the entity that governs them. Populism consciously pulls away from this requirement. In fact, it divides the citizens of a nation by splitting them into 'the people' and 'the others'—gradually populism develops into a process by itself that excludes 'the others' from participating in the governance process and relegating them into sub-citizens with ever diminishing rights. When this situation is entrenched in a nation, it is no more a liberal democracy.[60]

Populism is built on a belief that all people will have the same will and needs in a homogenous manner. Unfortunately, this is an untrue fallacy. In a pluralistic society, homogeneity cannot be enforced and after the initial euphoria of excluding 'the others', the supporters of populism will themselves fall prey to pluralism and divisiveness from within.[61] An assumption of homogeneity is fundamental to populism. However, in reality, every nation is a collection of diverse groups who may or may not be aligned with each other. Therefore, populism is directly opposed to democracy and its principle of inclusiveness. Populism takes the concept of majority rule to the next level of exclusion and the superimposition of the fundamentals of one social group over the others.[62] This process gradually grinds down democracy, since pluralism—the ability to find ways and means to live together as equal citizens—a crucial element of democracy is fully negated by populism.

Populism is built on the firm conviction that their own concepts are virtuous and therefore, by deduction, those of the 'enemy' are immoral and unworthy. Populist leaders find it easy to attack 'the others' as corrupt, self-seeking and conspirators against the people who are the good virtuous ordinary citizens. Populism shuns compromise, one of the virtues of decision-making in democracies. With compromise removed from the equation, normal societies are plunged into divisive zero-sum conflicts that gradually threaten and subsume the rights of minorities while disassembling institutional checks and balances.[63] In turn, this fight, at times physically violent, feeds back into populism in a vicious cycle that in itself becomes the raison d'etre for populism to exist. In this situation, unless the democratic institutions can fight back, the nation descends into anarchy, then autocracy and finally to a dictatorship where a directive 'top down' rather than 'bottom up' form of government prevails.

The modus operandi of populism and its dedicated leadership follow a predictable path to threaten, undermine and then demolish democracy. Analysis of historical cases demonstrates that the process starts with undermining the freedom of the press; weakening the independence of the justice system and rule of law; gradually gathering power to the executive while simultaneously dismantling legislative checks and balances; undermining and marginalising non-elected constitutional authority and institutions; and victimising minority groups, usually based on ethnicity, religion and race as 'the other' to be despised.[64] These actions are normally initiated from within the democratically elected government.

The flags have been raised in the USA and some other liberal democracies—the danger is here and now.

## The United States on the Brink or Why Democracies Fail

The US, as both the oldest constitutional democracy in the world and the self-proclaimed worldwide champion of democracy, has a chequered history of following fundamental democratic principles. The old Athenians who conceived the idea of democracy would have difficulty in recognising the US governance as a practice of democracy. They would consider it an oligarchy, where a few fortunate wealthy persons typically decide the rules of the political process and also who wins and loses elections. The Presidential Election of 2016 is a stark example of popular will and votes being pushed aside by the Electoral College—the oligarchs. In this election, Donald Trump the Republican candidate lost the popular vote to the Democrat

Hillary Clinton by more than 2.8 million votes but won 30 states and the decisive Electoral College with 304 electoral votes to Clinton's 227.[65] It is obvious that the US politicians, at least a sizeable majority, have become power-hungry, arrogant, self-serving individuals.

President Biden, in his recently delivered Memorial Day address to the nation, invoked democracy as the 'soul of America', while at the same time accepting that in the US, democracy was imperfectly practiced and is in peril.[66] However, the fact remains that democracy has been imperilled in the US in earlier times also. Before the American Civil War (1861-65), people of African origin, i.e., 'Black Men', were stripped of their right to vote and then of their citizenship itself. Just a decade after the end of the Civil War, a combination of legislation and violence made a mockery of democracy in the US.[67] The warning signs of a similar move are already visible in many states of the US. The US is facing a battle of ideology today to determine whether its brand of democracy will succeed or whether the entire concept of democracy—as accepted globally—will be discarded. It is a telling commentary that the day after the President's Memorial Day address, 100 scholars of repute who study democracy warned in an open statement that the Republican Party's efforts to radically reorganise the elections at the state level call into question whether the US will remain a democracy.[68]

The 2020 US Presidential Elections came precariously close to re-electing a President who had combined his private business interests with that of the White House, who openly embraced foreign dictators as the best leaders, politicised the justice department and at the end cast doubt on the veracity of the electoral process, the absolute foundation of democracy, and continues to do so eight months into a new Administration. With the insurrection on Capitol Hill on January 6, 2021, the US democracy came dangerously close to being dismantled.[69] The 2020 elections and their aftermath laid bare the deep flaws in the US electoral process, its practice of democracy, the manner in which its leaders are chosen and the way in which they govern. It was demonstrated that the flaws in the system—some as old as the nation itself and some of the more recent origins—could be easily weaponised by an authoritarian incumbent of the White House to dismantle the fundamentals of democracy in the country.[70]

The sad truth today is that the Republican Party does nothing to check the rampaging false rhetoric and accusations of the past President and is leading the nation towards an existentialist threat—the survival of the oldest constitutional democracy in the world rests on a delicate balance.

## Russia—Toying with Democracy

The erstwhile Soviet Union was a collective Communist dictatorship. On its collapse, in the late 1980s and early 1990s, Russia who donned the mantle of the old Soviet Union, and made some dramatic progress towards introducing a democratic order. In the last year of the Soviet Union and the first few years of Russia, the nation made a remarkable move toward holding real elections, protecting of civil liberties and the rule of law. Unfortunately, the march toward democracy stalled by the mid-1990s because of two main reasons. First, the overpowering weight of Communism's legacy of the historical experience of ignoring democratic values, and second, the failure of the leadership to build viable institutions to fill the vacuum left by the collapse of Communism.[71]

The result of the two failures was that power remained concentrated in the Executive Branch, centred on informal networks and personal connections, breeding nepotism and corruption. Further, the judicial and legislative institutions that were instituted were extremely fragile and could not stand up to the 'bull dozing' of the executive branch since there was no precedent to fall back upon. As a result, journalistic independence could not become entrenched in the new reality and the protection of civil liberties was extremely weak, even at its best.[72] When these challenges were combined with official corruption that remained pervasive and became endemic, failure of the fledgling experiment in democracy was a certainty.

For a little more than a decade after coming to power, till around 2013, Putin ruled over an over-managed democracy, winning votes because the voting public agreed with him and his policies, harking on his own leadership qualities and the competence of his government. From the mid-2010s, Russia's economic growth has stagnated and along with it, the regime has been faced with rising societal pressures. The reaction from the government has been increased repression and the building of an authoritarian regime based on elite unity has been shaping the political landscape.[73]

By 2019, the decline in democratic norms had reached a stage wherein 'Freedom House' had labelled Russia a 'consolidated authoritarian regime', giving it only 20 out of 100 in its Global Freedom Score. In the past few years, Russia has been struggling with a defunct electoral system, widely believed to be rigged, which makes its legitimacy very low. The civil society, which had embarked on grassroots political activism, has suffered a vicious backlash from the Kremlin. The government directly or indirectly owns or controls all the mainstays of what constitutes an independent media—television and radio stations, many national newspapers and almost all regional media.[74] There is no doubt that Russia remains 'authoritarian', with President Putin manipulating quasi-democratic institutions to generate legitimacy and distribute political power, mainly to informal institutions controlled or owned by the State. In Russia, reaching true democratic functioning remains a pipedream.

## Conclusion: The Quest for Liberal Democracies

Several safeguards can be erected to protect liberal democracies from populism and authoritarian onslaught: One, the health of the first line of defence—the press, judiciary, rule of law—can be monitored and remedial actions initiated early. The erosion of minority rights provides an early warning of deterioration and can be corrected. Two, the fears of the normal citizens, such as unlimited immigration overwhelming them economically and culturally, should not be allowed to be manipulated by populist and anti-liberal leadership and must be comprehensively addressed within the democratic process. Three, economic growth must be made inclusive and made into a broadly shared prosperity. Individual self-worth, status and dignity that come with a well-compensated job cannot be replaced with anything else.

So why do democracies fail if the safeguards can be erected and kept in place? With the recent events in the US, there is no doubt that the world is in the throes of a democratic gloom. In this dire assessment, it needs to be kept in mind that taken as part of the human evolution, democracy as a common practice is not even three centuries old, quite literally in its infancy.[75] Even today real democracy is an exception, not the rule; more a grand scheme of history.

The concept of democracy is deceptively simple: all members of a community should be equal, and all adults must join equally in its governance. As a corollary, no one should be able to enjoy unchecked power that leads to its arrogant abuse. Unfortunately, the concept goes against the basic instincts and impulses of fundamental human nature. Like all other animals, humans are also inherently aggressive and at the base, level seeks to survive and procreate. At that level, both these functions are achievable by subduing the 'other', manifested as a blind drive towards self-assertion, well hidden behind the façade of civilisation.[76] Scratch the surface and reality emerge faster than one can conceive.

A large part of world history is the story of leaders attempting to annihilate the 'other' or make them subservient, in an effort to cater for the majority impulses. Within this paradigm, democracy has only a fragile hold and needs careful nurturing to flourish. A person, a group, a 'people', or a nation must individually and collectively understand that living together means everyone is equal, with equal rights and responsibilities, irrespective of colour, creed, race or religion. This is a tall order, especially when historic wrongs are regularly brought up to create schisms or to facilitate the upliftment of a particular group, both antithesis for encouraging the entrenchment of democracy.

There is a discernible democratic recession worldwide with liberal democratic principles on the backfoot and receding in front of an audacious authoritarian onslaught. Further, long-term autocracies such as China and Russia have proven to be remarkably resilient and resourceful, providing a sort of 'living example' of the pitfalls of democracies. However, working against this trend is the global economic developments, which spreads outward to engulf and subsume anti-democratic notions. Expanded education, information transfer, and open travel have all contributed to the overall enhancement of broad human knowledge and awareness, creating an atmosphere most conducive to demanding the emergence of liberal democratic institutions.[77] There is a certainty that the quest for universal human freedoms will not stop until and unless liberal democracies ensure such freedoms are irrevocably established. Currently, such governments have not spread across the world, but there are indications of their spreading at various and differing rates in the most unlikely places. Projecting this trend forward into the middle future, it seems that a generational change in society towards liberal democratic values is inevitable.

New generations are increasingly critical of the hierarchical and deferential values of the older generation and reject them, looking to imbibe and practice universal, liberal, and egalitarian values. Only a truly embedded liberal democracy can support and absorb this fundamental shift in societal values. A society steeped in liberal values will normally be critical of the imposed authority of autocrats. To combat this trend, autocracies—like North Korea, Russia, China, Turkey and Venezuela—attempt to supplant liberal values by creating nationalistic cults, which require allegiance by all citizens. This is achieved through concerted propaganda that enforces and sustains autocratic 'strongman' rule.[78]

There is no doubt that currently, an illiberal public mood is sweeping across even established liberal democracies for myriad reasons, some enumerated above. The angst of the common people has generated support for 'strong leaders' who do not respect parliaments, senates and other institutions and are ready to run roughshod over all established democratic norms and processes. However, this phenomenon is bound to be of short-term attraction and strong liberal values will establish itself once the people realise the loss of freedoms that they encounter on the path of populism-fed authoritarian rule. The authoritarian attempt to redefine democracy will not hold water in the face of challenges from liberal democratic values.[79] Liberal values have long-term influence and have the capability to subsume the short-cycle authoritarian impulses built around temporary public opinion and support.

At its core democracy is about safeguarding freedoms—individual to minimise interference in private lives and collective to ensure the public discourse applies equally to all citizens. There is no denying that even matured democracies are in some troubled waters and rough seas at the moment. The population is split between support for authoritarian rule and liberal values. However, liberal values fostered by generations and the strong roots that it has among the younger generation provide genuine indications that liberal democracies will eventually triumph.[80] Franklin D. Roosevelt, the 32nd President of the US said, 'Let us never forget that government is ourselves and not an alien power over us. The ultimate rulers of our democracy are not a President and senators and congressmen and government officials, but the voters of this country.' It is time to remember these words.

## Notes


1. Moore, Bruce (ed.), *The Australian Concise Oxford Dictionary*, Fourth Edition, Oxford University Press, Melbourne, 2004, p. 368.
2. *The New International Webster's Comprehensive Dictionary of the English Language*, Trident Press International, FL, USA, 1996, p. 341.
3. Scrutiny of Acts and Regulations Committee, *Victorian Electronic Democracy, Final Report 2005*, at https://www.parliament.vic.gov.au/archive/sarc/E-Democracy/Final_Report/Glossary.htm. Accessed on July 1, 2021.
4. Columberg, Dumeni, *Report on Instruments of Citizen Participation in Representative Democracy*, Group pf European People's Party, Switzerland, March 25, 1997, at https://assembly.coe.int/nw/xml/XRef/X2H-Xref-ViewHTML.asp?FileID=7699&lang=EN. Accessed on July 1, 2021.
5. Rodrik, Dani, 'Populism and the Economics of Globalization', *Journal of International Business Policy*, June 2018, pp. 12-33.
6. For a detailed examination of this phenomenon see, Eichengreen, Barry, *The Populist temptation: Economic Grievance and Political Reaction in the Modern Era*, Oxford University Press, New York, 2018.
7. Chibber, Pradeep and Verma, Rahul, 'The BJP's 2014 'Modi wave': An Ideological Consolidation of the Right', *Economic and Political Weekly*, Volume 49, Issue No 39, September 27, 2014.
8. Lovenduski, Joni, 'The history of government from the earliest times', *Democratization*, Volume 5, 1998, Issue 4, pp. 197-212, September 27, 2007, at https://www.tandfonline.com/doi/abs/10.1080/13510349808403591?journalCode=fdem20. Accessed on July 1, 2021.
9. History.com Editors, *Ancient Greek Democracy*, August 19, 2019, at https://www.history.com/topics/ancient-greece/ancient-greece-democracy. Accessed on July 1, 2021.
10. History.com Editors, *Ancient Rome*, August 21, 2020, at https://www.history.com/topics/ancient-rome/ancient-rome. Accessed on July 1, 2021.
11. For an erudite analysis of the Italian 'republics' in medieval times read, Sismondi, Jean Charles Leonard de, *History of the Italian Republics in the Middle Ages*, Create space Independent Publishing Platform, California, November 21, 2014.
12. Navarro, Teressa, et al., *Democracy Development in England,* at https://www.sutori.com/story/democracy-development-in-england--aXc2vTeXauJdTW5aP4Q2PjnY. Accessed on July 1, 2021.

13. Bailey, Megan, *Series: Suffrage in America: The 15th and 19th Amendments*, at https://www.nps.gov/articles/series.htm?id=EA334AEE-A3B5-5979-737829A71446739C. Accessed on July 1, 2021. (This is a series of seven articles that cover the development of suffrage [the right to vote] for African American citizens in the USA from the earliest times.)
14. Reny, Tyler, 'Opinion: How the U.S. is Still Struggling with Universal Suffrage', *The Atlantic*, September 25, 2012, at https://www.theatlantic.com/politics/archive/2012/09/opinion-how-the-us-is-still-struggling-with-universal-suffrage/428883/. Accessed on July 1, 2021.
15. For a very early analysis of an 'ideal' democracy read, Brown, Jethro W., 'The True Democratic Ideal', *International Journal of Ethics*, Vol. 14, No. 2, (January 1904), pp. 137-150, at https://www.jstor.org/stable/pdf/2376137.pdf?refreqid=excelsior%3Aba46b8969fd655eff3620be37ed59b1a
16. 'Policy Recommendations: Strengthening Democracy', *Freedom House*, at https://freedomhouse.org/policy-recommendations/strengthening-democracy-abroad. Accessed on July 2, 2021.
17. Meyer-Resende, Michael, 'International Consensus: Essential Elements of Democracy', *Democracy Reporting International*, Berlin, October 2011 (the Report is also available for download as a pdf, at https://democracy-reporting.org/wp-content/uploads/2016/02/essential_elements_of_democracy_2.pdf).
18. Feulner, Edwin D., 'Preventing "The Tyranny of the Majority"', *The Heritage Foundation*, March 7, 2018, at https://www.heritage.org/conservatism/commentary/preventing-the-tyranny-the-majority. Accessed on July 2, 2021.
19. Hermens, Ferdinand A., 'The Tyranny of the Majority,' *Social Research*, vol. 25, no. 1, 1958, pp. 37-52. *JSTOR*, at www.jstor.org/stable/40982538. Accessed on July 2, 2021. (For an in-depth analysis of the challenge read, Nyirkos, Tamas, *The Tyranny of the Majority: History, Concepts and Challenges*, Routledge, Oxfordshire, 2018.)
20. Reuveny, Rafael and Quin Li, 'Economic Openness, Democracy and Income Inequality: An Empirical Analysis', *Journal of Comparative Political Studies*, Volume 36, Issue 5, June 1, 2003, at https://journals.sagepub.com/doi/abs/10.1177/0010414003036005004#. Accessed on July 2, 2021.
21. McCarty, Nolan, Poole, Keith T. and Rosenthal, Howard, 'Political Polarization and Income Inequality', *Social Science Research Network*, January 27, 2003, posted online 1 July 2008, at https://papers.ssrn.com/sol3/papers.cfm?abstract_id=1154098. Accessed on July 2, 2021.
22. Wolfendale, Jessica, 'Terrorism, Security and the Threat of Counterterrorism', *Studies in Conflict & Terrorism*, Volume 30, Issue 1, 2007, pp. 75-92, at https://www.tandfonline.com/doi/full/10.1080/10576100600791231?scroll=top&needAccess=true.
23. Mahajan, Gurpreet, 'Civil Societies and its Avtars: What Happened to Freedom and Democracy?', *Economic and Political Weekly*, Volume 34, No 20, May 15-21,

1999, pp. 1188-96, at https://www.jstor.org/stable/4407959. Accessed on July 2, 2021.

24. Peck, Richard and Harris, Nikos, 'Counting on the Court: The Preservation of Fundamental Freedoms and Liberties in the Era of the Security Revolution', *20 Supreme Court Law Review 2d*, 2003, posted on-line March 15, 2014, at https://papers.ssrn.com/sol3/papers.cfm?abstract_id=2347033. Accessed on July 2, 2021.
25. Henderson, Errol A. and Singer, David J., 'Civil War in the Post-Colonial World, 1946-92', *Journal of Peace Research,* Volume 37, Issue 3, May 1, 2000, at https://journals.sagepub.com/doi/abs/10.1177/0022343300037003001. Accessed on July 2, 2021.
26. Alatas, Syed Farid, 'Theories of Democratic and Authoritarian State Formation', *Democracy and Authoritarianism in Indonesia and Malaysia: The Rise of the Post-Colonial State*, Macmillan Press Ltd, London, 1997, pp. 19-43.
27. Henley, Jon, '2017 and the curious demise of Europe's centre-left', *The Guardian*, December 29, 2017, at https://www.theguardian.com/politics/ng-interactive/2017/dec/29/2017-and-the-curious-demise-of-europes-centre-left. Accessed on July 3, 2021.
28. Uberoi, Elise, Cracknell, Richard and Fella, Stefano, 'European Parliament elections 2019: results and analysis', Research Briefing, *House of Commons Library*, UK Parliament, London, June 26, 2019, at https://commonslibrary.parliament.uk/research-briefings/cbp-8600/. Accessed on July 3, 2021.
29. Daimond, Larry, 'Facing Up to the Democratic Recession', *Journal of Democracy*, Volume 26, Issue 1, January 2015, pp. 141-155, at https://www.journalofdemocracy.org/articles/facing-up-to-the-democratic-recession/. Accessed on July 3, 2021.
30. Ibid.
31. Diskin, Abraham, Diskin, Hanna, and Hazan, Reuven Y., 'Why Democracies Collapse: The Reasons for Democratic Failure and Success', *International Political Science Review*, Volume 26, No 3, 2005, pp. 291-309, at https://journals.sagepub.com/doi/pdf/10.1177/0192512105053787. Accessed on July 3, 2021.
32. This path is not being discussed further in this paper since a catastrophic failure of democracy through a military coup d'état has its own anti-dotes and repercussions in a contextual manner.
33. Case studies considered in this paper are taken from an extensive study conducted by Tom Ginsberg and Aziz Huq and published. Read, Ginsberg, Tom & Huq, Aziz, 'Democracy's "Near Misses"', *Journal of Democracy*, Volume 29, Issue 4, October 2018, pp. 16-30, at https://www.journalofdemocracy.org/articles/democracys-near-misses/. Accessed on July 3 , 2021.
34. For an in-depth analysis of the importance of independence of the judiciary read dissertation: Cho, Moohyung, *Rethinking Judicial Independence in Democracy and Autocracy*, Department of Political Science, Graduate School of Duke University,

2020, at https://dukespace.lib.duke.edu/dspace/bitstream/handle/10161/21523/Cho_duke_0066D_15882.pdf?sequence=1&isAllowed=y. Accessed on July 3, 2021.

35. Reuter, Ora John, 'Why Do Ruling Parties Extend Authoritarian Rule? Examining the Role of Elite Institutions and Mass Organisation', Working Paper Series 2021: 118, *The Varieties of Democracy Institute, Department of Political Science, University of Gothenburg*, April 2021, at https://www.v-dem.net/media/filer_public/3f/55/3f5554fb-f1e4-4a1d-8eb3-ce5c7d9619ff/wp_118_final.pdf. Accessed on July 3, 2021.
36. Csaky, Zselyke, et al., 'Nations in Transit 2021: The Antidemocratic Turn', *Freedom House*, Washington D.C., at https://freedomhouse.org/sites/default/files/2021-04/NIT_2021_final_042321.pdf. Accessed on July 3, 2021.
37. Schneider, Nancy, 'Free and Fair Elections are Elusive at the Best of Times', *Australian Outlook*, Australian Institute of International Affairs, Canberra, April 30, 2020, at https://www.internationalaffairs.org.au/australianoutlook/free-and-fair-elections-are-elusive-at-the-best-of-times/. Accessed on July 3, 2021.
38. Ham, Carolien van and Garnett, Holly Ann, 'Building impartial electoral Management? Institutional design, independence and electoral integrity', *International Political Science Review*, Volume 40, Issue 3, April 2019, at https://journals.sagepub.com/doi/full/10.1177/0192512119834573. Accessed on July 4, 2021.
39. Editors, 'The end of Soviet communism', *Britannica*, at https://www.britannica.com/event/the-collapse-of-the-Soviet-Union/The-rise-of-Yeltsin-and-the-foundation-of-post-Soviet-Russia. Accessed on July 4, 2021.
40. Editors at The Policy Circle, 'Foreign Policy: The Middle East', *The Policy Circle*, December 22, 2018, at https://www.thepolicycircle.org/brief/foreign-policy-brief-the-middle-east/. Accessed on July 4, 2021.
41. Vonyo, Tamas, 'Post-War Reconstruction and the Golden Age of Economic Growth', *European Review of Economic History*, Volume 12, No. 2, 2008, pp. 221-241. *JSTOR*, at www.jstor.org/stable/41378546. Accessed on July 5, 2021.
42. For a broad analysis of the impact of globalisation read, Swank, Duane, 'Globalisation, Domestic Politics, and Welfare State Retrenchment in Capitalist Democracies', *Social Policy and Society*, Volume 4, Issue 2, April 2005, pp. 183-195, Cambridge University Press, at https://www.cambridge.org/core/journals/social-policy-and-society/article/abs/globalisation-domestic-politics-and-welfare-state-retrenchment-in-capitalist-democracies/0391C95A6062C0D317CD4499025F158E. Accessed on July 5, 2021.
43. Mackintosh, Eliza, 'Report: Income inequality rising in most developed countries', *The Washington Post*, 16 May 2013, at https://www.washingtonpost.com/news/worldviews/wp/2013/05/16/report-income-inequality-rising-in-most-developed-countries/. Accessed on July 5, 2021.

44. Verick, Sher and Islam, Iyanatul, 'The Great Recession of 2008-2009: Causes, Consequences and Policy Responses', IZA Discussion Paper No. 4934, *Social Science Research Network*, at https://papers.ssrn.com/sol3/papers.cfm?abstract_id=1631069. Accessed on July 5, 2021.
45. Esses, Voctoria M., Medianu, Stelian, and Lawson, Andrea S., 'Uncertainty, Threat, and The Role of the Media in Promoting the dehumanization of Immigrants and Refugees' *Journal of Social Issues*, Volume 69, No 3, 2013, pp. 518-536, at https://scholar.google.com.au/scholar?q=Journal+of+Social+Issues+Vol+69+No+3&hl=en&as_sdt=0&as_vis=1&oi=scholart. Accessed on July 5, 2021.
46. Ogan, Chritine, Pennington, Rosemary, Venger, Olesya and Metz, Daniel, 'Who drove the discourse? News coverage and policy framing of immigrants and refugees in the 2016 U.S. presidential election', *Communications*, Volume 43, No. 3, 2018, pp. 357-378, at https://www.degruyter.com/document/doi/10.1515/commun-2018-0014/html. Accessed on July 5, 2021.
47. Melander, Charlotta and Florida, Richard, 'The Rise of Skills: Human Capital, the Creative Class and Regional Development', *Handbook of Regional Science*, 2021, at https://link.springer.com/content/pdf/10.1007/978-3-662-60723-7_18.pdf. Accessed on July 5, 2021.
48. Spence, Sean, 'Right-wing extremism: the new wave of global terrorism', *The Conversation*, October 23, 2020, at https://theconversation.com/right-wing-extremism-the-new-wave-of-global-terrorism-147975. Accessed on July 5, 2021.
49. Jones, Seth G., 'The Rise of Far-Right Extremism in the United States', CSIS Briefs, *Centre for Strategic & International Studies*, November 7, 2018, at https://www.csis.org/analysis/rise-far-right-extremism-united-states. Accessed on July 5, 2021.
50. For an in-depth analysis of the spread of right-wing extremism in the liberal democracies of Europe read, Merkl, Peter and Leonard Weinberg (eds), *Right-wing Extremism in the Twenty-First Century*, Routledge, London, April 2003.
51. D'Aspremont, J., *Legitimacy of Governments in the Age of Democracy*, January 4, 2007, at https://nyujilp.org/wp-content/uploads/2013/02/38.4-dAspremont.pdf. Accessed on July 6, 2021.
52. Holmes, Brenton, 'Citizens' engagement in policy making and the design of public services', Research paper No 1 2011–12, *Parliamentary Library of Australia*, Canberra, July 22, 2011, at https://www.aph.gov.au/about_parliament/parliamentary_departments/parliamentary_library/pubs/rp/rp1112/12rp01. Accessed on July 6, 2021.
53. Spry, Dr Max., 'The Executive Power of the commonwealth: its scope and limits', Research Paper No 28, 1995-96, *Parliamentary Library of Australia*, Canberra, May 20, 1996, at https://www.aph.gov.au/About_Parliament/Parliamentary_Departments/Parliamentary_Library/pubs/rp/RP9596/96rp28. Accessed on July 6, 2021.

54. Schmid, S.D., Piccoli, L., and Arrighi, J.T., 'Non-universal suffrage: measuring electoral inclusion in contemporary democracies', *European Political Science*, Issue 18, pp. 695-713, February 2019, at https://link.springer.com/article/10.1057/s41304-019-00202-8#citeas. Accessed on July 6, 2021.
55. Constant, Benjamin, 'The Spirit of Conquest and Usurpation and Their relation to European Civilization', in *Benjamin Constant: Political Writings*, translated and edited by Biancamaria Fontana, Cambridge University Press, Cambridge, 1988, p. 102.
56. Molloy David, 'What is populism, and what does the term actually mean?', BBC News, March 6, 2018, at https://www.bbc.com/news/world-43301423. Accessed on July 6, 2018.
57. Bryant, Octavia, and Moffit, Benjamin, 'What actually is populism? And why does it have a bad reputation?', *The Conversation*, February 6, 2019, at https://theconversation.com/what-actually-is-populism-and-why-does-it-have-a-bad-reputation-109874. Accessed on July 6, 2021.
58. Richter, Stephen, 'Are We Globalist Really Godless People? Globalism, elitism, populism and God', *The Globalist*, May 31, 2021, at https://www.theglobalist.com/are-we-globalists-godless-populism-elitism/. Accessed on July 6, 2021.
59. Goodwin, Matthew, 'National populism is unstoppable—and the left still doesn't understand it', *The Guardian* (Australian edition), November 8, 2018, at https://www.theguardian.com/commentisfree/2018/nov/08/national-populism-immigration-financial-crisis-globalisation. Accessed on July 6, 2021.
60. Roth, Kenneth, 'The Dangerous Rise of Populism: Global Attacks on Human Rights Values', *Introductory Essay, World Report 2017*, Human Rights Watch, 2017, at https://www.hrw.org/world-report/2017/country-chapters/global-4#. Accessed on July 6, 2021.
61. Plattner, Marc F., 'Democracies Past and Future: Populism, Pluralism, and Liberal Democracy', *Journal of Democracy*, Volume 21, Number 1, January 2010, Johns Hopkins University Press, Baltimore, Maryland, pp. 81-92.
62. Sadurski, Wojciech, 'Majority Rule, Democracy and Populism: Theoretical Considerations', *Legal Studies Research Paper Series No 20/01*, University of Sydney Law School, January 2020, at https://papers.ssrn.com/sol3/papers.cfm?abstract_id=3516981. Accessed on July 6, 2021.
63. Rostball, Christian F., 'Second-Order Political Thinking: Compromise vs Populism', *Political Studies* 69(3), February 2020, at https://www.researchgate.net/publication/339150234_Second-Order_Political_Thinking_Compromise_vs_Populism. Accessed on July 6, 2021.
64. Galston, William A., 'The populist challenge to liberal democracy', *Journal of Democracy*, Volume 29, Number 2, April 2018, at https://www.brookings.edu/wp-content/uploads/2018/04/04172018_gs_galston-democracy.pdf. Accessed on

July 7, 2021. Also read, Bernton, Edward, 'The Route to Authoritarian Power in Democracies: From the 1930s to the 2020s', *The Globalist*, July 24, 2021, at https://www.theglobalist.com/the-route-to-authoritarian-power-in-democracies-from-the-1930s-to-the-2020s/.

65. Beckwith, David C., 'United States Presidential Election of 2016', *Encyclopedia Britannica*, November 11, 2019, at https://www.britannica.com/topic/United-States-presidential-election-of-2016. Accessed on July 7, 2021.
66. 'Remarks by President Biden at the 153 National Memorial Day Observance', The White House, May 31, 2021, at https://www.whitehouse.gov/briefing-room/speeches-remarks/2021/05/31/remarks-by-president-biden-at-the-153rd-national-memorial-day-observance/. Accessed on July 7, 2021.
67. Editors of African American Heritage, 'Black Americans and the Vote', National Archives, at https://www.archives.gov/research/african-americans/vote. Accessed on July 7, 2021.
68. Open Statement, 'Statement of Concern; The Threats to American Democracy and the Need for National Voting and Election Administration Standards', *New America*, June 1, 2021, at https://www.newamerica.org/political-reform/statements/statement-of-concern/. Accessed on July 7, 2021.
69. Petras, George, Loehrke, Janet, et al., 'Timeline: How the storming of the U.S. Capitol unfolded on Jan. 6', USA Today News, January 7, 2021, at https://www.usatoday.com/in-depth/news/2021/01/06/dc-protests-capitol-riot-trump-supporters-electoral-college-stolen-election/6568305002/. Accessed on July 7, 2021.
70. Mohan, Lalit, 'US election system has serious flaws', *The Times of India*, October 21, 2020, at https://timesofindia.indiatimes.com/blogs/lalit-mohan-blog/us-election-system-has-serious-flaws/. Accessed on July 7, 2021. Also see, Norris, Pippa, *Why American Elections Are Flawed (And How to Fix Them)*, Cornell University Press, New York, 2017.
71. Bjorkman, Tom, 'Russian Democracy and American Foreign Policy', Brookings Policy Brief No 85, Brookings Institution, Washington D.C., July 1, 2001, at https://www.brookings.edu/research/russian-democracy-and-american-foreign-policy/. Accessed on July 7, 2021.
72. Ibid.
73. Orttung, Robert, 'Challenges in Building Russian Democracy', Wilson Centre, Washington D.C., April 12, 2010, at https://www.wilsoncenter.org/event/challenges-building-russian-democracyhttps://www.wilsoncenter.org/event/challenges-building-russian-democracy. Accessed on July 7, 2021.
74. Trickett, Nicholas, 'Nations in Transit 2020—Russia', Freedom House, January 2020, at https://freedomhouse.org/country/russia/nations-transit/2020. Accessed on July 7, 2021.

75. Connaughton, Aidan, Kent, Nicholas, and Schumacher, Shannon, 'How people around the world see democracy in 8 charts', Pew Research Centre, February 27, 2020, at https://www.pewresearch.org/fact-tank/2020/02/27/how-people-around-the-world-see-democracy-in-8-charts/. Accessed on July 7, 2021.
76. Ambrose, Vince, 'The Compatibility of Democracy and the Human Condition: the Quest for Objective Values', Honors Theses, Paper 257, Southern Illinois University, Carbondale, 2009, at https://opensiuc.lib.siu.edu/cgi/viewcontent.cgi?referer=https://www.google.com/&httpsredir=1&article=1272&context=uhp_theses. Accessed on July 8, 2021.
77. Eugster, Johannes, Ho, Giang, et al., 'How Knowledge Spreads', *Finance & Development*, Volume 55, No 3, September 2018, International Monetary Fund, at https://www.imf.org/external/pubs/ft/fandd/2018/09/globalization-and-how-knowledge-spreads-eugster.htm. Accessed on July 8, 2021.
78. Walker, Tony, 'The rise of Strongman politics', Paper 24, July 2018, La Trobe University, Melbourne, at https://www.latrobe.edu.au/news/articles/2018/opinion/the-rise-of-strongman-politics. Accessed on July 8, 2021.
79. Starr, Paul, 'Why Liberalism Works', *The American Prospect*, April 2007, Princeton University, at https://www.princeton.edu/~starr/articles/articles07/Starr.WhyLiberalismWorks.pdf. Accessed on July 10, 2021. Also read the same author's book *Freedom's Power: The True Force of Liberalism*, Basic Books, New York, 2007.
80. Deudney, Daniel, and G. John Ikenberry, 'The Myth of the Autocratic Revival: Why Liberal Democracy Will Prevail.' *Foreign Affairs*, Volume 88, No. 1, January-February 2009, pp. 77-93, *JSTOR*, at www.jstor.org/stable/20699435. Accessed July 10, 2021.

# 11

# India-South East Asia Security Cooperation

TEMJENMEREN AO

## Introduction

India and Southeast Asian countries are bound together by their shared history and culture. There has been steady progress in India's relations with Southeast Asia since the Look East Policy (LEP) was initiated in 1992; and the Act East Policy (AEP), announced in 2014, which continues to build on this. India has always considered Southeast Asia as a region of high economic and strategic priority. India's engagement in the region is primarily structured through the Association of Southeast Asian Nations (ASEAN), which is a rules-based regional process. The year 2022 marks thirty years of India-ASEAN relations, which continue to be shaped by the changing geopolitical environment. Beyond ASEAN with the emerging changes in contemporary global geopolitics and security environment, India and countries in Southeast Asia have articulated their convergence of interests including strengthening the partnerships to address common challenges critical for ensuring peace and stability in the region. The paper is a study on the changing nature of India's relations with Southeast Asian countries and how their converging interests are helping shape the security architecture of the region. The evolving nature and role of ASEAN towards addressing the security challenges such as maritime security and international terrorism, has enabled India to broaden its security partnership with Southeast Asian countries.

## ASEAN in the midst of the Evolving Security Environment

Since the establishment of ASEAN the security in the region has undergone considerable change. Under the Bangkok Declaration of 1967, the formal purpose of the ASEAN was to promote economic, social, cultural, scientific, and administrative fields cooperation and to promote regional peace and stability. In its declaration, ASEAN laid out the acknowledgement amongst all the members about their shared challenges and interests which could be overcome through partnership based on equality. The setting up of ASEAN was a consequent of the Cold War compulsions and the need to ensure that any form of expansionist aggression does not occur in the region. Further by undertaking conflict avoidance and management through dialogues amongst the members, was intended towards promoting regional reconciliation.[1]

The Bangkok Declaration also indicated a prerogative aspiration to manage regional order. At the ASEAN Foreign Ministers' Meeting in November 1971, there are a commitment to make Southeast Asia a Zone of Peace, Freedom, and Neutrality (ZOPFAN). An official commitment to political cooperation was expressed in a Declaration of ASEAN concord at the Bali Summit in February 1976 by the heads of the government. The ASEAN concord through the Treaty of Amity and Cooperation (TAC) laid out provisions for a norm-based regional order and for dispute settlement.[2] This became a necessary condition to ensure domestic stability and to lessen reliance on external powers for regional security. Over the decades through the various ASEAN-led mechanism, it has been successful in not only diffusing intra-regional conflicts but also in preventing new ones from arising.[3]

ASEAN's political and economic cooperation along with its aversion to formal defence cooperation were insufficient as it was not effective in addressing the evolving strategic environment in the region. By leaving out the security cooperation from the scope of ASEAN, the regional grouping wanted to keep its focus on the socio-economic development of the region. In the first few decades after the formation of the Association, much effort was towards building regional reconciliation which was essential for achieving peace and stability in the region. Therefore, security cooperation remained out of the purview of and sanctioned on a primarily bilateral basis. Notwithstanding ASEAN's efforts, the region continues to be plagued by a host of intra—regional and extra-regional tensions and challenges. With the end of the Cold War, the region was faced with a new and uncertain strategic environment marked by new security challenges. In the post-Cold War period, Southeast Asia also witnessed political transition amongst some of the ASEAN countries. This transition re-defined the political landscape in the region, making it more open and democratic which got filtered into the regional architecture that helped facilitate deeper and enhanced cooperation towards regional peace and security. ASEAN has been establishing new regional mechanisms to improve regional institutional capacity in order to respond to emerging security challenges some of which are transnational in nature.[4]

At the turn of the 21st century, Southeast Asia has witnessed the increasing economic and political assertiveness of extra-regional powers. ASEAN leaders agreed on the need to act collectively and enhance cooperation in order to address the economic and security challenges. At the Bali Summit on October 7, 2003, the leaders of the ASEAN Member States signed the Declaration of ASEAN Concord II or Bali Concord II, declaring their intention to establish an ASEAN Community. The ASEAN Community was founded on three pillars: (i) an ASEAN Security Community or ASC for political and security cooperation, (ii) ASEAN Economic Community or AEC for economic integration, and (iii) ASEAN Socio-Cultural Community or ASCC for socio-cultural cooperation. These three pillars are envisaged to be closely intertwined and mutually re-enforcing to ensure durable peace, stability, and prosperity in the region. While the AEC seeks to create a stable and highly competitive ASEAN economic region with the aim to establish a single market and production base, the ASCC aims to foster cooperation in social development targeted at raising the standard of living of the disadvantaged groups and rural populations. The ASC is envisaged to ensure peaceful processes are employed in the settlement of intra-regional differences and also address transboundary maritime issues and concerns.[5]

The ASC is intended to provide a regional framework to handle security matters and disputes within ASEAN. Following the adoption of the ASC, a number of regional initiatives to help promote political cooperation and deeper regional integration in ASEAN were laid out in the Vientiane Action

Programme (VAP). According to the VAP, the ASC is aimed at building 'a democratic, tolerant, participatory, and open community in Southeast Asia'.[6] The ASEAN Security Community Plan of Action, adopted at the 10th ASEAN Summit, stipulates that ASEAN shall work towards the convening of an annual ASEAN Defence Ministers' Meeting (ADMM). Against this background, the inaugural meeting of the ADMM was held in Kuala Lumpur on May 9, 2006. The "ADMM is the highest defence consultative and cooperative mechanism in ASEAN. The ADMM aims to promote mutual trust and confidence through greater understanding of defence and security challenges as well as enhancement of transparency and openness..." The key objectives of the ADMM are to promote peace and stability through dialogue and cooperation in defence and security. Since its inception, it has been able to build defence cooperation amongst the ASEAN member states in the areas such as maritime security, counter-terrorism, peacekeeping operations, humanitarian assistance and disaster relief, military medicine, and the defence industry. On October 12, 2010, the ADMM Plus was inaugurated as a platform for ASEAN and its eight Dialogue Partners, namely Australia, China, India, Japan, New Zealand, ROK, Russian Federation and the United States, to strengthen security and defence cooperation for peace, stability, and development in the region. The ADMM-Plus currently focuses on "... seven areas of practical cooperation, namely maritime security, counter-terrorism, humanitarian assistance and disaster management, peacekeeping operations, military medicine, humanitarian mine action and cyber security. Experts Working Groups (EWGs) have been established to facilitate cooperation in these areas..."[7]

ASEAN re-defined its institutional structure to help promote cooperation for peace and stability as it was a key to ensure economic progress amongst the member states. In this, the Bali Concord II which set out to establish the ASEAN Security Community as one of the three main pillars, added a new dimension to the regional security architecture. The need for building a security initiative amongst the ASEAN countries and its dialogue partners was intended to offer an alternative approach to security to that provided by military alliances. With ASEAN's primary purpose being the promotion of socio-economic cooperation the ever-changing security complexities required it to undertake conflict avoidance and management.

In its road towards establishing a more formal security arrangement, intra-regional as well as extra-regional factors played a significant role.

## Major Security Concerns for Southeast Asia

Following are the three major factors in the 21st century that has helped shape the narrative for building a formal security structure in Southeast Asia.

### *An Assertive China and the ongoing dispute in the South China Sea*

Four ASEAN countries are involved in the South China Sea (SCS) territorial and maritime boundary disputes with China. Malaysia and the Philippines claim jurisdiction over some of the Spratly Islands while Brunei claims jurisdiction over adjacent maritime space. China and Vietnam's major dispute in the SCS are over the Paracel and the Spratly islands. The contention over the Paracel islands is a bilateral dispute between Vietnam and China, while the dispute over the Spratly apart from the other three ASEAN members also includes Taiwan. According to China's self-declared maritime boundary—the 'nine-dash line'—the Paracel and the Spratly islands falls well within China's maritime boundary.[8]

Given the strategic significance of the South China Sea, it has led to the individual claims being defended in recent decades. Amidst regional competition, this has resulted in low intensity standoff between the Philippines and Vietnam (1998 and 1999) and between Taiwan and Vietnam in 1995. Meanwhile, larger-scale confrontations have taken place between China and Vietnam (1974, 1988, 1992 and 1994) as well as China and the Philippines (1995, 1996, 1997 and 1999). The dispute over the Paracel islands has in the past witnessed intense military engagement between the naval forces of China and Vietnam in January 1974. One of the bloodiest conflicts between the two countries occurred in 1988 when the Chinese and Vietnamese forces clashed at Fiery Cross Reef near Johnson Island. During the hostilities, the Vietnamese lost up to three vessels and seventy-seven crew members. In 1992, China reasserted its claim to exclusive sovereignty over the entire sub-region by passing a new "Law of the Territorial Sea and Contiguous Zone of the People's Republic of China". Following the military actions and China publishing a law on its territorial waters through which it proclaimed its maritime rights was seen as an assertive posturing and thereby increased ASEAN's apprehension.[9]

This move by China was also an outcome of the disintegration of the Soviet Union at the end of 1991 and the withdrawal of the US military presence from the Philippines in 1992. The withdrawal of US navy forces from Subic Bay created a vacuum which contributed to China's growing assertiveness being witnessed today. ASEAN has been keen to follow a common approach to peacefully resolve the disputes, in accordance with international law and the UN Convention on the Law of the Sea (UNCLOS). ASEAN sought to avoid both an escalation of the hostilities on the matter and the alienation of China which, by the time, had become a highly important trading partner in Southeast Asia. At a meeting of ASEAN's foreign ministries in Manila on July 22, 1992, a joint declaration was issued on the SCS. The declaration helped establish some sort of blueprint for governing behaviour in the SCS which paved the way for the Declaration on the Conduct of Parties in the South China Sea, known as DOC—which was signed on November 4, 2002, in Phnom Penh, by the foreign ministries of ASEAN and China. Signatories to the DOC pledged to find a peaceful and durable solution to differences and disputes amongst them in the SCS. The signatories also pledged to exercise self-restrain in the conduct of activities that would complicate or escalate disputes before the peaceful settlement was reached. The DOC was agreed to be the initial step towards a more binding Code of Conduct (COC). However, it did not alter China's behaviour in 1995 it occupied a small set of islands called Mischief Reef that are also claimed by the Philippines. China's occupation of Mischief Reef was well within the Philippines' EEZ. ASEAN was able to build a degree of solidarity over the issue by censuring China for its actions and reiterating its call for restraint based on the spirit of the DOC. This was followed by the Philippines navy who in 1996 reportedly engaged in a ninety-minute battle with three Chinese navy vessels.[10]

ASEAN called for the exercise of restraint through its Declaration on the South China Sea. This declaration ensured a unified ASEAN position that included the non-use of force along with the resolution of disputes by peaceful means. The declaration also urged the claimants, to explore greater cooperation in several fields such as navigation and cooperation against piracy and illicit drugs while leaving out discussion for the exploration of natural resources. The declaration also reiterated ASEAN's aim to have all parties accept and abide by the principle of the TAC as a basis for establishing a regional code of international conduct. While the ASEAN members agreed to the declaration, the Association was not successful in its attempt to acquire China's agreement to the declaration.[11] Further, the provisions laid out in the DOC were violated on several occasions. The military standoff between China and the Philippines in 2012 at Scarborough Shoal was one such crisis triggered when the navy of the later attempted to arrest and detain Chinese fishermen and their vessels for illegally obtaining endangered marine life. The situation in the SCS continues to remain tense with China, increasing its assertiveness over the disputed islands and reefs.[12]

While ASEAN has been pushing for the conclusion of the COC which would also include a restriction on the construction of new military bases in the sea; China has continued to increase its military presence in the region. In particular, China has increased its naval build-up along with the construction of artificial islands by increasing the area of landfills around the existing islands and reefs. The new infrastructure would be used to enhance radar coverage of the area, support a small presence of military personnel, and provide logistic support for ships patrolling the farther reaches of the SCS.[13] China's repeated intrusions into Vietnam's Exclusive Economic Zone (EEZ) off its central and southern coastlines have become one of the biggest challenges for Vietnam's foreign policy in terms of security and defence. In July 2019, there have been reports which suggested a large-scale stand-off between China and Vietnam's coastguard ships. The incident occurred after a Chinese oil exploration ship entered the contested waters near the Spratly Islands.[14]

ASEAN views these recurring incidents and their possible escalations affecting the stability and security, not to mention freedom of navigation. While ASEAN has been keen on following a common approach towards peacefully resolving the dispute. However, differences within the block remain in the approach toward achieving a settlement. The ASEAN ministerial meeting held in July 2012 at Phnom Penh highlighted these differences as the member states were not able to come to a consensus on a joint statement. The differences within ASEAN led to the then Indonesia's foreign minister Marty Natalegawa to meet with the leaders of Southeast Asia and negotiate a common ASEAN position. This led to the 'Six-Point Principles on the South China Sea', which reaffirmed ASEAN's commitment to a peaceful resolution of the dispute. China expressed its willingness to continue working alongside ASEAN towards adopting the COC.[15]

The COC, once concluded would put in place rules that are binding and help make the situation in the SCS more stable, through a mechanism that are effective to manage and control disputes, and facilitating deeper cooperation amongst all. The contestation over the demarcation of maritime borders in the South China Sea which in recent years has witnessed low-intensity engagements such as firing at fishing vessels by the navies of some of the claimants poses to be a major challenge as it also disturbs the regional stability, essential for promoting trade and commerce. The ongoing negotiation of the COC for the South China Sea between ASEAN and China requires an early conclusion which is in accordance with international law and the 1982 UNCLOS.[16]

### *Great Power Rivalry in the Indo-Pacific*

The geopolitical shift towards the Indo-Pacific region has resulted in the region becoming one of the major contested spaces in the globe amongst the major powers. In this region, we also have some of the major emerging countries whose future growth would be conditioned by a stable environment. These emerging countries are also involved in the competition for dominance while also safeguarding their respective interests from various security challenges. As discussed in the previous section, China's aggressive pursuit of its territorial claim over the South China Sea has led to the expansion of its navy. The militarisation such as the building of airstrips and other facilities for military purposes in the disputed waters is creating further security concerns in the region. Confronted by the China challenge the US has been expanding its strategic footprints in order to protect its interest in the Indo-Pacific.[17] Under President Trump, Asia became the centrepiece of US foreign policy. As per the National Security Strategy released in December 2017, China was seen as a challenge to American power, influence, and interest and it stated that the US was engaged in a geopolitical competition with Beijing. In May 2018, the US Pacific Command which is the oldest and largest unified combatant command was renamed the US Indo-Pacific Command (USINDOPACOM). Headquartered in Oahu, Hawaii, it is composed of nearly 330,000 service members and civilian employees and has forward bases in Japan, Guam, and South Korea. In mid-2019 the US Department of Defense released the 'Indo-Pacific Strategy Report' which explicitly claimed that the Indo-Pacific is the Pentagon's 'priority theatre'. The report sharpened the idea that the United States and China are engaged in a long-term struggle for influence and power in the Indo-Pacific.[18]

The emerging US narrative which is today focused on a rebalancing strategy is also engaged in fortifying the old as well as building a new alliance to confront the China challenge.[19] The establishment of the trilateral security partnership between Australia, the United Kingdom (UK), and the United States (US) (AUKUS) on September 15, 2021, is one such military alliance which is intended to address the emerging complexities in the Indo-Pacific.[20]

The emerging great power rivalry in the Indo-Pacific which is resulting in countries to increase their military footprints and building new alliances would lead to a further arms race in the region and will provoke other powers to act more aggressively. With the US-China competition in this region continuing to intensify, the Southeast Asian countries remain apprehensive about China's strategic intentions in particular its militarisation in the South China Sea. At the same time, some of the countries in the region have expressed unease over the US Indo-Pacific strategy (Free and Open Indo-Pacific) perceived by them as a direct response to China's more assertive approach.[21]

Southeast Asia given its geographical centrality in the Indo-Pacific, it has stressed on an ASEAN-centric regional architecture that is open, transparent, inclusive and rules-based. Indonesian Foreign Minister Ms Marsudi has stated that ASEAN being at the centre of the Indo-Pacific should not be silent and that in the 50 years of the existence of ASEAN it has never threatened others because the group always prioritized inclusiveness, cooperation and dialogue.[22] President Jokowi when delivering his speech at the plenary session of the 13th East Asia Summit (EAS) on November 15, 2018, conveyed Indonesia's vision of the "World Maritime Axis". The President explained that the Pacific and the Indian Oceans constitute a 'single geo-strategic theatre'. President Jokowi stressed on the need for ensuring that this region does not become a stage for disputes and unrest. Indonesia emphasised that efforts should be laid towards creating a peaceful region along the two oceans as the challenges are becoming more complex; such as the increasing instances of disputes over natural resources between nations and attempts to attain maritime supremacy for control over world trade routes, amongst regional players.[23]

The 'ASEAN Outlook on the Indo-Pacific' (AOIP) adopted in 2019 emphasises on the centrality of the ASEAN amidst the geopolitical shifts being witnessed in the region. Further, the ASEAN outlook on the Indo-Pacific is based on the principles of "…openness, transparency, inclusivity, a rules-based framework, good governance, respect for sovereignty, non-intervention, complementarities with existing cooperation frameworks, equality, mutual respect, mutual trust, mutual benefit and respect for international law, such as UN Charter, the 1982 UN Convention on the Law of the Sea, and three other relevant UN treaties and conventions, the ASEAN Charter and various ASEAN treaties and agreements and the EAS Principles for Mutually Beneficial Relations…".[24] The ASEAN Outlook on the Indo-Pacific focuses on three areas, namely maritime cooperation which also includes addressing crimes at sea, cooperation in connectivity to boost economic growth, and cooperation to realise sustainable development to achieve the SDGs target in an inclusive manner.[25]

### *Terrorism in Southeast Asia*

Terrorism in Southeast Asia is another key determinant of the region's political, military, and strategic alignments. It is regarded as the most serious security threat by all Southeast Asian countries. While Indonesia and the Philippines have home-grown terrorist networks as well as linkages to international terrorist organisations, Malaysia and Thailand have been used as transit points and temporary safe havens for some terrorist cells and individuals. Indonesia, Myanmar, the Philippines and Thailand (South) face insurgencies associated with separatist and Communist movements leading to violent conflicts between government security forces and armed rebels.[26]

The US administration's 'war on terror' and 'with us or against us' approach polarised both the political elites and the communities in

Southeast Asia by further exacerbating the already existing divisions in identity that have been a consequence of different social and religious histories. Other internal factors such as poor domestic security, the absence of secular education, high unemployment, and low standards of living, all contributed to the appeal of terrorist ideology. In the post-9/11 years the devastating terrorist attacks such as the Bali bombing in October 2002 and the 2009 Marriott and Ritz-Carlton bombing also build a unified perception across the region that terrorism is a concern for the world and the countries of Southeast Asia. In the case of Indonesia and in the wake of the economic crisis and the instability that followed, the country also had to content with other terrorist attacks in its capital along with several hotspots for religious and/or ethnic-based violence in various other locations within the country. In Malaysia, terrorism is predominately limited to a concern that the country continues to serve as a source of Islamic militancy rather than a victim of it. The Philippines meanwhile continues to suffer from both communist and Islamic insurgencies. In Laos, there remains occasional but limited occurrence of violence by ethnic minority groups in order to take over the Communist government. In the case of Myanmar, while it has not yet been a major source of terrorist activities beyond its own borders, the country has endured more than half a century of civil war and insurgency. In Thailand post-9/11 there has been a resurgence of the separatist movement in Southern Thailand that has generated large-scale violence.[27] Thailand also gained major international attention as a hideout and transit for Muslim-based extremist groups. An article in the Asian Wall Street Journal alleged that Al-Qaeda-linked Jemaach Islamiah (JI) has used Southern Thailand in January 2002 as a pivotal planning area for the Bali bombing. Given Thailand's location with porous borders, and a large Muslim minority population, in the age of global terrorism, it becomes a likely target of organisations like Al-Qaeda and JI. [28]

## India's Security Cooperation with Southeast Asia

### *ASEAN*

India's engagement in Southeast Asia is primarily structured through the ASEAN which is a rules-based open regional process. India became a sectoral dialogue partner of ASEAN in 1992 which was upgraded to a full dialogue partnership in 1996 and became a Summit level partner in 2002. The main forum for ASEAN security dialogue is the ASEAN Regional Forum (ARF) and India has been attending annual meetings of this forum since 1996 and has actively participated in its various activities. India signed the ASEAN's Treaty of Amity and Cooperation (TAC) in October 2003. India has also become part of ASEAN security dialogue initiatives such as the East Asia Summit established in 2005 and the ASEAN Defence Ministerial Meeting Plus established in 2010. In 2012 the relations got upgraded into a Strategic Partnership which has further enabled stronger cooperation in the area of security with ASEAN as well as with individual ASEAN states. At the 12th ASEAN-India Summit and the 9th East Asia Summit held in Nay Pyi Taw, Myanmar, in November 2014, the Prime Minister of India formally enunciated the Act East Policy (AEP). In 2018, ASEAN and India commemorated 25 years of dialogue partnership and 15 years of Summit-level partnership. Today India and ASEAN are focussed on creating a mechanism for maritime cooperation which would focus on addressing traditional and non-traditional security challenges. The need for expanding defence and security cooperation is emerging central to the India-ASEAN strategic partnership.[29] At the 18th ASEAN-India Summit held on October 28, 2021, significant progress was made in terms of the strategic partnership. The Joint Statement emphasized on building cooperation on priority areas as identified in the AOIP and strengthening the ASEAN-India Strategic Partnership for achieving peace and prosperity in the region.[30]

China's aggressive posturing in the region, particularly with regards to the territorial disputes in the South China Sea with several Southeast Asian countries, has pushed the regional states closer to the United States and also to view India, as a favourite as a potential balancer to China.[31] With the recent changes in contemporary global geopolitics, India and ASEAN have well-articulated the convergence of interests in the construct of the Indo-Pacific, demonstrated in India's Indo-Pacific Oceans Initiative (IPOI) and the AOIP. In 2022, ASEAN and India will complete their three decades of dialogue partnership. Faced with growing traditional and non-traditional challenges, politico-security cooperation is a key and an emerging pillar of

India-ASEAN relationship. India, therefore, places ASEAN at the centre of its Indo-Pacific vision.[32] However, India's engagement in the region goes beyond ASEAN, with the bilateral partnerships it shares with individual Southeast Asian countries making strong progress ever since the 'Look East' Policy was announced in 1992.

### *Indonesia*

Indonesia being one of the largest states in terms of geography and in influence in the region becomes a critical partner for India's expanding security engagement in Southeast Asia. While the relations date back to more than 1000 years the diplomatic relations are comparatively recent; established only after both nations attained their independence. In March 1951, India and Indonesia signed a Treaty of Friendship that helped lay the foundation for a sustained trade, cultural, military and diplomatic cooperation. Through the 'Look East' policy India was able to re-establish its relations with its Southeast neighbours in the economic and security spheres. The development of India's economic and security engagement, created the platform to further build on the India-Indonesia relations with the signing of a Defence Cooperation Agreement in 2001. This agreement stipulated the establishment of a Joint Defence Cooperation Committee (JDCC) to study and identify various possible fields of defence cooperation.[33] In the post-9/11 years, Indonesia experienced a string of major terrorist attacks such as the Bali bombing in October 2002, the 2009 Marriott and Ritz-Carlton bombings and the suicide bombers linked to Jamaah Ansharut Daulah (JAD) which attacked three churches across Surabaya, on May 13, 2018.[34] Indonesia which has been facing the impact of radical Islamic violence, today also faces the challenge of the growing scourge of Islamic State of Iraq and Syria (ISIS)-inspired terrorism.[35]

These events along with an emerging instable security environment helped set in motion the need for the expansion of the India-Indonesia relations which led to the establishment of the New Strategic Partnership during the visit of the then President Susilo Bambang Yudhoyono to India from November 21-23, 2005. According to the Joint Declaration, the New Strategic Partnership called for stronger defence relations.[36] In 2006, a defence cooperation agreement was signed and during the Indonesia-India Joint

Commission Meeting [JCM] in June 2007 it was agreed upon to accelerate the implementation of cooperation under the new strategic partnership and monitor progress through the mechanism of a Plan of Action. During the visit of the then Prime Minister Manmohan Singh to Indonesia in October 2013, strategic engagement, and defence and security cooperation in order to respond to common challenges were identified amongst the five focus areas in order to help strengthen the bilateral ties.[37]

While both countries have been a victim of terrorism, India's 26/11 terrorist attack showcased its vulnerabilities from the open seas. This encouraged both countries to expand their defence cooperation in their maritime space. Maritime security cooperation between India and Indonesia is perhaps the most significant aspect of the bilateral defence cooperation, considering the fact that together both countries control an area extending from the Bay of Bengal in the Indian Ocean to the Straits of Malacca. Further, Indonesia's location, combined with its naval forces, makes it a very important partner for India in order to ensure the security of the sea lanes of communication between Europe, West Asia, and Southeast Asia. Apart from engaging in the multi-nation MILAN naval exercise which started in 1995, both nations have been expanding their maritime cooperation in the area of coordinated patrols, joint bilateral or multilateral exercises, as well as humanitarian assistance and disaster relief. Joint naval exercises and patrols and regular port calls by respective navies have become a regular feature of the broader India-Indonesia defence cooperation.[38]

The announcement of the 'Act East' policy in 2014 provided the much-needed push to further propel the India-Indonesia relations. In December 2016, President Jokowi undertook a state visit to India during which both sides discussed the importance of maritime cooperation which would be critical for the stability of the surrounding region as well. The "Statement on Maritime Cooperation" during the visit provides a broad range of cooperation that included maritime security, maritime industry, maritime safety and navigation.[39]

India and Indonesia upgraded their partnership to a Comprehensive Strategic Partnership (CSP) in May 2018. The establishment of this new partnership provides the opportunity for deeper collaboration in the defence and security spheres. During the May 2018 meeting between President

Jokowi and PM Modi, both leaders acknowledged "the need to maintain maritime safety and security for peace, stability and sustainable economic growth and development in the maritime waters of the Indo-Pacific region as enshrined by UNCLOS and relevant international laws".[40] An agreement was also reached towards strengthening existing naval cooperation which includes bilateral Coordinated Patrols between the Navies initiated in 2002. Both sides also agreed to commence regular bilateral naval exercises and enhance information sharing related to maritime security in the Indo-Pacific region. Another significant aspect of this meeting was the agreement to give India economic and military access to the strategic island of Sabang which is located in the Indian Ocean.[41]

The Sabang port is approximately 90 nautical miles or 175 km from Indira Point, the southernmost tip of India's Andaman and Nicobar Islands. It is 40 metres (131 feet) deep and could be developed to accommodate both commercial vessels and submarines. The Sabang port as well as the Andamans straddles important sea lanes of trade and energy flow. Given the economic and strategic significance of this sea route, India and Indonesia have been expanding the deployment of their naval assets to safeguard their interests and ensure stability in the Indian Ocean. Being maritime neighbours that share a common vision the collaboration between India and Indonesia in the Sabang has a strategic tilt. Through the enhanced maritime cooperation under the CSP, Indonesia has allowed the berthing of IN ships in Sabang with INS Sumitra becoming the first warship to dock at the Sabang deep-sea port on July 11, 2018.[42] Further through the CSP it also enables widening the security cooperation to include exploration and uses of outer space for peaceful purposes.[43]

### *Malaysia*

Since the establishment of India-Malaysia diplomatic relations in 1957, the relations have grown at the economic and defence level. Malaysia is a littoral state of the Malacca Strait that links the Indian and the Pacific Oceans and more narrowly the Bay of Bengal to South China. Given the geostrategic significance of Malaysia, it becomes a key security partner for India; given that they share a common interest for a peaceful and stable regional environment which is necessary for development and growth. The signing of an MoU on Defence Cooperation in 1993 provided a framework for defence and security dialogues and cooperation through joint ventures, joint development projects, procurement, logistics, maintenance support, training, and education. Since then there have been high-level exchanges with visits by the Defence Ministers along with Staff talks between the three services being held regularly on an annual basis. This enabled exchange on strategic and security assessments which require further cooperation in areas of counter-terrorism, maritime security, disaster management, and peacekeeping operations. During the visit to Malaysia on October 26-28, 2010, by the then PM Manmohan Singh, a Framework for Strategic Partnership between the two countries was established. The framework for a strategic partnership was established with the intent to elevate the bilateral relations to the level of a long-term and strategic partnership. On November 23, 2015, during the official visit of PM Modi to Malaysia, both sides reaffirmed their determination to take the strategic partnership to the next level by deepening the existing areas of cooperation, while also exploring new areas.[44]

The positive outcomes of these interactions enabled deepening of the security cooperation especially in the maritime space. Defence initiatives such as joint exercises which include "Harimau Shakti"—a bilateral army exercise that is meant to prepare for the UN peacekeeping operations and assists in countering and strengthening counter-terrorism and counter-insurgency activities—are being held annually. The Indian Air Force training team was also deployed in Malaysia to train Malaysian pilots on the Su-30 SKM aircraft from 2008-2010. Maritime security which is critical for both the countries have enabled deeper cooperation for countering piracy at the sea and coordinating their research and rescue operation and response to natural disasters. In 2019, India's Chief of the Naval Staff visited Kuala Lumpur aimed towards strengthening maritime and naval cooperation. Both the navies have been regularly taking part in the Langkawi International Maritime and Aerospace Exhibition in Malaysia with Indian naval ships and coast guards making port calls at Malaysian ports. Malaysian naval ship has also regularly taken part in India's MILAN series of exercises.[45]

### *Philippines*

Since the launch of the "Look East" policy, the pace of high-level political and defence exchanges between India and the Philippines has increased due to the commonalities in the security challenges. At the turn of the 21st-century bilateral defence and security, interests were shaped to help build cooperation in order to combat against increasing terrorism, and transnational crimes including illicit drug trafficking. During the visit of the then Indian President Abdul Kalam Azad to the Philippines from February 3-6, 2006, an agreement for defence cooperation was signed which helped elevate the bilateral relations to a more strategic level. The agreement looked at enhancing defence cooperation through the exchange of military training expertise and information; exchange of military instructors/observers; exchange of visits of military aircraft and military naval vessels; exchange of information that is mutually beneficial, and other spheres of defence cooperation. India and the Philippines also signed a Joint Declaration for cooperation to combat international terrorism during the visit of Philippine President Gloria Macapagal Arroyo to India from October 4-6, 2007. Through this joint declaration, emphasis was towards information sharing, cooperation amongst law enforcement agencies, cooperation in capacity building and in the prevention and suppression of the financing of terrorist acts.[46]

In order to further strengthen the bilateral defence cooperation, the Joint Defence Cooperation Committee (JDCC) was constituted which had its first meeting in Manila in January 2012. The JDCC meetings reviewed and exchanged views on evolving regional security concerns as well as multilateral engagements. The two parties exchanged views on the future activities of cooperation that would further consolidate their defence and security relations, under this cooperation in the maritime space, has emerged as a major component.[47] This was further elaborated on during a meeting in New Delhi on March 9, 2018, between Department of National Defence Secretary Delfin Lorenzana and the then Indian Defence Minister Nirmala Sitharaman.[48] To further build on the levels of interoperability and ensure peaceful and secure seas for all, the Indian Navy has made a number of port visits to the Philippines. Indian Navy Vessel, INS Rana (D52) visited

Manila from October 23-26, 2018 and from October 23-26, 2019, Indian Navy ships—guided missile frigate INS Sahyadri and anti-submarine corvette INS Kiltan—made a port call at Manila.[49] On August 23, 2021, two ships of the Indian Navy, namely INS Ranvijay (Guided Missile Destroyer, D55) and INS Kora (Guided Missile Corvette, P61), carried out a Maritime Partnership Exercise with BRP Antonio Luna (Frigate, FF 151) of the Philippine Navy in the West Philippine Sea.[50]

Apart from the port calls and joint naval exercises, a bilateral MoU was signed between the Indian Navy and the Philippines Coast Guard on sharing of White Shipping Innovation in October 2019. The MoU seeks to enhance maritime security through sharing of information on non-military and non-government shipping vessels.[51] At the 4th Meeting of the India-Philippines Joint Commission on Bilateral Cooperation held on November 6, 2020, both sides agreed to further strengthen defence engagement and maritime cooperation, especially in military training and education, capacity building, regular goodwill visits, and procurement of defence equipment. Further, both countries agreed to enhance cooperation in the area of CT with information exchange between concerned agencies and support in terms of specialised training needs.[52] India and the Philippines on January 29, 2022, has formally signed a US$ 375 million contract for the BrahMos shore-based anti-ship missile system.[53] The conclusion of the contract has upgraded the India-Philippines defence ties to the next level.

### *Singapore*

India and Singapore have a history rooted in strong commercial, cultural, and people-to-people connections across a millennium. India was one of the first countries to establish diplomatic ties with Singapore in 1965. India and Singapore share similar concerns about the challenges posed by terrorism and extremism and have found it mutually beneficial to evolve a broad framework of security cooperation which also includes cyber security and combating drug trafficking. India and Singapore in October 2003 signed a Defence Cooperation Agreement. During the visit of PM Modi to Singapore in November 2015, which also marked the 50th anniversary of the India-Singapore diplomatic relations, a Joint Declaration on a Strategic Partnership was signed which elevated the relations to a Strategic

Partnership. Nine bilateral documents were signed in the areas of defence, maritime security, cyber security, narcotics trafficking, urban planning, civil aviation, and culture.[54]

India-Singapore relations are based on shared values and approaches which have enabled towards building of a strong defence partnership. India and Singapore have a longstanding and comprehensive partnership, which includes Annual Ministerial and Secretary-level dialogues; Staff level talks between three wings of armed forces; training of Singapore Army and Air Force in India; annual exercises including India's longest uninterrupted naval exercise with any other country (26th edition in 2019); ship visits from Navy and Coast Guard. Singapore participates in IONS and multilateral Exercise MILAN hosted by the Indian Navy. Singapore's membership of IORA and India's membership of ADDM Plus provides a platform for both countries to coordinate positions on regional issues of mutual concern. New developments include the inaugural Trilateral Maritime Exercise between India, Singapore and Thailand (SITMEX)—announced by PM Modi in his Keynote address at the 2018 Shangri La Dialogue—in September 2019 in Andaman Sea with the intention to conduct it annually at alternative locations. The two sides agreed to enhance maritime information exchange, intensify HADR cooperation, and explore cooperation in areas like geospatial data, cyber security and setting up of Joint Test Facilities under the Defence Testing Infrastructure Scheme of India.[55] The Indian PM during his visit to Singapore from May 31 to June 2, 2018, stated that the bilateral relation fulfils the criterion of strategic partnership in the true sense. During the meeting with PM Lee Hsien Loong, both sides emphasised the importance of defence and security in the bilateral strategic partnership. PM Modi stated that India and Singapore are natural partners with a shared vision and strong defence relations, evident in the India-Singapore naval exercise or SIMBEX which is entering its silver jubilee year. Other defence initiatives include regular military training as well as the recently concluded bilateral logistic agreement.[56] Both leaders discussed the issue of combating cyber security, extremism and terrorism, which was described as a major threat and an important area of bilateral cooperation. Given their shared concern on the global and regional challenges both sides reaffirmed their principled views on maritime security which include openness, inclusiveness, transparency, and peaceful settlement of disputes on the basis of international law, including the 1982 United Nations Convention on the Law of the Sea, while also reaffirming their commitment to a rules-based order.

### *Thailand*

Thailand was one of the first countries to establish diplomatic relations with India in 1947; and 2022 would mark the completion of 75 years. In the 21st century with a shift in the concept of security due to the changing nature of threat, it altered bilateral defence engagement amongst States. India and Thailand were no exceptions with the partnership expanding to include strategic cooperation in the field of counter-terrorism and other forms of non-traditional threats. Defence cooperation between India and Thailand in the area of counter-terrorism over the years has increased in scope. During the State visit of the then Prime Minister of Thailand, Yingluck Shinawatra to India from January 24-25, 2012, both sides while unequivocally condemning terrorism in all its forms and manifestations recognised the common threats to national security from transnational crimes, including international terrorism. The 6th meeting of the Joint Working Group on Security Cooperation held in New Delhi on May 25-26, 2011, provided an opportunity to discuss the issue of terrorism in a comprehensive manner. A bilateral MoU on Defence cooperation was signed during the January 2012 Thailand PM's visit. In the area of counter-terrorism according to the MoU, both sides resolved to significantly enhance bilateral cooperation in combating terrorism, including restricting transnational movement and unauthorised stay of known terrorists in each other's countries. The two leaders resolved to commit their countries to improve sharing of intelligence, the development of more effective counter-terrorism policies, enhance liaison between law enforcement agencies, provide assistance in the areas of border and immigration control to stem the flow of terrorist-related material, money and people and specific measures against transnational crimes, through the already existing mechanisms between Thailand and India.[57]

During the visit of Thailand's Deputy Prime Minister and Defence Minister to India in March 2016, a wide variety of security cooperation were discussed. These included intelligence sharing, counter-terrorism, and cyber security. In the same year when PM Chan-o-cha visited New Delhi, while condemning terrorism, both India and Thailand agreed to enhance substantive cooperation for addressing this increasing threat from non-traditional security; which also included counter-terrorism.[58]

The India-Thailand relations have also increased its military engagement in the maritime space this was necessary as the event of 9/11 which brought out the vulnerabilities of the seas. This further broadens the scope of the bilateral security cooperation to ensure the safety of sea lanes of communication (SLOCs), seaborne military threats but also non-conventional threats to human beings such as low-intensity armed conflicts, narcoterrorism, maritime piracy, and arms trafficking in the sea. Thus, securing the maritime space in the new century expanded to not only protect one's territory but also secure the sea lines necessary for the free flow of trade and commerce.[59]

There has been close interaction and increasing exchanges between the armed forces of India and Thailand. At the inaugural bilateral India-Thailand Defence Dialogue which took place in December 2001, both sides agreed to work together on matters relating to defence and security, such as coordinated patrol, combating transnational crimes, terrorism, and maritime piracy. The Indo-Thailand Joint Working Group on security cooperation established in 2003 has provided a useful framework to push forward cooperation in maritime fields including security cooperation to include counter-terrorism and military cooperation. In the area of maritime security cooperation, India and Thailand have been cooperating through multilateral naval exercise. Indian Navy's exercise MILAN provided this very opportunity in fostering closer cooperation among navies of countries in the Bay of Bengal and the Indian Ocean region. In February 1995, India, Indonesia, Thailand, Singapore, and Sri Lanka participated with their warships in the first MILAN exercise. Since then MILAN exercise has been a biennial naval exercise with the list of participating countries increasing from the original five to include Australia, Bangladesh, Brunei, Malaysia, Maldives, Myanmar, Mauritius, New Zealand, the Philippines and Seychelles. Apart from the biennially held MILAN exercise, both navies also interact in other multilateral fora such as the Indian Ocean Naval Symposium (IONS), and the Western Pacific Naval Symposium (WPNS).[60]

The need to further deepen bilateral security cooperation in the marine domain led to the Indo-Thailand Coordinated Patrolling or Indo-

Thai CORPAT initiated and launched in 2006. The 25th edition of the CORPAT was held from January 23 to 31, 2018. The aim of this exercise is to engage in coordinated patrolling, anti-piracy exercise, and search and rescue exercise. India is also an 'Observer Plus' country in the multilateral Cobra Gold exercise held in Thailand. Further, India and Thailand on October 25-26, 2015 in New Delhi held a Joint Task Force on Maritime Security. During Thai Prime Minister Chan-o-cha's visit to New Delhi in June 2016, both sides expressed a keen interest in enhancing cooperation in the maritime domain including anti-piracy cooperation, security of sea lanes of communication including coast guard cooperation to maintain peace and ensure the safety and security of navigation in the Indian Ocean. In this connection, during the visit, it was agreed to work towards the completion of the negotiation for the signing of the White Shipping Agreement between India and Thailand.[61]

### *Vietnam*

India's relations with Vietnam are based on a long history of cultural ties which have continued to evolve on the bases of shared and sustained cooperation between the two nations. The location of Vietnam in East Asian waters, adjacent to China and overlooking the PLA Navy submarine base on Hainan Islands, makes it a key strategic partner.[62] Historically, Vietnam had an adverse relationship with China, having fought its last war with China in 1979.[63] China and Vietnam's major dispute in the South China Sea is over the Paracel and the Spratly islands. The contention over the Paracel islands is a bilateral dispute between Vietnam and China, while the dispute over the Spratly includes five Southeast Asian nations, Taiwan and China. The issue between Vietnam and China over the Paracel islands has been intense with military engagement between the naval forces of China and South Vietnam taking place in January 1974. While today Vietnam has a normalised its relations with Beijing, with whom it has also established a CSP in March 2013, yet it is also one of the most strident voices in Southeast Asia that speak out against China's unilateral actions in the South China Sea.[64] This has helped in the building of a strategic cooperation between India and Vietnam where the defence partnership is specifically directed at capacity building and training. India shares a long-term commitment with Vietnam to help prepare its navy to absorb modern and advanced technologies to play a greater role as a strategic partner.[65]

In the post-Cold War period, both nations began to deepen their strategic cooperation with defence emerging as a major area of cooperation. The first Memorandum of Understanding was signed in 1994, a formal Defence Protocol in March 2000 where both nations signed agreements on joint military exercises, joint campaigns on anti-piracy in the South China Sea and anti-insurgency training. In 2003 a Joint Declaration was signed which binds both nations to conduct periodic high-ranking visits including the expansion of cooperation in the defence and security spheres. The signing of the MoU on Defence Cooperation by the two Defence Ministers in November 2009 has helped build closer interaction between the two nations through regular defence dialogue, training, exercises, Navy and Coast Guard ship visits, along with capacity building.[66] The continued and increasing bilateral defence cooperation enabled the establishment of the Strategic Partnership in 2007 which was elevated to a Comprehensive Strategic Partnership in September 2016, during the visit of India's Prime Minister to Vietnam.[67] Defence and security cooperation between India and Vietnam has today become an important element of the CSP.

Apart from regular visits of high-ranking military delegations and port calls, the two countries have to built ties on the procurement of weaponry and military hardware, capacity building, and collaboration in the area of warship building and repair. In terms of maritime cooperation, Indian ships have been regularly making friendly port calls to Vietnam. In February 2016, for the very first time, a Vietnamese ship participated in the International Fleet Review at Vishakhapatnam.[68] In December 2020, the Indian Navy took part in the "passage exercise" with the Vietnamese Navy in the SCS as part of effort to boost maritime cooperation between the two countries.[69] Further, both nations have signed MoU on Cyber Security to enhance cooperation in the non-traditional security domain, along with enhancing cooperation in the area of counter-terrorism, transnational crimes, and disaster management and response.[70]

During the visit of the then Vietnamese President Tran Dai Quang to New Delhi from March 2-4, 2018, the leader emphasised on the ongoing bilateral security cooperation which according to him would be crucial for maintaining peace, stability, growth, and prosperity in the entire region. In his meeting with Prime Minister Modi, he expressed his appreciation for India's contribution to defence ties and support for Vietnam in United Nations peacekeeping operations. President Quang and PM Modi also underlined the importance of maintaining peace and stability, and peaceful solutions to disputes, in accordance with international law, including the 1982 United Nations Convention on the Law of the Sea (UNCLOS). They also underscored the need to fully and effectively implement the Declaration on the Conduct of Parties in the East Vietnam Sea (DOC) and the establishment of a Code of Conduct (COC) for the maritime area.[71] India's President, Mr Ram Nath Kovind during his visit to Vietnam in November 2018, both sides agreed to effectively implement the Joint Vision Statement on Viet Nam-India Defence Cooperation for the period of 2015-2020. They agreed to step up cooperation in human resources training, and promote collaboration between the Army, Air Force, Naval and Coast Guard of the two countries, as well as strengthen cooperation in other maritime domains including anti-piracy, security of sea lanes, and exchange of white shipping, etc.[72] During the visit to Vietnam in May 2019, the Vice President of India, Mr M Venkaiah Naidu, both sides agreed to further strengthen the bilateral cooperation in defence and security.[73]

### *Other Key Security Partners for India in Southeast Asia*

As India continues to build its security cooperation with countries in Southeast Asia, Brunei Darussalam is also strategically significant. In 2016 India and Brunei have signed a defence pact which looks to enhance defence cooperation which includes conducting joint military exercises, hosting visits of naval ships, cooperating between defence industries and exchanging & training military officers. Over the past several years, defence relations between the two countries have been expanding. The cooperation is by way of regular official level defence exchanges, visits of naval and coast guard ships, training and joint exercises and participation in each other's defence exhibitions/expositions, etc. Officials of the Defence Ministries from both countries held a virtual meeting in January 2021.[74] The MoU on Defence Cooperation was renewed for a further period of five years in May 2021. One area for closer India-Brunei security cooperation could be in the maritime domain. Although Brunei is not geographically proximate to the Andaman Sea, this maritime arena would be suitable for the country to participate in joint military exercises in order to boost its naval preparedness and enhance defence relations, especially with India.[75]

Myanmar given its geographical proximity with India and with whom we share a long land border of over 1600 km and a maritime boundary in the Bay of Bengal, makes it an important strategic partner. Over the years New Delhi has been increasing its defence cooperation with Myanmar which is important for promoting the development and security of India's Northeastern states. The border areas of Myanmar allegedly are being used by separatist groups, such as the National Socialist Council of Nagaland (NSCN).[76] Both countries have increased their defence cooperation along their shared border which includes a coordinated border security operation against militant groups. In May 2019, the armies of India and Myanmar carried out a three-week-long coordinated operation in their respective border areas, targeting several militant groups operating in Manipur, Nagaland, and Assam. According to defence sources during the operation called 'Operation Sunrise 2' the camps of several militant outfits which included the Kamtapur Liberation Organisation, the National Socialist Council of Nagaland (Khaplang), the United Liberation Front of Assam (I) and the National Democratic Front of Bodoland, were targeted.[77] In 2019 during the visit of Senior General Min Aung Hlaing, Commander-in-Chief of Myanmar's Defence Services—who is currently the Chairman of the State Administration Council of Myanmar—a new MoU on bilateral defence cooperation was signed. Through the enhanced defence cooperation both countries are looking at also strengthening their maritime security through joint surveillance, capacity building, and developing new infrastructure. India has also supplied defence equipment to Myanmar including the indigenously built torpedoes for its Navy delivered in 2019.[78]

India and Cambodia have been expanding their cooperation in diverse fields that include security and defence. Bilateral defence cooperation between the two countries has been continuing with the conduct of regular training programmes and ship visits by the Indian Navy and the Indian Coast Guard.[79] During the visit of Cambodian PM Samdech Hun Sen to India in 2018, both sides signed a joint statement in support of safety and security in the Indo-Pacific and advocated for a peaceful resolution of maritime issues based on international law. In the joint statement, both sides expressed a keen interest in enhancing cooperation in the maritime domain, which included the promotion of peace and security; which is critical for both the countries. The two sides also called for a concerted global effort to eliminate terrorism, including blocking the source of terror financing and dismantling terrorist bases. The defence ties would be further enhanced through exchanges of senior-level defence personnel and capacity building projects.[80]

India also shares an excellent relationship with Lao PDR with both sides engaged in a wide range of discussions with regard to bilateral cooperation, region and global issues of common interest. Indian Army has been undertaking training programmes for the Lao People's Army with both sides agreed carrying out an exchange of visits at the level of high-ranking military officers.[81] Another country of significance is Timor Leste; located between the Indian and Pacific Oceans; this makes it strategically important. After its independence from Indonesia in 2002, India's relations have been limited to capacity-building projects funded through various government aid programmes. While bilateral defence engagements have been sparse, Timor Leste did participate for the first in the India naval multinational exercise Milan in 2018.[82]

## Conclusion

The security cooperation between India and countries in Southeast Asia continues to factor in the emerging regional events and global uncertainties. The security challenges from terrorism in the post-9/11 era, to the emerging security dimensions in the maritime space, to increasing assertion by some countries over the disputed waters in the South China Sea, and the emerging great power rivalry in the Indo-Pacific. These factors not only impact the region's internal and external security but are seen as an impediment to the free flow of trade and commerce. The Indo-Pacific provides a host of opportunities as well as challenges that have brought India and ASEAN countries in a common platform. India and ASEAN countries that share common values and principles would need to continue building on their cooperation for the promotion of security and stability.

## Notes

1. "Indonesia", *National Intelligence Estimate (NIE 55-68), US Department of States,* December 31, 1968, at https://nsarchive2.gwu.edu/NSAEBB/NSAEBB242/1968_NIE-55-68.pdf, Accessed on December 12, 2021.
2. Joseph Chinyong Liow, *Dictionary of the Modern Politics of Southeast Asia,* Routledge, Oxon, 2015, pp. 82-83.
3. Munmun Majumdar, *Indonesia: Primus Inter Pares in ASEAN,* Rajat Publications, New Delhi, 2003, pp. 8-15.
4. Mely Caballero-Anthony, "Reflections on Political Change, democratic transitions, and regional security in Southeast Asia", in Mely Caballero-Anthony (ed.), *Political Change, Democratic Transitions and Security in Southeast Asia,* Routledge, Oxon, 2010, p. 138.
5. Joseph Chinyong Liow, n. 2, pp. 86-87.
6. Mely Caballero-Anthony, n. 4, pp. 138-139.
7. "ASEAN Defence Ministers Meeting (ADMM)", *ASEAN,* at https://asean.org/asean-political-security-community/asean-defence-ministers-meeting-admm/. Accessed on December 12, 2021.
8. John Reed, "South China Sea: Fishing on the Frontline of Beijing's Ambitions", *Financial Times,* January 24, 2019, at https://www.ft.com/content/fead89da-1a4e-11e9-9e64-d150b3105d21. Accessed on January 10, 2022.
9. Christopher B. Roberts, *ASEAN Regionalism: Cooperation, values and institutionalization,* Routledge, Oxon, 2015, pp. 79-80.
10. Joseph Chinyong Liow, n. 2, pp. 138-140.
11. Christopher B. Roberts, n. 9, pp. 79-80.
12. Joseph Chinyong Liow, n. 2.
13. Jeremy Page and Julian E. Barnes, "China Expands Island Construction in Disputed South China Sea", *The Wall Street Journal,* February 18, 2015, at http://www.wsj.com/articles/china-expands-island-construction-in-disputed-south-china-sea-1424290852. Accessed on January 9, 2022.
14. Ravi Shankar, "Vietnam, China Showdown in South China Sea: Implications for India", *Bharat Shakti,* August 5, 2019, at https://bharatshakti.in/vietnam-china-showdown-in-south-china-sea-implications-for-india/. Accessed on January 10, 2022.
15. Joseph Chinyong Liow, n. 2, p. 139.
16. "Wang Yi, "Responds to Four Questions on the Consultations on the Code of Conduct in the South China Sea (COC)", *The South China Sea Issue,* August 1, 2019, at https://www.fmprc.gov.cn/nanhai/eng/wjbxw_1/t1685673.htm. Accessed on January 15, 2022.

17. Renato Cruz De Castro, "The Case of the Philippines", in Ash Rossiter and Brendon J Cannon (eds.), *Conflict and Cooeration in the Indo-Pacific: New Geopolitical Realities,* Routledge, Oxon, 2020, pp. 158-160.
18. Michael R. Auslin, *Asia's New Geopolitics: Essays on Reshaping the Indo-Pacific,* Hoover Institution Press, Stanford, 2020, pp. 171-175.
19. Renato Cruz De Castro, n. 17, pp. 158-160.
20. Remarks by President Biden, Prime Minister Morrison of Australia, and Prime Minister Johnson of the United Kingdom Announcing the Creation of AUKUS, The While House, September 15, 2021, at https://www.whitehouse.gov/briefing-room/speeches-remarks/2021/09/15/remarks-by-president-biden-prime-minister-morrison-of-australia-and-prime-minister-johnson-of-the-united-kingdom-announcing-the-creation-of-aukus/. Accessed on January 27, 2022.
21. Temjenmeren Ao, "AUKUS: ASEAN and the New Alignment, ICWA, October 18, 2021, at https://www.icwa.in/show_content.php?lang=1&level=3&ls_id=6487&lid=4459. Accessed on January 15, 2022.
22. "ASEAN crafts position on US 'Free and Open Indo-Pacific' Strategy", *Nikkei Asian Review,* August 2, 2018, at https://asia.nikkei.com/Politics/International-relations/ASEAN-crafts-position-on-US-Free-and-Open-Indo-Pacific-strategy. Accessed on January 28, 2022.
23. "President Jokowi Presented the Indo-Pacific Concept at the EAS Summit", Ministry of Foreign Affairs, Republic of Indonesia, November 16, 2018, at https://www.kemlu.go.id/en/berita/Pages/President-Jokowi-Presented-the-Indo-Pacific-Concept-at-the-EAS-Summit.aspx. Accessed on January 28, 2022.
24. "ASEAN Outlook on the Indo-Pacific", at https://asean.org/storage/2019/06/ASEAN-Outlook-on-the-Indo-Pacific_FINAL_22062019.pdf. Accessed on February 12, 2022.
25. Yuen Foong Khong, "Michal Leifer and the pre-requisites of regional order in Southeast Asia", in Joseph Chinyong Liow and Ralf Emmers (eds), *Order and Security in Southeast Asia: Essays in memory of Michael Leifer,* Routledge, Oxon, 2006, pp. 32-33.
26. Tin Maung Maung Than, "Politics and Security in Southeast Asia: Trends and Challenges", in Daljit Singh (ed.), *Political and Security Dynamics of South and Southeast Asia,* ISEAS, Singapore, 2007, p. 80.
27. Christopher B. Roberts, n. 9, pp. 82-85.
28. Lt Col. N. K. Chhibber and Col. S. K. Shishodia, "India-Thailand Relations", in Sanjay Kumar (ed.) *India-Thailand Bilateral Relations*, Mohit Publication, New Delhi, 2013, p. 130.
29. Dipanjan Roy Chaudhury, "India, ASEAN leaders agree to boost maritime cooperation", *The Economic Times,* January 28, 2018, at https://economictimes.

indiatimes.com/news/defence/india-asean-leaders-agree-to-boost-maritime-cooperation/articleshow/62654982.cms. Accessed on February 12, 2022.

30. "Chairman's Statement of the 18th ASEAN-India Summit 28 October 2021", *ASEAN,* October 28, 2021, at https://asean.org/wp-content/uploads/2021/10/70.-Final-Chairmans-Statement-of-the-18th-ASEAN-India-Summit.pdf. Accessed on December 2, 2021.
31. Shishir Upadhyaya, *India's Maritime Strategy: Balancing Regional Ambitions and China,* Routledge, Oxon, 2020, p. 142.
32. "India-ASEAN Relations", *Ministry of External Affairs,* August 2018, at https://mea.gov.in/aseanindia/20-years.htm. Accessed on January 12, 2022.
33. Pradeep Kaushiva and Om Prakesh Dahiya, "India-Indonesia Defence cooperation in the Indo-Pacific Region", in Rajiv K Bhatia and Rahul Mishra (eds), *The Peacock and the Garuda: An Overview of India-Indonesia Relations,* KW Publishers, New Delhi, 2015, pp. 114-115.
34. Karina M. Tehusijarana and Moses Ompusunggu, "What is JAD? Terror group behind Mako Brimob riot, Surabaya bombings", *The Jakarta Post,* May 14, 2018, at http://www.thejakartapost.com/news/2018/05/14/what-is-jad-terror-group-behind-mako-brimob-riot-surabaya-bombings.html. Accessed on December 15, 2021.
35. Superintendent Craig Riviere, "The Evolution of Jihadist-Salafism in Indonesia, Malaysia and The Philippines, and its impact on security in Southeast Asia", *Indo-Pacific Strategic papers, The Centre for Defence and Strategic Studies, Australian Defence College,* November 2016, at http://www.defence.gov.au/ADC/Publications/IndoPac/Riviere_IPSP.pdf. Accessed on December 9, 2021.
36. "Joint Declaration between the Republic of India and the Republic of Indonesia", Ministry of External Affairs, Government of India, November 23, 2005, at https://mea.gov.in/bilateral-documents.htm?dtl/7067/Joint+Declaration+between+the+Republic+of+India+and+the+Republic+of+ Indonesia. Accessed on February 12, 2022.
37. Vibhanshu Shekhar, *Indonesia's Rise: Seeking Regional and Global Roles,* Pentagon Press, New Delhi, 2014, pp. 133 and 139.
38. Pradeep Kaushiva and Om Prakesh Dahiya, n. 33, pp. 115-119.
39. "India-Indonesia Joint Statement during the State visit of President of Indonesia to India", Ministry of External Affairs, Government of India, December 12, 2016, at http://mea.gov.in/bilateral-documents.htm?dtl/27805/IndiaIndonesia+Joint+Statement+during+the+State+visit+of+President+of+Indonesia+to+India. Accessed on December 2, 2021.
40. "Shared Vision of India-Indonesia Maritime Cooperation in the Indo-Pacific", Press Information Bureau, May 30, 2018, at https://pib.gov.in/newsite/PrintRelease.aspx?relid=179630. Accessed on December 2, 2021.

41. "India and Indonesia Agree Naval Cooperation at Sabang", The Maritime Executive, May 30, 2018, at https://www.maritime-executive.com/article/india-and-indonesia-agree-naval-cooperation-at-sabang. Accessed on December 2, 2021.
42. "India's Tsunami Relief for Indonesia Supplements a Strategic Pacific Twist", Strategic News International, October 3, 2018, at https://sniwire.com/2018/10/03/indias-tsunami-relief-for-indonesia-supplements-a-strategic-pacific-twist/. Accessed on December 2, 2021.
43. n. 40.
44. "India-Malaysia Relations", Ministry of External Affairs, January 2017, at https://www.mea.gov.in/Portal/ForeignRelation/Malaysia_Jan_2017.pdf. Accessed on January 28, 2022.
45. Jyot Shikhar Singh, "India-Malaysia Defence Cooperation", Centre for Security and Strategy Studies, June 3, 2021, at https://www.cescube.com/vp-india-malaysia-defence-cooperation. Accessed on February 3, 2022.
46. "PH-India Relations", *Embassy of the Philippines, New Delhi, India*, at https://newdelhipe.dfa.gov.ph/index.php/2014-04-14-03-09-43. Accessed on November 11, 2021.
47. "Bilateral Political and Cultural Relations", Embassy of India, Manila, Philippines, at https://www.eoimanila.gov.in/page/bilateral-political-and-cultural-relations/. Accessed on November 11, 2021.
48. "PH-India Relations", Embassy of the Philippines, New Delhi, at https://newdelhipe.dfa.gov.ph/index.php/2014-04-14-03-09-43. Accessed on November 11, 2021.
49. "INS Sahyadri and INS Kiltan on 4 day port call at Manila", Rakshak News, October 23, 2019, at https://www.rakshaknews.in/en/military-en/ins-sahyadri-and-ins-kiltan-on—4-day-port-call-at-manila/. Accessed on November 11, 2021.
50. "Maritime Partnership Exercise between Indian Navy and the Philippines Navy—23 August 2021", Ministry of Defence, August 23, 2021, at https://pib.gov.in/PressReleasePage.aspx?PRID=1748328. Accessed on November 11, 2021.
51. "PHL, India sign agreements on maritime security, other areas", *Business World*, October 18, 2019, at https://www.bworldonline.com/phl-india-sign-agreements-on—maritime-security-other-areas/. Accessed on November 11, 2021.
52. "4th India-Philippines Joint Commission on Bilateral Cooperation", Ministry of External Affairs, November 6, 2020, at https://mea.gov.in/press-releases.htm?dtl/33168/4th_India__Philippines_Joint_Commission_on_Bilateral_Cooperation. Accessed on November 11, 2021.
53. "India, Philippines ink $375 million deal for BrahMos missiles", *The Economic Times*, January 29, 2022, at https://economictimes.indiatimes.com/news/defence/india-philippines-ink-375-million-deal-for-brahmos-missiles/articleshow/89188501.cms. Accessed on February 1, 2022.

54. "India-Singapore Relations", Ministry of External Affairs, January 2018, at https://www.mea.gov.in/Portal/ForeignRelation/Singapore_new_updated.pdf. Accessed on January 29, 2022.
55. "India-Singapore Relations", High Commission of India, Singapore, January 2020, at https://www.hcisingapore.gov.in/pages?id=eyJpdiI6I1QyQ0ZQR1FpdWwxMF1DUnM4YWxMdmc9PSIsInZhbHVlIjoiOTFHaGhPbjd3UjIzSDcwblp2K1M0UT09IiwibWFjIjoiNGQ5ZjNiMzZhNDE1MGVmODEyNWMxNjA4ZThhMzM0YTQyNzQyYTgyYjc1ZjQ2MDkzNDRmMGUxYzk3MDZjYjVhNCJ9&subid=eyJpdiI6IlR6dkRBaU9KblBLUENcL2p0UGxBVDBBPT0iLCJ2YWx1ZSI6ImdkV0gwS0xCRldQdUgyK2VzR1JPN2c9PSIsIm1hYyI6IjNhZTA4YmIyZDZiNWMyOTgyZjAyOTczZjI2N2M1OWIwMDJhZjExNDRkNmEwNzU3NmNlYTFhOTQ2MmMzNzg0NjcifQ==. Accessed on January 20, 2022.
56. "Prime Minister's Speech at the Business-cum-Community Event, Singapore (May 31, 2018)", Ministry of External Affairs, May 31, 2018, at http://www.mea.gov.in/Speeches-Statements.htm?dtl/29936/Prime_Ministers_Speech_at_the_BusinesscumCommunity_Event_Singapore_May_31_2018. Accessed on January 20, 2022.
57. "Joint Statement by India and Thailand on the State Visit of Prime Minister of Thailand Yingluck Shinawatra to India", Press Information Bureau, January 25, 2012, at http://pib.nic.in/newsite/PrintRelease.aspx?relid=79931. Accessed on January 15, 2022.
58. "Joint Statement by India and Thailand on the occasion of the State visit of PM of the Kingdom of Thailand Gen Prayut Chan-o-cha to India", Ministry of Foreign Affairs of the Kingdom of Thailand, June 17, 2016, at http://www.mfa.go.th/main/contents/files/media-center-20160617-191718-448815.pdf. Accessed on January 15, 2022.
59. Vibhanshu Shekhar, "India's Maritime Security and ASEAN: Issues of Narcoterrorism, Piracy and Poaching", in P. V. Rao (ed.), *India and ASEAN: Partners at Summit*, KW Publishers, New Delhi, 2008, pp. 195-196.
60. Hari Saran, "Indo-Thailand Maritime Cooperation in the Changing World", in Sanjay Kumar (ed.) *India-Thailand Bilateral Relations*, Mohit Publication, New Delhi, 2013, pp. 73-75.
61. "Joint Statement by India and Thailand on the occasion of the State visit of PM of the Kingdom of Thailand Gen Prayut Chan-o-cha to India", Ministry of Foreign Affairs of the Kingdom of Thailand, June 17, 2016, at http://www.mfa.go.th/main/contents/files/media-center-20160617-191718-448815.pdf. Accessed on January 15, 2022.

62. Shishir Upadhyaya, *India's Maritime Strategy: Balancing Regional Ambitions and China,* Routledge, Oxon, 2020, p. 155.
63. Tridib Chakraborti, "Rising India-Vietnam Ties in the Emerging Security Architecture of the Asia-pacific Region", in Rajiv K Bhatia, Vijay Sakhuja and Vikash Ranjan (eds), *India-Vietnam; Agenda for Strengthening Partnership,* Shipra Publication, New Delhi, 2013, pp. 104-105.
64. John Reed, "South China Sea: Fishing on the Frontline of Beijing's Ambitions", *Financial Times,* January 24, 2019, at https://www.ft.com/content/fead89da-1a4e-11e9-9e64-d150b3105d21. Accessed on December 12, 2021.
65. Shishir Upadhyaya, *India's Maritime Strategy: Balancing Regional Ambitions and China,* Routledge,: Oxon, 2020, p. 156.
66. P. V. Rao, "India and Vietnam: Forging a Durable Strategic Partnership", in Vijay Sakhuja (ed.), *India-Vietnam Strategic Partnership: Exploring Vistas for Expanded Cooperation,* Pentagon Press, New Delhi, 2011, pp. 152-153.
67. "Press Statement by Prime Minister during his visit to Vietnam [September 3, 2016]", Ministry of External Affairs, September 3, 2016, at https://mea.gov.in/outoging-visit-detail.htm?27363/Press+Statement+by+Prime+Minister+during+his+visit+to+Vietnam+September+03+2016. Accessed on January 15, 2022.
68. Le Thi Hang Nga, "The East Sea Issue and its Impact on Vietnam-India Relations", in G Jayachandra Reddy (ed.) *Vision of Ho Chi Minh: India-Vietnam Relations,* UGC Centre for Southeast Asian & Pacific Studies, Tirupati, 2017, p. 169.
69. S D Pradhan, "India and Vietnam: Strengthening of defence relations", *The Times of India,* July 2, 2021, at https://timesofindia.indiatimes.com/blogs/ChanakyaCode/india-and-vietnam-strengthening-of-defence-relations/. Accessed on February 2, 2022.
70. Tridib Chakraborti, n. 63, pp. 114-118.
71. Duy Khang, "Vietnam, India strive for $15bn bilateral trade turnover by 2020", Tuoi Tre News, March 4, 2018, at https://tuoitrenews.vn/news/politics/20180304/vietnam-india-strive-for-15bn-bilateral-trade-turnover-by-2020/44351.html. Accessed on January 15, 2022.
72. "India-Vietnam Joint Statement during State Visit of President to Vietnam", Ministry of External Relations, November 21, 2018, at https://www.mea.gov.in/bilateral-documents.htm?dtl/30615/IndiaVietnam_Joint_Statement_during_State_Visit_of_President_to_Vietnam. Accessed on January 10, 2022.
73. "Press Statement by Vice President during his Official visit to Vietnam", Ministry of External Affairs, May 10, 2019, at https://mea.gov.in/outoging-visit-detail.htm?31240/Press+Statement+by+Vice+President+during+his+Official+visit+to+Vietnam. Accessed on January 15, 2022.

74. "India-Brunei Bilateral Relations", High Commission of India, Brunei Darussalam, January 2022, at https://www.hcindiabrunei.gov.in/page/india-brunei-bilateral/. Accessed on February 11, 2022.
75. Mustafa Izzuddin, "Envisioning the potential in India-Brunei Relations", Institute of South Asian Studies Insights, March 4, 2020, at https://www.isas.nus.edu.sg/papers/envisioning-the-potential-in-india-brunei-relations/. Accessed on February 10, 2022.
76. Michael Martin, "Prime Minister Modi and Myanmar's Military Junta", Centre for Strategic and International Studies, November 22, 2021, at https://www.csis.org/analysis/prime-minister-modi-and-myanmars-military-junta. Accessed on February 1, 2022.
77. "India, Myanmar conduct joint operation to destroy militant camps in Northeast", *The Hindu*, June 16, 2019, at https://www.thehindu.com/news/national/india-myanmar-conduct-joint-operation-to-destroy-militant-camps-in-northeast/article27956142.ece. Accessed on February 1, 2022.
78. Ankit Panda, "India, Myanmar Conclude Defence Cooperation Agreement", *The Diplomat*, July 30, 2019, at https://thediplomat.com/2019/07/india-myanmar-conclude-defense-cooperation-agreement/. Accessed on February 11, 2022.
79. "India-Cambodia Relations", Ministry of External Affairs, October 2017, at https://www.mea.gov.in/Portal/ForeignRelation/1_Cambodia_November_2017.pdf. Accessed on February 11, 2022.
80. Shubhajit Roy, "India, Cambodia to boost maritime, defence cooperation, *The Indian Express*, January 28, 2018, at https://indianexpress.com/article/india/india-cambodia-to-boost-maritime-defence-cooperation-5041837/. Accessed on February 14, 2022.
81. "Agreed Minutes of the Ninth Joint Commission Meeting on Bilateral Cooperation between India and Lao PDR (November 23, 2018)", Ministry of External Affairs, November 23, 2018, at https://www.mea.gov.in/bilateral-documents.htm?dtl/30627/Agreed+Minutes+of+the+Ninth+Joint+. Accessed on February 15, 2022.
82. Shishir Upadhyaya, n. 65.

# 12

# The Resurgence of Taliban Post 9/11

MOHIT SHARMA

With the signing of the historic Doha Deal between the Taliban and the United States on February 29, 2020, the stage was set for the Taliban to come to power whether unilaterally or in power-sharing. The elected government of Afghanistan was deemed to be in a manageable position until the US troops started to withdraw. The world witnessed an absolute Taliban blitzkrieg after that, and it took them no time to shift from rural stronghold to knock at the urban district centres. A week later, Kabul fell as the Afghan forces surrendered to the Taliban without a significant clash. An Islamic Emirate has been set up again after 24 years under the leadership of Mullah Hassan Akhund. Ostensibly, the takeover of Afghanistan by the Taliban presents an enigma that took the world by surprise. Taliban, however, have been on a path of resurgence since 2002 when the global community dismissed them after being reduced to ashes. This chapter analyses the major drives of Taliban resurgence and how the Taliban was able to reorganise and eventually strengthen themselves throughout two decades.

The Taliban are predominantly a Pashtun, Islamic Fundamentalist group that returned to power in Afghanistan in 2021 after 20 years of insurgency. It was Pashtun king Ahmad Shah Durrani who founded the modern state of Afghanistan in 1747. Although he established a solid Pashtun-based Afghan identity, he left a dangerous legacy that would make Afghanistan vulnerable.[1] Unlike Western monarchs who restrained feudal barons and imposed a centralised system, Durrani maintained a decentralised tribal system that allowed tribal chiefs to retain their authority.[2] He ruled indirectly through power brokers. Afghanistan became a confederation of independent tribal fiefdoms with bare minimum aspects of statehood. Afghans who got used to such a system would never appreciate the externally imposed Eurocentric state system. Pashtuns have always been disinclined to accept any kind of central authority—even at the cost of insecurity and discord. Throughout the period of insurgency, the Taliban witnessed transformation and disruption of society at large and side-lining of old tribal hierarchies.[3] The Talib leaders commanded power in religious courts, and Mullahs set up a different structure for conflict management. Nevertheless, what made Taliban so potent is the capacity of the insurgency to find receptive support among the population who are willing to lay down their lives for the cause.[4] This is the basis for this Ethno-religious and Ethno-nationalist explanation. In the theoretical conceptualisation of post-9/11 resurgence, Pashtun Nationalism and Islamism are two major drivers. Taliban believe that any government in Kabul should belong to Pashtuns. Taliban seized upon pre-existing isolationist and anti-foreign sentiment.

Around 70 per cent of Taliban come from Pashtun belts. Over time, they have come to identify Islam with a mixture of tribal customs, Quranic concepts, Hanafi legal tradition, and Pashtunwali (chivalrous tribal codes of Pashtuns). The Afghan Islamicists have failed to resolve the dichotomy of 'Tribe vs Ummah', Clan vs State & Religion.[5] This failure of Political Islam has had repercussions on the way extremist elements exploited this vacuum. Some of these Pashtunwali customs are diligently followed by Taliban, which also paves the way for their amelioration. Few of them are thereby listed: 'Melmastia'—Profound respect for guests of all races, religions, and tribes; 'Badal'—Revenge for any wrong committed Pashtuns highly follow this tradition; 'Nanawatay'—Protection is given to a person who requests it against his enemy; 'Zemaka'—to inspire Pashtuns to defend the land and property against insurgents; 'Nang'—safeguarding the honour of family and oneself.[6] Taliban have successfully managed to integrate Islam and Pashtunwali. They claim that their rise was due to their widely resonating promises of security and justice and their belief in obedience. Taliban refers to Quranic verses and Hadees while talking about the process of establishing an Emirate. According to them, Islam comes with social unity, which can only come under an Emirate, and an Emirate can only be established if there is obedience.[7] As there is no universally accepted definition of Sharia law, it means a mix of Pashtunwali, Hanafi legal tradition, and some decontextualized Quranic Verses for the Taliban. They underscore three golden principles of Islam and justify their struggle upon the basis: 'Qisas' (Revenge for Wrong), 'Zina' (Dignity of human to be protected), and 'Jihad' (The fight for freedom).[8] The Mujahideen invoked Quranic verses manipulatively to strengthen their cause; for instance, they often refer to a verse from 'Al-Baqarah', "that a small group would succeed against a larger group with the order of God and He is with those who are patient". Taliban's Islamic motifs have acted as a powerful tool for mobilisation and legitimisation that kept the door open even for non-Pashtuns to join the Taliban ranks. Reference to Islam provides Taliban with a support base that creates the appearance of cohesion in an otherwise ethnically and politically heterogeneous community.[9]

## The Initial Collapse and Regrouping (2002-04)

After the American onslaught during 'Operation Enduring Freedom', the Taliban suffered losses to the extent of extinction. The polycentric structure (explained ahead) enabled Taliban to regroup and sustain the American strikes.[10] Polycentrism is not to be confused with Fragmentation. The former implies multiple chains of command, whereas the latter implies competing chains of command.[11] The uniqueness of polycentrism and de-centralisation attribute a USP: their Modus Operandi is more resilient in the face of counter-insurgency efforts driven by modern technologies.[12] Taliban were quick to learn that negotiating from a position of weakness would not fetch them anything. The early regrouping started around 2002 in the South. Shah Wali Kot became the central hub of Taliban activity in Kandahar. In the East, Nangarhar became the ground for Taliban activity. Several small shuras were set up initially in Pakistan—significant ones being Spin Ghar, Ijraya Shura and Gardi Jangal Shura.[13] These shuras were set up near the Pakistan-Afghanistan border. Fighters relied upon weapons left over by the Taliban inside Afghanistan. These shuras did not have the resources to establish any shadow governance or even pay salaries to fighters. Instead, they relied on religious taxes, smugglers, and donations from businessmen.[14] These shuras were different from the later bigger Shuras like Quetta as they were structured as a small party and not some entourage of a leader. With more funds, a bigger council called Rahbari Shura or Leadership council was set up in 2003. It also became famous by the name of Quetta Shura. The founding members include Mullah Abdul Ghani Baradar (former deputy minister of Defence in the 1st Emirate 1996-2001 and now deputy leader of Islamic Emirate of Afghanistan), Mullah Dadullah, Mullah Faruq, Mohammad Akhtar Mansur (former leader of Taliban killed in an American drone strike), and Gul Agha Ishaqzai (close collaborator of Mullah Omar, the founding leader of Taliban). Their initial aim was not to overthrow the Afghan regime formed under the leadership of Hamid Karzai but to put pressure on the American and Kabul administration to force them to seek accommodation with the Taliban.[15] Mullah Baradar is told to have reached out to Karzai for an amicable settlement. However, the then American Secretary of Defence, Donald Rumsfeld, strictly forbade Karzai to entertain any Taliban reconciliation advances. This miscalculation would later come to haunt United States' administration.

## Formation of Quetta Shura and its administration

Quetta Shura was formed in 2003 and was operating along with other shuras. By 2005, it launched commissions to implement policies decided by leadership. Central leadership had to operate through consensus, and the chain of command operated through networks. The Shadow governors were put in districts and provinces. In a vertical chain of command, a group of 2000 men were formed called 'Loy Mahazes', who was placed in charge of a Commander. Any Taliban leader could establish his own Loy Mahaz if he had the required number of fighters, but there were established rules that every Commander had to follow. The group commander had to report to the district governor, who had to report to the provincial governor.[16] Taliban's formal entry into an area would be preceded by an organised propaganda effort that laid the ground for an active insurgency. This often entailed making use of Mullahs. The persistence of the abusive attitude of local Afghan government officials and humiliation of local elders often created a base for support of the insurgency. Taliban would then launch an intimidation campaign with increasing threats to pro-government elements. The expansion also meant absorbing existing resistance fronts and co-optation of non-Taliban networks. These included former commanders of

Jamat-e-Islami and Hizb-e-Islami. Taliban exploited local rivalries among Uzbeks and Tajiks. Where Taliban did not enjoy extensive community support, Madrassas seemed to be the primary source of recruitment.[17]

Structure of Taliban:[18]

- Deputy Governor
- Military Commission
- Finance Commission
- Preaching and Guidance Commission
- Culture and Information Commission
- Education Commission
- Health Commission

Military and Finance commissions had more significance than others. The major task of the Finance commission included investing the financial resources of the Taliban in legal business and properties. Governors were supposed to supervise and perform all critical activities related to finance and logistics. The creation of Loy Mahaz is also linked to the fact that some donors would only transfer funds to their protégé among Taliban leaders. The internal organisation of loy mahaz varied among themselves. All Mahazes needed district and provincial representatives to coordinate with other Taliban, but they were free to organise themselves. In 2005, a 'Council of Front Leaders' (Mahaz Shura) was set up to solve disputes among insurgents. From 2005-10, Quetta shura became increasingly dependent upon the multiplication of Loy Mahazes to maintain their fighting power. A system of double funding was in practice whereby the leadership paid mahaz according to their numerical strength, and also mahaz were able to raise funds independently.[19] However, these loy mahazes were vulnerable as it depended upon the status of their leader. As the mahaz got bigger and better funded, it became more difficult for the governor to control it. So, there were common occurrences of infighting between Loy Mahaz and governor's groups and amongst themselves. It was mainly the leadership provided by Mullah Baradar then that kept these fighting units together somehow.

In the early days of the insurgency, local taxation accounted for the maximum share of revenue, including taxation of ISAF supply convoys and war booty.[20] External donors gradually replaced it. United Nations sources indicate that 31 per cent of Taliban revenue did not accrue to leadership but stayed with local commanders. There were attempts by the leadership to force commanders to hand over tax revenue to finance or military commission, but that could not fructify. Commanders were able to get a concession from the council, and they could spend revenue on their groups as they desired and only report to the Quetta Shura about the amount and how it was spent. A basic rule had been established that taxes and voluntary contributions would pay for the salaries of fighters while weapons and ammunition were to be provided by the leadership.[21]

## Alternate Centres of Power: Haqqani Network and Peshawar Shura

It was not just vertical polycentrism but also horizontal, establishing two shuras parallelly-Miran Shah Shura controlled by Haqqanis and Peshawar Shura. These shuras not just undermined Quetta but also competed with it. Sometimes, they got even more powerful than the Quetta and were able to fund the central Taliban leadership.

Haqqani Network: In North Waziristan, Jalaluddin Haqqani and his entourage took refuge in 2001 and reorganised immediately. The group called itself Haqqani Shabaka or Haqqani Network. Haqqanis constituted a large number of foreign fighters and were supplemented by Al-Qaeda and FATA region insurgents. The Haqqanis established Miran Shah Shura in 2003. Pakistan decided to pour in money to fund the Taliban when Haqqanis started showing the capability to fight. Initially, they started operations in Paktia and Khost province and later spread to Paktika and Logar. They accepted the suzerainty of Quetta Shura but operated autonomously. Around 2006, they started to send combat troops to districts under the control of Rahbari Shura. Jalaluddin retired in 2007 owing to ill health, and the reins were taken over by his son Sirajuddin Haqqani who demanded representation in the Quetta leadership aggressively. Such was the autonomy that he even withdrew the recognition of Quetta-appointed governors in their provinces.[22] However, an agreement was reached where governors would be appointed by Quetta but were put under the superior authority of Miran Shah representative. The strength of Haqqanis came from their better organisational structure and cohesiveness. Revenues extracted were to be necessarily transferred to the Finance Commission of Miran Shah.[23]

Haqqanis are champions of asymmetric warfare. With time, they developed their own brand of Jihadism. They have been receiving uninterrupted support from Al-Qaeda since 2002. They did venture out in Syria and Iraq but primarily have restricted themselves to their region. Pakistani fighters are directly recruited to their rank, and the Pakistani establishment controls the Haqqani leadership. They focus on high-profile Fedayin attacks and targeted assassinations. Their tactics have also been influenced by Iran's Islamic Revolutionary Guard Corps (IRGC) during 2012-15. They have a bit different military system from Quetta. Their structure comprises:[24]

- Zerbati Commission—to manage village-level militias
- Delayez Commission—to manage full-time mobile units
- Fedayin Commission—for special ops and suicide attacks
- De Minema Commission—to manage IED teams.

Haqqanis have the only functioning Fedayin commission that operates throughout Afghanistan. They imported suicide tactics from Iraq and have never abandoned them. There are specific madrassas maintained by Haqqanis that have been turned into specialised factories for suicide training in the FATA region.[25] Haqqani Network for long had maintained a Kabul City front, which was completely isolated from other Taliban groups. It was considered that other groups were more liable to be infiltrated by western spies. Haqqanis have carried out some of the most horrendous attacks, including the 2008 attack on the Indian embassy in Kabul.

Peshawar Shura—the first attempt to establish any command centre for jihad in the eastern part was the Ijraya Shura.[26] The elements of Hizb-e-Islami had always been prominent in the East, and hence its former members filled the ranks of Ijraya Shura. Another faction split from Hizb-e-Islami and formed Shamsatoo Mahaz,[27] based upon the Shamsatoo refugee camp in Peshawar. In around 2005, Shamsatoo was offered Arab and Pakistani support if it joined Ijaraya Shura. Over the years, the boundary between former Hizb-e-Islamis and Taliban blurred and Shamsatoo and Ijraya Shura merged to join Peshawar Shura in 2005.

Peshawar had a very distinctive feature as it focussed on recruitment from high schools and universities. Peshawar Shura operated in Nangarhar, Kunar, Nuristan and Laghman. Under the influence of ISI, another faction by the name of Toor-e-Pagri was merged into Peshawar Shura. By 2010, the shura felt strong enough to claim the monopoly of authority over large parts of Afghanistan. Governors appointed by Quetta were marginalised and were subjected to the authority of Peshawar provincial leaders. By 2012, Peshawar banned other networks and insisted that it would operate as a single entity. It established its own Peshawar military commission, and other Shuras, including Quetta, started to bow to Peshawar's financial superiority. Foreign sponsors from the Middle East threw their lot with them owing to the military weakness of Quetta around this time. It was only around 2016 when Peshawar's might saw an end, and the supremacy of Quetta Shura was established again with the defection of Qari Baryal, the head of Peshawar Military Commission.[28] Peshawar Shura also expanded in the North, where it recruited many non-Pashtuns. A separate mahaz exclusively of non-Pashtuns was established called Jundullah Mahaz[29] by the initiative of Qari Baryal.[30] Taliban always suffered from long supply lines and problematic logistics in the North. With the control of the North, the logistical problems were eased. Peshawar Shura also offered more promotion opportunities and better financial conditions.

Like Haqqanis, Peshawar also had Pakistani and Arab fighters. The inclusion of Toor-e-Pagri resulted in Pakistani infiltration, and many Pakistani groups formally joined. Some of them being Jamiat-e-Ulema, Lashkar-e-Jhangvi, Lashkar-e-Islam, Jaish-e-Mohammad, and Sepah-e-Sahaba. Peshawar Shura established a new system of 'Nizami Massuleen' meant to be professional military leaders and operate from a separate chain of command of governors.[31] This was often the bone of contention between different shuras as other shuras like Quetta did not employ these nizami massuleen. With the coming of the nizamis, Taliban turned into a professional guerrilla force. Personal allegiance to charismatic mullahs was de-emphasized in favour of membership in the movement as a whole. The office of Nizami Massuleen was later relegated when Quetta Shura assumed complete control of the Taliban movement.

## Adaptations and Innovations of Taliban

Afghanistan has been witnessing war for the last three decades. Afghans, cognisant of their limited capabilities, have employed innovative tactical ways to fight their enemies. Once a tactic proves successful, the Taliban refine it to make it fit their circumstances and then deploy it at the operational level.[32] Taliban have been changing their methods constantly, making them sustain such a prolonged insurgency. Taliban now might have control of all territory. However, when they were outmanned and outgunned on the battlefield, they constantly struck at the weakness of the Afghan Government and Western coalition forces. Taliban were never as politically vulnerable as their adversaries and hence could employ historical narrative of 'Jihad' or 'fighting the invaders' to circumvent questions regarding their actions.[33] Taliban identified their hitting targets such as logistical convoys and not adequately defended posts, similar to what Mujahideen did during anti-Soviet jihad. Taliban controlled the battlefield operational tempo by forcing US and NATO troops to commit mistakes that they used to their advantage.[34] This refers to issues of collateral damage, civilian deaths, and human rights. Western forces have devised some rules of engagement (ROE) in order to lessen civilian deaths. Taliban recognise this as a self-imposed limitation on the part of coalition forces and hence tend to exploit these restraints to maximise their chances.[35] Contrary to the fact that Taliban are mindless fanatics, they have grown into a sophisticated army fighting to endure and defensive jihad. Their strategy is reflected by: seeking haven in cities like Karachi, running circles around the Afghan Government through effective public relations and information operations, bringing the fight to Kabul through expanded use of IEDs, establishing shadow government institutions to bring law to rural areas where corruption was rampant.[36] Taliban has always been aware of their weakness, and hence they avoided symmetrical combat at all costs to minimise losses. From 2009 onwards, the Taliban pulled out their full-time mobile units and left behind local fighters who could easily hide in the villages. Part-time fighters got prominence in Taliban machinery. They brought with them many advantages—they were cheaper than mobile groups, more knowledgeable about the local area, could operate underground and were easier to recruit.[37]

Some specific tactical changes include Improved fire control using coordinated, a disciplined volley of RPGs against specific targets and multiple firing positions, better fire coordination with combined arms and manoeuvring units, improved anti-armour tactic, improved cover and concealment using 'karez' irrigation ditches which provide good cover.[38] Taliban have been very effective in their use of mines. Until 2007, most mines were made with military explosives. Later they started to manufacture it using fertilisers produced in Pakistan. Miran Shah Shura even had a specific mines commission. Taliban could secure small arms, machine guns, rocket launchers, and recoilless guns but surprisingly could not source TNT for IED manufacturing. This hints that Pakistan hosts were somehow constraining the ability of the Taliban to escalate military technologies.[39] Taliban resorted to intimidation campaigns where they used their intelligence network inside the government apparatus for hunting down collaborators. Another tactic they employed was the infiltration of Afghan Security Forces. The Green on Blue insider attacks had a major debilitating impact. In 2011, the Taliban set up the 'Dawat-o-Irshad' commission to encourage defections from security forces.[40]

The adaptations had some considerable impact. The regular operation by ISAF troops in Taliban-held areas were reduced as they started consolidating their controlled areas. This also resulted in a lesser number of ISAF casualties. They developed an IED development centre in Pakistan where new technologies were developed. The major objective of IED was to limit the mobility of US and NATO forces and keep them out of village areas. The capacity of the Taliban to absorb large losses became one of their great strengths. The expanded use of suicide bombings came at a time they were also expanding their organisation. The purpose was to show the Taliban's commitment and determination in their struggle and exhibit the Afghan government's vulnerability and their failure to protect average civilians.[41] Another tactic used was frequent assassination attacks, especially in Southern Afghanistan. The modus operandi of Taliban has been simple—to target important officials like governors or police chiefs with command-detonated IEDs or suicide attacks[42] and shoot at sight for mid-level bureaucrats. Again, the primary goal of the assassination campaign is to reverse security gains in the disputed areas and discredit their enemies' most celebrated achievement—Governance and Authority.[43]

## Taliban Leadership

If not for the operational efficiency of commanders, the Taliban would not have been able to revive amidst growing counter-insurgency operations. Especially in Southern and South-Eastern parts, the Taliban saw fierce commanders who got primarily famous or infamous and penetrated deep into rural households. With the establishment of Loy Mahaz in 2005, the stature of commanders rose as they got the required autonomy to manage their own mahaz.[44] The leadership provided during the initial stages of insurgency was so significant that later the need for a leader was not required. This eventually became the strength of the Taliban movement. The first leaders to establish their mahaz were Mullah Dadullah, Mullah Baradar, Mullah Faruq, and Mullah Ibrahim. This also resulted in infighting, but it never got enough to shatter the organisation as a whole.

***Mullah Dadullah:*** In the South, Mullah Dadullah launched an operation and expanded the influence of Quetta Shura. Dadullah was a powerful commander and cruel as well. While leading a Taliban operation in Hazarajat in 1998, he ordered massacres of Shias. Soon he was appointed to lead all operations in the South. Even all senior commanders used to bow to him, including Baradar and Mullah Faruq Ibrahim.[45] Dadullah had a personal rapport with Deobandi leaders in Karachi and raised money from a large Pashtun population in the city.[46] However, owing to his brutality, he earned some enemies as well. Haqqanis saw Dadullah Mahaz as an opportunity to expand influence into Southern Afghanistan.

In the East, few Taliban Commanders had a sizeable following. There was no Eastern Dadullah.[47] Former foreign affairs minister in the first Islamic Emirate, Mullah Kabir, was dispatched to the East. He failed to gather support among the small shuras. Here new fronts were forming outside the influence of Quetta much before even Peshawar Shura was launched. Kabir wanted southern Durrani tribes to settle in the East, but the local Taliban did not want their leaders to be from Kandahar.[48]

***Mullah Abdul Ghani Baradar:*** Mullah Baradar was best known of all Taliban political leaders and de-facto head of Quetta Shura. Baradar's relationship with ISI deteriorated in 2009 as he started working on a reconciliation deal with Kabul.[49] His major funding came from Arab Gulf sources through ISI. As that stopped, Baradar started to survive on Iranian funding[50] and kept the Taliban military system together somehow. After helping found the Taliban movement in 1994, he developed his profile as a military strategist and commander. He was the primary reason for loy mahaz coherence, as he used to mediate and resolve disputes. Baradar attempted to centralise power in his hands and also got partially successful, but it soon ended in 2010 when Pakistani authorities arrested him.[51] After his arrest, the fear of the Taliban crumbling grew, but Mullah Akhtar Mansur's leadership managed it. Mullah Baradar again rose into prominence when he was released from Pakistani detention.

*Mullah Akhtar Mansur:* He was elected as a successor of Mullah Omar, though in a controversial selection. He brought back Quetta Leadership from their period of adversity. Mansur brought the news of the death of Mullah Omar in 2015 during a power struggle within Taliban. Mansur was recognised for his administrative qualities more than military capability. He had an influential role in reviving Taliban in the Southern Afghanistan after 2001. After being appointed as a leader, he won loyalties of most Taliban factions. Through diplomatic manoeuvring, he brought much of Taliban funding under his control. However, Mullah Mohammad Yakub (son of Mullah Omar) posed an obstacle to Mansur's leadership.

The leaders of the Military Commission have been very significant in the Taliban movement. *Abdul Qayum Zakir,* who led the Quetta Military Commission till 2014 was relatively independent of Pakistani pressure as he was closer to Iran. He belongs to a very conservative, hard-line faction within the Taliban. Qari Baryal, erstwhile leader of Peshawar Military Commission and now Governor of Kabul Province in the new Taliban administration was instrumental in the expansion of the Taliban. US Military described Baryal as 'al-Qaeda associated Taliban leader'. He began his career as Hizb-e-Islami cadre, and rose through the ranks of Taliban to lead forces in central and north-eastern Afghanistan. Baryal was a key commander in what NATO called 'Kabul Attack Network'. This network pooled fighters from Taliban, Al-Qaeda, Islamic Jihad Union, Islamic Movement of Uzbekistan[52]. Baryal group facilitated movement of weapons, explosives, and suicide bombers from the Pakistan border to Kabul.

***Sirajjudin Haqqani:*** After Jalaluddin Haqqani retired in 2007 due to ill health, his son Sirajjduin Haqqani took over the reins. Keeping in line with the tradition of Haqqanis, he took asymmetric warfare to a higher level. Like his father, he has been the go-between for Al-Qaeda and Taliban on both sides of the Afghanistan-Pakistan border.[53] He had been actively overseeing the planning and execution of attacks on the International Security Assistance Force (ISAF), Afghan officials and civilians, mostly in eastern and south-eastern Afghanistan. With Sirajuddin as a leader, Haqqanis' activities ranged from extortion and ransom to investments in firms abroad through front companies.[54] Sirajuddin made sure that hardlines within the Taliban would always be placed in the higher echelons. Therefore, any international dialogue with the Taliban cannot proceed without Haqqanis or in other sense without Pakistan on board.

## Role of Pakistan in Taliban movement

Since its formation in 1947, Pakistan has always considered Religion and religious forces as a strategic weapon and a tool of foreign policy, both foreign and domestic. The time of Zia-ul-Haq saw complete convergence of religious 'Right' and Pakistan military. Soviet invasion of Afghanistan in 1979 changed the geopolitical equation of the region. Pakistan decided to oppose the Soviet invasion politically and more actively by supplying material benefits to Afghan resistance forces. The success of this policy led Pakistan to conceive Mujaheddin as a major tool of its Afghan policy. Though after the death of Zia, Pakistan saw successive civilian governments of Benazir Bhutto and Nawaz Sharif, but they could not bypass the general parameters of military as Army retained its pivotal influence on the formulation of domestic and foreign policy agendas and political process remained beholden to dictates and machinations of generals.[55]

***The 1990s-2000:*** From 1990s, Pakistan's objectives were clear regarding its blatant support for mujahideen forces and then later Taliban: opening up trade routes to Central Asia, including natural gas pipeline between Turkmenistan and Pakistan, and to gain 'strategic depth' in Afghanistan.[56] Pakistan military and ISI wanted for strategic reasons to secure its western borders to guarantee the security of Pakistan in the eventuality of war with its Eastern neighbour. Also, geo-economic reasons had a role in Pakistan backing the Taliban. Pakistan did not want Northern Alliance, especially India, to gain control of Central Asian markets via Afghanistan. Taliban movement from its beginning was under Pakistani patronage. The nature of its funding, weaponry and training suggests the same. From 1994 onwards, ISI agents were attached to Taliban forces and provided them with tactical and professional support.

Amir Sultan Tarar, also known as Colonel Imam, was instrumental in Pakistan's policy in Afghanistan. He had known many Taliban leaders since Soviet Jihad days and developed a close rapport with Mullah Omar. Posted as Pakistan's consul general, first in Kandahar and then in the western Afghan city of Heart, he emerged as a key adviser to the Taliban leaders. Also, he acted as a conduit for arms and money.[57] The Taliban operations received substantial assistance from the Pakistan Army's XI Corps at Peshawar as most of the arms supply source for the Taliban came from army depots.[58] The funding that Saudi Arabia provided to Afghan fighters also subsidized militant Sunni organisations in Pakistan. ISI was the main conduit for arms, ammunition and fuel supplies from Pakistan to the Taliban in their fight against an opposition alliance based in the North, while the agency's officers served as military advisers to the Taliban.[59]

***Post 9/11:*** After the 9/11 attack and the subsequent Operation Enduring Freedom against Al-Qaeda in Afghanistan, Pakistan shifted its course from overt to covert support. President Musharraf decided to proactively participate in 'Global War on Terror' initially to the dismay of clergy in Pakistan. However, it readily became apparent that Pakistan had no intentions to give up the Taliban in their frontier areas. With the war on Iraq in 2003, equations in Afghanistan changed rapidly. The US was diverted from Afghan theatre to Iraq. ISI did not let go of the opportunity provided by the American involvement in Iraq and hence cultivated the Taliban on its own terms. Apart from providing sanctuary and support to the Taliban, Pakistan has also timely arrested Taliban leaders who stepped out of line, including the deputy leader of the Taliban, Mullah Abdul Ghani Baradar. The support of Pakistan to Taliban insurgency is reinforced by its aspiration to influence Pashtuns in the border belt—across the Durand line.[60] Pakistan wanted to subdue the cause of Pashtunistan in Khyber Pakhtunkhwa and FATA. ISI is embedded in Quetta Shura, either as participants or observers, and the agency is involved at the highest level of insurgency.[61]

From 2003-2004, Pakistan operated training camps for Taliban recruits, and facilitated the supply of funds, equipment and arms from Gulf countries. The Pakistani army established medical facilities for Taliban fighters and even provided covering fire at border crossings. Communications intercepts showed that Taliban commanders were liaising with Pakistani military officers to ensure safe passage across the border.[62] In June 2006, a joint US, NATO and Afghan intelligence assessment concluded that the ISI provided a vital sanctuary for the Taliban and paid and pressured them to fight. As Ahmed Rashid puts it, 'over time evidence slowly collected by US and NATO intelligence officers on the ground showed a systematic and pervasive system of ISI collusion.'[63]

Pakistan also tends to exploit ethnic fault lines in Afghanistan to its advantage. Taliban, from its beginning, had dominance of Ghilzai Pashtuns, who historically have been arch-rivals of Durrani Pashtuns (Members of which have occupied senior positions in the Afghan Government). Taliban had a minimal representation of Durranis. The Pakistani Government had a long-term bias against Durrani tribes because they are said to support the idea of Pashtunistan and claims to Pakistani territory. Hence Pakistan looked further into subtribes of Durranis and courted those which more suited its cause. The ISI attempted to appoint more Alizai Durranis, a subtribe of Durrani, into the leadership council to increase its control over the movement. Increasing Durrani representation on the Shura helps to strengthen the authority of the movement, given Afghanistan's long tradition of Durrani rulers, and give Pakistan more leverage in any possible negotiations.[64]

*Arrests in 2010:* Pakistan carried out arrests of many Taliban and Al-Qaeda operatives in 2010, including Mullah Baradar. Apparently, this seemed a big victory as far as 'War on Terror' was concerned, but in reality, this was a recalibration from Pakistan's side. ISI took out the unruly elements from the Quetta Shura and exerted more control thereafter. This was when moderates within the Taliban, under the leadership of Mullah Baradar, were reaching out to the Afghan Government for reconciliation.

Pakistan wanted any reconciliation to occur through its own interlocutors and in a manner mindful of Pakistani interests. Therefore, Pakistan began a series of arrests of many Taliban members making sure its grip on Quetta Shura was not loosened. With the second term of the Obama Presidency in the United States, withdrawal of all American troops seemed inevitable then. Hence Islamabad did everything within its power to inject itself more vigorously into the strategic direction of insurgency.[65] Though American withdrawal took a decade more to fructify, Pakistan always wanted to secure three elements whenever the withdrawal happened: a friendly government in Kabul that includes Pakistani clients in the top policy circles, ejection of India from Afghanistan or a very reduced Indian presence, and to have significant influence over Afghanistan's strategic choices and geopolitical direction.[66]

***2014 onwards: Pakistan's role in Intra-Taliban Feud:*** With the emergence of different mahazes led by different commanders, factions within Taliban were set to grow. From 2010-2015 Taliban saw much infighting amongst themselves, but Pakistan manipulatively held Taliban under its clutches by encouraging reconciliation between disgruntled leaders. It all started with the assertiveness of Abdul Qayum Zakir, the head of the Quetta Military Commission. He earned many enemies when he started to go for a change in administrative systems. He wanted Peshawar-style reforms with the introduction of Nizami Masuleen in areas under his control. This became a bone of contention between him and other leaders of Quetta Shura like Akhtar Mansur who wanted to retain the old governorship system.[67] Zakir was the blue-eyed boy of the ISI and cooperated with Peshawar Shura leadership to become a key recipient of funds from there and used those to fund his mahaz. After Baradar's arrest in 2010 by Pakistan authorities, Zakir formed his own loy mahaz and attracted many of Baradar's men.[68] Zakir was the star of Quetta Shura between 2009-13. He drew strength from aligning with Peshawar. He was offered the post of deputy leader of Quetta Shura, but he declined, knowing fully well that he could exert more power by being head of the Quetta Military Commission.[69] When differences between Zakir and others grew, he decided to form his 'New Quetta Shura' with the assistance of some old Taliban leaders.[70] At the insistence of Pakistan, the factions of Zakir and Mansur were reconciled. However, Zakir was sacked from the leadership of the Military Commission, and Pakistan changed its policy and turned towards Akhtar Mansur. Mansur consolidated control by reigning in Zakir and other mahazes and reclaimed the funds that went to the Peshawar council. A fall in funding to Peshawar eventually forced it to fold up and surrender autonomy to Quetta Shura. Pakistan brought Sirajjudin Haqqani to Mansur's side when there was serious trouble between Akhtar Mansur and Mullah Yakub (son of Mullah Omar) in 2015, even when Sirajuddin had good personal relations with Mullah Yakub.[71] At the insistence of Pakistan, Sirajjudin Haqqani was offered deputy leadership of the Taliban. Pakistan wanted an agreement between factions and approached moderates like Mullah Baradar to cooperate with Akhtar Mansur and threatened a crackdown on Taliban leadership if the agreement was not reached. However, after Sirajuddin Haqqani came to exert power in Central Taliban Leadership, Akhtar Mansur felt side-lined.[72] It is probable that Pakistan slyly wanted Haqqani to rise to Taliban echelons at the cost of others. Akhtar was eventually killed in an American drone strike while he was returning from Iran. Nobody knows what those negotiations with Iran were. In around 2016, all differences within Taliban were mostly settled. Taliban started to grow in strength again then onwards. Qari Baryal, Zakir and Sirajjudin Haqqani met in Waziristan in 2015 to agree on a set of priorities and to make inroads into heavy populated urban centres.[73] This was the start of the new Taliban offensive.

Taliban will always retain their presence and never get obliterated as long as Pakistan plays its complex game—playing simultaneously with both the Western world and the Global Islamist network and retaining importance in the eyes of both.[74] Pakistan allowed the US to go vigorously after Al-Qaeda while supporting Taliban at the same time. By this, Pakistan retained US interest in the region and kept itself active in Afghan politics. This allows Pakistan to be a constant recipient of Western aid. The US has a long-standing relationship with the military establishment in Pakistan which has undermined civilian and democratic institutions in the country.[75] President Musharraf's campaign into tribal areas of Pakistan failed, resulting in unequal treaties that they had to sign with TTP representatives in FATA. Thus, a vast support base for the Afghan Taliban was always ready for them whenever needed. With the Talibanisation of the Afghanistan-Pakistan border, it became easy to establish sanctuaries and training camps, use the area to transport arms and ammunition, and it became a fertile ground for recruitment.

The recent comments of former US Defense Secretary Ashton Carter are insightful. He said, "Make no mistake: The Taliban operated from Pakistan consistently. It is no accident that Osama Bin Laden was in Abbottabad. It is no accident that [Sirajuddin] Haqqani is running the place now. Where did Haqqani spend the last couple of decades? In Western Pakistan."[76]

Faiz Hameed, the previous director of ISI, visited Kabul just before the announcement of the new Taliban interim government. When it was announced, it included many leaders of the Haqqani network at important posts.

## Weak Governance

The United States chose Hamid Karzai in 2001 as President of the Republic of Afghanistan as he was close to the Bush administration. Karzai initiated state-building in Afghanistan and made some visible and quantifiable gains in the revival of democracy. Throughout his tenure, Karzai had constantly emphasized the need for the West to re-strategise the war on terror and address the institutional source of terrorism that emanates from Pakistan.[77] Though the blame on Pakistan is undeniable, his own Government was not without weaknesses. This section would deal with the lacunae in the administration, which led to the resurgence of Taliban.

***Factionalism and lack of Consensus:*** The political system established after Bonn Conference in 2001 was inclusive, participatory and representative of social and political diversity but was marred by factionalism. The appointed interim cabinet relied on two major groups of people: Former Mujahideen members of the Northern Alliance and Afghan technocrats living in exile in western countries.[78] As they had different experiences and different socio-political backgrounds, they never got along. The ethnic divide made matters worse as many former mujahideen were non-Pashtuns while technocrats were Pashtuns. Karzai tried to correct the ethnic imbalance, but his actions were primarily seen anti-Mujahideen by non-Pashtuns, especially Tajiks. Appointments in the cabinet and in various ministries were controversial. Each minister treated his ministry as a personal fiefdom and tried to fill various positions, high and low, with their relatives, friends and members of their ethnic groups.[79] Corruption and nepotism got so prevalent that no administrative reforms could correct the situation. This not only scarred the legitimacy of the government but also affected the fight against the Taliban.

***Reconstruction and Development:*** Reconstruction and Development projects were deemed to be effective tools in counter-insurgency. However, in reality, the successful examples of such projects were few. The amount of aid pledged was much less than what was needed. The Afghan Government initially estimated the total cost of reconstruction at $30 billion. However, in May 2008, it disclosed that it required an additional $50 billion to fund a 5-year developmental plan. According to a study by the Agency Coordinating Body for Afghan Relief (ACBAR), until the beginning of 2008, only $15 billion was disbursed, though the number pledged was $25 billion.[80] Another problem was that a large portion of the 'delivered' amount was returned to the donor countries through contracting and subcontracting. The salaries for 'advisors' and 'experts' were extremely high, about 40 per cent according to the ACBAR study.[81] This was exacerbated by a lack of transparency, accountability, corruption in NGOs and lack of coordination in international assistance. West paid more attention to economic development, and the functioning state institutions, and judiciary were relegated. Though the Provincial Reconstruction Team (PRT) concept was put in place, they were managed by foreign actors, and locals had no say in it, further marginalising the population.[82]

***Local Governance:*** After coming to power, he filled important portfolios and appointed governors who were politically allied with him and side-lined others with whom he did not have good personal relations.[83] As a result, many local leaders came up to the scene like Ismael Khan in Herat, Ustad Ata in Jowzjan, Ustad Rabbani in Badakhshan and others. The local leaders controlled a sizeable amount of territory but did little to rebuild the state. Border transits, customs and tolls were under the control of these commanders, and they used all legal/illegal trade and cross-border commerce to fill their pockets rather than using the resources for public good or building of state institutions.[84] Also, these strong local leaders accrued foreign aid as there was no oversight mechanism for aid outside of

Kabul. Both international and Afghan forces were unable to extend their influence beyond the city limits of Kabul. Though resources were poured into establishing the interim government, not much emphasis was given to maintaining and strengthening governance at the provincial level. In the absence of administrative and security support, the Taliban found it easy to build alternate administration and extended their influence into areas where initially they had little traction.[85] The biggest victims of this security and administrative void were the police and judiciary who were already poorly paid and inadequately armed.

***Issues with Ghani Administration:*** The Government led by Ashraf Ghani, too, was unable to withstand the challenges. Ghani's approach to governance was part of the problem. Though he should be credited for his expression of interest in long-term state development but made folly of not engaging domestic political actors.[86] He made enemies with local power brokers who had maintained strong regional security networks—the likes of Abdul Rashid Dostum in North, Atta Mohammad Noor in Balkh, Ismael Khan in Herat. Ghani was left with few allies because of his centralised decision-making. His state-centric approach might have been better if his regime had got more time. He did miscalculate his internal domestic opposition and external support. His governing strategy failed as he did not adjust to changing circumstances.[87] The other political actors, too, have their share in the downfall of the Islamic Republic. Ghani's rival Abdullah Abdullah had been contesting Presidential elections for long. Both never got along, and Abdullah even held a parallel inauguration for President, rejecting the election results.[88] Other domestic politicians too focussed on their own political futures. Mir Rahmani, Younus Qanooni took no time to fly to Islamabad when Kabul fell in 2021 to retain some political influence via the Pakistani government. However, they lost on both fronts as they weakened the country and did not obtain anything from the new Taliban Government.

***Afghanistan National Defence and Security Forces:*** Afghanistan National Defence and Security Forces (ANDSF) were infected by centrifugal tendencies arising from various challenges like logistical, lack of cohesion, factionalism, and infiltration by the Haqqanis.[89] The fact that the majority of the soldiers in the Army were illiterate had been a reason for its inefficiency as providing advanced western weapons and management systems to uneducated forces without apt training created long-term dependencies.[90] The US Government was ill-prepared to conduct Special Security Assistance (SSA) Programs of the scope required in Afghanistan.[91] The early US liaison with independent militias undermined the role of the Afghan National Army and Police. An increasing number of insider attacks too brought down the morale. The US military plans for ANDSF were created under politically constrained timelines rather than a realistic assessment of Afghan readiness. As the security situation deteriorated, combat operations became the immediate goal, and the need to professionalise ANDSF got secondary. Though ANDSF fought bravely over the last two decades, they were let down by leadership failures.

Political interference impeded any reforms in ANDSF. Rather than being a proactive and aggressive force, it was mostly defensive and reactive. ANDSF did very little in risk analysis, assessment or contingency planning. The overall result was that they simply could not keep pace with changing security environment.

## Where did International Assistance go Wrong?

After 20 years of costly international state-building efforts, the Government of Afghanistan fell in the summer of 2021 in a matter of weeks. This segment assesses why international projects in Afghanistan fell short of their aims.

***Subnational Governance:*** International community tried to strengthen subnational governance by enhancing its capacity and accountability, but it suffered from three major shortcomings. First, assistance project were aimed to build trust and strengthen linkages between state and citizens. However, they failed to acknowledge that the major communication barrier between people and the government was not technical but political.[92] In Afghanistan, the patronage networks and informal consultative mechanisms are valued more than a constitutional and legal framework. Second, they aimed to build the capacity of district and provincial councils, but training efforts could not see satisfactory results because these bodies did not have clear authority or roles. Third, there was no meaningful decentralisation of authority and power away from Kabul. Westerns emphasized the importance of local governance, but their approach to improving it was ill-defined in conceptualisation and implementation.[93]

*ISAF focus on the South:* The bulk of western resources went to Southern Afghanistan in the districts of Kandahar and Helmand, which eventually helped Taliban insurgents there.[94] Taliban used to tactically retreat from areas whenever the surge in troops happened and return when they would leave. With the diversion provided by the war in Iraq, the United States got complacent regarding security architecture in Afghanistan. Concentrating more on the South left the North open for the Taliban to strengthen their position there.[95] Southern Afghanistan lies on the border with Pakistan, so the Taliban always had a refuge whenever they felt vulnerable. Historically, the Taliban were weak in Northern provinces, but a passive response by coalition forces allowed the Taliban to gain strength and local support.

Taliban found a response to deal with the US's 'kill and capture campaign' and 'drone war' by their spree of targeted assassinations.[96] Taliban mirrored the tactic used against them by taking down western officers, civil servants, even tribal leaders and religious leaders.[97] Another blunder was little commonality in planning, policies, expectations, and reporting schemes among various contributors.[98] Under a UN mandate and leadership of NATO, 40 nations contributed to five regional commands, and 26 nations led PRTs. All the countries viewed the situation differently depending upon where they were situated in Afghanistan.[99] The NATO troops contributing countries also had to deal with domestic opposition at home due to civilian casualties and their own soldiers. NATO's unwillingness to take on more casualties made them too much dependent on air power. In doing so, it lost hope of winning over the population as the South relentlessly witnessed a plethora of airstrikes.[100] Capt. Leo Docherty, a former British officer in Helmand, said they adopted the same approach as the US and described the campaign as "a textbook case of how to screw up a counter-insurgency."[101]

All factors interacted and reinforced one another in deadly ways. President Biden's decision to withdraw American troops also resulted in the withdrawal of all international forces along with associated contractors.[102] Afghan military had recently got US-made UH-6 Black Hawks, but there was no time to train Afghan pilots and crew to operate these new advanced and complex machines.[103] As multiple 'Special Inspector General for Afghanistan Reconstruction (SIGAR) reports suggest, the US Government was not properly prepared to build an Afghan army and police capable of protecting the country from external and internal threats. US officials believed that they could solve the insecurity problem by pouring more resources into Afghan institutions. This could not address the concerns as there was no enforcement or oversight mechanism. "The U.S. government consistently underestimated the time to rebuild Afghanistan and created unrealistic timelines and expectations that prioritized quick spending. These choices increased corruption and reduced the effectiveness of programs."[104] To rebuild any country, one requires a detailed understanding of its social, economic and political dynamics. The US forced western models onto Afghan institutions, imposed the formal rule of law on a country that addressed the majority of its disputes through informal means and struggled to mitigate the cultural barriers to supporting women and girls.[105] The officials often empowered power brokers who hunted on the population and diverted western aid from its intending recipients to enrich and empower themselves.[106]

## Engaging with the Taliban

The Process of Reconciliation always brings with it two opposing aspects. On the one hand, Reconciliation is thought to be one of the best ways to overcome social conflict.[107] The international turn to reconciliation with the Taliban does not seem surprising that way. On the other hand, reconciliation involving sub-state Terrorists has been seen with scepticism.[108] A conflict resolution negotiation works during the initial stage of insurgency.[109] If the insurgency has been prolonged and the other side has gained considerable acceptance among the local population, the insurgents have no incentive to obey regulations. This explains why ceasefire agreements with Taliban did not work. Reconciliation began to take shape when Taliban started to get de-coupled from Al-Qaeda under Western conceptions. This began during the second Obama administration, during which the term 'Taliban and al-Qaeda' was replaced with 'al-Qaeda and its allies'.[110] However, it was Kabul that first came up with its peace process plan in 2010. Its significant constituents were 'Reconciliation' and 'Re-integration', the former aimed at Taliban leadership in Pakistan and the latter at mid-level Taliban fighters.[111] Since it was Kabul-led, many countries like India too supported it, but it could not be conceptualised as the US started to reach out to the Taliban directly and announced a strategy to integrate 'non-ideologically committed' insurgents.[112] Obama replaced the word 'War on Terror' with 'Overseas Contingency Operation'. For any Kabul administration, two major challenges identified were (a) How to mainstream the process of Political Reconciliation with the Taliban under the constitutional framework; and (b) How to lead the Reconciliation process given the role of powerful entities in the politics of the region.[113] Any peace initiative that came forward failed to manage divergent perceptions, factional interests, patronage networks, and informal power structures at all levels.[114] Besides, a strategic communication strategy[115] was needed to counter any terror campaign and an efficient counter-insurgency strategy that integrates the local population in building local governance and economic development. US-Taliban deal in 2020 left Taliban with little incentive to follow broad-based regional approaches and strengthen state institutions. The deal legitimised Taliban, an insurgent organisation while undermining the Afghan Government, with which the US had signed Bilateral Security Agreement. The deal shifted the balance of power towards Taliban, and it created conditions for a state collapse.[116] Taliban exploited the cover of the peace agreement to manoeuvre into position across the country, encircling important districts and province capitals while also limiting US military strength. The sense of betrayal from the Doha agreement deepened the spat between Ghani, Abdullah and Karzai, thus weakening any chances of a robust interim government.[117] President Biden might have reassured the American people that their objectives were over in Afghanistan and they never came for nation-building. However, the chaos that emanates from their embarrassing departure is bound to bite back not just them but also other countries that have invested their capital and energies in Afghanistan for the last 20 years.

## Conclusion

From $1 trillion surges to the complete withdrawal of Western troops and the resulting establishment of the Taliban Government after two decades, this should count amongst the most surreal episodes in the history of modern International Relations.[118] The hybrid of state-building and counter-insurgency became fatal in Afghanistan. Taliban had its own vision for establishing security, governance and the rule of law. They sold it in the name of Sharia from within tribal structures and appealed to the rural population.[119] The more the military was deployed against them, the more they presented themselves as a bastion of Jihad.

All the drives of Taliban Resurgence that have been discussed also tend to give an insight into a prediction of what lies ahead. As long as Pakistan presents itself as an all-weather friend of Islamist groups, the Taliban will have its significance maintained in Afghanistan irrespective of whether it stays in power. The old intra-Taliban rivalry might erupt again, for example, between Alizai and Nurzai tribes. Long-standing Alizai commanders in the field like Sardar Ibrahim and Mullah Zakir have always been loyal to the deceased Akhtar Mansour. This group was set against the larger faction of Nurzai Taliban loyal to current Emir Haibatullah Akhundzada.[120] So, the infighting between Taliban factions will happen but it is expected to be resolved at the behest of Pakistani mediation as has happened in the past. Now the Taliban seek the support and legitimacy of the International Community. Central Asian Republics have started meeting with them as they face the most threat from extremism spilling into their side. Not much could be expected on whether big and middle power will formally recognise the Taliban this time. However, there is a sense that business and economic interests will be back on track gradually as the Taliban regime settles. However, the Taliban should not be formally recognised until women and minorities face repression in Afghanistan and Afghan soil being used as a hub for training for militants to be deployed in other countries.

UN team that monitors the Taliban, in its 2021 report said that the Taliban still has very strong ties with al-Qaeda. Yet, the UN reported that, the Taliban have started to "tighten control over al-Qaeda by gathering information on foreign terrorist fighters and registering and restricting them."[121] Taliban still provides them with protection in exchange for resources and training. According to the same report around 500 al-Qaeda fighters still have their presence in Afghanistan. Taliban simultaneously is fighting Islamic State-Khorasan (IS-K) which has around 2000 fighters in Afghanistan. They will continue to attack major cities and the overall security architecture looks far from promising.

## Notes

1. Kareem Kamel, "Understanding Taliban Resurgence: Ethno-Symbolism and Revolutionary Mobilization," Studies in Ethnicity and Nationalism, pp. 66-82.
2. Ibid.
3. A.L.V Linschoten and F. Kuehn, *The Taliban Reader: War, Islam, and Politics* , Oxford University Press, New York, 2018, p. 30.
4. Kamel, n. 1.
5. Ahmed Rashid, *Taliban: Islam, Oil, and the New Great Game in Central Asia,* I.B. Tauris Publishers, London, 2020, p. 87.
6. Hassan Abbas, *The Taliban Revival: Violence and Extremism on the Pakistan-Afghanistan Frontier,* Yale University Press, London, 2014, p. 18.
7. Linschoten and Kuehn, n. 3, p. 159.
8. Ibid., p. 111.
9. Kamel, n. 1.
10. Antonio Giustozzi, *The Taliban at War, 2001-2018,* Oxford University Press, New York, 2019, p. 15.
11. Ibid.
12. Ibid.
13. Ibid., p. 34.
14. Ibid., p. 35.
15. Ibid., p. 40.
16. Ashley Jackson and Rahmatullah Amiri, "Insurgent Bureaucracy: How the Taliban makes Policy," United States Institute of Peace, no. 153, 2019, p. 7.
17. Ibid., p. 22.
18. Guistozzi, n. 10, p. 68.
19. Ibid., p. 72.
20. Ibid., p. 83.
21. Ibid., p. 82.
22. Ibid., p. 87.
23. All shuras had established their individual commissions, including military, finance and others.
24. Ibid., p. 93.
25. Ibid., p. 94.
26. Ibid., p. 96.
27. Shamsatoo mahaz was created in 1988 by orders of Gulbuddin Hekmatyar (leader of Hizb-e-Islami).

28. Ibid.
29. Ibid., p. 106.
30. Mullah Qari Baryal led Peshawar Military Commission and is known for his charismatic persona. He was sacked from the position under the pressure of Mullah Zakir and Pakistan. When Peshawar Shura was subsumed in Quetta Shura around 2014-15, he left and formed his autonomous mahaz called 'Shura of the North' with the help of Iranian and later Russian funding.
31. Ibid., p. 172.
32. Thomas H. Johnson, "Taliban adaptations and innovations," *Small Wars and Insurgencies*, vol. 24, no. 1, 2013, pp. 3-27.
33. Ibid., p. 5.
34. Ibid., p. 6.
35. Ibid.
36. Ibid., p. 7.
37. Guistozzi, n. 10, p. 202.
38. Johnson, n. 32, p. 7.
39. Guiztozzi, n. 10, p. 152.
40. Ibid., p. 159.
41. Johnson, n. 32, p. 12.
42. UNAMA, Afghanistan: Annual Report 2010 Protection of Civilians in Armed Conflict, 13.
43. Johnson, n. 32, p. 13.
44. Guistozzi, n. 10, p. 69.
45. Ibid., p. 46.
46. Ahmed Rashid, *Descent into Chaos: The United States and the Failure of Nation Building in Pakistan, Afghanistan and Central Asia,* Penguin Publishers, New York, 2008.
47. Guistozzi, no. 10, p. 58.
48. Ibid., p. 59.
49. Ibid., p. 73.
50. Ibid.
51. Ibid., p. 79.
52. Bill Roggio, "Taliban appoints Kabul Attack Network Commander as provincial governor", *FDD's Long War Journal,* at https://www.longwarjournal.org/archives/2021/11/taliban-appoints-kabul-attack-network-commander-as-provincial-governor.php
53. https://www.un.org/securitycouncil/sanctions/1988/materials/summaries/individual/sirajuddin-jallaloudine-haqqani

54. Gretchen Peters, "Haqqani Network Financing: The Evolution of an Industry," *CTC at West Point*, July 2012, at https://ctc.usma.edu/wp-content/uploads/2012/07/CTC_Haqqani_Network_Financing-Report__Final.pdf
55. Ijaz Ahmad Khan, "Understanding Pakistan's Pro-Taliban Afghan Policy," *Pakistan Horizon*, vol. 60, no. 2, 2007, pp. 141-157.
56. Anthony Davis, "Riding the Taliban Tiger: The price Pakistan pays for creating a monster", *Asia week*, at www-cgi.cnn.com
57. Zahid Hussain, *Frontline Pakistan: The Struggle with Militant Islam*, Columbia University Press, New York, 2007.
58. Brian Cloughley, *A History of the Pakistan Army*, Oxford University Press, New York, 2001, p. 395.
59 A.Z. Hilali, *US-Pakistan Relationship: Soviet Invasion of Afghanistan*, Ashgate Publishing Limited, London, 2005, p. 248.
60. Matt Waldman, "The Sun in the Sky: The Relationship between Pakistan's ISI and Afghan Insurgents," *Carr Centre for Human Rights Policy*, Discussion Paper 18, 2010.

    The 'Durand line', formalized in 1893, created a border between what was then British India with Afghanistan. It effectively divided the Pashtun nation into two parts and is thus rejected by many Pashtuns on both sides of the border. Notably, some 25 million Pashtuns are living in Pakistan, perhaps double the number in Afghanistan. Pakistan's support for the Afghan insurgency is perhaps also reinforced by fears that India is seeking to bolster insurgents in Baluchistan, a south-western province of Pakistan.
61. Ibid.
62. Rashid, n. 46, p. 223.
63. Ibid., p. 222.
64. Tribal Analysis Center. 2009. '*The Quetta Shura: a tribal analysis*'. Williamsburg: Tribal Analysis Center.
65. Ashley J. Tellis, "Beradar, Pakistan and the Afghan Taliban: What Gives?," Carnegie Endowment for International Peace, 2010.
66. Ibid.
67. Guistozzi, n. 10, p. 170.
68. Ibid., p. 124.
69. Ibid.
70. Ibid., p. 138.
71. Ibid., p. 110.
72. Ibid., p. 263.
73. Ibid., p. 238.
74. Vishal Chandra, *The Unfinished War in Afghanistan 2001-2014*, Pentagon Press, New Delhi, 2015, p. 191.

75. Ibid.
76. Ajmal Ahmady, "Why Afghanistan Fell: An Insider's Account of What Went Wrong," *Foreign Affairs*, October 2021.
77. Chandra, n. 74, p. 190.
78. Najibullah Lafraie, "Resurgence of the Taliban Insurgency in Afghanistan: How and Why?," *International Politics*, vol. 46, no. 1, 2009, pp. 102-113.
79. Ibid.
80. Ibid.
81. Ibid.
82. Gilles Dorronsoro, "The Taliban's Winning Strategy in Afghanistan," Carnegie Endowment for International Peace, 2009, p. 17.
83. Ibid.
84. Ibid., p. 18.
85. Ibid., p. 19.
86. Ahmady, n. 76.
87. Ibid.
88. Ibid.
89. Chandra, n. 74, p. 172.
90. Special Inspector General for Afghanistan Reconstruction Report, October 2017.
91. Ibid.
92. Frances Z. Brown, "Aiding Afghan Local Governance: What Went Wrong?," Carnegie Endowment for International Peace, 2021.
93. Ibid.
94. Dorrensoro, n. 82, p. 29.
95. Ibid.
96. Johnson, n. 32, p. 14.
97. Ibid.
98. Alison M Coady and Hussein Solomon, "Afghanistan's arrested Development: combating Taliban resurgence with an eye for lasting peace," *South African Journal of International Relations*, vol. 16, no. 1, 2009, pp. 103-114.
99. Ibid.
100. Rashid, n. 46, p. 441.
101. Christina Lamb, "Soldier Quits as Blundering Campaign Turns into Pointless War," *The Sunday Times*, September 10, 2006.
102. Ahmady, n. 76.
103. Ibid.
104. Special Inspector General for Afghanistan Reconstruction Report, August 2021, titled What we Need to Learn: Lessons from Twenty Years of Afghanistan Reconstruction.
105. Ibid.

106. Ibid.
107. Judith Renner and Alexander Spencer, "De-antagonising the Other: Changing Constructions of the Taliban and the Possibility of Reconciliation," *Global Society*, vol. 27, no. 4, 2013, p. 476.
108. Ibid.
109. The conflict resolution theory by William Zartman talks about the ripe time for negotiations to take place.
110. Ibid., p. 489.
111. Chandra, n. 74, p. 123.
112. Ibid., p. 130.
113. Ibid., p. 125.
114. Ibid., p. 300.
115. Ibid., p. 323.
116. Ahmady, n. 76.
117. Ibid.
118. Rory Stewart, "The last days of Intervention: Afghanistan and the Delusions of Maximalism," *Foreign Affairs*, vol. 100, no. 6, 2021, p. 60.
119. Ibid., p. 67.
120. United Nation Security Council Report, 27 May 2020, S/2020/415.
121. Lindsay Maizland, "The Taliban in Afghanistan," Council on Foreign Relations, September 2021, at https://www.cfr.org/backgrounder/taliban-afghanistan#chapter-title-0-3.

# 13

# Taliban Takeover: Emerging Dynamics in Central Asia

POONAM MANN

The rapid takeover of Afghanistan by the Taliban on August 15, 2021 and the resultant chaos intensified fear among the Central Asian Republics (CARs).[1] There emerged new challenges and risks that posed threat to their security and stability, however, increasing their salience. The main cause of concern for them remained the spillover effects from the Taliban takeover that includes an increase in refugee flow and the resultant humanitarian crisis, resurgence of radical ideology, drug-trafficking and economic challenges. Therefore, maintaining stability and ensuring security was one of their primary concerns. Consequently, the reaction from the Central Asian countries, especially from the frontline states of Tajikistan, Turkmenistan and Uzbekistan was very swift. Besides, with the speedy pace of developments in Afghanistan, the reaction from global powers, regional players and even from the Taliban itself was equally quick and it signifies a major shift in the geostrategic context for CARs. In this context, the present paper will evaluate the various choices that CARs have made to deal with the existing challenges and how much room do they have to manoeuvre. Further, the paper will also analyse the great power influence vis-à-vis the common threat of the Taliban at play into the regional dynamics.

## Brief Background

A Taliban-controlled Afghanistan is not new for the CARs. Over the last three decades, they have undergone a number of waves of heightened anxiety over the situation in Afghanistan.

For instance, the Taliban expanded rapidly across Afghanistan in 1990s after the CARs gained independence from the USSR in 1991. It is also believed that the five-year long Tajik civil war (1992-1997) was partly fuelled by groups operating out of bases in Afghanistan, thus, bringing instability to the southern borders of Central Asia.[2] From 1996 to 2001, when the Taliban ruled most of Afghanistan for the first time, their expansion was seen as a threat to the fragile regional security.[3] Moreover, two incursions by an extremist organisation known as Islamic Movement of Uzbekistan (IMU) posed a considerable security risk to the countries of the region. The Republic of Uzbekistan and Kyrgyzstan were targeted by the militants linked to IMU in 1999 and 2000. Among the major attacks attributed to them were (i) a series of bomb attacks in Tashkent in February 1999 where 16 people were killed and 128 injured, (ii) the militants entered southern Kyrgyzstan through Tajik-Afghan border and took several hostages while fighting the local forces.[4] IMU used Afghan territory for training, funding and its transnational terrorist operations. Taliban's expanding support to IMU and its growing aspirations to transform itself from a national movement into more of a regional force created a wave of panic among the leaders of CARs.[5] However, its activities were largely curtailed after the US-led "war on terrorism" in Afghanistan post-9/11, when NATO forces took control over most of the Afghan provinces in 2001-2002. Though the group fought alongside the Taliban and Al-Qaeda against the coalition forces, but it suffered heavy losses and to an extent, lost its ability to easily penetrate to the Central Asian region through Afghanistan.[6]

Besides, all the five Central Asian countries were very quick in providing their whole-hearted support to the US and its coalition forces. They monopolised on the need for coordinated and effective actions of all countries and international organisations to curb the menace of international terrorism, rather Uzbekistan and Kyrgyzstan granted the US military access to their territories. Tajikistan, Kazakhstan and Turkmenistan also opened up their airspace for coalition overflights and channelling humanitarian aid to Afghanistan.[7] Obviously, their readiness to assist the US and coalition forces in "war against terrorism" stemmed from their own security concerns and they sought to draw international attention over it.

However, this cooperation between CARs, the US and the NATO forces suffered a setback when in mid-2000s a series of "colour revolutions" hit some of the post-Soviet Republics including Kyrgyzstan. These "colour revolutions" were perceived as a part of Western democratisation agenda.[8] Hence, in 2005 Astana Summit of Shanghai Cooperation Organisation (SCO), Presidents of Kazakhstan, Kyrgyzstan, Tajikistan and Uzbekistan signed the SCO declaration that "... the member countries of the Shanghai Cooperation Organisation consider it necessary that respective members of the anti-terrorist coalition set a final timeline for their temporary use of...objects of infrastructure and stay of their military contingents on the territories of SCO member states."[9] Subsequently, Uzbekistan terminated its military agreement with the US to use its Karshi-Khanabad airbase for US operations in Afghanistan.[10] Barring Turkmenistan,[11] rest of the four Central Asian countries expressed their faith in the Regional Anti-Terrorist Structure (RATS) of SCO as the main vehicle to combat "three evils"—terrorism, separatism and extremism in the region. Nonetheless, later, considering the overall security situation in Afghanistan and its possible repercussions, the relations between the US and the Central Asian countries did get normalised, but it took some time. It was in early 2008 that Uzbekistan permitted US military personnel under NATO command to transit through an airbase near Termez, which was being operated by Germany at that time. In April 2008, the then Uzbek President Islam Karimov attended the NATO summit in Bucharest, Romania and affirmed Uzbekistan's readiness to discuss the transit of non-lethal goods and equipment by NATO to Afghanistan through Uzbekistan. In May 2009, it allowed the US and NATO to use its Navoi airport for transporting non-lethal supplies to Afghanistan.[12] In 2009, the then Kyrgyz President Kurmanbek Bakiyev announced the closure of the Manas airbase that it had given to the US forces on lease and was considered to have served as the 'premier air mobility hub' for operations in Afghanistan. It was speculated that the decision was spurred by Russia which offered Kyrgyzstan a substantial amount of grants and loans. However, later that year the Kyrgyz government revised its decision to let the US use its Manas airbase as a 'transit centre'. The Kyrgyz Government agreed to lease it for five years, which would be renewed annually. This decision was taken considering the security situation in Afghanistan.[13] The CARs also played a significant role in the transportation of supplies to support NATO and US operations in Afghanistan, as a part of the Northern Distribution Network (NDN). In 2009, the US was successful in acquiring permission from Kazakhstan, Kyrgyzstan, Tajikistan and Uzbekistan to use their territories to transport non-lethal supplies.[14] Specifically, this route became very important in November 2011, when Pakistan blocked its vital NATO supply routes into Afghanistan in response to NATO's attack on Pakistan's border checkpoints.[15] Reportedly, in late 2011, almost three-fourths of the non-lethal surface shipments to Afghanistan were transported through NDN.[16] Moreover, the CARs also provided humanitarian, financial and technical assistance for the reconstruction and development of Afghan society.[17]

Unfortunately, another wave of anxiety over the situation in Afghanistan hit the Central Asian region when the decision to withdraw the US and International Security Assistance Force (ISAF) troops from Afghanistan in 2014, was announced. At that point of time, it was believed that the complete withdrawal of US and ISAF forces from Afghanistan could cause more instability in the country and the security situation in Afghanistan will further deteriorate. It might further, upset the fragile regional balance that was underpinned by the efforts of the international community to restrict Afghanistan's challenges within the country.[18] Central Asian countries, being the immediate neighbours of Afghanistan, would be the first one to feel the change, especially the republics of Tajikistan, Turkmenistan and Uzbekistan. The major concerns of these countries revolved around the issues of national security and political stability. For them, the situation in Afghanistan would pose long-term security threats, such as:

1. The Taliban would allow the Central Asian Islamic radicals, to create their sanctuaries along Afghanistan's border with the CARs and such a possibility could threaten the stability of these countries as there was considerable potential for radicalisation in the region.
2. Another major concern was cross-border drug-trafficking. Since the borders between Afghanistan and CARs (especially Tajikistan) are very porous and difficult to monitor, they form the major supply route for the drug-trade to carry drugs to Europe. These routes also provide for an influx of arms and associated criminality and are hardly controlled.[19]

3. The leaders of CARs were also worried that the worsening of security situation in Afghanistan could lead to an increased influx of refugees in their countries.

Hence, three of these countries were consistently involved in the processes related to Afghanistan. On the other hand, Kazakhstan and Kyrgyzstan were comparatively less involved as they do not share physical borders with Afghanistan. Nonetheless, each of these republics adopted different approaches to deal with their southern neighbour. For Instance, Uzbekistan emphasised on the fact that since, Afghan problem cannot be resolved through force alone, therefore, targeted economic assistance could probably would help in reducing the conflict potential inside Afghanistan. So, it participated in an array of social and economic projects in Afghanistan that included building bridges, railways, power grids, etc. to assist NDN, ISAF's supply routes to Afghanistan through Central Asia.[20] Tajikistan, on the other hand, shares very strong religious, linguistic and cultural links with Afghanistan, thus, it adopted a very cautious approach toward the war-torn country. It relied mostly on collaborative efforts through bilateral and multilateral relationships. Mostly, it rendered its support through its collaboration with Russian-based organisations and agreements.[21] Turkmenistan adheres to the policy of 'permanent neutrality', hence, did not participate in the International military operations in Afghanistan. Despite its 497-mile shared border with Afghanistan, Turkmenistan remained cautious in criticising the Taliban and its leadership. In fact, it maintained a close and constant (though unofficial) relationship with the Taliban and instructed its media outlets to self-censor and not to portray the Taliban government in a negative light.[22] This reluctance to criticise the Taliban government, probably, stemmed from Ashgabat's quest to expand and explore new markets for its gas exports in South Asia and lower down its dependency on Russia and China.[23] Kazakhstan and Kyrgyzstan were comparatively less affected countries as they do not have shared borders with Afghanistan, but they did establish a formal relationship with Afghanistan. Their shared view was that international efforts should be geared towards making Afghanistan more economically stable and less dependent on international humanitarian aid so that it can develop financial ties with its extended neighbourhood and become a more attractive destination for investment. Afghanistan was also seen as an important transit centre between Central and South Asia.[24]

Simultaneously, the influence of Russia and China, which always existed, grew immensely as the CARs saw the opportunities that the continues deepening of relationship with these two countries provided. In addition, the non-interference of Russia and China in the internal matters of these mostly authoritarian regimes also added to the comfort of CARs in dealing with them.

For Russia, the CARs have always been a part of their sphere of influence and vice-versa. Russia has always been more concerned about the spillover effects of Afghanistan's chaos into CARs and the resultant impact on Russia, especially, terrorism and drug-trafficking. Hence, President Putin was one of the first foreign leaders to call the then US President Bush in the wake of 9/11 attacks and pledged his support for the US-led 'war against terrorism' in Afghanistan. However, over the years, Moscow became concerned about the growing US presence in Central Asia, which is considered as an integral part of its own security zone.[25] Russian leadership's uneasiness was quite evident in 2005 when the Russian Ministry of Defence newspaper stated that "it is becoming evident that Washington, having completed the Military Phase of the Afghan campaign, does not intend to roll back its military presence or political influence in Central Asia which had become possible precisely because of Afghanistan and the Taliban".[26] Further, the Russian Government became very suspicious about US plans of connecting Central Asia and Afghanistan into a unified economic zone. In 2005, the US floated the concept of the 'Greater Central Asia Partnership' and in 2011 'New Silk Road Initiative'. Russia considered these US initiatives as a move to contain Russia geopolitically. However, with the closing down of NATO's Manas Transit Centre in Kyrgyzstan, in 2014, seemingly Russia finally got its way. Nonetheless, its fear of chaos in Afghanistan after the ISAF's withdrawal persisted as Russia's Ministry of Foreign Affairs stated that even after "thirteen years of ISAF presence in Afghanistan, its activities did not lead to the stabilisation of the situation in that country. Multifaceted security threats, including religious extremism, terrorism, narco-crime ... not only continue to exist but exhibit an escalatory trend."[27] Thus, the security considerations took priority in the Russian approach not only towards

Afghanistan, but the whole Central Asian region. For Russia, the main security implications of the US/NATO withdrawal from Afghanistan were more related to Central Asia. To address these concerns it adopted a two-pronged approach to strengthen its position in its strategic backyard, i.e., (i) security cooperation, (ii) Economic integration, by promoting multi-lateral cooperation and various integrating projects among the post-soviet republics like, Eurasian Economic Union (EAEU), CIS Anti-Terrorist Centre and Collective Security Treaty Organisation (CSTO), etc. In addition, Russia in partnership with China made successful attempts to bind the CARs closer through multilateral initiatives like SCO.

Like Russia, China was also concerned about the post-September 2001 geopolitical environment in the region when the US established its military bases in the heart of Central Asia. It also resisted and countered the Western security and economic moves in the region.[28] In fact, China's foreign policy thinking presented two contrasting moves at that time. On the one hand, it supported US military action in Afghanistan,[29] which provided Beijing with an opportunity to reframe its security operations against the Uyghur separatist groups in Xinjiang as a part of larger international struggle against terrorism.[30] On the other hand, US military bases in Uzbekistan and Kyrgyzstan raised alarm bells in China's foreign policy circles. It feared that the permanent US presence could add to the array of US bases in Asia which could encircle China. Further, China viewed US bases in Central Asia as a part of its unilateralist security policy that was explicitly opposed by China in its "New Security Concept" of that time.[31] Although by 2001, Beijing was successful in developing a relatively successful approach towards the CARs in social, economic and security spheres bilaterally but it was trying to strengthen this cooperation through multilateral diplomacy as well. For that, it tried to reinvigorate SCO as a viable regional security organisation. In this context, China's efforts were supported by some of the missteps taken by the US in handling the CARs. For instance, the US response to the Andijan events in Uzbekistan and Tulip revolution in Kyrgyzstan in 2005, was seen as America's attempt to overthrow the status quo of authoritarian regimes of the region and promotion of West's democratic agenda in the CARs. The countries like Uzbekistan and Kyrgyzstan, clearly, viewed it as at odds with US global war on terrorism. Thus, China along with Russia was able to contrast it with the SCO's principles of "non-interference in the internal matters of any state" and was able to draw Uzbekistan and Kyrgyzstan firmly back into their orbit.

On the question of ISAF's withdrawal from Afghanistan, the main concerns for China were influx of terrorists trained in Afghanistan, which included Uyghur separatists who were claiming independence of Xinjiang Uyghur Autonomous Region (XUAR), drugs and weapon trafficking, inter-ethnic clashes, cross-border crime, etc. which could have a negative impact on China's security and stability. Central Asian region was seen as the region where terrorist activities might be revived. Consequently, a noticeable rise in China's activities was witnessed on the eve of ISAF withdrawal. For instance, besides, strengthening the SCO mechanism, it supported Afghanistan's bid to become an SCO observer member and Afghanistan was granted the status of an Observer State in the SCO in 2012. China, also emphasised on strengthening of SCO's security cooperation and a regional solution to the Afghan problem. Besides, there was a substantial amount of increase in frequent high-level visits to the neighbouring countries and China vigorously pursued bilateral, trilateral and multilateral dialogues with countries surrounding Afghanistan. One of the important tools it adopted was to enhance multi-lateral cooperation between Central Asia and South Asia. In this endeavour, it initiated its own new silk road initiative under One Belt One Road, which was announced by President Xi Jinping in 2013 during his visit to Kazakhstan.[32] Over the years, China's policy in Central Asian region has evolved to an extent that it has emerged as the main economic partner of the CARs. At the same time, it has been conscious of Russian sensitivities and has not stepped in Russia's shoes with regard to the security aspect of the relationship. In fact, both Russia and China have adopted a cooperative approach in the pursuance of their respective policies in the CARs.

On the other hand, the leaders of the CARs through their multi-vector foreign policy have maintained a balanced approach towards China and Russia. However, ever since their independence, the CARs have faced persisting apprehensions vis-à-vis Afghanistan. The first time Taliban showed up at their doorstep when all the five CARs had been independent for a mere five years, therefore, there was a reason for the leaders of these countries to get concerned. But now, after their 30 years of independence, the Central Asian region is generally considered as a stable region and over a period of time, they have had considerable time to strengthen their position. Also, they are now more familiar with the Taliban. In this context, during the swift takeover of Afghanistan by the Taliban on August 15, 2021, the CARs were better prepared to make their choices to deal with the subsequent challenges. For instance, in the weeks when US forces were approaching to their final withdrawal, many of the Central Asian republics bolstered their military presence near the borders with Afghanistan.[33] Focusing on the potential security threats emanating from Afghanistan, they participated in bilateral and multilateral military exercises too.[34] Since, the Taliban-led government assured that the territory of Afghanistan will not be used against the interests of third countries, hence, will not pose any threat to the countries of the Central Asian region,[35] subsequently, the CARs adopted a very pragmatic approach toward the Taliban.

## Taliban takeover of Afghanistan on 15th August 2021 and the CARs' Response

All the Central Asian countries wish to have a stable and secure government in Afghanistan so that the spillover effects of destabilisation could be prevented across their borders. The leaders of these countries do realise that although Afghanistan may not be a very lucrative market for them to trade with but is very crucial for connecting the Central Asian region to the vast South Asian consumer market of more than 1.5 billion people.[36] Besides, to materialise many of the important infrastructural projects that run through Afghanistan, like, Central Asian—South Asian Electricity Transmission Project (CASA-1000), Turkmenistan-Afghanistan-Pakistan-India Gas Pipeline (TAPI), Central Asia's outreach to the warm waters via Iran through Chabahar Port, Turkmenistan-Afghanistan-Pakistan Power Interconnection (TAP) project, a secure and stable Afghanistan is very important. Moreover, all the CARs are keen to fructify their policy of diversification to lessen their dependence on any one or two major powers. Keeping these interests in mind, the CARs (except Tajikistan) softened their rhetoric against the Taliban and expressed their intentions of "Friendship and Good Neighbourliness" with the Taliban-ruled Afghanistan. However, the old and persisting fears like uncontrolled migration and resultant refugee crisis, influx of extremist elements and drug-trafficking, etc. still remained an area of deep concern. Therefore, during the takeover march of Afghanistan by the Taliban, the CARs displayed a strong response.

### *CARs preparation for the Taliban Takeover*

As the Taliban forces started taking control over the territories of Afghanistan's borders with the Central Asian region towards the end of June 2021, each Central Asian country responded differently, despite facing similar security implications from these incursions. For instance, Uzbekistan started with its military preparedness. It conducted tactical military exercises, in late June 2021, near the Afghan border and also sent more troops near the border. In July 2021, it conducted joint military exercises with Russian troops in Samarkand province of Uzbekistan.[37] In August 2021, Uzbekistan also participated in a virtual summit of Collective Security Treaty Organisation (CSTO) (though the country is not a member of this organisation), where the discussion revolved around the need to make extra efforts to develop cooperation among the member states in counteracting the challenges emanating from Afghanistan.[38] Later, Uzbek forces held a joint training exercise with their Russian counterparts along the Uzbek-Afghan border at Termez Field Training Camp and joint drills with Tajikistan in response to the deteriorating security situation in the region.[39]

Similarly, Tajikistan, amidst rising instability in Afghanistan, puts its armed forces on high alert and relocated thousands of its troops along its 1,344 km long border with Afghanistan. It also conducted a combat-readiness check exercise, which was considered as a biggest exercise in the history of independent Tajikistan.[40] In fact, to check the readiness of the military assets, Tajik President Emamoli Rahmon visited Mir and Panj—two of the Afghan-Tajik border posts in an effort to boost the morale of its armed forces and arouse patriotic sentiments among the soldiers and emphasising on the significance of their mission to protect the border amidst rising threats from Afghanistan.[41] Further, besides Russia and Uzbekistan, it also conducted anti-terror military drills with China to show mutual determination to fight terrorism and effectively respond to the possible threats emanating from Afghanistan.[42]

Turkmenistan, reportedly, also reacted by rushing its armed forces to the Afghan border with heavy military equipment. However, officially, it rejected these reports by underlying the fact that there are strong bonds of love and friendship between Turkmen and Afghan people and thus, do not require any military equipment.[43]

Initially, the countries of the region were somewhat unclear about how to respond to the unfolding situation in Afghanistan. Although militaries of the three Central Asian countries bordering with Afghanistan were put on high alert, however, no direct engagement of them with the Taliban forces took place. Also, the CARs abstained from condemning the Taliban forces for their advances in Afghanistan at the cost of Afghan Government's control. Besides, the Taliban also released multiple statements assuring their Central Asian neighbours that they will pose no threat to the security of any of them.[44]

Taliban's return to power in Afghanistan is a reality now. Seemingly, all the CARs agree on the fact that the Taliban-led Afghanistan is a key part of their region and they have to deal with it. Therefore, based on their respective interests, they are trying to take a pragmatic approach to the new regime in Afghanistan.

### *Central Asian Republics' approach toward the Taliban*

All the Central Asian countries adopted a very cooperative attitude in response to the developments in Afghanistan. All of them assisted in the evacuation efforts out of Afghanistan.

- Uzbekistan facilitated the transit of thousands of Afghan nationals and foreigners out of Afghanistan. It hosted hundreds of Afghan pilots and their families who fled Afghanistan and reportedly reached out to the US for their relocation.[45] It allowed European military aeroplanes to fly evacuees from Kabul to airports in Tashkent, Navoi and Bukhara and from here, they were flown out to Europe on special chartered flights.[46]
- Tajikistan also made itself available as a transit point for evacuations of Afghan nationals to a third country.[47]
- Kazakhstan made itself available for the relocation of the United Nations Assistance Mission in Afghanistan (UNAMA) staff in Almaty. The temporary office in Almaty may be used as a hub for UN staff to

rotate in and out of Afghanistan, depending upon the security situation in the country.[48]

- Kyrgyzstan also earned praise when the government announced that it will issue 500 student visas to Afghans as a humanitarian gesture.[49]
- Turkmenistan announced that it would allow flights evacuating foreign nationals out of Afghanistan to use their air space.[50]

### *Position on accepting Refugees from Afghanistan*

With the fall of Afghan Government, the country also fell into the grips of a humanitarian crisis. The Taliban takeover created panic among the people and fearful people got desperate to leave the country. Many of them tried to flee to the North. Taking into consideration the seriousness and sensitive nature of refugee crisis, the CARs adopted quite firm but divergent approaches towards the refugees coming from Afghanistan to their countries. All the countries except Tajikistan made it clear that they will not be accepting the refugees coming from Afghanistan after the Taliban takeover.

Uzbekistan denied the entry of refugees from Afghanistan, but despite that hundreds of Afghan soldiers entered into Uzbekistan. Some of the refugees were being kept in the tent camps, at the same time the Uzbek Government was clear that they will not stay there. Some of the refugees were sent back after negotiations with the Taliban.[51] A statement from the ministry of foreign affairs said that "To ensure security ... the Uzbek-Afghan border is completely closed and no crossing through the Termez security checkpoint is allowed."[52]

Besides, Uzbek President's special envoy on Afghanistan, Ismatilla Ergashev, made it clear that "Uzbekistan is not a signatory to the 1951 convention on the status of refugees and its own laws does not have any provisions for granting anyone refugee status. Hence taking into account external and internal factors, there are no legal grounds to provide asylum on our territory for Afghan citizens...."[53]

Considering that the influx of refugees from Afghanistan could undermine the domestic security, the republics of Kazakhstan, Kyrgyzstan and Turkmenistan also refused to accept refugees from Afghanistan.[54] Although, the republics of Kazakhstan and Kyrgyzstan were ready to accept the ethnic Kazakhs and ethnic Kyrgyz to their respective countries but

Turkmenistan refused to accept even the ethnic Turkmen to its country. Tajikistan Government, on the other hand, was open to accept 100,000 refugees. In fact, the Tajik residents were also open to accepting the refugees from Afghanistan.[55] Reportedly, Tajik Government has also allocated seventy hectares of its territory to accommodate potential Afghan refugees.[56]

All of these countries were very apprehensive to allow refugees because they fear that many of the extremist militants may enter their countries in the guise of refugees. Second, It would add up the social and economic cost to the countries, i.e., it could put a burden on the public resources of the host countries, fuel labour market pressure and could lead to the social tensions. Third, they want to maintain good relations with the Taliban as they have a lot at stake in terms of their pipelines and infrastructural project passing through Afghanistan.

Keeping these factors in mind, the Central Asian leaders showed no inclination to maintain the status quo with the Taliban, therefore, they tried to keep the lines of communication open with them.

### *Dealing with the Taliban-led Government*

All the CARs have called for the formation of an inclusive government in Afghanistan that involves various rival groups. However, Uzbekistan and Turkmenistan's friendly posturing toward the Taliban is a clear reflection of their priorities.

**Uzbekistan** has established contacts with the interim government in Afghanistan. Uzbek foreign minister Mr. Abdulaziz Kamilov made it clear that "We are pursuing a friendly policy with Afghanistan based on the principles of mutual respect, equality, non-interference in the internal affairs and consideration of mutual interests".[57] He further added that "At present, the interim Taliban Government that has come to power is seeking international recognition ... we must not allow the transformation of this country into the so-called "rogue-state", as was the case in the 1990s".[58] A peaceful and stable Afghanistan is one of the main drivers of Uzbekistan's policy towards the Taliban and a lot will depend on the Taliban that how it will deal with the militant groups present in the country. Moreover, being a land-locked country, Uzbekistan is looking for a breakthrough in South Asia and Afghanistan has the prospects to connect Central Asian region with the South Asian region. Therefore, economic and transport—infrastructure is another important driver of Uzbekistan's engagement with the Taliban.[59]

**Turkmenistan,** on the other hand, started engaging the Taliban much before the fall of Kabul and became one of the first countries to send humanitarian aid after the Taliban took over the country. When, the US decided to withdraw its forces from Afghanistan, the situation became very volatile, one of the main concerns of Turkmen Government was to prevent the armed incursions of extremist elements from its shared border with Afghanistan and to check the influx of migrant refugees. The government took the diplomatic route and hosted Taliban representatives in Ashgabat in July 2021, to deal with this concern.[60] Second, Energy issues also factor in establishing close relations with the Taliban for Turkmenistan. Turkmenistan does not have a significant industrial base to support its economy and its economy largely depends on its gas exports (mainly to China and Russia). It is also trying hard to diversify its exports and reach out to the big South Asian markets. Hence, it wants positive signals from the Taliban to support its TAPI[61] project. This was expressed by the Minister of Foreign Affairs of Turkmenistan, Mr. R. Meredov, during his visit to Afghanistan and meeting with the high-ranking officials of the interim government in Kabul on October 30-31, 2021. During the visit, he expressed "Turkmenistan's readiness to work in close cooperation and have constructive dialogue with the new state structures of Afghanistan, underlining the fact that Turkmenistan, as a neighbouring state is deeply interested in political stability and security of the Afghan people, and, thus, wanted to resolve contradictions by peaceful, political-diplomatic means."[62] During the talks issue of promoting the construction of infrastructural projects like TAPI was also given due consideration to which Defense Minister Mullah Mohammad Yaqoob of the Taliban-led interim government assured the Turkmen side that they will "spare no effort" in ensuring the security of infrastructure projects like TAPI.[63] Although the project TAPI has been marred by many political, economic and security-related complications, however, Turkmenistan is pushing hard for its completion.

**The Republics of Kazakhstan and Kyrgyzstan** do not share their physical borders with Afghanistan. They reacted comparatively slowly to the 2021 events in Afghanistan than Uzbekistan, Turkmenistan and Tajikistan.

Initially, the Kazakh Government declined to engage extensively with the new Taliban regime. Their major concern was the safety of their embassy in Kabul and the diplomats over there. The government also insisted on establishing an inclusive government in Kabul. Seemingly, Kazakhstan and Kyrgyzstan followed the Russian lead under the Collective Security Treaty Organisation (CSTO) platform to deal with the crisis.[64] However, later, representatives of both countries (separately) met the Taliban leaders and rendered their support to deal with the humanitarian crisis in Afghanistan. Kyrgyzstan's high-level delegation to Kabul interacted with the Taliban officials on September 23, 2021, and expressed their support to have a friendly relations with them and assured that they will not interfere in the internal matters of Afghanistan.[65] Similarly, on September 9, 2021, Kazakh President Mr. Kassym—Zhomart Tokayev stated that his country is ready for establishing business contacts with the new Afghan authorities. He, further, stated that it is very important "that Afghanistan should become a stable, sovereign and united state, living in peace with itself and its neighbours … for that it is imperative to solve the acute humanitarian crisis there".[66] With a package of 500-kilo medical products for humanitarian assistance, a Kazakh delegation led by the trade and integration minister visited Afghanistan to discuss trade, transit routes and other economic cooperation between the two countries.[67] Clearly, though both the countries do not share their physical borders with Afghanistan, but cannot remain unaffected from the threats and challenges an unstable Afghanistan could pose. Therefore, above-mentioned Central Asian countries have tried to contribute towards the humanitarian crisis that emerged in the country post-US withdrawal on individual basis and are trying to engage them.

However, **Tajikistan** has taken a very hardline stance toward the Taliban. Tajikistan shares an extensive mountainous border with Afghanistan which is very difficult to control. It is also a transit stop for most of the drug-traffic from Afghanistan to Russia and Europe. It should also be taken into account that in the late 1990s, Tajikistan was a key supporter of the Northern Alliance in Afghanistan, which was fighting the Taliban. There is a considerable population of ethnic Tajiks in Afghanistan. Thus, unlike other Central Asian countries, Tajikistan did not rush to establish its ties with the Taliban, rather it took a very critical view. Tajik President Emomali Rahmon condemned the Taliban-led Government for failing to form an inclusive government and he remained very vocal about Afghanistan's misfortunes under the Taliban. He stated that "Tajikistan will not recognize any other government formed in this country formed through oppression and persecution, without taking into account the position of the entire Afghan people, especially all of their national minorities".[68] He, in fact, awarded the prestigious Order of Ismoli Somoni (country's highest award) posthumously, to ethnic Tajik leaders Ahmed Shah Massoud and former President of Afghanistan Burhanuddin Rabbani.[69] These gestures underscored Tajikistan's resolve to resist establishing official relations with the Taliban regime. Moreover, there were persistent rumours also that Tajikistan has provided tacit support to the National Resistance Front of Afghanistan, led by Ahmad Massoud (son of Ahmed Shah Massoud).[70]

There are multiple factors that drive Tajikistan's critical stance toward the Taliban. For instance, Tajikistan, being the cradle of Tajik identity, for President Rahmon, it could be a moral obligation to support ethnic Tajiks in Afghanistan. By being the Taliban's toughest critic, the situation has allowed the President to strengthen ethno-nationalism in the country[71] and win people's support. Further, President Rahmon was able to gather a lot of international spotlight. He was invited by the French President Emmanuel Macron to France. During his visit on October 13, he got assurances from the French President of possible assistance as the country was dealing with the aftermath of the Taliban takeover of Afghanistan.[72] He also met with President of the European Council Charles Michel, the EU's foreign affairs chief Josep Borrell, and other international officials during the same trip and discussed about the security issues on Tajik-Afghan border.[73]

The above discussion highlights the different stands adopted by the CARs towards the current Afghan regime on the basis of their national interests. However, a coordinated regional approach was missing which could have given them substantial leverage while dealing with Afghanistan. The major powers who have always been interested in the region due to their strategic location once again have been trying to make a play for the region.

## US, Taliban and Central Asia: Quest for Military Bases

Ever since the announcement of the US troops withdrawal from Afghanistan by September 11, 2021 (that also marked the 20th anniversary of the attacks on the twin towers and Pentagon), there were speculations that the US was exploring options to reposition some of its bases in Central Asia. It was reported by the *Wall Street Journal* that with the increasing pace of the drawdown, the US military commanders wanted new bases around the region not only for their troops to support the Afghan government but also to keep the Taliban insurgency in check and monitor other extremist organisations.[74] Similar reports were published in the New York Times that as the withdrawal of the US forces proceeds ... "the Pentagon, American spy agencies and Western allies are refining their plans to deploy a less visible but still potent force in the surrounding areas as a part of their wider counter-terrorism and surveillance strategy".[75] To achieve the objective, the report highlighted that "drones, long-range bombers and spy networks could be used (in case they are required) in an effort to prevent Afghanistan from re-emerging as a terrorist base to threaten the United States".[76] The report also affirmed that the Pentagon was in talks with the authorities of the republics of Kazakhstan, Uzbekistan, and Tajikistan, regarding the repositioning of their forces.[77] Moreover, the US Secretary of State Antony Blinken called up Kazakhstan's Deputy Prime Minister and Foreign Minister Mukhtar Tileuberdi[78] and Uzbekistan's Foreign Minister Kamilov[79] on April 22, 2021, ahead of their virtual meeting under the C5+1 framework. Following these calls and the virtual meeting on April 23, 2021, Zalmay Khalilzad, the US special representative for Afghanistan reconciliation paid a visit to Uzbekistan and Tajikistan in May 2021. Though it was not made clear that the base access was discussed during his visit, but it could be inferred from this increased US engagement that it was trying to form a new narrative for its policy towards the region.

This was certainly a more obvious option for the US as it has military bases in the region earlier also (from 2001-2014) Today, the geo-political configuration in the region is quite different. A lot has changed, specifically, Russia and China's position in the region has strengthened manifold and at the same, their relationship with the US has sharply deteriorated. Second, this time the Central Asian leadership directly engaged with the

Taliban leaders and are negotiating to make peace deals. They are now better prepared to militarily resist the Taliban threat. Third, out of the five CARs, three could be considered as viable countries to have US military bases, i.e., Tajikistan, Kyrgyzstan and Uzbekistan. However, Uzbekistan's defence doctrine does not allow to have foreign military bases on its territory and Tajikistan and Kyrgyzstan Tajikistan and Kyrgyzstan are the members of Russian-led CSTO and any presence of foreign troops on their territories has to be endorsed by the security pact.[80] Besides, none of the CARs had shown their keenness for the same.[81]

## Russian and Chinese Concerns in Central Asia vis-à-vis the Taliban

As the Taliban forces took charge of Afghanistan, Russia's security presence in Central Asia and diplomatic involvement in Afghanistan grew rapidly. Russia's main concern was to ensure the Taliban preventing extremists from causing problems in the Central Asian region, especially in Tajikistan. It was also concerned about the presence of self-proclaimed Islamic State (IS) and other organised groups and what if they start targeting Central Asia and Russia itself again.

Second, Russia fears about the uncontrolled weapon transfers to the Taliban and the threat of extremists among the refugees crossing into Central Asia and drug-trafficking.[82] Consequently, Russia increased its military presence in the region. Though it already had military bases in Tajikistan and Kyrgyzstan. Its 201st Military Base in Tajikistan is considered to be the largest military base in a foreign country, with about 7,000 troops, 96 tanks, eight helicopters, five ground attack aircraft, and many other military pieces of equipment.[83] Its military base in Kyrgyzstan is 20 km east of the capital, Bishkek which is hosting Russian Air Force units since 2003.[84] Keeping in mind the emerging threat perceptions from Afghanistan, Russia wants to further improve its military bases there. Although it is supporting the militaries of Central Asian countries with various activities like joint military exercises, arms sales, training and assistance programmes, etc., but it is eager to strengthen the combat readiness of its military bases in Tajikistan and Kyrgyzstan.[85]

Meanwhile, Russia was also apprehensive about US intentions of relocating its military facilities to Central Asia. President Putin objected to any role for the US forces in CARs, when he met his US counterpart, President Biden on June 16. In this context, his Deputy Foreign Minister, Sergei Ryabkov made it clear that "Russia do not see how any form of U.S. military presence in Central Asia might enhance the security of the countries involved and/or of their neighbours. It would definitely NOT be in the interests of Russia".[86]

Similarly, China would also not like to see the return of US bases in Central Asia. Though in the early 2000s, China's concerns about Taliban support for Xinjiang-based separatist and extremist groups impelled China to view the US efforts as fitting to its own security interests, but since then China's relations with the US have deteriorated sharply. Beijing now sees the US presence in Afghanistan as an attempt to contain China's regional ambitions. Therefore, Beijing will oppose America's military expansion to Central Asia—a critical region for its westward push.[87] For China, Central Asia is a buffer zone between instability in Afghanistan and Xinjiang. Though it is considered as one of the leading economic players in Central Asia but to protect its investments in the region and protect the region from becoming a safe haven for Uighurs, China is gradually expanding its security footprints in the Central Region. Initially, China has developed security cooperation with CARs through regional organisations like SCO. But lately, it was reported that China has built a military outpost in Tajikistan with facilities in the country's mountainous Gorno-Badakhshan province near the Afghan border.[88] Similarly, it has expanded its military exercises with the CARs, has transferred surveillance technologies to Central Asian cities and its private security companies have also increased their activities to protect China's Belt and Road Initiative infrastructure projects.[89]

With respect to the Taliban takeover of Afghanistan, while the Chinese did not expect it to happen so quickly, but they did a quick reset of their Afghan policy and adopted a cautious and pragmatic approach. China has not recognised the Taliban-led Afghan government yet, but assured that "China will push for reconciliation and reconstruction in Afghanistan with respect and at the request of the Afghan people".[90]

Considering the above-mentioned factors, the Taliban takeover in Afghanistan enhances the prospects for cooperation between Russia, China and CARs. Amidst this powerplay, the CARs have got enough to manoeuvre with their independent approach towards the Afghan crisis. They have not only adopted a cooperative attitude towards the major players in their proximity, but are also reaching out to other regional players like, India, Iran, Japan, South Korea, Pakistan, etc. to continue with their long-standing balancing acts. Here, India figures prominently in the security calculus of Afghanistan vis-à-vis Central Asian Republics.

## Plausible cooperation between India and Central Asia Post August 2021

Afghanistan is one of the key areas of cooperation between India and CARs, where they have major stakes. The developments in Afghanistan after the withdrawal of US troops presents new challenges and risks to the security and stability of both, at the same time both are concerned about the subsequent humanitarian crisis. Recognising their shared views and concerns, i.e., the formation of a truly representative and inclusive government, preserving the rights of women, children and other minority groups, combatting terrorism and drug-trafficking, the central role of the UN and providing immediate humanitarian assistance to the Afghan people, India hosted three back-to-back summits with the CARs.

- 3rd meeting of the India-Central Asia Dialogue at Foreign Ministerial level on December 19, 2021.
- 3rd edition of the Delhi Regional Security Dialogue on Afghanistan at the National Security Advisor level, where among others representatives of all the five CARs participated.
- 1st India-Central Asia Summit at the Head of the States level on January 27, 2022.

One of the purposes behind holding these summits was to build a regional consensus on the emerging situation in Afghanistan. There was a unanimous recognition among all about the need to address the mounting economic and humanitarian crisis in Afghanistan and help the Afghan people. Although, there are no easy/early solutions for this problem but regular discussions and consultations among the stakeholders are very necessary to find means and ways to help Afghanistan. All the above three back-to-back summits between India and CARs can be seen through this prism.

Though like the rest of the international community, India has not recognised the Taliban regime, but, it has shown solidarity for the people of Afghanistan by joining the efforts to respond to the crisis. For instance;

- India has embarked US$ 26.7 million to Afghanistan.[91]
- In December 2021, India sent a consignment of two tonnes of medicine as a part of its humanitarian assistance to Afghanistan.[92]
- India supported United Nations Security Council's resolution to grant exemption from sanctions for humanitarian assistance to Afghanistan.[93]
- India has committed to deliver 50,000 metric tonnes of wheat through multiple consignments for the Afghan people. So far four consignments have been delivered.[94]

Though these little gestures are too little to consolidate India's position in Afghanistan because of its limited relations with the Taliban. Hence, by engaging with other regional actors, India can work out a strategy to get the Taliban to work on a more inclusive government. However, the possibility of such an outcome is a wait-and-watch game.

## Conclusion

The rapid takeover of Afghanistan by the Taliban has shocked the whole world and Central Asia is no exception. Concerns over the security and stability of the region, porous borders, uncontrolled migration etc. pose serious challenges for the Central Asian governments. Since, the CARs were dealing with the presence of the Taliban in Afghanistan and the threat of their presence in Afghanistan over the past thirty years, so they are trying to deal with them pragmatically. Their policies towards Afghanistan have evolved over the past three decades and the geopolitical landscape of the region and the security situation has considerably changed. Also, in the present context, geo-economics has taken a precedence over geopolitics. As brought out earlier in the paper with regards to China and Russia. Russia as a security provider and contributor of the Central Asian economy through remittances, while China as the leading economic partner and investor in physical infrastructure for its own Belt and Road Initiative are the major player in the region. However, as a part of their diversification strategy CARs are trying to engage with the Taliban to get access to the South Asian markets as Afghanistan provides them with the opportunities for trade and transit routes connecting Central and South Asia. Thus, it is in the best interest of all the CARs to have a stable Afghanistan.

## Notes

1. Central Asian Republics include-Republic of Kazakhstan, the Kyrgyz republic, Tajikistan, Turkmenistan and Uzbekistan constitute five Central Asian Republics.
2. Nargis Kassenov, "Kazakhstan's Policy toward Afghanistan", in Amin Saikal and Kirill Nourzhanov (eds), *Afghanistan and its Neighbours after the NATO Withdrawal*, Lexington Books, London, 2016, p. 100.
3. Poonam Mann. "Taliban at the Doorstep of Central Asia", *Strategic Analysis*, vol. XXV, no. 1, April 2001, pp. 139-142.
4. Poonam Mann, "Religious Extremism in Central Asia", *Strategic Analysis*, vol. XXV, no. 9, December 2001, pp. 1029-1044.
5. Poonam Mann, "Central Asia: From Islamic Revivalism to Extremism", *World Focus*, vol.23, no. 1, January 2002, pp. 15-16.
6. Reuel R. Hanks, "Uzbekistan, Afghanistan, Desecuritization, and Regional Security", in Amin Saikal and Kirill Nourzhanov (eds), *Afghanistan and its Neighbours after the NATO Withdrawal*, Lexington Books, London, 2016, p. 88.
7. Poonam Mann," The Role of Neighbours: Central Asian Republics", in Sreedhar (ed.), *Afghanistan in Transition*, Indian Council of World Affairs, New Delhi, 2003, pp. 62-73.
8. Nargis Kassenova, "Kazakhstan's Policy toward Afghanistan", in Amin Saikal and Kirill Nourzhanov (eds), *Afghanistan and its Neighbours after the NATO Withdrawal*, Lexington Books, London, 2016, p. 101.
9. "Declaration of Heads of Member States of SCO", *China Daily*, July 5, 2005, updated on June 12, 2006, at http://www.chinadaily.com.cn/china/2006-06/12/content_6020345.htm. Accessed on January 16, 2016.
10. Daniel Kimmage, "Central Asia: SCO –Shoring Up The Post-Soviet Status Quo", July 8, 2005, at https://www.rferl.org/a/1059771.html. Accessed on January 16, 2016.
11. Turkmenistan pursues the policy of 'permanent neutrality' hence is not a member of SCO.

12. Jim Nicole, "Central Asia: Regional Developments and Implications for U.S. Interests", Congressional Research Service (CRS) Report for Congress RL 33458, March 21, 2014, pp. 65-66, at https://sgp.fas.org/crs/row/RL33458.pdf. Accessed on July 15, 2021.
13. Ibid., pp. 67-68.
14. Andrew C. Kuchins, et al., "The Northern Distribution Network and the Modern Silk Road: planning for Afghanistan's Future", Centre for Strategic and International Studies, Washington DC, December 2009, pp. 8-9, at https://csis-website-prod.s3.amazonaws.com/s3fs-public/legacy_files/files/publication/091217_Kuchins_NorthernDistNet_Web.pdf. Accessed on July 15, 2021.
15. "Pak stops NATO supplies after raid kills 28", November 26, 2011, at https://www.news18.com/news/india/pak-stops-nato-supplies-after-raid-kills-28-422566.html. Accessed on July 15, 2021.
16. Nicole, n. 11, p. 71.
17. For details see, Hamed Saboori, "Kazakhstan's role in Afghanistan's reconstructions", *The Daily Outlook Afghanistan*, September 15, 2014, at http://outlookafghanistan.net/topics.php?post_id=11071. Accessed on July 17, 2021; Nargis Kassenova, "Relations Between Afghanistan and Central Asian States after 2014: Incentives, Constrains and Prospects", Stockholm International Peace Research Institute (SIPRI), Sweden, May 2014, at https://www.sipri.org/sites/default/files/files/misc/SIPRI14wcaNK.pdf. Accessed on July 20, 2021.
18. Johan Norberg and Erika Holmquist (eds), *ISAF's withdrawal from Afghanistan: Central Asian Perspectives on Regional Security*, Conference Report, Almaty, May 22-23, 2013, p. 19.
19. For details see, UN Office on Drugs and Crime (UNODC), "Opiate Flows Through Northern Afghanistan and Central Asia: A Threat Assessment", UNODC, Vienna, 2012.
20. Azamjon Issabaev, "Uzbekistan and Afghanistan—security challenges post-2014", in Johan Norberg and Erika Holmquist (eds), *ISAF's withdrawal from Afghanistan—Central Asian perspectives on regional security* (Conference Report, Almaty May 22-23, 2013), June 2014, at file:///C:/Users/HP/Downloads/FOIR3880%20(2).pdf. Accessed on August 1, 2021.
21. Timothy A. Krambs, "Central Asia and Afghanistan Security Dilemma: Amelioration, Retrograde, or Status Quo? Central Asia's role in Regional Security Regarding Afghanistan after 2014", *Connections*, Vol. 12, No. 2, Spring 2013, pp. 10-11.
22. Igor Rotar, "Can Ashgabat Reconcile Kabul with the Taliban?", *Eurasia Daily Monitor*, vol. 11, issue. 69, April 11, 2014, at http://Jamestown.org/program/can-ashgabat-reeconcile-kabul-with-the-taliban/. Accessed on August 1, 2021.

23. Dante Schulz, "Turkmenistan's Deviated Approach to the Taliban Explained", September 8, 2021, at https://www.caspianpolicy.org/research/security-and-politics-program-spp/turkmenistans-deviated-approach-to-the-taliban-explained-13229. Accessed on December 12, 2021.
24. Murat Laumulin, "Regional efforts of the Central Asian states Regarding Afghanistan", in Johan Norberg and Erika Holmquist (eds), *ISAF's withdrawal from Afghanistan—Central Asian perspectives on regional security* (Conference Report, Almaty, May 22-23, 2013), June 2014, p. 70.
25. Kirill Nourzhanov, "Russia's Afghanistan Policy after 2014—Staying at an Arm's Length and Preparing for the Worst", in Amin Saikal and Kirill Nourzhanov (eds), *Afghanistan and its Neighbors after the NATO Withdrawal*, Lexington Books, London, 2016, pp. 163-164.
26. Ibid., p. 164.
27. Ibid., pp. 165-166.
28. Alexander Cooley, *Great Games, Local Rules: The new Great Power Contest in Central Asia*, Oxford: Oxford University Press, 2012, p. 4.
29. "US wins support from China", October 19, 2001, at https://edition.cnn.com/2001/WORLD/asiapcf/east/10/19/bush.jiang.apec/index.html. Accessed on August 13, 2021.
30. Chein-peng Chung, "China's War on Terror: September 11 and Uighur Separatism", *Foreign Affairs*, vol. 81, no. 4, July-August 2002, p. 10.
31. Cooley, n. 28, p. 81.
32. Justyna Szczudlik—Tatar, "China's Evolving Stance on Afghanistan: Towards More Robust Diplomacy with Chinese Characteristics", No. 28 (58), October 2014, at https://www.files.ethz.ch/isn/184324/PISM%20Strategic%20File%20no%2022%20(58).pdf. Accessed on September 12, 2021.
33. "Tajikistan Holds Massive Combat-Readiness Check Amid Rising Instability in Neighbouring Afghanistan", July 22, 2021, at https://www.rferl.ofg/a/tajikistan-readiness-drill-afghamistan/31371522.html. Accessed on August 1, 2021; "Turkmenistan: As Taliban arrives at the gates, diplomats and army scramble", *Akhal-Teke: A Turkmenistan Bulletin*, July 13, 2021, at https://eurasianet.org/Turkmenistan-as-taliban-arrives-at-the-gates-diplomats-and-army-scramble. Accessed on August 31, 2021.
34. Catherine Putz, "With Eyes on Afghanistan, Russian Military Exercises in Central Asia", *The Diplomat*, August 4, 2021, at https://thediplomat.com/2021/08/with-eyes-on-afghanistan-russian-military-exercises-in-central-asia/. Accessed on September 5, 2021; "Russia-led-bloc concludes drills near Afghan border to boost Tajik security", October 24, 2021, at https://www.reuters.com/world/asia-pacific/Russia-led-bloc-concludes-drills-near-afghan-border-boost-tajik-security-2021-10-23. Accessed on December 12, 2021; Laura Zhou, "China

conducts anti-terror drill with Tajikistan, as Afghan spillover worries grip Central Asia", *South China Monitoring Post*, August 18, 2021, at https://www.scmp.com/news/china/diplomacy/article/3145532/china-conducts-anti-terror-drill-tajikistan-afghan-spillover. Accessed on August 31, 2021.

35. Vladimir Isachenkov, "Russian envoy expects Taliban not to threaten Central Asia", Associated Press, July 14, 2021, at https://apnews.com/article/europe-government-and-politics-russia-asia-central-asia-0b42f13a960bfbcca0fc448243cf42c4. Accessed on August 31, 2021; "Uzbek Foreign Minister Discusses Cooperation With Taliban Leaders", October 8, 2021, at https://www.rferl.org/a/uzbek-foreign-minister-taliban/31499921.html. Accessed on October 10, 2021; "As Tajikistan mobilizes 20,000 troops, Taliban says it poses no threat", July 6, 2021, *Eurasianet*, at https://eurasianet.org/as-tajikistan-mobilizes-20000-troops-taliban-says-it-poses-no-threat. Accessed on October 8, 2021.
36. Navbahor Imamova, "Uzbekistan Conference attracts Global Interests in Central Asia", July 20, 2021, at https://www.voanews.com/a/south-central-asia_uzbekistan-conference-attracts-global-interest-central-asia/6208490.html. Accessed on October 29, 2021.
37. Bruce Pannier, "Then and Now: Concerns about a Taliban-led Afghan Spillover into Central Asia", July 12, 2021, at https://www.rferl.org/a/taliban-central-asia/31354914.html. Accessed on September 2, 2021.
38. CSTO intends to strengthen the borders of Central Asia with Afghanistan, August 24, 2021, *News Central Asia*, at http://www.newscentralasia.net/2021/08/24/csto-intends-to-strengthen-the-borders-of-central-asia-with-afghanistan/. Accessed on September 2, 2021.
39. "Russian bombers & Spetsnaz train in Afghan border drills with Uzbekistan & Tajikistan, as Taliban advances", August 7, 2021, at https://www.rt.com/russia/531427-afghanistan-border-military-drills/. Accessed on September 2, 2021.
40. "Tajikistan Holds Massive Combat-Readiness Check Amid Rising Instability In Neighbouring Afghanistan", July 22, 2021, at https://www.rferl.org/a/tajikistan-readiness-drill-afghanistan/31371522.html. Accessed on August 1, 2021.
41. "President Emomali Rahmon Visits Border Detachments in Panj and Mir Said Ali Hamadoni Districts", *KHOVAR—National Information Agency of Tajikistan*, July 16, 2021, at https://eng.khovar.tj/2021/07/president-emomali-rahmon-visits-border-detachments-in-panj-and-mir-said-ali-hamadoni-districts/. Accessed on August 1, 2021.
42. Laura Zhou, "China conducts anti-terror drills with Tajikistan as Afghan spillovers worries grip Central Asia", *South China Morning Post*, August 18, 2021, at https://www.scmp.com/news/china/diplomacy/article/3145532/china-conducts-anti-terror-drill-tajikistan-afghan-spillover. Accessed on September 9, 2021.

43. "Turkmenistan: As Taliban arrives at the gates, diplomats and army scramble", *Akhal-Teke: A Turkmenistan Bulletin*, July 13, 2021, at https://eurasianet.org/turkmenistan-as-taliban-arrives-at-the-gates-diplomats-and-army-scramble. Accessed on August 31, 2021.
44. Umida Hashimova, "Greater Coordination in Central Asian Responses to Afghan Border Troubles", *The Diplomat*, July 19, 2021, at https://thediplomat.com/2021/07/greater-coordination-in-central-asian-responses-to-afghan-border-troubles/. Accessed on August 9, 2021.
45. Mihra Rittmann and Huge Williamson, "Uzbekistan should do more to help Afghans", Human Rights Watch, September 8, 2021, at https://www.hrw.org/news/2021/09/08/uzbekistan-should-do-more-help-afghans. Accessed on October 20, 2021; Navbahor Imamova, "Right Groups fear for Safety of Defecting Afghan Pilots", September 1, 2021, at https://www.voanews.com/a/south-central-asia_rights-groups-fear-safety-defecting-afghan-pilots/6210239.html. Accessed on October 20, 2021.
46. "U.S. Military Withdrawal and Taliban Takeover in Afghanistan: FAQs", *CRS Report*, September 17, 2021, at https://crsreports.congress.gov/product/pdf/R/R46879, pp 52-53. Accessed on October 20, 2021.
47. Ibid.
48. UN statement on temporary relocation of the UNAMA staff to Almaty", Press Release, August 20, 2021, at https://kazakhstan.un.org/en/140984-un-statement-temporary-relocation-unama-staff-almaty. Accessed on October 20, 2021.
49. " Kyrgyzstan to issue 500 student visas as humanitarian assistance for Afghanistan—national security chief", AKI Press, August 16, 2021, at https://akipress.com/news:661509:Kyrgyzstan_to_issue_500_student_visas_as_humanitarian_assistance_for_Afghanistan_-_national_security_chief/. Accessed on October 20, 2021.
50. "Turkmenistan: Taliban of Brothers", Akhal Teke—A Turkmenistan Bulletin, August 24, 2021, at https://eurasianet.org/turkmenistan-taliban-of-brothers. Accessed on August 31, 2021.
51. Jonathan Meyer, "Forceful Displays and Soft Rhetoric: Central Asia's Response to Developments in Afghanistan", *Foreign Policy Research Institute*, August 25, 2021, at https://www.fpri.org/article/2021/08/forceful-displays-and-soft-rhetoric-central-asias-response-to-developments-in-afghanistan/. Accessed on March 30, 2022.
52. "Central Asia refuses to accept Afghan Refugees", Institute for War and Peace Reporting (IWPR), September 8, 2021, at https://iwpr.net/global-voices/central-asia-refuses-accept-afghan-refugees. Accessed on March 30, 2022.
53. "Uzbekistan says has no grounds to host Afghans awaiting U.S. visas", Reuters, July 22, 2021, at https://www.reuters.com/world/asia-pacific/uzbekistan-says-has-no-grounds-host-afghans-awaiting-us-visas-2021-07-22/. Accessed on September 9, 2021.

54. n. 52.
55. "Central Asian Countries are not open to accept Afghan Refugees", CABAR, September 3, 2021, at https://cabar.asia/en/central-asian-countries-are-not-ready-to-accept-afghan-refugees. Accessed on September 21, 2021.
56. Avaz Yuldashev, "Tajikistan says it will not be able to accept massive flow of Afghan Refugees", Asia-Plus, September 2, 2021, at http://www.asiaplustj.info/ru/news/tajikistan/politics/20210902/Tadzhikistan-zayavil-chto-ne-smozhet-prinyat-massovii-potok-afganskih-bezhentsev. Accessed on September 21, 2021.
57. Georgi Gotev, "Foreign Minister: Uzbekistan is promoting 'pragmatic relations' with Afghanistan", November 15, 2021, at http://www.euractiv.com/section/global-europe/interview/foreign-minister-uzbekistan-is-promoting-pragmatic-relationss-with-afghanistan/. Accessed on December 24, 2021.
58. Ibid.
59. Bruce Pannier, "Uzbekistan Has Good Reasons To Be On Good Terms With The Taliban", September 23, 2021, at http://www.rferl.org/a/Uzbekistan-taliban-business-relations/31474600.html. Accessed on September 30, 2021.
60. Fabio Indeo, "Turkmenistan's ambivalent foreign policy towards Afghanistan", CABAR, July 29, 2021, at https://www.cabar.asia/en/Turkmenistan-s-ambivalent-policy-towards-afghanistan-taliban-advance-and-rising-instability-along-the-shared-border. Accessed on September 30, 2021.
61. TAPI is Turkmenistan-Afghanistan-Pakistan-India Gas Pipeline project.
62. "A visit of the Government Delegation of Turkmenistan to Afghanistan", Ministry of Foreign Affairs of Turkmenistan, October 30-31, 2021, at https://www.mfa.gov.tm/en/news/2866. Accessed on November 16, 2021.
63. Ibid.
64. Richard Weitz, "Central Asia's Taliban Surprise", September 16, 2021, at https://www.mei.edu/publications/central-asias-taliban-surprise. Accessed on October 20, 2021.
65. Bruce Pannier, "Kazakhstan, Kyrgyzstan open channels with the Taliban", October 1, 2021, at httpss://www.gandhara.rferl.org/a/Kazakhstan-kyrgyzstan-taliban/31487601.html. Accessed on October 20, 2021.
66. "Kazakhstan ready for business contacts with new Afghan authorities—Tokayev", September 9, 2021, at http://Interfax.az/view/844505. Accessed on October 20, 2021.
67. "Kazakhstan Delegation visits Kabul to discuss Trade, Cooperation with Taliban", December 25, 2021, at httpss://www.rferl.org/a/Kazakh-trrade-delegation-visits-kabul/3162607.html. Accessed on January 12, 2022.
68. "Meeting with Minister of Foreign Affairs of the Islamic Republic of Pakistan Makhdoom Shah Mahmood Qureishi", President of the Republic of Tajikistan, August 25, 2021, at http://www.prezident.tj/ru/node/26368/lakhsh. Accessed on November 1, 2021.

69. "Signing of Executive Order on awarding Order of Ismoili Somoni to former Minister of Defense of the Islamic Republic of Afghanistan, National Hero of Afghanistan Ahmad Shah Massoud", September 2, 2021, President of Republic of Tajikistan, at https://www.president.tj/en/node/26473. Accessed on November 1, 2021 and "Signing of Executive Order on awarding Order of Ismoili Somoni to former President of Afghanistan Burhanuddin Rabbani", September 2, 2021, President of Republic of Tajikistan, at https://www.president.tj/en/node/26472. Accessed on November 1, 2021.
70. Temur Umarov, "Why Tajikistan is Taking a Stand Against the Taliban", *The Moscow Times*, October 26, 2021, at https://www.themoscowtimes.com/2021/10/26/why-tajikistan-is-taking-a-stand-against-the-taliban-a75413
71. Mélanie Sadozaï, "Taliban at the border: A new Regime Neighboring Tajikistan", Central Asia Programme, October 22, 2021, at https://centralasiaprogram.org/taliban-border-regime-neighboring-tajikistan. Accessed on November 10, 2021.
72. "France's Macron Hosts Tajik Leader For Talks On Afghanistan", Agence France Presse, October 13, 2021, at https://www.barrons.com/articles/france-s-macron-hosts-tajik-leader-for-talks-on-afghanistan-01634129707. Accessed on October 20, 2021.
73. Ana-Maria Anghelescu, "Tajik President Emomali Rahmon's European Tour", *The Diplomat*, October 26, 2021, at https://thediplomat.com/2021/10/tajik-president-emomali-rahmons-european-tour/. Accessed on October 26, 2021.
74. Vivian Salama *and* Gordon Lubold, "Afghan Pullout Leaves U.S. Looking for Other Places to Station Its Troops", *The Wall Street Journal*, May 8, 2021, at https://www.wsj.com/articles/afghan-pullout-leaves-u-s-looking-for-other-places-to-station-its-troops-11620482659. Accessed on May 12, 2021.
75. Eric Schmitt and Helene Cooper, "How the U.S. Plans to Fight from Afar After Troops Exit Afghanistan", *The New York Times*, April 27, 2021, at https://www.nytimes.com/2021/04/15/us/politics/united-states-al-qaeda-afghanistan.html. Accessed on April 29, 2021.
76. Ibid.
77. Ibid.
78. "Secretary Blinken's Call with Kazakhstan Deputy Prime Minister and Foreign Minister Tileuberdi", US Department of State, April 22, 2021, at https://www.state.gov/secretary-blinkens-call-with-kazakhstan-deputy-prime-minister-and-foreign-minister-tileuberdi/. Accessed on May 10, 2021.
79. "Secretary Blinken's Call with Uzbekistan Foreign Minister Kamilov", US Department of State, April 22, 2021, at https://www.state.gov/secretary-blinkens-call-with-uzbekistan-foreign-minister-kamilov/. Accessed on May 10, 2021.
80. Vladimir Isachenkov, "Russia against US troops in Central Asia near Afghanistan", July 13, 2021, at https://apnews.com/article/joe-biden-government-and-politics-

russia-europe-afghanistan-b1cc3ba07b4ebcdaa44a7af69ea3f90c. Accessed on August 8, 2021.

81. Ibid.
82. Paul Stronski, "Forget Schadenfreude, what does the Kremlin Really Think About Afghanistan", August 30, 2021, at https://carnegieendowment.org/2021/08/30/forget-schadenfreude-what-does-kremlin-really-think-about-afghanistan-pub-85230. Accessed on September 21, 2021.
83. Vusala Abbasova, "Russia Pledges Military Assistance to Central Asian Allies", Caspian News, July 31, 2021, at https://caspiannews.com/news-detail/russia-pledges-military-assistance-to-central-asian-allies-2021-7-31-0/. Accessed on September 21, 2021.
84. Ibid.
85. Ibid.
86. Michael R Gordon, "Putin Rejected Role for US forces Near Afghanistan at Summit with Biden", *The Wall Street Journal,* August 19, 2021, at https://www.wsj.com/articles/putin-rebuffed-u-s-plans-for-bases-near-afghanistan-at-summit-with-biden-11629398848. Accessed on September 21, 2021.
87. Emil Avdaliani, "Russia, China, and the Prospects of US Military Bases in Central Asia", August 12, 2021, at https://chinaobservers.eu/russia-china-and-the-prospect-of-us-military-bases-in-central-asia/. Accessed on September 21, 2021.
88. Asim Kashgarian, "China, Russia working together on Security Threats in Central Asia", October 27, 2021, at https://www.voanews.com/a/china-russia-working-together-on-security-threats-in-central-asia/6288233.html. Accessed on November 1, 2021; also see, Reid Standish, "From A Secret Base in Tajikistan, China's War on Terror Adjusts To a New Reality", October 14, 2021, at https://gandhara.rferl.org/a/tajikistan-china-war-on-terror-afghan/31509370,.html. Accessed on October 20, 2021.
89. Ibid.
90. Stefanie Kam, "The fall of Taliban and its implications for China, *East Asia Forum*, September 21, 2021, at https://www.eastasiaforum.org/2021/09/21/the-fall-of-afghanistan-and-its-implications-for-china/. Accessed on September 23, 2021.
91. "India looking forward to a long-lasting cooperation with Afghanistan", Khaama Press, February 5, 2022, at https://www.khaama.com/op.ed-india-looking-forward-to-a-long-lasting-cooperation-with-afghanistan-98763/. Accessed on March 18, 2022.
92. Nayanima Basu, "India sends medicine to Afghanistan, Taliban says 'thank you', relations very vital", *The Print*, December 12, 2021, at https://www.theprint.in/diplomacy/india-sends-medicines-to-afghanistan-taliban=says-thank-you-relations-very-vital/780341/. Accessed on March 18, 2022.

93. "India supports UNSC resolution to grant exemption from sanctions for humanitarian assistance to Afghanistan: TS Trimurti", *The Times of India,* December 23, 2021, New Delhi.
94. "India sends fourth consignment of 2,000 MTs of wheat to Afghanistan", *The Print,* March 15, 2021, at https://www.theprint.in/world/india-sends-fourth-consignment-of-2000-mts-of-wheat-to-afghanistan/874744/. Accessed on March 18, 2022.

# 14

# Is India's 'Net Security Provider' Status in the Indian Ocean Region Shrinking?

JOSHY M PAUL

> "... while to other countries the Indian Ocean is only one of the important oceanic areas, to India, it is a vital sea. Her lifelines are concentrated in that area, her freedom is dependent on the freedom of that water surface. No industrial development, no commercial growth, no stable political structure is possible for her unless her shores are protected.... The Indian Ocean must therefore remain truly Indian." (K.M. Panikkar )*

> "India is strategically located vis-à-vis both continental Asia as well as the IO Region.... The seas surrounding India have been a theatre of superpower rivalry in the past, and continue to be a region of heightened activity from and by extra-regional navies on account of global security concerns." (Annual Report of Ministry of Defence, 2004)**

The Indo-Pacific region is going to be the contested zone for dominance in the 21st century. It has two parts—the eastern and western—the former is the western Pacific in which a US-China rivalry is undergoing, while the western part is the Indian Ocean where a Sino-Indian competition could take place sooner rather than later. With its sophisticated anti-access and

* K.M. Panikkar, *India and the Indian Ocean,* Allen and Unwin, London, 1945, p. 84.

** Ministry of Defence, "Annual Report 2003-2004", Government of India, p. 9, at https://www.files.ethz.ch/isn/155965/India%20%202004.pdf. Accessed on October 10, 2021.

area denial capability, China has been able to push the war theatre beyond the first island chain which includes East China and South China Seas.[1] It is now consolidating its dominance in the South China Sea and expanding its power influence into the Indian Ocean. China's Indian Ocean strategy is to dominate the ocean by taking ownership of economic activity and guaranteeing the security of the waterbody. This would marginalise India's status as a 'net security provider' in the Indian Ocean Region (IOR). This is in consonance with Chinese President Xi Jinping's "China Dream" project through which China is seeking to emerge as a "true maritime great power (MGP)" by the middle of the century when China celebrates the centenary of the establishment of the People's Republic of China (PRC) in 2049.[2] At that time it might attempt to ensure that its surrounding seas and the waterbody it depends on for energy and trade interests are the Chinese's oceans. In this regard, its actions targeting the Indian Ocean will affect Indian interests because the Indian Ocean is critical to India's energy and trade lifelines.

Chinese President Xi Jinping's "China Dream" of national rejuvenation, which he announced in 2012 and was elaborated on at the First Session of the 12th National People's Congress in March 2013, envisioned that China should emerge as a 'true maritime power' with a strong navy and a moderately prosperous nation by the middle of the century.[3] Although his predecessor, Hu Jintao, had set the platform for converting China into a maritime power, Xi has sought the maritime power concept in an assertive and expanded manner. This includes creating artificial islands in the disputed South China Sea SCS, lingering friction with other disputants such as Japan, the Philippines, and Vietnam, challenging the US supremacy in the East China Sea and the South China Sea, and giving 'open seas protection' mandate for People's Liberation Army Navy (PLAN). Xi's MGP strategy is comprehensive and has been expanded in all areas and "is being used to embolden China's economic philosophy and, in conjunction with other national-security goals, to project a vision of future national greatness".[4]

Ever since Xi took over as the Chinese President in 2013, China's national security strategy has undergone a significant transformation. You Ji argues that Xi has been "instrumental in changing China's passivity into an assertive strategy" to protect China's claims.[5] Xi Jinping pointed out that "building a maritime power was an integral part of China's socialist undertaking because the importance of the sea had become more apparent with respect to developing the national economy, improving ecosystems, and competing for international politics".[6] Under Xi, China is on the cusp of transforming from traditional land power into a maritime power and the initiatives such as the 21st century Maritime Silk Road (MSR), the maritime component of Xi's grand strategy of the Belt and Road Initiative (BRI) can be seen as an important pillar of Xi's China 'dream' project. At the 19th National Congress of the Chinese Communist Party held in October 2017, President Xi announced that China would invest as much as US$ 900 billion over 10 years in infrastructural development, across the whole of the IOR.[7] Through the MSR China is building ports and other infrastructures which can be used as strategic assets for China during a crisis. Importantly, PLA Navy will secure access to berthing facilities along with the MSR ports, leading to a Chinese permanent naval presence in IOR.

Today Chinese navy is the largest in the world in terms of tonnage and are more ships on the production line. Its naval ships construction spree started along with China's "going out" strategy in the previous decade. It had 216 ships in 2005 that increased to 348 in 2021, according to the latest Congressional Service Report.[8] The new inventory into the Navy has sped up since Xi came to power. For instance, between 2014 and 2018, China launched more submarines, warships, amphibious vessels, and auxiliaries than the number of ships currently serving in the individual navies of Germany, India, Spain, and the United Kingdom.[9] China commissioned 18 ships into its armoury in 2016 alone and another 14 were inducted in 2017, while US Navy commissioned only 5 and 8 ships respectively during the same period.[10] There has been a major transformation during this period from a regional and technologically-inadequate navy to one that is global, upgraded, and capable of multiple missions far from China's ports. Its current destroyers are technologically at par with the US Navy's, the only area in which China is lagging behind the US is the aircraft carrier.[11] The latest series of nuclear-armed submarines have the capabilities to contribute to PLAN's missions of anti-submarine warfare (ASW), nuclear deterrence, and power projection. China has increased its nuclear submarine building facilities and the new facility can produce one SSN a year and one SSBN every two years—meaning there will be eight more SSNs and about four more SSBNs by 2030.[12] "By 2030, it is estimated that the PLAN will consist of some 550 ships: 450 surface ships and ninety-nine submarines".[13] Certain Chinese scholars argue that "China should consider deploying two oceangoing fleets, centred around aircraft carriers—[sic] the Pacific fleet and the Indian Ocean Fleet."[14]

In 2018, China launched the world's largest destroyer, Type 055 class destroyer with a displacement capacity of over 11,000 tonnes, demonstrating China's technical capability in building advanced systems and its blue-water naval capabilities.[15] The Type 055 class destroyer is expected to perform major command and control functions in far seas operations and will likely serve as the primary escort of China's aircraft carrier strike groups in blue-water operations.[16] Since then China has launched five such destroyers which are under various stages of operational requirements.[17] China launched its second aircraft carrier, indigenously-built Type-001A Shandong, in April 2017, which underwent maiden sea trials the following June, and was commissioned in December 2019.[18] The *Shandong* can operate up to 36 Shenyang J-15 fighters, a Chinese copy of the Sukhoi Su-33, as well as several helicopters.[19] It usesa ski-ramp to launch aircraft and participated for the first time in an exercise in the South China Sea (SCS) in May 2021.[20] The first one *Liaoning* is originally a Soviet cruiser carrier, retrofitted by China and launched in 2012, with *Shandong* PLAN has become a true two-carrier navy.[21] A third, larger, vessel is also under construction, and Beijing's long-term carrier plan has generated considerable sources of concern across the globe. As per various reports, China plans to build a fleet of somewhere between four and ten by 2030.[22] This suggests that at least one aircraft carrier can make its presence in the Indian Ocean throughout the year, it would be more if China were to go for higher numbers, making China a formidable military power in the IOR. With this expected force level, it is believed that China would be able to project its power beyond the second island chain by 2030/35, to satisfy the force required to satisfy Xi's "Chinese Dream" of rejuvenation of the Chinese nation by 2049.

With the expansionist propensity towards the Indian Ocean, PLAN has been given the right to 'protect' Chinese MSR assets in distant ocean spaces. Termed it as "far seas protection" operations for the PLAN, the 2015 Defence

White Paper calls for the need to "develop a modern maritime military force structure commensurate with its national security and development interests, safeguard its national sovereignty and maritime rights and interests, protect the security of strategic SLOCs (sea lanes of communication) and overseas interests, and participate in international maritime cooperation, to provide strategic support for building itself into a maritime power".[23] Quite obviously, the geographical area denotes as "far seas" is the Indian Ocean where PLAN has been mandated to exercise "offshore waters defence" activities.[24] PLAN will be a 'strategic force' in the Indian Ocean with multifarious activities which include; protection of Chinese assets (MSR), search and rescue operations, humanitarian assistance and disaster relief (HADR) operations, anti-piracy operations, UN peacekeeping operations, and above all will facilitate China's military strategy of "strategic deterrence and maritime counterattack."[25] PLAN's real military role would indeed evolve as and when a crisis emerged either in East Asia over Taiwan Strait or in the Indian Ocean area itself such as prevention of the SLOCs by rivals or security crisis in a littoral state in which Beijing expects the Chinese Navy should be the first foreign force to be providing security assistance for the home country. Chinese Navy's larger and permanent presence in the IOR risks the Indian Navy's manoeuvrability in its home waters and also will render the 'net security provider' status insignificant.

## China's Indian Ocean Strategy for Strategic Dominance

For many reasons, China would not be able to perform the same kind of military (naval) dominance in the IOR as it seeks to establish in the "near seas" which include the Yellow Sea, the East China Sea, and the South China Sea. Near Seas are the primary areas of security concern for China, and the defence capabilities that have been developed are to protect coastal areas and the adjacent waters, i.e., the near seas. And its immediate rival is the United States, superior power to China in all formats. Also, China is far from a free-rider on neighbourhood diplomacy, its territorial disputes with the neighbouring countries in the East and South China Seas can disrupt its far seas ambitions. Besides, the Senkaku/Diayou problem hinders Beijing from seeking full-fledged naval dominance in the western Pacific. Even if China settles the Taiwan problem in its favour and US failed to intervene in support of Taiwan, it will not be acceptable to Japan. So, diverting naval capabilities from the western Pacific to the Indian Ocean for full-spectrum dominance is a risky matter for China. Of course, PLAN is pursuing to become a two-ocean navy, but it will face significant challenges from the Indian, Australian and US Navies in the Indian Ocean. In this respect, the Chinese strategy has been seeking to get strategic dominance in the Indian Ocean than military dominance.[26]

Strategic dominance has multiple dimensions. Getting strategic dominance in a particular region means that the dominant power has no rival from that region to hurt its interests. It ensures a favourable regional order which caters to unfettered military access across the region both in times of peace and in crisis. It would help to get a controlling stake over resources the region trades with itself and other countries. Also, the regional countries' economic dependence on the dominant power increases because it will be the main source of finance, both as a major investor and a trade facilitator. Eventually, it contributes to better economic and security cooperation between them and the dominant power. The Chinese strategy is to secure access to ports in strategic locations to gain an economic and strategic advantage during peacetime as well as in a conflict. China's military dominance of the Indian Ocean water is highly unlikely due to distance and China's inadequate military capability to become a full-fledged two-ocean navy. At the same time, the Chinese strategic dominance of the IOR is very much imperative for securing its energy and trade interests, especially during a China-US military confrontation over Taiwan in the western Pacific. Beijing's major worry is preventing its SLOCs from rival powers during a crisis in East Asia. The US or Indian dominance of the Indian Ocean would severely cripple China's economic and security interests during a war in East Asia. In this regard, deterring others' dominance of the Indian Ocean is a major part of China's "open seas protection" strategy. For that it seeks to emerge as a predominant naval power in the Indian Ocean or no rival power, regional like India or extra-regional like the US and its allies, to dominate the ocean and challenge Chinese commercial as well as security interests in the region. For China, instead of a full spectrum of military dominance, its strategy is to establish a strategic dominance in the Indian

Ocean and for that, it has adopted two methods; asset accumulation, and naval expansionism.

## China's Asset Accumulation in the IOR

When China became a net importer of oil in 1993, its concern over the protection of the SLOCs became a major security issue because more than 80 per cent of its hydrocarbon had to traverse through the Indian Ocean and to cross the narrow Malacca Strait where it had no stake on it. This concern was amply raised by Chinese President Hu Jintao in 2003 noting that "certain powers have all along encroached on and tried to control navigation through the [Malacca] Strait."[27]As the energy security concern topped the security calculation in China's Indian Ocean strategy, Beijing sought to acquire assets and bases in the Indian Ocean littorals, popularly known as "String of Pearls" and major pearls in this asset/bases strategy were Gwadar in Pakistan, Hambantota in Sri Lanka, and Chittagong in Bangladesh. China planned to build dual-use ports, commercial ports which can be used for anchoring naval ships, in these countries who were expected to become China's close partners as the investment relationship progressed. However, the strategy received pushback from India and other major powers across the globe and questioned the motivation behind the new strategy as they believed it was China's military expansionist strategy toward the Indian Ocean region.[28] However, Bangladesh gradually withdrew from giving its territory to Chinese-made ports, while China continued its agenda with Gwadar and later Hambantota.

With the MSR strategy China forcefully pursued its asset accumulation in the IOR and this time it expanded to all corners as well as most of the littoral countries. Like the erstwhile powers, the Portuguese, the Dutch, and the British, Beijing is pursuing the imperial model of acquiring assets at strategic locations along the trade routes in distant waters which would allow Beijing to get a firm foothold in the waterbody. Without having a dominant position in the Indian Ocean, China would remain as an East Asian power only, far away from the great power of the 21st century. Indeed, as an emerging great power, it cannot rely on others for protecting trade interests concerning the Indian Ocean. It requires berthing facilities for the Chinese naval ships to make a permanent presence in the IOR and some of the MSR assets would facilitate the basing requirements of the PLAN. A dominance in waterbody and control of the land trade route under the Silk Road connectivity to the European theatre China could emerge as an 'unparalleled' great power—a continental-cum-maritime great power—by the middle of the 21st century.[29] Xi's China dream is a 'Eurasian great power' with a strong maritime footprint in three waters—western Pacific, Indian Ocean, and the Mediterranean Sea—by the middle of the 21st century.[30]

In the Indian Ocean region, certain Chinese investments are a continuation of the previous ones under the "string of pearls" strategy. However, the MSR projects are comprehensive in nature, helping the host country to overcome its infrastructure bottlenecks and to become part of a China-led new international order. China has specifically focused on countries whose locations and political systems are suited for China: democratic countries tend to follow transparency and accountability for foreign investments, while semi-authoritarian governments rely on the regime's image.[31] Hardly few countries are purely democratic in the region, like India, instead, most of them are authoritarian or semi-democratic with authoritarian tendencies.[32] The countries that have joined the MSR from the Indian Ocean littorals are Pakistan, Sri Lanka and Myanmar in the northern Indian Ocean; Djibouti, Yemen, Oman, Kenya, Tanzania and Mozambique in the western Indian Ocean; the Seychelles and Madagascar in the central south Indian Ocean, and island states of Sri Lanka and the Maldives in the middle. This has helped China to establish its presence in all parts of the Indian Ocean region. Major projects being undertaken by China in these countries are the China-Pakistan Economic Corridor ($62 billion) in Pakistan; in Sri Lanka, in the form of Hambantota port and $6.8 billion worth of infrastructure projects; for Bangladesh, $1.03 billion worth of investment by 2018, and has committed another $7 billion for 27 infrastructure projects; in Myanmar, $9 billion China-Myanmar Economic Corridor (CMEC), Kyaukphyu port of $1.3 billion; and a $10 billion port project at Bagamoyo, Tanzania as well multipurpose port projects in Kenya (Lamu) and Djibouti (Doraleh) connected with rail and road towards other countries of the East African region.

The Chinese strategy is to create a Chinese economic region centred on ports which are mostly at strategic locations in the Indian Ocean region.

Like the erstwhile colonial powers who ruled the ocean by controlling the entry points, China has also attempted to get a stake in the entry points to the Indian Ocean. Beijing had earlier planned to build a $14 sea port-cum—city development project at Melaka Gateway in Malaysia, on the entry point from east to the Indian Ocean, which is now cancelled by the local government in November 2020.[33] Chinese projects in Djibouti, a multipurpose port at Doraleh, and a naval base at Obock, are important as it stands at the entry point from the west, and also the mouth of the Indian Ocean up to the Mediterranean Sea, so that it can monitor both the narrow but busy trade routes. Hambantota and Feydhoo Finolhu are closer to the busy trade routes crossing the Indian Ocean. Beijing has recently stepped up the pace of MSR investments in East Africa. According to Beijing-based China-Africa Business Council (CABC) report released in September 2021 Chinese investments in Africa grew from $2.71 billion in 2019 to $2.96 billion in 2020, while cumulative investment increased from $210 million in 2000 to $47 billion in 2020.[34] Recently, Tanzania has decided to revive the Chinese proposal of a $10 billion port project at Bagamoyo, a move that would greatly enhance China's strategic presence in the western Indian Ocean.[35] Given the demand for foreign investment for infrastructure improvement and economic growth, Tanzania might allow China to build its second naval base in Africa. With the footholds in the entry points and strategic locations in the Indian Ocean region, China would get more strategic leverage than any other country, even for the largest resident power India.

In most cases, however, the economic viability of this magnitude of investment is highly questionable because it is dependent entirely on Chinese investments in the economic region.[36] Similarly, MSR ports will have to compete with either existing ports, such as Singapore, Colombo and Dubai, or with other Chinese ports to make each port commercially viable. For instance, the Melaka Gateway project in Malacca Strait will have to compete with other MSR ports, such as Kuantan as well as Singapore, which is currently the world's busiest transhipment hub. Similarly, Hambantota port is close to the busiest East-West trade route but has to compete with the busiest Colombo port, and has not emerged as a big transhipment hub, despite China holding the port ownership. Besides, the major source of export from the region is not industrial products, like in East Asia, but energy and other natural resources, and for that, the region does not require so many ports. Certain port projects are economically unviable at any cost, however, China is keen to not only keep these projects under their hold but are ready to pump more money into them. The pattern of Chinese investments in Sri Lanka is a case in point that after spending almost $1.5 billion for the Hambantota port project, the commerciality of the port became abysmally low, even though it is only 10 nautical miles from one of the world's busiest shipping lanes.[37] Notably, the lease amount of $1.12 billion which has been infused into the Hambantota project was used to bolster the country's foreign reserves, not to pay off China Exim bank, which means that China has virtually written off the debt.[38] Similarly, in the case of Chinese investments in CPEC, it was reportedly said that "Chinese officials were admitted privately that they expect to lose 80 per cent of their investments in Pakistan".[39] The reason for the Chinese commitment to continue the investment as well as taking control of ports in the Indian Ocean region has been China's strategic motivation to continue these countries closer to Beijing. Also, ports at the strategic locations offer Beijing "a front-row seat to spy on rival navies", such as Indian, American, and Australian naval operations.[40] With the investments in port 'assets', China is trying to strengthen its relationship with Myanmar, Pakistan, Bangladesh, Sri Lanka, Maldives, Tanzania and Mozambique in a bid to counter India in the Indian Ocean region. However, except for Pakistan and Myanmar, which are traditionally political allies of China, other countries are 'hedging' their relationship between India and China for their economic gains.[41]

## China's Naval Expansionism towards the Indian Ocean

China's first overseas naval expedition as well as the first overseas deployment was to the Indian Ocean, showing Beijing's long-term ambitions set out decades ago for expanding its dominance up to the third island chain.[42] When the Chinese military was weak it had sought to ensure that no rival power dominate the Indian Ocean and it provided its support for the regional countries' demand for declaring the Indian Ocean as a 'zone of peace' at the United Nations.[43] However, as China became militarily powerful and its trade and other economic interests expanded, it envisioned to reach out to the distant waters to make its naval power felt like a strong maritime nation.

When Xi became the president of China he identified naval assertiveness in the regional waters and expansionism towards the distant waters are the primary component of demonstrating China's maritime power capability. This was also inconsonant with Liu's island chains strategy that between 2010 and 2020 China should have established its naval dominance between the second and third island chains.[44] This suggests that China is on the cusp of expanding its naval dominance from the near seas to the far seas.

China began to execute its assertiveness in the maritime domain during the latter part of the first decade of the 21st century when it came to the conclusion that following the 2008 financial crisis the United States would not get back its glory as it had enjoyed during the unipolar moment. US' capacity to influence the outcome across the globe is waning, thus generating an opportunity for China to carve out its sphere of influence in the East. Since China had shed its continental security strategy long back for being a naval power, it now realised that the maritime area is vast and open to establishing its dominance as no regional power has the capacity to challenge Chinese power. It has gradually upped the ante in maritime territorial disputes and even sometimes used its armed guards to seize the islands in the South China Sea. It has created artificial islands in the SCS which would help it put legal claims over the entire SCS as China's Exclusive Economic Zone (EEZ). Besides, it has militarised these artificial islands and set up hangars for fighter aircraft, fixed-weapons positions, barracks, administration buildings, and communication facilities in other Paracel island groups in the SCS.[45] The largest islands in both the Spratlys and Paracels are now capable of deploying advanced fighter aircraft and surface-to-air and anti-ship cruise missiles.[46] Undoubtedly, China's dominance of the South China Sea is almost over, it faces little resistance from the regional states, while has kept external powers at bay from involving territorial disputes in the SCS.

The Chinese naval supremacy in the East Asian waters is almost certain. Its anti-access area-denial (A2/AD) capability is a proven system to deter the US forces' advancement towards the land and also could prevent reinforcement of US troops in the western Pacific.[47] It has reduced the gap with the US Navy both in quantitative and qualitative terms and is now predominant if not absolute naval power in the western Pacific. For the US, its priority is to protect its homeland from the threat of China rather than focusing on its preponderance and hegemony in the western Pacific. This has emboldened China for taking an assertive position against its regional rivals, both small and big, and seeking to establish its order in East Asia. China is using varied techniques short of military confrontation in the East Asian waters to intimidate other regional navies and signalling that the cost will be unbearable if they were to confront the Chinese navy. It also uses 'maritime militias' known as the People's Armed Forces Maritime Militia (PAFMM), a government-supported armed fishing force operating under the patronage of the Chinese Coast Guard and PLA Navy in the SCS—to scare away the fishermen of other countries.[48] This shows that China's consolidation of the South China Sea is real and complete without using regular force thus avoiding military confrontation with other disputants in the region. This can be a template for China to establish its dominance in other waters, especially in the Indian Ocean.

China has eyed its dominance in the Indian Ocean with the 'far seas protection strategy', and building a two-ocean navy. The expansionist and offensive nature of the strategy was demonstrated in the *Science of Military Strategy*, a blue book of China's defence first published in 2002, while the 2013 edition explains that in future China's navy will "elevate offence from the campaign and tactical levels to the strategic level."[49] It further says, China "cannot wait for the enemy to attack," but rather should engage in "strategic attack activities."[50] Indeed, the "open seas protection" strategy is the last stage of PLAN's gradual expansion from the coastal navy into a world-class navy capable of undertaking missions in faraway regions. As an emerging great power, China shows that it is capable of deploying its naval force for security missions in faraway regions. According to the 2015 white paper the PLAN has been tasked to "safeguard its national sovereignty and maritime rights and interests, protect the security of strategic SLOCs and overseas interests, and participate in international maritime cooperation, to provide strategic support for building itself into a maritime power".[51] China claims that its deployment of naval force in the Indian Ocean has been to protect its MSR assets and to secure the ocean from piracy and other non-traditional security threats, apart from the military doctrine of 'deterrence and counter-attack'.[52]

China's first-ever overseas naval deployment mission was to the Indian Ocean in 2008 to participate in the anti-piracy operations in the Gulf of

Aden. China claimed that the naval deployment was a cooperative exercise of a responsible power dealing with an international security issue and worked with other international groupings such as the United States established Combined Task Force 151 (CTF-151), NATO's Operation Allied Protector, and the European Union organised Operation Atalanta, under the United Nations Security Council Resolution 1851, which encouraged member states to take a more active role in fighting pirates off the coast of Somalia.[53] China viewed international security cooperation as a medium to show its capabilities as well as projecting its naval strength to the outside world. At the same time, China's naval deployment in the Indian Ocean was the culmination of long-term strategy experimented with in a gradual manner; formulating policies, creating domestic awareness for projecting the need for a blue water navy, and a full-fledged power projection. For instance, the 2004 white paper suggested the requirement for 'defensive' operations in the external waters by extending the maritime 'strategic frontier' from the near seas to the far seas with "expanding the space and extending the depth for offshore defence operations".[54] The 2006 defence white paper had provided the Navy for conducting "independent operations" and emphasised "enhancing PLAN's capabilities for integrated maritime operations" in distant waters.[55] It also highlighted the need for PLA Navy to an increased role in China's international cooperation. The naval deployment was projected with great fanfare in China as a show of military strength, for instance, on the day the Chinese mission was launched, Wu Shengli, commander of the PLAN, announced, "It's the first time we go abroad to protect our strategic interests armed with military force."[56]

Though the piracy was faded away by 2012 as a result of the increased naval deployment of various navies, China continued its deployment albeit vigorously. According to the statistics of Atlanta, piracy was almost completely eradicated by 2012: while 176 attacks were recorded in 2011, there were only 35 in 2012, and after that only two unsuccessful piratical activities, one in 2017 and another one in 2019.[57] On the other hand, the PLA Navy has been continuously deploying two to three vessels throughout the year in the Gulf of Aden.[58] Since 2009 China has been sending a minimum of three task forces to the Indian Ocean region every year, and each task force will have a minimum of three ships; a guided-missile destroyer, a missile frigate, and a supply vessel, and spend 3-4 months for the escort operations in the Indian Ocean.[59] In 2017, 14 ships were deployed for anti-piracy operations in the Indian Ocean, and between 2015 and 2019, there were six submarines in China deployed for the same purpose.[60] According to former Indian Navy chief Admiral Sunil Lamba, "at any given time there are six to eight PLAN warships in the northern Indian Ocean", which are "permanently present and they have three to four survey vessels or hydrographic vessels".[61] China is considering the anti-piracy operations to gain far seas experience and to enhance its power projection capability and for that, it has deployed advanced naval ships and nuclear submarines, though nuclear submarines are unsuited for such operations, Chinese officials referred to as a "combat readiness patrol," or "blue-water training," in the Indian Ocean.[62] China has multiple objectives in its deployment of naval ships to the Indian Ocean: certain deployments are training exercises for the crew in the far seas area; some are for nontraditional security purposes, while some are to give political signals to its adversaries that China is a formidable power in the IOR. For instance, it dispatched a fleet of two Type 052D destroyers, a 054A frigate, and a 071 dock landing ship to the Indian Ocean in February 2018 as part of the 'Blue 2018 A' exercise, which was held amid the political stalemate going on in the Maldives.[63] The Type 052D destroyer is considered the Chinese equivalent to the American AEGIS destroyer and will be the primary escort ship for the Chinese carrier strike group.[64] China has been deploying all its advanced systems in the Indian Ocean to get acclimatisation for its crew in the region and also gather domain awareness, necessary for military operations in distant waters, especially during a crisis period.

To enhance its presence in the Indian Ocean and avoid infrastructure bottlenecks for PLAN's longer deployment in the waters, China set up its first overseas naval at Obock, Djibouti in 2015. China claims that the Obock naval base, which became operational in 2017, is not a military base as such, but a "logistical support facility" for the PLAN, "mainly used to provide rest and rehabilitation for the Chinese troops taking part in escort missions in the Gulf of Aden and waters off Somalia, UN peacekeeping and humanitarian rescue"[65] Notwithstanding the Chinese claims, however, it can host around 2,000 military personnel, not only of the Navy but also the Army and particularly its special forces.[66] China has recently constructed a new 1,110-foot pier capable of accommodating an aircraft carrier, and also the facility is capable of handling the new Type 075 amphibious assault ship, which is being positioned at the core of China's land warfare capabilities.[67] Satellite imagery shows that the Djibouti naval base is a large military fortress where China has stationed "armoured vehicles such as ZBD-09 infantry fighting vehicles and ZTL-11 assault gun vehicles, armed with an array of automatic cannons, anti-tank missiles, and large-calibre guns".[68] Africa has become China's new destination for its BRI drive, with large investments in 'dual-use' ports, one on the Atlantic coast and another one on the Indian Ocean side. *Nikkei Asia* reported in June 2021 that China is mulling to set up its second naval base in the Indian Ocean at Bagamoyo in Tanzania, where the Tanzanian government has revived the $10 dollar port project with Chinese assistance, and the port may be used as a ship repair hub for the Chinese PLA Navy, "or perhaps even more".[69] With naval bases in Cambodia, Djibouti and Tanzania, China could overcome bottlenecks and the 'distant power dilemma' in the Indian Ocean, while these facilities would provide a strategic boost for China, it helps in the protection of the SLOCS, anti-piracy operations, enhances China's role in international peacekeeping, and can monitor the movements of rival navies.

## Implications for India

With the MSR China has built new kinds of alliances and partnerships aimed at enhancing Chinese power and prestige on political, economic, and diplomatic levels in the IOR area. Consistent with its maritime great power status, MSR will help China get a strategic dominance of the Indian Ocean, along with the East Asian waters. Chinese maritime power will be a combination of wider economic presence, strong political connections with the littoral countries, and enhanced military capabilities across the Indo-Pacific region. China's interests in the Indian Ocean are not just to protect its trade routes and energy supplies but to become a major source of economic activity, and security guarantor in the IOR. The Chinese capital will accelerate local industrialisation and economic advancement of regional countries, as China has been engaged in bilateral infrastructure projects, trade, and investment cooperation with them, and also it can tap its huge domestic market.[70] China's billions of dollars of investments in the littoral countries will increase their exports, and Chinese shipping companies are going to carry such products through the Indian Ocean to the outside world. This means that China is going to be the financier, producer, carrier of goods, and a major source of market for these countries. In case of any crisis to this economic activity in the waters of the Indian Ocean happens, China would be the natural choice as a guarantor of the trade. Similarly, the BRI participants from the IOR are mostly low or middle-income countries that badly needed foreign capital and trade opportunities to sustain their economies. With a large number of investments in these countries, China can manipulate its choices of foreign policies of them at various multilateral forums, including at the United Nations. This will enhance China's naval presence as a 'legitimate stakeholder' in the security of the Indian Ocean region. Taking ownership of the economic activity in and around the Indian Ocean would help China move away from an East Asian power to a trans-Oceanic power in the Indo-Pacific.

Western scholars have opined about the India-China competition is going to take place in the 21st century in the Indian Ocean for dominance in the waterbody. However, the actual competition between the two is to be to win over the smaller island countries because their strategy and relationship with India and China would determine who would have more sway in the strategic dynamics of the IOR. Both India and China are providing financial aid and assistance to the smaller island countries, while they act smartly to receive the benefits from both sides. The hedging strategy that these smaller countries are pursuing is to gather great advantages for them as they are able to manage their independence, and not become a vassal states despite a large amount of BRI money is being pumped into these countries by China. When they found a crisis in their relationship with China they turn to India. In October 2021, Sri Lanka awarded West Container Terminal (WCT) in the sprawling Colombo port to India's Adani Group in a Public-Private Partnership at the cost of $700 million, adjoining the Chinese-operated Colombo International Container Terminal (CICT).[71]

Undoubtedly, Beijing is emerging as an additional and perhaps an alternate security provider for the Indian Ocean littoral countries. Chinese naval ships could be the first vessel to be called on in a security crisis that happened in littoral countries as PLAN ships are being widely deployed across the Indian Ocean. At the same time, large Chinese naval deployment for the protection of its BRI 'assets' and trade interests would lead to friction with the Indian Navy in the future over 'area of operations' as PLAN ships may come closer to India's Exclusive Economic Zones, constraining Indian Navy's manoeuvrability in its backyard. China has already demonstrated its intention to test the Indian Navy's resolve to counter the PLAN in the Indian Ocean in an incident that happened in the eastern Indian Ocean in December 2019 when the Chinese research ship, *Shiyan-1*, was caught operating in the waters around Port Blair until the Indian Navy expelled it.[72]

It is highly unlikely that China could establish a full-spectrum military dominance in the Indian Ocean. The distance, strategic priorities, and naval capabilities prevent China for an East Asian model for the IOR. Instead, it would follow the South China Sea style of slow and steady escalatory tactics to deny Indian dominance in the Indian Ocean. As a distant power, China requires formal military bases and alliances in the Indian Ocean littorals for a full spectrum dominance of the water body. However, the regional countries are averse to providing their soil for the military purpose for China as it would hurt their relationship with the largest neighbour India. Similarly, even though PLAN has achieved blue-water naval capability, its strategic force arsenals lack depth both in terms of quantity and quality to project power as a counterforce beyond the second island chain. China operates a small number of nuclear-powered attack submarines (SSNs) and a small number of nuclear-powered ballistic missile submarines (SSBNs), most of China's submarines are non-nuclear-powered attack submarines aimed at securing the near seas.[73] Even if China could settle the Taiwan problem in its favour, still it would not be able to shift its arsenals to the Indian Ocean because China could see another formidable challenger in Japan. Even if the US would not allow China to become a free rider in East Asia, the US is enhancing its capability to deter China locally.

With the asset accumulation in the IOR, China is seeking a legitimate stakeholder position in the IOR. A legitimate power status could counter the criticism of Chinese 'hegemonism' and 'expansionism' rhetoric in the PLAN's expansionism efforts to the Indian Ocean. If China establishes real military bases in the Indian Ocean then it would face strong pushback from littoral countries, while the sustained deployment of PLAN as a stakeholder could negate such anti-China sentiments. However, without adequate logistical support facilities, the Chinese Navy would face significant difficulty in its operations in the Indian Ocean. It requires reliable access to facilities in key points around the region to sustain its military operations in the IOR. It would be difficult for Chinese naval ships had to come back to Chinese facilities in East Asia for fuel and resupply. In this respect, it seeks cooperation with the littoral countries to get easy access for its naval vessels for its sustained naval presence in the Indian Ocean and BRI would facilitate such cooperation between China and the littoral countries. To this end, China has leased ports in strategic locations in the Indian Ocean including Kyaukphyu in Myanmar, Hambantota in Sri Lanka, Feydhoo Finolhu in the Maldives, Gwadar in Pakistan. Lamu in Kenya, Bagamoyo in Tanzania, and Doraleh and Obock in Djibouti. This is contrary to the US-style permanent facilities in the western Pacific. In the earlier case, 'string of pearl' was seeking approval for access for naval vessels, but the MSR focuses on port-centred economic development activity so that the targeted country will become interdependent on China, leaving less room for countervailing measures against China by rival powers. Zack Cooper of Washington-based CSIS posits, "China is following in the traditional path of other rising powers; it is expanding its military operations to match its interests abroad". These assets would help China "to refuel or resupply naval vessels and in terms of anti-piracy operations and familiarization with other regional militaries" in peacetime, while it will provide many "opportunities in terms of protecting trade routes, bases, and ships during wartime".[74]

With various strategic assets that China has set up in islands and littoral states, China is going to be a vital state in the economic activity, and security dynamics of the Indian Ocean region. Almost one-third of Chinese BRI investments are going to take place in the littoral area of the Indian Ocean region. Most of the countries that have joined the MSR are in dire need of investments for their infrastructure development as well as for exports to sustain their economy more competitive. With the MSR China has emerged as the main source of financial assistance for these countries' demand for money, which will make the relationship between China and the host countries closer. This will make the poor countries vulnerable to the Chinese pressure to take positions favouring China or prevent them from taking advantage of their rivals. China could use the "real estate" assets to either benefit them or can prevent others from taking advantage. With the MSR China seeks overall strategic leverage in the Indian Ocean as commercial 'assets' are the means to achieve strategic ends. The relationship between the recipient and the investor becomes stronger and the recipients' foreign policy may become a hostage for the investor's interests. In a way, Chinese strategic dominance in the Indian Ocean region is real and going to increase in the coming years.

China has been quietly creating its order without challenging the US, rather following the footsteps of the US but with modifications. West has used commercial tools such as foreign aid, export credits, and benevolent out-flow of capital to wield economic and political interests abroad. China also uses foreign aid and export credits, and a major objective of Chinese economic assistance is to gain strategic influence not only in one particular country but at the regional level. With the outflow of Chinese capital and trade connectivity that will help to establish China as an engine of regional development, the MSR recipient countries will become long-term reliable partners of China. This will provide China getting assistance from the friendly littoral countries for the PLAN during a crisis in East Asia.

As a result, the Chinese strategy to the IOR is to deny India of its 'net security provider' status and establish itself in that role in the region. Its naval ships are available throughout the year for security contingencies in and around the waterbody. As of now, Pakistan and Bangladesh have purchased naval systems which include submarines from China, while more countries would show interest to buy arms from China.[75] Though the acquisition is a purely commercial deal, China may use its financial strength by providing aid-cum-purchase mechanism to win friends from the region. China provided grants and loans of around $1 billion to Sri Lanka, which include arms and ammunition, during the final stages of its fight with the LTTE.[76] China is providing financial aid to countries like the Maldives and the Seychelles and Madagascar for various infrastructure projects to strengthen their cooperation with China. It could turn into military aid in the future as these countries face various types of non-traditional security threats. Also, the need to protect Chinese assets will legitimise increased PLAN deployment in the Indian Ocean, which will also provide security assistance for the regional countries on demand. As China enhances its economic and military presence in the Indian Ocean region, China would become the provider of 'public goods' in and around the IOR. This would ultimately render India's status as a 'net security provider' redundant.

## Policy Options for India

Besides strengthening its naval capabilities to emerge as a preponderant power in the IOR, India needs to activate as a 'leader', not as a facilitator, in the Indian Ocean region. India should consider the Indian Ocean region in three parts: The Bay of Bengal, The Island States, and the Gulf and Africa region. First, the current Bay of Bengal Initiative for Multi-Sectoral Technical and Economic Cooperation (BIMSTEC) needs to be strengthened by an enhanced focus on economic and security agendas. India must take a proactive step to strengthen the Bay of Bengal sub-regional cooperation in the name of, such as, 'Bay of Bengal Economic Community' comprising the eastern part of the Indian Ocean states through enhanced economic and security cooperation, which will ensure a bulwark against China's expansionism to the Indian Ocean region. India is not part of the two major regional groupings in Asia that have come into effect in recent times, which include Regional Comprehensive Economic Partnership (RCEP) and the Comprehensive and Progressive Agreement for Trans-Pacific Partnership (CPTPP), so a Bay of Bengal Economic Community will help to strengthen India's engagement with the Southeast Asian countries. Earlier ASEAN had objected to such a grouping as they wanted to keep ASEAN homogeneity intact, but now selected member countries have been joined in other sub-regional groupings which include Mekong Sub-regional Cooperation comprising southern provinces of China and Mekong river basin countries,[77] and the CPTPP, wherein only Singapore, Malaysia, Vietnam, and Brunei have joined. Like China gets the strategic leverage in peninsular Southeast Asia through the Mekong cooperation, India can effectively strengthen its position in the eastern Indian Ocean through a Bay of Bengal Economic Community.

Second, India needs to increase its engagement with the island states through bilateral aid, investment, and security assistance. New Delhi has already provided such assistance in the form of financial aid of $2 billion to the Maldives,[78] $100 million Line of Credit to Mauritius to help procurement of defence assets,[79] and joint investment in Sri Lanka's petroleum storage facility at Trincomalee[80] as well as the container terminal facility at the Colombo port.[81] On security matters, India must consider the IOR, not as a sub-region of the Indo-Pacific, but as much weight as given to the larger Indo-Pacific. Earlier, from 2011 to 2014, National Security Advisors of India, Sri Lanka and the Maldives met thrice on the security matters concerning the ocean, but abandoned for a while, then resuscitated in November 2020, where they discussed ways of enhancing maritime security cooperation in the Indian Ocean region (IOR).[82] Following the fifth deputy NSA level meeting in August 2021, the maiden '*Colombo Security Conclave* (CSC) *Focused Operation*' was conducted between the three navies on November 27 and 28, 2021.[83] At the deputy NSA level meeting, they identified "four pillars" of cooperation in Marine Safety and Security, Terrorism and Radicalisation, Trafficking and Organised Crime, and Cyber Security.[84] Like the Quad is being evolved from an official meeting to the summit level, the trilateral NSA meeting has to grow to the level of state heads so that larger security issues such as China's naval expansionism can be discussed, which would address India's concerns and leverage strategically.

Third, India has to promote a cooperative security framework for the western and north-western Indian Ocean area where other major powers' presence is strong. The US has naval bases in Bahrain and Diego Garcia, and France is a resident power, while UK, Germany and Russia are seeking increased presence in the region, and all are pursuing a strategic partnership with India. To strengthen New Delhi's bond with the West Asian and African countries, New Delhi pronounced SAGAR (Security and Growth for All in the Region) in 2015, and Asia-Africa Growth Corridor or AAGC with Japan in 2017 to counter the Chinese BRI along with the Indian Ocean littoral countries of Africa. This would boost India's economic presence in the region while engaging with other major powers will stabilise the security dynamics of the region.

## Notes

1. Congressional Research Service, "China Naval Modernization: Implications for U.S. Navy Capabilities—Background and Issues for Congress", May 21, 2020, at https://

assets.documentcloud.org/documents/6927913/China-Naval-Modernization-Implications-for-U-S.pdf. Accessed on October 21, 2021.

2. *China Daily*, "Structuring the Chinese Dream", January 25, 2014, at http://usa.chinadaily.com.cn/opinion/2014-01/25/content_17257856.htm. Accessed on November 10, 2021.
3. *China Daily*, "Chinese dream' is Xi's vision", March 18, 2013, at http://www.chinadaily.com.cn/china/2013npc/2013-03/18/content_16315025.htm. Accessed on November 24, 2021.
4. James R. Holmes and Toshi Yoshihara, "China's Navy: A Turn to Corbett?," U.S. Naval Institute *Proceedings* (December 2011), pp. 42-46, at https://www.usni.org/magazines/proceedings/2010/december/chinas-navy-turn-corbett. Accessed on December 2, 2021.
5. You Ji, " Deciphering Beijing's Maritime Security Policy and Strategy in Managing Sovereignty Disputes in the China Sea", *RSIS Policy Brief*, October 1, 2013, RSIS, NTU, Singapore, at https://www.rsis.edu.sg/rsis-publication/rsis/216-deciphering-beijings-maritime/#.XifmUdR97Gg. Accessed on November 30, 2021.
6. Kejin Zhao and Hao Zhang, "Projecting Political Power: China's Changing Maritime Strategy", *The Chinese Journal of International Politics*, vol. 12, no. 4, 2019, pp. 229-261.
7. Sukjoon Yoon, "Xi Jinping's Chinese Dream in the Indian Ocean Region: Time to Move beyond Outdated Maritime Strategies", in Jagannath P. Panda and Titli Basu, (eds), *China-India-Japanin the Indo-Pacific: Ideas, Interests, and Infrastructure,* Pentagon Press, New Delhi, 2018, p. 137.
8. Congressional Research Service, "China Naval Modernization: Implications for U.S. Navy Capabilities—Background and Issues for Congress", December 2, 2021, p. 7, at https://sgp.fas.org/crs/row/RL33153.pdf. Accessed on December 20, 2021.
9. CSIS China Power, "How is China modernizing its navy?", at https://chinapower.csis.org/china-naval-modernization/. Accessed on November 25, 2021.
10. "How is China Modernising its navy", CSIS China Power, September 1, 2021, at https://chinapower.csis.org/china-naval-modernization/. Accessed on November 28, 2021.
11. Jon Harper, "Eagle vs Dragon: How the U.S. and Chinese Navies Stack Up", National Defense, September 3, 2020, at https://www.nationaldefensemagazine.org/articles/2020/3/9/eagle-vs-dragon-how-the-us-and-chinese-navies-stack-up. Accessed on November 30, 2021.
12. Nick Danby, "China's navy looms larger", *Harvard Political Review*, October 5, 2019, at http://harvardpolitics.com/world/prcnavy/. Accessed on December 31, 2021.
13. James E. Fanell, "China's Global Naval Strategy and Expanding Force Structure: Pathway to Hegemony" *Naval War College Review*: vol. 72, no. 1, 2019, pp. 11-45.

14. Christopher Colley, "A Future Chinese Indian Ocean Fleet?" *War on the Rocks*, April 2, 2021, at https://warontherocks.com/2021/04/a-future-chinese-indian-ocean-fleet/. Accessed on July 31, 2021.
15. Rick Joe, "All You Need to Know About China's New Stealth Destroyer", *The Diplomat*, June 8, 2018, at https://thediplomat.co.m/2018/06/all-you-need-to-know-about-chinas-new-stealth-destroyer/ Accessed on July 31, 2021.
16. *The Week*, "China set to showcase game-changing warship at the navy parade", April 19, 2019, at https://www.theweek.in/news/world/2019/04/19/china-set-showcase-game-changer-warship-at-navy-parade.html. Accessed on July 31, 2021.
17. Franz-Stefan Gady , "China's Navy Commissions First-of-Class Type 055 Guided Missile Destroyer", *The Diplomat*, January 13, 2020, at https://thediplomat.com/2020/01/chinas-navy-commissions-first-of-class-type-055-guided-missile-destroyer/. Accessed on July 31, 2021.
18. *Business Standard*, "China's 1st indigenous aircraft carrier to be combat-ready by 2020: Report", October 27, 2020, at https://www.business-standard.com/article/international/china-s-1st-indigenous-aircraft-carrier-to-be-combat-ready-by-2020-report-120102701577_1.html. Accessed on July 26, 2021.
19. Greg Waldron, "Beijing commissions its second aircraft carrier", *Flight Global*, December 18, 2019, at https://www.flightglobal.com/defence/beijing-boosts-its-carrier-power-with-shandong-commissioning/135830.article. Accessed on August 31, 2021.
20 *Global Times*, "China's 2nd aircraft carrier group holds 1st drill in 2021 in S. China Sea, 'training for combat preparedness'," May 2, 2021, at https://www.globaltimes.cn/page/202105/1222578.shtml. Accessed on August 26, 2021.
21. *Global Times*, "Aircraft carrier Liaoning's latest voyage lays down foundation for enhanced night combat", August 8, 2021, at https://www.globaltimes.cn/page/202108/1230896.shtml. Accessed on August 20, 2021.
22. America's Indo-Pacific Command suggests that China will operate four carriers by 2025. British defence intelligence reckons that it may have as many as five by 2030. The expert consensus is that China plans eventually to build a fleet of somewhere between six and ten. For details, see *The Economist*, "China's next aircraft carrier will be its biggest", July 1, 2021, at https://www.economist.com/china/2021/07/01/chinas-next-aircraft-carrier-will-be-its-biggest. Accessed on December 20, 2021.
23. "China's Military Strategy 2015", Ministry of National Defence, People's Republic of China, Beijing, May 2015, at http://eng.mod.gov.cn/Database/WhitePapers/2015-05/26/content_4586713.htm. Accessed on December 21, 2021.
24. Shishir Upadhyaya, "Expansion of Chinese maritime power in the Indian Ocean: implications for India", *Defence Studies*, vol. 17, no. 1, 2017, pp. 63-83.
25. "China's Military Strategy 2015", n. 23.

26. Joshy M Paul, "China's Naval Strategy towards the Indian Ocean under Xi Jinping", *Air Power Journal*, vol. 16 no. 4, 2021 (October-December), pp. 99-120.
27. Marc Lanteigne, "China's Maritime Security and the 'Malacca Dilemma', *Asian Security*, vol. 4, no. 2, 2008, pp. 143-161.
28. Gurpreet S. Khurana, "China's 'String of Pearls' in the Indian Ocean and Its Security Implications. *Strategic Analysis*, vol. 32, no. 1, 2008, pp. 1-39.
29. Joshy M. Paul, "China's 'Marching West' Strategy: Creating a Eurasian Great Power", *Defence and Diplomacy*, vol. 10, no. 2, 2021, pp. 75-86.
30. Elizabeth Threlkeld, "China's Eurasian Ambitions: Ground Realities of Great-Power Competition", *Asia Policy*, vol. 15, no. 3, 2020, pp. 134-138.
31. Benjamin Barton, "Leveraging the "String of Pearls" for strategic gains? An assessment of the Maritime Silk Road Initiative's (MSRI) economic/security nexus in the Indian Ocean Region (IOR)" *Asian Security*, vol. 17, no. 2, 2021, pp. 216-235.
32. Ibid.
33. *Strait Times*, "Controversial Melaka port project scrapped by state govt", November 21, 2020, at https://www.straitstimes.com/asia/se-asia/controversial-melaka-port-project-scrapped-by-state-govt. Accessed on December 21, 2021.
34. *Xinhua*, "China's investment stock in Africa exceeds 47 bln USD" September 9, 2021, at http://www.news.cn/english/2021-09/09/c_1310178126.htm. Accessed on December 23, 2021.
35. *Nikkei Asia*, "China looks to East Africa for second Indian Ocean foothold", June 30, 2021, at https://asia.nikkei.com/Politics/International-relations/Indo-Pacific/China-looks-to-East-Africa-for-second-Indian-Ocean-foothold. Accessed on January 8, 2022.
36. Mathew and Jonathan Funaiole, "China's Maritime Silk Road Initiative: Economic Drivers and Challenges". *CSIS Briefs*. April 2, 2018, at https://csis-website-prod.s3.amazonaws.com/s3fs-public/publication/180717_FunaioleHillman_ChinaMaritimeSilkRoad.pdf. Accessed on January 10, 2022.
37. Abdul Rahman Shah, "China's Belt and Road Initiative: The Way to the Modern Silk Road and the Perils of Overdependence" *Asian Survey*, vol. 59, no. 3, pp. 407-428.
38. Deborah Brautigam and Meg Rithmire, "The Chinese 'Debt Trap' Is a Myth", *The Atlantic*, February 6, 2021, at https://www.theatlantic.com/international/archive/2021/02/china-debt-trap-diplomacy/617953/?utm_source=facebook&utm_medium=social&utm_campaign=share&fbclid=IwAR1zrlu1O18po26vLZfQFARDnlfvnKqHWQbtdPa8qqG0dB-kLX5vUNVEgu4. Accessed on January 15, 2022.
39. Shah, n. 37, p. 418.
40. Jane Perlez, "The US Casts Wary Eye on Australian Port Leased by Chinese" *New York Times*. March 20, 2016, at https://www.nytimes.com/2016/03/21/world/australia/china-darwin-port-landbridge.html. Accessed on January 14, 2022.

41. Darren Lim and Rohan Mukherjee, "Hedging in South Asia: balancing economic and security interests amid Sino-Indian competition", *International Relations of the Asia-Pacific*, vol. 19, no. 3, 2019, pp. 493-522.
42. China's first overseas naval expedition was to the Indian Ocean in November 1985, under the direct supervision of the then PLAN commander Admiral Liu Huaqing, see, Christopher D. Yung, et al., "China's Out of Area Naval Operations: Case Studies, Trajectories, Obstacles, and Potential Solutions", *China Strategic Perspectives, No. 3,* 2010, National Defense University Press, Washington, DC.
43. Gurnam Singh, "China and the Indian Ocean Region" *China Report*, vol. 20, no. 3, 1984, pp. 15-23.
44. As per Liu's island chain (first, second and third) strategy, China will be able to expand its influence gradually into "far sea" in three stages; "in the first stage, from 2000 to 2010, China was to establish control of waters within the first island chain that links Okinawa Prefecture, Taiwan and the Philippines. In the second stage, from 2010 to 2020, China would seek to establish control of waters within the second island chain that links the Ogasawara island chain, Guam and Indonesia. In the final stage, from 2020 until 2040, China would have to be able to exercise its naval power in the south Pacific and Indian Oceans, using aircraft carriers as a key component of its military force". For details, see, Stacy A. Pedrozo, " China's Active Defense Strategy and its Regional Impact", Council on Foreign Relations, January 27, 2010, at https://www.cfr.org/report/chinas-active-defense-strategy-and-its-regional-impact. Accessed on January 8, 2022.
45. Feng Zhang, "China's long march at sea: explaining Beijing's South China Sea strategy, 2009–2016", *The Pacific Review*, vol. 33. no. 5, 2020. pp. 757-787.
46. Asia Maritime Transparency Initiative, "China's new Spratly island defences", December 13, 2016, at https://amti.csis.org/chinas-new-spratlyisland-defenses/. Accessed on January 18, 2022.
47. "The China Syndrome", *The Economist*, June 9, 2012.
48 Gregory Poling, "China's Hidden Navy", *Foreign Policy*, June 25, 2019, at https://foreignpolicy.com/2019/06/25/chinas-secret-navy-spratlys-southchinasea-chinesenavy-maritimemilitia/. Accessed on January 8, 2022.
49. Shou Xiaosong, (ed.), *Science of Military Strategy*, Military Science Beijing, 2013, p. 107.
50. Ibid., p. 2016.
51. "China's Military Strategy 2015", The State Council Information Office of the People's Republic of China, Beijing, May 2015, at http://eng.mod.gov.cn/Database/WhitePapers/index.htm. Accessed on January 8, 2022.
52. Ibid.
53. Silvia Burke, "Explaining China's Participation in Anti-Piracy Operations in the Gulf of Aden", May 2009, MIT, at https://ocw.mit.edu/courses/political-

science/17-408-chinese-foreign-policy-fall-2013/assignments/MIT17_408F13_ExplinigChina.pdf. Accessed on January 12, 2022.

54. Information Office of the State Council of the People's Republic of China, "China's National Defense in 2004", December 2004, Beijing, at http://en.people.cn/whitepaper/defense2004/defense2004.html. Accessed on January 8, 2022.

55 Information Office of the State Council of the People's Republic of China, "China's National Defense in 2006", Beijing, December 2006, at http://en.people.cn/whitepaper/defense2006/defense2006(2).html. Accessed on January 8, 2022.

56 AFP "Chinese Navy Off on Historic Anti-Piracy Mission," *Space Daily*, December 26, 2008, at https://www.spacedaily.com/reports/Chinese_navy_off_on_historic_anti-piracy_mission_999.html. Accessed on January 8, 2022.

57. Shishir, n, 24; Combined Maritime Force (CMF), "CTF 151: Counter-Piracy," Combined Maritime Forces, December 2020, at https://combinedmaritimeforces.com/ctf-151-counter-piracy/. Accessed on January 13, 2022.

58. David Brewster, "The Changing Balance of Power in the Indian Ocean: Prospects for a Significant Chinese Naval Presence", in David Michel and Ricky Passarelli (eds.), *Sea Change: Evolving Maritime Geopolitics in the Indo-Pacific Region*, Stimson Centre, December 2014, at https://www.stimson.org/wp-content/files/file-attachments/SEA-CHANGE-WEB.pdf. Accessed on January 10, 2022.

59. Koh Swee Lean Collin, "China-India Rivalry at Sea: Capability, trends, and challenges," *Asian Security*, vol, 15, no. 1, 2019, pp. 5-24.

60. Ibid.

61. *Hindustan Times*, "'Keeping a close eye on Chinese presence in the Indian Ocean,' says Admiral Lanba", March 13, 2019.

62. Silvia Burke, "Explaining China's Participation in Anti-Piracy Operations in the Gulf of Aden", May 2009, MIT, at https://ocw.mit.edu/courses/political-science/17-408-chinese-foreign-policy-fall-2013/assignments/MIT17_408F13_ExplinigChina.pdf. Accessed on January 8, 2022.

63. *The Hindu*, "China Deploys Warships in the Indian Ocean", February 20, 2018, at https://www.thehindu.com/news/international/china-deploys-warships-in-indian-ocean/article22808463.ece. Accessed on September 15, 2021.

64. Eric Wertheim, "China's Luyang III/Type 052D Destroyer Is a Potent Adversary", *US Naval Institute Proceedings*, January 2020, at https://www.usni.org/magazines/proceedings/2020/january/chinas-luyang-iiitype-052d-destroyer-potent-adversary. Accessed on December 15, 2021.

65. Jean-Pierre Cabestan, "China's Military Base in Djibouti: A Microcosm of China's Growing Competition with the United States and New Bipolarity", *Journal of Contemporary China*, vol. 29, no. 125, 2020, pp. 731-747.

66. Ibid.

67. *Nikkei Asia*, "China adds carrier pier to Djibouti base, extending Indian Ocean reach", April 27, 2021, at https://asia.nikkei.com/Politics/International-relations/Indo-Pacific/China-adds-carrier-pier-to-Djibouti-base-extending-Indian-Ocean-reach. Accessed on December 15, 2021.
68. H I Sutton, "Satellite Images Show That Chinese Navy Is Expanding Overseas Base", *Forbes*, May 10, 2020, at https://www.forbes.com/sites/hisutton/2020/05/10/satellite-images-show-chinese-navy-is-expanding-overseas-base/?sh=7a0118a68691. Accessed on December 10, 2021.
69. *Nikkei Asia*, "China looks to East Africa for second Indian Ocean foothold", June 30, 2021, at https://asia.nikkei.com/Politics/International-relations/Indo-Pacific/China-looks-to-East-Africa-for-second-Indian-Ocean-foothold. Accessed on December 15, 2021.
70. Hong Yu, "Motivation behind China's 'One Belt, One Road' Initiatives and Establishment of the Asian Infrastructure Investment Bank", *Journal of Contemporary China*, vol. 26, no. 105, pp. 353-368.
71. *The Mint*, "India counters China in Sri Lanka with $700 million port deal", October 1, 2021, at https://www.livemint.com/news/india/india-counters-china-in-sri-lanka-with-700-million-largest-foreign-investment-port-deal-11633046975815.html. Accessed on January 10, 2022.
72. *South China Morning Post*, "Chinese research vessel expelled by Indian warship for operating near Andaman and Nicobar Islands", December 4, 2019, at Chinese research vessel expelled by Indian warship for operating near Andaman and Nicobar Islands | South China Morning Post (scmp.com). Accessed on January 10, 2022.
73. Congressional Research Service, "China's Military: The People's Liberation Army (PLA)," June 4, 2021, at https://sgp.fas.org/crs/row/R46808.pdf. Accessed on January 10, 2022.
74. Zack Cooper, "Security Implications of China's Military Presence in the Indian Ocean," *CSIS Briefs*, April 2, 2018, at https://www.csis.org/analysis/security-implications-chinas-military-presence-indian-ocean. Accessed on January 8, 2021.
75. Satoru Nagao, "The Growing Militarization of the Indian Ocean Power Game and Its Significance for Japan", Sasakawa Peace Foundation, July 10, 2018, at https://www.spf.org/iina/en/articles/nagao-india-powergame.html. Accessed on January 10, 2022.
76. Peter Layton, " How Sri Lanka Won the War", *The Diplomat*, April 9, 2015, at https://thediplomat.com/2015/04/how-sri-lanka-won-the-war/. Accessed on January 6, 2022.
77. Lu Guangsheng, "China Seeks to Improve Mekong Sub-Regional Cooperation: Causes and Policies", *RSIS Policy Report*, February 2016, at https://www.rsis.edu.sg/wp-content/uploads/2016/02/PR160225_China-Seeks-to-Improve-Mekong.pdf. Accessed on January 10, 2022.

78. Nayanima Basu, "Delhi's financial aid to Male exceeds $2 billion as the Maldives returns to 'India First'", *The Print*, August 13, 2020, at https://theprint.in/diplomacy/delhis-financial-aid-to-male-exceeds-2-billion-as-maldives-returns-to-india-first/481052/. Accessed on January 8, 2021.
79. *Business Standard*, "India offers $100 mn LoC to Mauritius to help procurement of defence assets", February 23, 2021, at https://www.business-standard.com/article/current-affairs/india-offers-100-mn-loc-to-mauritius-to-help-procurement-of-defence-assets-121022201251_1.html. Accessed on January 8, 2021.
80. *Live Mint*, "Sri Lanka, India ink deal to jointly redevelop strategic Trincomalee Oil Tanker Complex", January 6, 2022, at https://www.livemint.com/news/india/sri-lanka-india-ink-deal-to-jointly-redevelop-strategic-trincomalee-oil-tank-complex-11641488870616.html. Accessed on January 12, 2021.
81. *The Mint*, n. 71.
82. Vishal Tiwari, "4th NSA-level Meeting Held Between India, Sri Lanka And Maldives; Ajit Doval Attends", *Republic World*, November 29, 2020, at https://www.republicworld.com/world-news/rest-of-the-world-news/4th-nsa-level-meeting-held-between-india-sri-lanka-and-maldives-ajit-doval-attends.html. Accessed on January 8, 2021.
83. Press Information Bureau, "Colombo Security Conclave Focused Operation between India, the Maldives and Sri Lanka", November 28, 2021, at https://pib.gov.in/PressReleasePage.aspx?PRID=1775797. Accessed on January 8, 2021.
84. *The Hindu*, "India, Sri Lanka, and Maldives to collaborate on security", August 6, 2021, at https://www.thehindu.com/news/international/india-sri-lanka-maldives-to-collaborate-on-security/article35775231.ece. Accessed on January 5, 2021.